A Mary
Wilkins
Freeman
Reader

A MARY
WILKINS
FREEMAN
READER

Edited by Mary R. Reichardt

University of Nebraska Press, Lincoln and London

Introduction
© 1997 by the
University of
Nebraska Press
All rights reserved
Manufactured in
the United States of
America
⊛ The paper in this
book meets the
minimum
requirements of
American National
Standard for
Information
Sciences—
Permanence of
Paper for Printed
Library Materials,
ANSI Z39.48-1984.
Library of Congress
Cataloging-in-
Publication Data
Freeman, Mary
Eleanor Wilkins,
1852–1930.
A Mary Wilkins
Freeman reader /
edited by Mary R.
Reichardt. p.   cm.
Includes biblio-
graphical refer-
ences. ISBN 0-8032-
1998-9 (cloth : alk.
paper).—ISBN 0-
8032-6894-7 (pbk.
: alk. paper)
1. New England—
Social life and
customs—Fiction.
2. Ghost stories,
American—New
England.
I. Reichardt, Mary R.
II. Title.
PS1711.R45   1997
813'.4—dc20
96-20358 CIP

CONTENTS

INTRODUCTION

Mary R. Reichardt

"I suppose it seems to you as it does to me that everything you have heard, seen, or done, since you opened your eyes on the world, is coming back to you sooner or later, to go into stories," thirty-seven-year-old Mary Eleanor Wilkins wrote in 1889 to friend and fellow author Sarah Orne Jewett.[1] Wilkins had reason at the time to reflect on her own fiction's origin and to ponder its future direction. In the six years between 1883 and 1889 she had seen fifty-two of her adult short stories into print: forty-nine in the three prestigious Harper's publications, *Harper's Bazar*, *Harper's Monthly*, and *Harper's Weekly*, and three elsewhere (*Lippincott's Magazine*, *The Detroit Free Press*, and *Cosmopolitan*). Capitalizing on her remarkable appeal, the Harper's firm had already collected twenty-eight of those stories into *A Humble Romance and Other Stories* (1887), and a second collection was under way (*A New England Nun and Other Stories*, 1891).

In 1889, then, Mary Wilkins Freeman was approaching the height of her success. She had already written several of the stories that would secure her place in American literature as a local-color realist and, as more recent criticism shows, as a participant in the tradition of New England women's writing—stories such as "A New England Nun," "A Village Singer," and "A Church Mouse." In the following year, she would pen more such works, including "A Poetess," "The Revolt of 'Mother,'" and "Louisa." In fact, among the fifty-two stories that comprise her first two collections, many of the author's strongest and most characteristic stories can be found, including those most often anthologized today.

Reviewers were lavish in their praise. Considered a protégée of influential editor and writer William Dean Howells and other advocates of the "new" realism in literature, Freeman drew accolades for her portraits of the "pathos and beauty of simple lives"; for the "biting force" of her "short, terse sentences, written in the simplest, homeliest words"; and for her accurate depiction of rural and impoverished New England life.[2] Her concentration on the sensitive consciences and stubborn wills of her characters led some to compare her work favorably with Nathaniel Hawthorne's. She quickly gained an international reputation as well with the publication of British editions of her work; in 1890 an English critic remarked on "something like a craze" for Mary Wilkins's stories.[3] Reporters sought her out at the Randolph, Massachusetts, home where, after the death of her parents and only remaining sibling, Wilkins had taken up residence with her childhood friend, Mary Wales, and Wales's family. Those same reporters churned out articles that satisfied a public eager for such intimate details as the author's appearance ("a little frail looking creature with a splendid quantity of pale brown hair and dark blue eyes with a direct look"); the furnishings of her private rooms ("warm colors predominate, and bright bits of bric-a-brac"); her reading selections (Scott, Dickens, Thackeray, Hardy, Tolstoy, and Dostoevsky); and her supposed resemblance to the New England nun of her famous story ("Miss Wilkins leads by no means a cloistered life. Boston is only half an hour's ride from her home").[4] In particular they marveled that one so young could write so compellingly about the plight of the destitute and the elderly—Freeman had already formed the lifelong habit of allowing her audience to believe she was ten years younger than she actually was.

Freeman's correspondence at the time shows her amusement with her quick rise to fame. In a letter to *Harper's Bazar* editor Mary Louise Booth, she chuckled at her meeting with two Boston artists who were enthusiastically distributing her stories around town: "But the funniest thing is—the two of them . . . have bought *thirteen* of my books and given [them] away. Just fancy my seeing people who had bought *thirteen* of my books. I thought it was the most comical thing."[5] But her work's success was also a very serious matter to Freeman. For one thing, her celebrity brought her a wide circle of friends, including such writers as Jewett and Hamlin Garland and such editors as Booth, Kate Upson Clark, and Henry Mills Alden. Lacking an immediate family, Freeman found these relationships—some of which lasted a lifetime—increasingly important. "I begin to see that there is one beautiful thing which comes from this kind of work, and the thing I have the most need of, I think," she wrote in 1885. "One is going to find friends because of it; and when one has no one of their very own, one does need a good many of these, who come next."[6] Moreover, Freeman's writing was closely tied to her self-concept; she often refused to read negative reviews of her fiction and later in life poignantly asserted that her work was "all I came into the world for, and [I] have failed dismally if it is not a success."[7]

Perhaps the greatest reason for Freeman's concern about her work's success was her early experience with poverty. Her father, Warren Wilkins, had failed in attempts at carpentry in Randolph and then at running a general store in Brattleboro, Vermont. To Mary's shame, in 1877 when Mary was twenty-five, necessity forced the family to move into the wealthy home of a local minister, where her mother, Eleanor Wilkins, began work as housekeeper. Indeed, the poorhouse was never far from Freeman's imagination: it threatens many of her female protagonists, particularly those in her early works such as "Louisa," "A Church Mouse," and the novel *Pembroke*. Searching for the means to contribute to the family's income and, upon the death of her parents, to secure her own welfare, Freeman abandoned her desire to be a painter and began to write. She first tapped into the market for children's literature and was gratified to see her stories and poems appear, sometimes anonymously, in several prominent children's magazines, including *Wide-Awake* and *St. Nicholas*. But they did not pay. Thus years later, at the age of seventy-four, she could still remember clearly the excitement of receiving her first check for twenty-five dollars from *Harper's Bazar*.[8] Though her fiction was soon commanding extraordinarily high prices, she rarely deviated from the daily habit she had formed in these early years of keeping to her room until she produced at least fifteen hundred words.

Freeman's early stories reflect many of the themes and techniques that would animate much of her fiction throughout her long career. Usually set in post–Civil War New England villages much like the shoe-manufacturing Massachusetts towns of Freeman's youth, the stories most often concern characters striving to maintain their dignity or independence in the face of some threat. As such, Freeman's protagonists are frequently those most trapped by social or religious customs, by circumstance, or in constricting relationships—women, the elderly, the impoverished, the outcast. Of the sixty-nine stories written between 1882 and 1891, the majority involve women protagonists who must resort to some unexpected or even extreme behavior in order to preserve self-respect. Elderly Hetty Fifield takes up residence in a church when no other dwelling is offered her in "A Church Mouse"; Candace Whitcomb purposely antagonizes the congregation that ousted her from her job as soloist in "A Village Singer"; and Sarah Penn challenges her husband by moving her family into a barn when he rejects her plea for a new house in "The Revolt of 'Mother.'" A number of these stories involve courtship situations, another common theme in Freeman's fiction. Esther Barney refuses to marry a man whose stubborn pride has made him the town laughingstock in "A Conflict Ended"; a young woman scorns her mother's choice of a suitor for her in "Louisa"; and Louisa Ellis backs out of a fifteen-year engagement when she discovers her fiancé loves another woman in "A New England Nun." Some Freeman protagonists win their battles—Hetty Fifield is allowed to remain in the church, Sarah Penn gets her new house—and some, though overtly failing or capitulating, achieve a modicum of inner victory. Agitated beyond their strength, both Betsey Dole of "A Poetess" and Candace Whitcomb of "A Village Singer" die, for example, but the last lines of both stories suggest they have triumphed morally over their opponents.

Underlying the majority of Freeman's stories is an examination of the human will poised between the demands of duty and propriety on the one hand and the forces of self-pride and individual fulfillment on the other. Outwardly quiet, decorous lives are in reality often so racked with frustration that they eventually erupt. The narrator's description of Martha Elder, the protagonist of "The Balsam Fir," typifies Freeman's many stories of rebellion in spirit if not always in fact: "But it was very different with [Martha] from what people thought. Nobody dreamed of the fierce tension of her nerves as she sat at her window sewing. . . ; nobody dreamed what revolt that little cottage roof, when it was covered with wintry snows, sometimes sheltered." Freeman studies her characters when they are near the breaking point, at the moment of extreme stress or decision.

One source of such tension is religion. Heeding the promptings of conscience, Freeman's protagonists frequently find themselves as odds with religious convention; this in turn leads to unrelenting social censure in a village that insists upon rigid conformity. Freeman captures well the hypocrisy of a Christianity devoid of spirit in such tales as "Life-Everlastin'," in which Luella Ansel refuses to be pressured into belief before she herself experiences need of it; "An Independent Thinker," in which Esther Gay scandalizes her neighbors by practicing her own form of charity instead of attending church; and "The Balking of Christopher," in which Christopher Dodd suddenly rebels against the tenets of an orthodoxy he can no longer accept. Besides religion, Freeman's characters contend with myriad other social dictates, including restrictions on style of dress and housekeeping practices. In fact, any behavior that marks a villager as "different" or "odd" invites vicious gossip and warrants a visit from the town minister or selectman. Women in particular risk being labeled "witches" in an environment not substantially different from that which led to hanging such offenders two centuries before. Because she tends sick animals and a deaf-and-dumb child, the protagonist of "Christmas Jenny," for example, is suspected of witchcraft by townsfolk to whom "everything out of the broad, common track was a horror."

Her interest in the human psyche also led Freeman to write of the tendency of the intractable will and hypersensitive conscience toward neurosis. Like Hawthorne, Freeman often explores the psychology of those so "set" in one track they are unable to deviate from it. Dogged stubbornness marks a number of her protagonists, including Marcus Woodman of "A Conflict Ended," who for years sits on the church steps during Sunday service after quarreling with the minister. Martha Patch's scrupulous honesty nearly culminates in her death from starvation as she sews quilts for her neighbors in "An Honest Soul." In addition, several of Freeman's female protagonists become "love-cracked" after being rejected by their lovers; others disappointed in love, such as Evelina Adams of "Evelina's Garden," attempt to exert control over younger women's courtships so as to compensate for what they themselves have lost. Throughout her career, Freeman remained fascinated by the human conscience seared with guilt and the human will grown obstinate: along with many of her short stories, several of her novels are premised on these themes.

Freeman discovered her subject matter by carefully observing the life around her, by "sharp[ening her] eyes and ears to see and hear everything in the whole creation."9 Sympathy for a chained dog she witnessed at an old lady's birthday party provided the "germ" for "A New England Nun," and the image of a forlorn little girl she could not get out of her head evolved over the years into several tales, including "The Lost Ghost." Once at her desk, she allowed her stories to develop organically, often expressing surprise at the turn her characters or plot had taken. Remaining loyal to the Harper's firm, she allotted them the first right to her best material; in turn, she profited from the advice of her editors—especially Booth—as she polished her grammar and honed the techniques of magazine fiction. The typical Freeman story opens in the midst of the central conflict and moves swiftly to its climax; plot is developed by clipped, laconic dialogue, often in New England dialect, and narration is kept to a minimum. Given this dramatic style, it is easy to understand Freeman's interest in playwriting: she wrote several during her life, achieving some success with the production of *Giles Corey: Yeoman* (1893). Later and longer stories such as "Evelina's Garden" and "Eglantina" exhibit heavier narration, no doubt a result of the author's increased concentration on novel writing. However, Freeman was quite capable of returning to the compressed style and the vigorous, spontaneous effect of dialogue whenever she wished. Her occasional stories featuring first-person narrators are particularly lively.

Freeman's eye for detail is superb; nuances of dress, houses and household furnishings, food, and gift giving are subtle but influential forces in her works, revealing depth of character and, in many cases, shallowness as well. The title character of "The Revolt of Sophia Lane" flouts the useless gifts given her niece, returning every one of them; two feuding sisters are reunited by their care for a doll in "The Reign of the Doll"; and Louisa's three aprons and her repeated sewing of the same fine linen seam in "A New England Nun" eloquently express her craving for order and tranquillity. A further, often-overlooked hallmark of Freeman's fiction is her penchant for ironic twists of plot and the fine, often sardonic humor that accompanies such development. A jilted woman's bird viciously attacks the bridal hat of her ex-lover's fiancée in "The Parrot"; despite Sarah Penn's firm and reiterated pleading for a new house in "The Revolt of 'Mother,'" her husband confesses he had "no idee" she was in earnest; and an elderly couple eagerly await their wealthy neighbors' yearly vacation so they can take up residence on the house's stately porch in "The Outside of the House." Indeed, Freeman's best short fiction is compelling in theme and deft in technique, leaving the reader with much to ponder.

Freeman's prolific short-story writing and the rapid success she enjoyed in the first part of her career came with mixed blessings. In constant demand, she complied as much as possible with solicitations from numerous publications for holiday tales—*Harper's*, *Ladies' Home Journal*, *Century*, *Woman's Home Companion*, *Lippincott's*, and *The Detroit Free Press*, among others. In fact, of her adult canon of 247 short stories, more than 50 were written for Christmas, Valentine's Day, Easter, or Halloween editions of magazines and newspapers. Always a practical woman, she expressed few qualms about such writing on demand, regarding it as her bread and butter. Predictably, some of these stories are formulaic and trite; others, however, such as "Christmas Jenny," "The Balsam Fir," and "The Revolt of Sophia Lane," succeed despite their holiday themes. Freeman's early success had a further repercussion: once her reputation was established, she felt more at liberty after 1891 to experiment with her work. Though she continued to write successful village stories with her trademark themes all her life, she was artistically ambitious and sought to try her hand at other genres as well. She increasingly turned her energies to the novel: *Jane Field* was first serialized in 1892, and thirteen more, ranging in subject matter from an exposé of New England millworking conditions (*The Portion of Labor*) to a historical romance set in the South (*The Heart's Highway*), followed steadily through 1917. In addition, she produced poetry, plays, children's stories, nonfiction prose, and even motion-picture scripts. Indeed, the sheer bulk and variety of Freeman's canon are remarkable, attesting to a professional author dedicated to her work; however, then as now, Freeman's distinction in American literature rests on her many fine short stories and one or two of her novels, including *Pembroke* (1894).

More important, as Freeman began to experiment with different genres, she explored new types of short stories as well. Since the fiction she actually wished to write was that which exhibited "more symbolism, more mysticism,"[10] she ventured in mid-career away from the stark realism and contemporary settings of her early tales. Her lifelong interest in the New England past resulted in a number of historical pieces, six of which were collected in *Silence and Other Stories* (1898). The plot of one of these, "Evelina's Garden," unfolds across several generations of a genteel New England family; a later mystery story, "The Gold," is one of several set during the American Revolution. Freeman also embarked on a series of symbolic stories, investigating the psychic connections between animals, flowers, and trees on the one hand and humans on the other. Readers will find four such tales here: "Arethusa" and "The Parrot," originally collected in *Understudies* (1901); and "The Balsam Fir" and "The Great Pine," originally collected in *Six Trees* (1903). Always sensitive to nature and animals—she particularly loved flowers and cats—Freeman perceptively examines in these works the subtle influence of the natural world on the human psyche. In "The Great Pine," for example, a sailor who has deserted his wife and children learns through repeated contact with a magnificent pine tree to transcend his selfishness; eventually, he is able to return to his family to make amends. "Who shall determine the limit at which the intimate connection and reciprocal influence of all forms of visible creation upon one another may stop?" the narrator of the tale rhetorically queries.

In addition, Freeman penned a number of ghost stories, a genre that evidently came naturally to her. Friends and acquaintances alike recounted how an evening gathering usually ended in the author's droll spinning of supernatural yarns while they relaxed around the fireplace. Six ghost stories were collected in *The Wind in the Rose-Bush and Other Stories of the Supernatural* (1903); two of these are reprinted in this volume. In "Luella Miller," a vampire-like woman unwittingly sucks the life out of all those who must care for her, and in "The Lost Ghost," the spirit of a horribly abused little girl returns from the dead to seek her mother.

Freeman's literary experiments in mid-career coincided with significant changes in her personal life. On 1 January 1902, after a prolonged engagement eagerly followed by the press, she wed Charles Manning Freeman, a wealthy coal and lumber dealer and trained, though no longer practicing, medical doctor. Marrying at the age of forty-nine did not come without some trauma for Freeman: though happy to shed the public's perception of her as a "nunlike" spinster, she worried that her duties as a married woman would interfere with her career. Moreover, she never felt at home in Charles's hometown of Metuchen, New Jersey, where she moved after the wedding; she found herself bored by the staid upper-class social life there and ostracized when she satirized it in such thinly veiled works as *The Butterfly House* (1912). A few contented years followed, but her life was soon soured by Charles's drinking and drug habits. Seven years after their marriage, he was hospitalized for alcoholism in a New York sanitorium; during the next decade, his condition deteriorated enough to warrant confinement in a series of hospitals and mental institutions. Mary Freeman legally separated from her husband in 1922. Charles died the following year, leaving his wife only a single dollar in his will.

Despite the increased complications of her personal life, Freeman succeeded in giving high priority to her writing after her marriage. From 1902 to 1930—the year of her death at the age of seventy-eight—she published 7 novels and 105 stories for adults. After her series of historical, symbolic, and supernatural stories, she resumed writing short fiction primarily with her characteristic village themes: the "rebellions" of those who, after much long-suffering, suddenly can endure no more ("The Revolt of Sophia

Lane," "The Balking of Christopher"); family relationships and the mending of quarrels ("The Selfishness of Amelia Lamkin," "The Reign of the Doll"); relationships in courtship and marriage ("Eglantina"); and the quiet triumphs of the poor and elderly ("The Outside of the House"). Twenty-six of these later stories were collected by Harper's in *The Givers* (1904), *The Fair Lavinia and Others* (1907), and *The Winning Lady and Others* (1909). She also wrote a series of stories with child-protagonists, collected in *The Copy-Cat and Other Stories* (1914). And as she had done earlier with a slender volume entitled *The People of Our Neighborhood* (1898), she produced a cycle of interrelated village stories united by a common character (Sarah Edgewater) and a common setting (Barr Center). Entitled *Edgewater People* (1918), it was her last volume of new material. Many more stories from this period, including several patriotic war stories, were not collected during her lifetime.

Though for the most part Freeman's themes in this period echo those found in her earlier work, some change is apparent. A number of later stories evince a boldness and cynicism that her early work lacks. The satire is more biting, the irony more trenchant. Through the delightfully frank voice of Lily Talbert, for example, "The Old-Maid Aunt" ridicules society's scorn of single women past the age of thirty. Knowing such prejudice firsthand, Freeman dealt with the plight of "spinsters" in much of her fiction; this piece, however, confronts the issue head-on with unrelenting satire. "Here I am the old-maid aunt," Lily announces at the beginning of the narrative. "Not a day, not an hour, not a minute . . . passes that I do not see myself in [others'] estimation playing that role as plainly as if I saw myself in a looking-glass." And "Old Woman Magoun," a tragic tale of an elderly woman who attempts to protect her granddaughter from sexual abuse by the girl's own father, is perhaps the darkest and most bitter of all Freeman's tales. Summarizing Freeman's tone in this and other such stories, one critic has rightly commented that "as Freeman becomes angrier and bolder, her women become angrier and bolder. . . . [Her] cynicism is made urgent by the explosiveness of this theme."[11]

Feeble and ailing in her last years, Freeman nevertheless wrote steadily until her death. Although her output diminished considerably in her last decade, she published her final story in 1928 (only two years before she succumbed to heart failure) and left at least five story manuscripts unfinished. By that time, however, the post–World War I "masculine" mood of the country and corresponding changes in literary tastes had rendered her village themes and particular brand of "feminine" subject matter passé. Disheartened by her waning popularity, in 1926 Freeman cautioned an aspiring author that "everything is different since the War. . . . As nearly as I can understand the situation, there is in arts and letters a sort of frantic impulse for something erratic, out of the common. . . . I am none too sure of a market for my own wares. . . . I am about as bewildered by the whole situation as you are."[12] So diminished was her reputation by the time of her death that Henry Wysham Lanier, who selected twenty-five stories for *The Best Stories of Mary E. Wilkins* in 1927, apologized in his preface for having to remind his audience who the author was: "Indeed, to one who was a reader in the 'nineties, it seems almost ludicrous to 'introduce' Mary E. Wilkins. (Just a little like introducing Babe Ruth anywhere in the United States, in these latter days!)"[13] Despite this decline, however, a number of honors brightened Freeman's final years, helping to keep her work from total obscurity. In 1925 she received the first William Dean Howells Medal for fiction from the American Academy of Arts and Letters and the following year was one of the first women elected to membership in the National Institute of Arts and Letters. Ornamental doors installed posthumously at the American Academy of Arts and Letters in New York and inscribed "to the Memory of Mary E. Wilkins Freeman and the Women Writers of America" continue to bear witness to the accomplishments of a remarkable and influential American author.

It has sometimes been claimed that all of Freeman's best stories were published by 1891 and that her writing fell off significantly thereafter. Although it is certainly true that many of the stories published in her first two collections are consistently excellent, it is also true that, though decidedly more uneven, her later work reveals interesting and powerful tales as well. Modern readers are largely unfamiliar with the bulk of this writing: only four post-1891 stories have appeared in the three collections of Freeman's stories published since 1974.[14] Seeking to remedy this gap, my *Uncollected Stories of Mary Wilkins Freeman* (Mississippi, 1992) brought together twenty heretofore "lost" stories, nineteen of them originally published after 1891. However, one must return to Lanier's 1927 *Best Stories* to find a wide selection of previously collected material that spans Freeman's career. Still found on some library shelves, Lanier's volume has served its purpose well over the years as the first and—up to now—only substantial edition of Mary Wilkins Freeman's stories drawn from most of her original thirteen collections.

A *Mary Wilkins Freeman Reader* will thus prove a welcome addition to Freeman scholarship, providing the general reader and the student of American literature alike with an updated edition of the best and most representative of Freeman's short fiction. Its generous sampling of stories comes from twelve of her collections and represents over three decades of her career. Arranged chronologically by date of collection, the selections allow readers a sense of the author's development as a writer over time. Part One reprints eleven tales from the fifty-two that comprised *A Humble Romance and Other Stories* (1887) and *A New England Nun and Other Stories* (1891), the collections that made Freeman famous and ensured her position in American literary history. As a group, the village tales here typify the themes and techniques that concerned the author all her life and that came to define her art. Part Two includes eight stories out of the five collections (originally totaling thirty-five stories) that Freeman published in mid-career: *Silence and Other Stories* (1898); *The Love of Parson Lord and Other Stories* (1900); *Understudies* (1901); *Six Trees* (1903); and *The Wind in the Rose-Bush and Other Stories of the Supernatural* (1903). Included in this section are a number of the author's "experiments" in literary form and theme: historical, symbolic, and ghost stories.

Part Three contains eight stories from the fifty published in Freeman's last five collections: *The Givers* (1904); *The Fair Lavinia and Others* (1907); *The Winning Lady and Others* (1909); *The Copy-Cat and Other Stories* (1914); and *Edgewater People* (1918). This final section also includes one piece that, strictly speaking, is not a short story. "The Old-Maid Aunt" was commissioned by William Dean Howells as a chapter for his "collective" novel, *The Whole Family* (1908). A literary gimmick, the novel brought together—anonymously, when first serialized in *Harper's Bazar*—the efforts of twelve popular writers of the day, including Howells, Henry James, Alice Brown, and Elizabeth Stuart Phelps. Asked to follow Howells's introductory chapter concerning a father musing on his daughter's recent engagement, Freeman took evident delight in deliberately subverting the homely tone and benign characterization that the—to Freeman—woefully reactionary Howells had hoped to establish.[15] "The Old-Maid Aunt" discloses Freeman in one of her more strident and candid moods, an effect enhanced by its first-person narration.

Though large and uneven, Freeman's canon of adult short fiction reveals many gems; it is not a simple task to choose from among her many fine tales. My years of reading and research have convinced me that approximately fifty or sixty stories deserve serious critical attention—certainly an impressive number by any standard. Note needs to be made, therefore, about further criteria used to select the stories readers will encounter here. First, this anthology is limited to those stories collected in Freeman's lifetime; a volume of the best of the one hundred uncollected tales has recently been published elsewhere. Second, stories were chosen with an eye toward representing most of the broad categories of short fiction Freeman produced (village stories, symbolic stories, holiday stories, ghost stories, etc.) as well as representing most of the collections in which they were published. Of her thirteen collections, only *The People of Our Neighborhood* (1898) was excluded: its interrelated pieces are really sketches more than short stories. Finally, because the relationship between criticism and literature is, in the ideal, a reciprocal one, stories that have received recent scholarly attention were given some priority. In the last ten years, for example, critics have examined "Christmas Jenny," "Evelina's Garden," "Arethusa," "Eglantina," "The Balking of Christopher," "The Lost Ghost," and "The Selfishness of Amelia Lamkin," among others. And of course, scholarship continues on better-known stories such as "A New England Nun," and "The Revolt of 'Mother.'"

Appreciation for Freeman's writing has, in fact, increased steadily over the last decade. All but dismissed as a minor local-color realist throughout much of this century, she is today considered, along with Sarah Orne Jewett, the foremost delineator of New England life at the turn of the century. More important, her work now occupies a significant position in the history of American women's fiction in general and in the development of the American short story in particular. Witnessing to this positive reassessment, a number of important scholarly books on Freeman have appeared since 1985, including an edition of her letters, a literary biography, a collection of critical essays, and several full-length studies of her fiction. In addition, more than forty articles or book chapters and at least twenty Ph.D. dissertations dealing solely or in part with Freeman's writings have been produced since that date. Given the extent of this recent interest, it is all the more imperative that readers have ready access to the stories themselves. By bringing together Freeman's most skillful and characteristic short fiction, *A Mary Wilkins Freeman Reader* fulfills that need, providing at once an attractive assortment for the casual reader and a definitive text for the literary scholar.

∾

Each of the Freeman stories in this volume is taken from its original collection. The date by each story title is that of the story's first magazine publication. In an effort to be faithful to the text as originally published, variations in spelling and punctuation have been maintained. Only obvious typographical errors have been corrected.

NOTES

1. Freeman to Sarah Orne Jewett, 10 December 1889, *The Infant Sphinx: Collected Letters of Mary E. Wilkins Freeman*, ed. Brent L. Kendrick (Metuchen NJ: Scarecrow, 1985), 99.

2. "Mary E. Wilkins," *Bookman* (1 December 1891): 102; Charles Miner Thompson, "Miss Wilkins: An Idealist in Masquerade," *Atlantic Monthly* 83 (May 1899): 669.

3. "Notes," *The Critic* (London) 14 (23 August 1890): 101.

4. Mina C. Smith, "Mary Wilkins at Home," *Boston Evening Transcript*, 12 June 1890, 4; Albert Doyle, "A New England Recluse," *Donahoe's Magazine* 35 (March 1896): 287; Joseph E. Chamberlin, "Authors at Home: Miss Mary E. Wilkins at Randolph, Mass.," *The Critic* (New York) 29 (5 March 1898): 155–56; Albert D. Vandam, "Women Worth Knowing: Mary E. Wilkins," *Atalanta* (London) 5 (November 1891): 94.

5. Freeman to Mary Louise Booth, 15 May 1888, Kendrick, *Infant Sphinx*, 88.

6. Freeman to Booth, 21 April 1885, Kendrick, *Infant Sphinx*, 62.

7. Freeman to William Harlowe Briggs, 1 February 1928, Kendrick, *Infant Sphinx*, 424.

8. "American Academy Honors Two Women," *New York Times*, 24 April 1926, sec. 1, p. 7.

9. Freeman, "Good Wits, Pen and Paper," in *What Women Can Earn: Occupations of Women and Their Compensation*, ed. G. H. Dodge et al. (New York: Frederick A. Stokes, 1899), 28.

10. Freeman to Fred Lewis Pattee, 5 September 1919, Kendrick, *Infant Sphinx*, 382.

11. Alice Glarden Brand, "Mary Wilkins Freeman: Misanthropy as Propaganda," *New England Quarterly* 50 (March 1977): 84, 97.

12. Freeman to Jean O'Brien, 27 February 1926, Kendrick, *Infant Sphinx*, 401–2.

13. *The Best Stories of Mary E. Wilkins*, ed. Henry Wysham Lanier (New York: Harper and Brothers, 1927), vii.

14. Michele Clark's *"The Revolt of 'Mother'" and Other Stories* (New York: Feminist Press, 1974) and Marjorie Pryse's *Selected Stories of Mary E. Wilkins Freeman* (New York: Norton, 1983) contain stories from Freeman's first two collections only. Barbara Solomon's *Short Fiction of Sarah Orne Jewett and Mary Wilkins Freeman* (New York: NAL Penguin, 1979) reprints four post-1891 stories: "One Good Time," "The Lombardy Poplar," "The Selfishness of Amelia Lamkin," and "Old Woman Magoun."

15. A full account of Freeman's deliberate "travesty" of the novel and Howells's subsequent ire can be found in Alfred Bendixen's "It Was a Mess! How Henry James and Others Actually Wrote a Novel," *The New York Times Book Review*, 27 April 1986, 3, 28–29.

SELECTED BIBLIOGRAPHY

Primary Works

Adult Short Story Collections

A Humble Romance and Other Stories. New York: Harper and Brothers, 1887.
A New England Nun and Other Stories. New York: Harper and Brothers, 1891.
The People of Our Neighborhood. Philadelphia: Curtis, 1898.
Silence and Other Stories. New York: Harper and Brothers, 1898.
The Love of Parson Lord and Other Stories. New York: Harper and Brothers, 1900.
Understudies. New York: Harper and Brothers, 1901.
Six Trees. New York: Harper and Brothers, 1903.
The Wind in the Rose-Bush and Other Stories of the Supernatural. New York: Doubleday, Page, 1903.
The Givers. New York: Harper and Brothers, 1904.
The Fair Lavinia and Others. New York: Harper and Brothers, 1907.
The Winning Lady and Others. New York: Harper and Brothers, 1909.
The Copy-Cat and Other Stories. New York: Harper and Brothers, 1914.
Edgewater People. New York: Harper and Brothers, 1918.
The Best Stories of Mary E. Wilkins. Ed. Henry Wysham Lanier. New York: Harper and Brothers, 1927.

The Uncollected Stories of Mary Wilkins Freeman. Ed. Mary R. Reichardt. Jackson: University Press of Mississippi, 1992.

Novels and Plays

Jane Field. New York: Harper and Brothers, 1893.
Giles Corey, Yeoman: A Play. New York: Harper and Brothers, 1893.
Pembroke. New York: Harper and Brothers, 1894.
Madelon. New York: Harper and Brothers, 1896.
Jerome, A Poor Man. New York: Harper and Brothers, 1897.
The Jamesons. New York: Doubleday and McClure, 1899.
The Heart's Highway, A Romance of Virginia in the Seventeenth Century. New York: Doubleday, Page, 1900.
The Portion of Labor. New York: Harper and Brothers, 1901.
The Debtor. New York: Harper and Brothers, 1905.
By the Light of the Soul. New York: Harper and Brothers, 1906.
"Doc" Gordon. New York: Authors and Newspapers Association, 1906.
The Shoulders of Atlas. New York: Harper and Brothers, 1908.
The Whole Family: A Novel by Twelve Authors. By William Dean Howells et. al. New York: Harper and Brothers, 1908.
The Butterfly House. New York: Dodd, Mead, 1912.
The Yates Pride: A Romance. New York: Harper and Brothers, 1912.
An Alabaster Box. With Florence Morse Kingsley. New York: D. Appleton, 1917.

Book-Length Secondary Works

Foster, Edward. *Mary E. Wilkins Freeman.* New York: Hendricks House, 1956.
Glasser, Leah Blatt. *In a Closet Hidden: The Life and Work of Mary E. Wilkins Freeman.* Amherst: University of Massachusetts Press, 1996.
Kendrick, Brent L., ed. *The Infant Sphinx: Collected Letters of Mary E. Wilkins Freeman.* Metuchen NJ: Scarecrow, 1985.
Marchalonis, Shirley, ed. *Critical Essays on Mary Wilkins Freeman.* Boston: G. K. Hall, 1991.
Reichardt, Mary R. *Mary Wilkins Freeman: A Study of the Short Fiction.* New York: Twayne, 1997.
————. *A Web of Relationship: Women in the Short Stories of Mary Wilkins Freeman.* Jackson: University Press of Mississippi, 1992.
Westbrook, Perry D. *Mary Wilkins Freeman.* Rev. ed. Boston: Twayne, 1988.

Part One

Stories from
A Humble Romance (1887)
A New England Nun (1891)

An Honest Soul

1884

"Thar's Mis' Bliss's pieces in the brown kaliker bag, an' thar's Mis' Bennet's pieces in the bed-tickin' bag," said she, surveying complacently the two bags leaning against her kitchen-wall. "I'll get a dollar for both of them quilts, an' thar'll be two dollars. I've got a dollar an' sixty-three cents on hand now, an' thar's plenty of meal an' merlasses, an' some salt fish an' pertaters in the house. I'll get along middlin' well, I reckon. Thar ain't no call fer me to worry. I'll red up the house a leetle now, an' then I'll begin on Mis' Bliss's pieces."

The *house* was an infinitesimal affair, containing only two rooms besides the tiny lean-to which served as wood-shed. It stood far enough back from the road for a pretentious mansion, and there was one curious feature about it—not a door nor window was there in front, only a blank, unbroken wall. Strangers passing by used to stare wonderingly at it sometimes, but it was explained easily enough. Old Simeon Patch, years ago, when the longing for a home of his own had grown strong in his heart, and he had only a few hundred dollars saved from his hard earnings to invest in one, had wisely done the best he could with what he had.

Not much remained to spend on the house after the spacious lot was paid for, so he resolved to build as much house as he could with his money, and complete it when better days should come.

This tiny edifice was in reality simply the L of a goodly two-story house which had existed only in the fond and faithful fancies of Simeon Patch and his wife. That blank front wall was designed to be joined to the projected main building; so, of course, there was no need of doors or windows. Simeon Patch came of a hard-working, honest race, whose pride it had been to keep out of debt, and he was a true child of his ancestors. Not a dollar would he spend that was not in his hand; a mortgaged house was his horror. So he paid cash for every blade of grass on his lot of land, and every nail in his bit of a house, and settled down patiently in it until he should grub together enough more to buy a few additional boards and shingles, and pay the money down.

That time never came: he died in the course of a few years, after a lingering illness, and only had enough saved to pay his doctor's bill and funeral expenses, and leave his wife and daughter entirely without debt, in their little fragment of a house on the big, sorry lot of land.

There they had lived, mother and daughter, earning and saving in various little, petty ways, keeping their heads sturdily above water, and holding the dreaded mortgage off the house for many years. Then the mother died, and the daughter, Martha Patch, took up the little homely struggle alone. She was over seventy now—a small, slender old woman, as straight as a rail, with sharp black eyes, and a quick toss of her head when she spoke. She did odd housewifely jobs for the neighbors, wove rag-carpets, pieced bed-quilts, braided rugs, etc., and contrived to supply all her simple wants.

This evening, after she had finished putting her house to rights, she fell to investigating the contents of the bags which two of the neighbors had brought in the night before, with orders for quilts, much to her delight.

"Mis' Bliss has got proper handsome pieces," said she—"proper handsome; they'll make a good-lookin' quilt. Mis' Bennet's is good too, but they ain't quite ekal to Mis' Bliss's. I reckon some of 'em's old."

She began spreading some of the largest, prettiest pieces on her white-scoured table. "Thar," said she, gazing at one admiringly, "that jest takes my eye; them leetle pink roses is pretty, an' no mistake. I reckon that's French caliker. Thar's some big pieces too. Lor', what bag did I take 'em out on! It must hev been Mis' Bliss's. I mustn't git 'em mixed."

She cut out some squares, and sat down by the window in a low wooden rocking-chair to sew. This window did not have a very pleasant outlook. The house was situated so far back from the road that it commanded only a rear view of the adjoining one. It was a great cross to Martha Patch. She was one of those women who like to see everything that is going on outside, and who often have excuse enough in the fact that so little is going on with them.

"It's a great divarsion," she used to say, in her snapping way, which was more nervous than ill-natured, bobbing her head violently at the same time—"a very great divarsion to see Mr. Peter's cows goin' in an' out of the barn day arter day; an' that's about all I do see—never git a sight of the folks goin' to meetin' nor nothin'."

The lack of a front window was a continual source of grief to her.

"When the minister's prayin' for the widders an' orphans he'd better make mention of one more," said she, once, "an' that's women without front winders."

She and her mother had planned to save money enough to have one some day, but they had never been able to bring it about. A window commanding a view of the street and the passers-by would have been a great source of comfort to the poor old woman, sitting and sewing as she did day in and day out. As it was, she seized eagerly upon the few objects of interest which did come within her vision, and made much of them. There were some children who, on their way from school, could make a short cut through her yard and reach home quicker. She watched for them every day, and if they did not appear quite as soon as usual she would grow uneasy, and eye the clock, and mutter to herself, "I wonder where them Mosely children can be?" When they came she watched their progress with sharp attention, and thought them over for an hour afterwards. Not a bird which passed her window escaped her notice. This innocent old gossip fed her mind upon their small domestic affairs in lieu of larger ones. To-day she often paused between her stitches to gaze absorbedly at a yellow-bird vibrating nervously round the branches of a young tree opposite. It was early spring, and the branches were all of a light-green foam.

"That's the same yaller-bird I saw yesterday, I do b'lieve," said she. "I recken he's goin' to build a nest in that ellum."

Lately she had been watching the progress of the grass gradually springing up all over the yard. One spot where it grew much greener than elsewhere her mind dwelt upon curiously.

"I can't make out," she said to a neighbor, "whether that 'ere spot is greener than the rest because the sun shines brightly thar, or because somethin's buried thar."

She toiled steadily on the patchwork quilts. At the end of a fortnight they were nearly completed. She hurried on the last one morning, thinking she would carry them both to their owners that afternoon and get her pay. She did not stop for any dinner.

Spreading them out for one last look before rolling them up in bundles, she caught her breath hastily.

"What hev I done?" said she. "Massy sakes! I hevn't gone an' put Mis' Bliss's caliker with the leetle pink roses on't in Mis' Bennet's quilt? I hev, just as sure as preachin'! What shell I do?"

The poor old soul stood staring at the quilts in pitiful dismay. "A hull fortni't's work," she muttered. "What shell I do? Them pink roses is the prettiest caliker in the hull lot. Mis' Bliss will be mad if they air in Mis' Bennet's quilt. She won't say nothin', an' she'll pay me, but she'll feel it inside, an' it won't be doin' the squar' thing by her. No; if I'm goin' to airn money I'll airn it."

Martha Patch gave her head a jerk. The spirit which animated her father when he went to housekeeping in a piece of a house without any front window blazed up within her. She made herself a cup of tea, then sat deliberately down by the window to rip the quilts to pieces. It had to be done pretty thoroughly on account of her admiration for the pink calico, and the quantity of it—it figured in nearly every square. "I wish I hed a front winder to set to while I'm doin' on't," said she; but she patiently plied her scissors till dusk, only stopping for a short survey of the Mosely children. After days of steady work the pieces were put together again, this time the pink-rose calico in Mrs. Bliss's quilt. Martha Patch rolled the quilts up with a sigh of relief and a sense of virtuous triumph.

"I'll sort over the pieces that's left in the bags," said she, "then I'll take 'em over an' git my pay. I'm gittin' pretty short of vittles."

She began pulling the pieces out of the bed-ticking bag, laying them on her lap and smoothing them out, preparatory to doing them up in a neat, tight roll to take home—she was very methodical about everything she did. Suddenly she turned pale, and stared wildly at a tiny scrap of calico which she had just fished out of the bag.

"Massy sakes!" she cried; "it ain't, is it?" She clutched Mrs. Bliss's quilt from the table and laid the bit of calico beside the pink-rose squares.

"It's just the same thing," she groaned, "an' it came out on Mis' Bennet's bag. Dear me suz! dear me suz!"

She dropped helplessly into her chair by the window, still holding the quilt and the telltale scrap of calico, and gazed out in a bewildered sort of way. Her poor old eyes looked dim and weak with tears.

"Thar's the Mosely children comin'," she said; "happy little gals, laughin' an' hollerin', goin' home to their mother to git a good dinner. Me

a-settin' here's a lesson they ain't larned in their books yit; hope to goodness they never will; hope they won't ever hev to piece quilts fur a livin',
without any front winder to set to. Thar's a dandelion' blown out on that
green spot. Reckon thar *is* somethin' buried thar. Lordy massy! *hev* I got to
rip them two quilts to pieces agin an' sew 'em over?"

Finally she resolved to carry a bit of the pink-rose calico over to Mrs.
Bennet's and find out, without betraying the dilemma she was in, if it were
really hers.

Her poor old knees fairly shook under her when she entered Mrs. Bennet's sitting-room.

"Why, yes, Martha, it's mine," said Mrs. Bennet, in response to her agitated question. "Hattie had a dress like it, don't you remember? There was
a lot of new pieces left, and I thought they would work into a quilt nice.
But, for pity's sake, Martha, what is the matter? You look just as white as a
sheet. You ain't sick, are you?"

"No," said Martha, with a feeble toss of her head, to keep up the deception; "I ain't sick, only kinder all gone with the warm weather. I reckon I'll
hev to fix me up some thoroughwort tea. Thoroughwort's a great strength-
ener."

"I would," said Mrs. Bennet, sympathizingly; "and don't you work too
hard on that quilt; I ain't in a bit of a hurry for it. I sha'n't want it before
next winter anyway. I only thought I'd like to have it pieced and ready."

"I reckon I can't get it done afore another fortni't," said Martha, trembling.

"I don't care if you don't get it done for the next three months. Don't go
yet, Martha; you ain't rested a minute, and it's a pretty long walk. Don't
you want a bite of something before you go? Have a piece of cake? You
look real faint."

"No, thanky," said Martha, and departed in spite of all friendly entreaties to tarry. Mrs. Bennet watched her moving slowly down the road,
still holding the little pink calico rag in her brown, withered fingers.

"Martha Patch is failing; she ain't near so straight as she was," remarked
Mrs. Bennet. "She looks real bent over to-day."

The little wiry springiness was, indeed, gone from her gait as she crept
slowly along the sweet country road, and there was a helpless droop in her
thin, narrow shoulders. It was a beautiful spring day; the fruit-trees were
all in blossom. There were more orchards than houses on the way, and
more blooming trees to pass than people.

Martha looked up at the white branches as she passed under them. "I kin smell the apple-blows," said she, "but somehow the goodness is all gone out on 'em. I'd jest as soon smell cabbage. Oh, dear me suz, kin I ever do them quilts over agin?"

When she got home, however, she rallied a little. There was a nervous force about this old woman which was not easily overcome even by an accumulation of misfortunes. She might bend a good deal, but she was almost sure to spring back again. She took off her hood and shawl, and straightened herself up. "Thar's no use puttin' it off; it's got to be done. I'll hev them quilts right ef it kills me!"

She tied on a purple calico apron and sat down at the window again, with a quilt and the scissors. Out came the pink roses. There she sat through the long afternoon, cutting the stitches which she had so laboriously put in—a little defiant old figure, its head, with a flat black lace cap on it, bobbing up and down in time with its hands. There were some purple bows on the cap, and they fluttered; quite a little wind blew in at the window.

The eight-day clock on the mantel ticked peacefully. It was a queer old timepiece, which had belonged to her grandmother Patch. A painting of a quaint female, with puffed hair and a bunch of roses, adorned the front of it, under the dial-plate. It was flanked on either side by tall, green vases.

There was a dull-colored rag-carpet of Martha's own manufacture on the floor of the room. Some wooden chairs stood around stiffly; an old, yellow map of Massachusetts and a portrait of George Washington hung on the walls. There was not a speck of dust anywhere, nor any disorder. Neatness was one of the comforts of Martha's life. Putting and keeping things in order was one of the interests which enlivened her dulness and made the world attractive to her.

The poor soul sat at the window, bending over the quilt, until dusk, and she sat there, bending over the quilt until dusk, many a day after.

It is a hard question to decide, whether there were any real merit in such finely strained honesty, or whether it were merely a case of morbid conscientiousness. Perhaps the old woman, inheriting very likely her father's scruples, had had them so intensified by age and childishness that they had become a little off the bias of reason.

Be that as it may, she thought it was the right course for her to make the quilts over, and, thinking so, it was all that she could do. She could never have been satisfied otherwise. It took her a considerable while longer to finish the quilts again, and this time she began to suffer from other causes than mere fatigue. Her stock of provisions commenced to run low, and her money was gone. At last she had nothing but a few potatoes in the house to eat. She contrived to dig some dandelion greens once or twice; these with the potatoes were all her diet. There was really no necessity for such a state of things; she was surrounded by kindly well-to-do people, who would have gone without themselves rather than let her suffer. But she had always been very reticent about her needs, and felt great pride about accepting anything for which she did not pay.

But she struggled along until the quilts were done, and no one knew. She set the last stitch quite late one evening; then she spread the quilts out and surveyed them. "Thar they air now, all right," said she; "the pink roses is in Mis' Bennet's, an' I ain't cheated nobody out on their caliker, an' I've airned my money. I'll take 'em hum in the mornin', an' then I'll buy somethin' to eat. I begin to feel a dreadful sinkin' at my stummuck."

She locked up the house carefully—she always felt a great responsibility when she had people's work on hand—and went to bed.

Next morning she woke up so faint and dizzy that she hardly knew herself. She crawled out into the kitchen, and sank down on the floor. She could not move another step.

"Lor sakes!" she moaned, "I reckon I'm 'bout done to!"

The quilts lay near her on the table; she stared up at them with feeble complacency. "Ef I'm goin' to die, I'm glad I got them quilts done right fust. Massy, how sinkin' I do feel! I wish I had a cup of tea."

There she lay, and the beautiful spring morning wore on. The sun shone in at the window, and moved nearer and nearer, until finally she lay in a sunbeam, a poor, shrivelled little old woman, whose resolute spirit had nearly been her death, in her scant nightgown and ruffled cap, a little shawl falling from her shoulders. She did not feel ill, only absolutely too weak and helpless to move. Her mind was just as active as ever, and her black eyes peered sharply out of her pinched face. She kept making efforts to rise, but she could not stir.

"Lor sakes!" she snapped out at length, "how long *hev* I got to lay here? I'm mad!"

She saw some dust on the black paint of a chair which stood in the sun, and she eyed that distressfully.

"Jest look at that dust on the runs of that cheer!" she muttered. "What if anybody come in! I wonder if I can't reach it!"

The chair was near her, and she managed to stretch out her limp old hand and rub the dust off the rounds. Then she let it sink down, panting.

"I wonder ef I *ain't* goin' to die," she gasped. "I wonder ef I'm prepared. I never took nothin' that shouldn't belong to me that I knows on. Oh, dear me suz, I wish somebody would come!"

When her strained ears did catch the sound of footsteps outside, a sudden resolve sprang up in her heart.

"I won't let on to nobody how I've made them quilts over, an' how I hevn't had enough to eat—I won't."

When the door was tried she called out feebly, "Who is thar?"

The voice of Mrs. Peters, her next-door neighbor, came back in response: "It's me. What's the matter, Marthy?"

"I'm kinder used up; don't know how you'll git in; I can't git to the door to unlock it to save my life."

"Can't I get in at the window?"

"Mebbe you kin."

Mrs. Peters was a long-limbed, spare woman, and she got in through the window with considerable ease, it being quite low from the ground.

She turned pale when she saw Martha lying on the floor. "Why, Marthy, what is the matter? How long have you been laying there?"

"Ever since I got up. I was kinder dizzy, an' hed a dreadful sinkin' feelin'. It ain't much, I reckon. Ef I could hev a cup of tea it would set me right up. Thar's a spoonful left in the pantry. Ef you jest put a few kindlin's in the stove, Mis' Peters, an' set in the kettle an' made me a cup, I could git up, I know. I've got to go an' kerry them quilts hum to Mis' Bliss an' Mis' Bennet."

"I don't believe but what you've got all tired out over the quilts. You've been working too hard."

"No, I 'ain't, Mis' Peters; it's nothin' but play piecin' quilts. All I mind is not havin' a front winder to set to while I'm doin' on't."

Mrs. Peters was a quiet, sensible woman of few words; she insisted upon carrying Martha into the bedroom and putting her comfortably to bed. It was easily done; she was muscular, and the old woman a very light weight. Then she went into the pantry. She was beginning to suspect the state of affairs, and her suspicions were strengthened when she saw the bare shelves. She started the fire, put on the tea-kettle, and then slipped across the yard to her own house for further reinforcements.

Pretty soon Martha was drinking her cup of tea and eating her toast and a dropped egg. She had taken the food with some reluctance, half starved as she was. Finally she gave in—the sight of it was too much for her. "Well, I will borry it, Mis' Peters," she said; "an I'll pay you jest as soon as I kin git up."

After she had eaten she felt stronger. Mrs. Peters had hard work to keep her quiet until afternoon; then she would get up and carry the quilts home. The two ladies were profuse in praises. Martha, proud and smiling. Mrs. Bennet noticed the pink roses at once. "How pretty that calico did work in," she remarked.

"Yes," assented Martha, between an inclination to chuckle and to cry.

"Ef I ain't thankful I did them quilts over," thought she, creeping slowly homeward, her hard-earned two dollars knotted into a corner of her handkerchief for security.

About sunset Mrs. Peters came in again. "Marthy," she said, after a while, "Sam says he's out of work just now, and he'll cut through a front window for you. He's got some old sash and glass that's been laying round in the barn ever since I can remember. It'll be a real charity for you to take it off his hands, and he'll like to do it. Sam's as uneasy as a fish out of water when he hasn't got any work."

Martha eyed her suspiciously. "Thanky; but I don't want nothin' done that I can't pay for," said she, with a stiff toss of her head.

"It would be pay enough, just letting Sam do it, Marthy; but, if you really feel set about it, I've got some sheets that need turning. You can do them some time this summer, and that will pay us for all it's worth."

The black eyes looked at her sharply. "Air you sure?"

"Yes; it's fully as much as it's worth," said Mrs. Peters. "I'm most afraid it's more. There's four sheets, and putting in a window is nothing more than putting in a patch—the old stuff ain't worth anything."

When Martha fully realized that she was going to have a front window, and that her pride might suffer it to be given to her and yet receive no insult, she was as delighted as a child.

"Lor sakes!" said she, "jest to think that I shall have a front winder to set to! I wish mother could ha' lived to see it. Mebbe you kinder wonder at it, Mis' Peters—you've allers had front winders; but you haven't any idea what a great thing it seems to me. It kinder makes me feel younger. Thar's the Mosely children; they're 'bout all I've ever seen pass *this* winder, Mis' Peters. Jest see that green spot out thar; it's been greener than the rest of the yard all the spring, an' now thar's lots of dandelions blowed out on it, an' some clover. I b'lieve the sun shines more on it, somehow. Law me, to think I'm going to hev a front winder!"

"Sarah was in this afternoon," said Mrs. Peters, further (Sarah was her married daughter), "and she says she wants some braided rugs right away. She'll send the rags over by Willie to-morrow."

"You don't say so! Well I'll be glad to do it; an' thar's one thing 'bout it, Mis' Peters—mebbe you'll think it queer for me to say so, but I'm kinder thankful it's rugs she wants. I'm kinder sick of bed-quilts somehow."

A Conflict Ended

1886

In Acton there were two churches, a Congregational and a Baptist. They stood on opposite sides of the road, and the Baptist edifice was a little farther down than the other. On Sunday morning both bells were ringing. The Baptist bell was much larger, and followed quickly on the soft peal of the Congregational with a heavy brazen clang which vibrated a good while. The people went flocking through the street to the irregular jangle of the bells. It was a very hot day, and the sun beat down heavily; parasols were bobbing over all the ladies' heads.

More people went into the Baptist church, whose society was much the larger of the two. It had been for the last ten years—ever since the Congregational had settled a new minister. His advent had divided the church, and a good third of the congregation had gone over to the Baptist brethren, with whom they still remained.

It is probable that many of them passed their old sanctuary to-day with the original stubborn animosity as active as ever in their hearts, and led their families up the Baptist steps with the same strong spiritual pull of indignation.

One old lady, who had made herself prominent on the opposition, trotted by this morning with the identical wiry vehemence which she had manifested ten years ago. She wore a full black silk skirt, which she held up inanely in front, and allowed to trail in the dust in the rear.

Some of the stanch Congregational people glanced at her amusedly. One fleshy, fair-faced girl in blue muslin said to her companion, with a laugh: "See that old lady trailing her best black silk by to the Baptist. Ain't it ridiculous how she keeps on showing out? I heard some one talking about it yesterday."

"Yes."

The girl colored up confusedly. "Oh dear!" she thought to herself. The lady with her had an unpleasant history connected with this old church quarrel. She was a small, bony woman in a shiny purple silk, which was strained very tightly across her sharp shoulder-blades. Her bonnet was quite elaborate with flowers and plumes, as was also her companion's. In fact, she was the village milliner, and the girl was her apprentice.

When the two went up the church steps, they passed a man of about fifty, who was sitting thereon well to one side. He had a singular face—a mild forehead, a gently curving mouth, and a terrible chin, with a look of strength in it that might have abashed mountains. He held his straw hat in his hand, and the sun was shining full on his bald head.

The milliner half stopped, and gave an anxious glance at him; then passed on. In the vestibule she stopped again.

"You go right in, Margy," she said to the girl. "I'll be along in a minute."

"Where be you going, Miss Barney?"

"You go right in. I'll be there in a minute."

Margy entered the audience-room then, as if fairly brushed in by the imperious wave of a little knotty hand, and Esther Barney stood waiting until the rush of entering people was over. Then she stepped swiftly back to the side of the man seated on the steps. She spread her large black parasol deliberately, and extended the handle towards him.

"No, no, Esther; I don't want it—I don't want it."

"If you're determined on setting out in this broiling sun, Marcus Woodman, you jest take this parasol of mine an' use it."

"I don't want your parasol, Esther. I—"

"Don't you say it over again. Take it."

"I won't—not if I don't want to."

"You'll get a sun-stroke."

"That's my own lookout."

"Marcus Woodman, you take it."

She threw all the force there was in her intense, nervous nature into her tone and look; but she failed in her attempt, because of the utter difference in quality between her own will and that with which she had to deal. They were on such different planes that hers slid by his with its own momentum; there could be no contact even of antagonism between them. He sat there rigid, every line of his face stifened into an icy obstinacy. She held out the parasol towards him like a weapon.

Finally she let it drop at her side, her whole expression changed.

"Marcus," said she, "how's your mother?"

He started. "Pretty well, thank you, Esther."

"She's out to meeting, then?"

"Yes."

"I've been a-thinking—I ain't drove jest now—that maybe I'd come over an' see her some day this week."

He rose politely then. "Wish you would, Esther. Mother'd be real pleased, I know."

"Well, I'll see—Wednesday, p'rhaps, if I ain't too busy. I must go in now; they're 'most through singing."

"Esther—"

"I don't believe I can stop any longer, Marcus."

"About the parasol—thank you jest the same if I don't take it. Of course you know I can't set out here holding a parasol; folks would laugh. But I'm obliged to you all the same. Hope I didn't say anything to hurt your feelings?"

"Oh no; why, no, Marcus. Of course I don't want to make you take it if you don't want it. I don't know but it would look kinder queer, come to think of it. Oh dear! they are through singing."

"Say, Esther, I don't know but I might as well take that parasol, if you'd jest as soon. The sun is pretty hot, an' I might get a headache. I forgot my umbrella, to tell the truth."

"I might have known better than to have gone at him the way I did," thought Esther to herself, when she was seated at last in the cool church beside Margy. "Seems as if I might have got used to Marcus Woodman by this time."

She did not see him when she came out of church, but a little boy in the vestibule handed her the parasol, with the remark, "Mr. Woodman said for me to give this to you."

She and Margy passed down the street towards home. Going by the Baptist church, they noticed a young man standing by the entrance. He stared hard at Margy.

She began to laugh after they had passed him. "Did you see that fellow stare?" said she. "Hope he'll know me next time."

"That's George Elliot; he's that old lady's son you was speaking about this morning."

"Well, that's enough for me."

"He's a real good, steady young man."

Margy sniffed.

"P'rhaps you'll change your mind some day."

She did, and speedily, too. That glimpse of Margy Wilson's pretty, new face—for she was a stranger in the town—had been too much for George Elliot. He obtained an introduction, and soon was a steady visitor at Esther Barney's house. Margy fell in love with him easily. She had never had much attention from the young men, and he was an engaging young fellow, small and bright-eyed, though with a nervous persistency like his mother's in his manner.

"I'm going to have it an understood thing," Margy told Esther, after her lover had become constant in his attentions, "that I'm going with George, and I ain't going with his mother. I can't bear that old woman."

But poor Margy found that it was not so easy to thrust determined old age off the stage, even when young Love was flying about so fast on his butterfly wings that he seemed to multiply himself, and there was no room for anything else, because the air was so full of Loves. That old mother, with her trailing black skirt and her wiry obstinacy, trotted as unwaveringly through the sweet stir as a ghost through a door.

One Monday morning Margy could not eat any breakfast, and there were tear stains around her blue eyes.

"Why, what's the matter, Margy?" asked Esther, eying her across the little kitchen-table.

"Nothing's the matter. I ain't hungry any to speak of, that's all. I guess I'll go right to work on Mis' Fuller's bonnet."

"I'd try an' eat something if I was you. Be sure you cut that velvet straight, if you go to work on it."

When the two were sitting together at their work in the little room back of the shop, Margy suddenly threw her scissors down. "There!" said she, "I've done it; I knew I should. I've cut this velvet bias. I knew I should cut everything bias I touched to-day."

There was a droll pucker on her mouth; then it began to quiver. She hid her face in her hands and sobbed. "Oh, dear, dear, dear!"

"Margy Wilson, what is the matter?"

"George and I—had a talk last night. We've broke the engagement, an' it's killing me. An' now I've cut this velvet bias. Oh, dear, dear, *dear*, dear!"

"For the land's sake, don't mind anything about the velvet. What's come betwixt you an' George?"

"His mother—horrid old thing! He said she'd got to live with us, and I said she shouldn't. Then he said he wouldn't marry any girl that wasn't willing to live with his mother, and I said he wouldn't ever marry me, then. If George Elliot thinks more of his mother than he does of me, he can have her. I don't care. I'll show him I can get along without him."

"Well, I don't know, Margy. I'm real sorry about it. George Elliot's a good, likely young man; but if you didn't want to live with his mother, it was better to say so right in the beginning. And I don't know as I blame you much: she's pretty set in her ways."

"I guess she is. I never could bear her. I guess he'll find out—"

Margy dried her eyes defiantly, and took up the velvet again. "I've spoilt this velvet. I don't see why being disappointed in love should effect a girl so's to make her cut bias."

There was a whimsical element in Margy which seemed to roll uppermost along with her grief.

Esther looked a little puzzled. "Never mind the velvet, child: it ain't much, anyway." She began tossing over some ribbons to cover her departure from her usual reticence. "I'm real sorry about it, Margy. Such things are hard to bear, but they can be lived through. I know something about it myself. You knew I'd had some of this kind of trouble, didn't you?"

"About Mr. Woodman, you mean?"

"Yes, about Marcus Woodman. I'll tell you what 'tis, Margy Wilson, you've got one thing to be thankful for, and that is that there ain't anything ridickerlous about this affair of yourn. That makes it the hardest of anything, according to my mind—when you know that everybody's laughing, and you can hardly help laughing yourself, though you feel 'most ready to die."

"Ain't that Mr. Woodman crazy?"

"No, he ain't crazy; he's got too much will for his common-sense, that's all, and the will teeters the sense a little too far into the air. I see all through it from the beginning. I could read Marcus Woodman jest like a book."

"I don't see how in the world you ever come to like such a man."

"Well, I s'pose love's the strongest when there ain't any good reason for it. They say it is. I can't say as I ever really admired Marcus Woodman much. I always see right through him; but that didn't hinder my thinking so much of him that I never felt as if I could marry any other man. And I've had chances, though I shouldn't want you to say so."

"You turned him off because he went to sitting on the church steps?"

"Course I did. Do you s'pose I was going to marry a man who made a laughing-stock of himself that way?"

"I don't see how he ever come to do it. It's the funniest thing I ever heard of."

"I know it. It seems so silly nobody 'd believe it. Well, all there is about it, Marcus Woodman's got so much mulishness in him it makes him almost miraculous. You see, he got up an' spoke in that church meeting when they had such a row about Mr. Morton's being settled here—Marcus was awful set again' him. I never could see any reason why, and I don't think he could. He said Mr. Morton wa'n't doctrinal; that was what they all said; but I don't believe half of 'em knew what doctrinal was. I never could see why Mr. Morton wa'n't as good as most ministers—enough sight better than them that treated him so, anyway. I always felt that they was really setting him in a pulpit high over their heads by using him the way they did, though they didn't know it.

"Well, Marcus spoke in that church meeting, an' he kept getting more and more set every word he said. He always had a way of saying things over and over, as if he was making steps out of 'em, an' raising of himself up on 'em, till there was no moving him at all. And he did that night. Finally, when he was up real high, he said, as for him, if Mr. Morton was settled over that church, he'd never go inside the door himself as long as he lived. Somebody spoke out then—I never quite knew who 'twas, though I suspected—an' says, 'You'll have to set on the steps, then, Brother Woodman.'

"Everybody laughed at that but Marcus. He didn't see nothing to laugh at. He spoke out awful set, kinder gritting his teeth, 'I will set on the steps fifty years before I'll go into this house if that man's settled here.'

"I couldn't believe he'd really do it. We were going to be married that spring, an' it did seem as if he might listen to me; but he wouldn't. The Sunday Mr. Morton begun to preach, he begun to set on them steps, an' he's set there ever since, in all kinds of weather. It's a wonder it 'ain't killed him; but I guess it's made him tough."

"Why, didn't he feel bad when you wouldn't marry him?"

"Feel bad? Of course he did. He took on terribly. But it didn't make any difference; he wouldn't give in a hair's breadth. I declare it did seem as if I should die. His mother felt awfully too—she's a real good woman. I don't know what Marcus would have done without her. He wants a sight of tending and waiting on; he's dreadful babyish in some ways, though you wouldn't think it.

"Well, it's all over now, as far as I'm concerned. I've got over it a good deal, though sometimes it makes me jest as mad as ever to see him setting there. But I try to be reconciled, and I get along jest as well, mebbe, as if I'd had him—I don't know. I fretted more at first than there was any sense in, and I hope you won't."

"I ain't going to fret at all, Miss Barney. I may cut bias for a while, but I sha'n't do anything worse."

"How you do talk, child!"

A good deal of it was talk with Margy; she had not as much courage as her words proclaimed. She was capable of a strong temporary resolution, but of no enduring one. She gradually weakened as the days without her lover went on, and one Saturday night she succumbed entirely. There was quite a rush of business, but through it all she caught a conversation between some customers—two pretty young girls.

"Who was that with you last night at the concert?"

"That—oh, that was George Elliot. Didn't you know him?"

"He's got another girl," thought Margy, with a great throb.

The next Sunday night, coming out of meeting with Miss Barney, she left her suddenly. George Elliot was one of a waiting line of young men in the vestibule. She went straight up to him. He looked at her in bewilderment, his dark face turning red.

"Good-evening, Miss Wilson," he stammered out, finally.

"Good-evening," she whispered, and stood looking up at him piteously. She was white and trembling.

At last he stepped forward suddenly and offered her his arm. In spite of his resentment, he could not put her to open shame before all his mates, who were staring curiously.

When they were out in the dark, cool street, he bent over her. "Why, Margy, what does all this mean?"

"Oh, George, let her live with us, please. I want her to. I know I can get along with her if I try. I'll do everything I can. Please let her live with us."

"Who's *her*?"

"Your mother."

"And I suppose *us* is you and I? I thought that was all over, Margy; ain't it?"

"Oh, George, I am sorry I treated you so."

"And you are willing to let mother live with us now?"

"I'll do anything. Oh, George!"

"Don't cry, Margy. There—nobody's looking—give us a kiss. It's been a long time; ain't it, dear? So you've made up your mind that you're willing to let mother live with us?"

"Yes."

"Well, I don't believe she ever will, Margy. She's about made up her mind to go and live with my brother Edward, whether or no. So you won't be troubled with her. I dare say she might have been a little of a trial as she grew older."

"You didn't tell me."

"I thought it was your place to give in, dear."

"Yes, it was, George."

"I'm mighty glad you did. I tell you what it is, dear, I don't know how you've felt, but I've been pretty miserable lately."

"Poor George!"

They passed Esther Barney's house, and strolled along half a mile farther. When they returned, and Margy stole softly into the house and upstairs, it was quite late, and Esther had gone to bed. Margy saw the light was not out in her room, so she peeped in. She could not wait till morning to tell her.

"Where have you been?" said Esther, looking up at her out of her pillows.

"Oh, I went to walk a little way with George."

"Then you've made up?"

"Yes."

"Is his mother going to live with you?"

"No; I guess not. She's going to live with Edward. But I told him I was willing she should. I've about made up my mind it's a woman's place to give in mostly. I s'pose you think I'm an awful fool."

"No, I don't; no, I don't, Margy. I'm real glad its all right betwixt you and George. I've seen you weren't very happy lately."

They talked a little longer; then Margy said "Good-night," going over to Esther and kissing her. Being so rich in love made her generous with it. She looked down sweetly into the older woman's thin, red-cheeked face. "I wish you were as happy as I," said she. "I wish you and Mr. Woodman could make up too."

"That's an entirely different matter. I couldn't give in in such a thing as that."

Margy looked at her; she was not subtle, but she had just come out triumphant through innocent love and submission, and used the wisdom she had gained thereby.

"Don't you believe," said she, "if you was to give in the way I did, that he would?"

Esther started up with an astonished air. That had never occurred to her before. "Oh, I don't believe he would. You don't know him; he's awful set. Besides, I don't know but I'm better off the way it is."

In spite of herself, however, she could not help thinking of Margy's suggestion. Would he give in? She was hardly disposed to run the risk. With her peculiar cast of mind, her feeling for the ludicrous so keen that it almost amounted to a special sense, and her sensitiveness to ridicule, it would have been easier for her to have married a man under the shadow of a crime than one who was the deserving target of gibes and jests. Besides, she told herself, it was possible that he had changed his mind, that he no longer cared for her. How could she make the first overtures? She had not Margy's impulsiveness and innocence of youth to excuse her.

Also, she was partly influenced by the reason which she had given Margy: she was not so very sure that it would be best for her to take any such step. She was more fixed in the peace and pride of her old maidenhood than she had realized, and was more shy of disturbing it. Her comfortable meals, her tidy housekeeping, and her prosperous work had become such sources of satisfaction to her that she was almost wedded to them, and jealous of any interference.

So it is doubtful if there would have been any change in the state of affairs if Marcus Woodman's mother had not died towards spring. Esther was greatly distressed about it.

"I don't see what Marcus is going to do," she told Margy. "He ain't any fitter to take care of himself than a baby, and he won't have any housekeeper, they say."

One evening, after Marcus's mother had been dead about three weeks, Esther went over there. Margy had gone out to walk with George, so nobody knew. When she reached the house—a white cottage on a hill—she saw a light in the kitchen window.

"He's there," said she. She knocked on the door softly. Marcus shuffled over to it—he was in his stocking feet—and opened it.

"Good-evening, Marcus," said she, speaking first.

"Good-evening."

"I hadn't anything special to do this evening, so I thought I'd look in a minute and see how you was getting along."

"I ain't getting along very well; but I'm glad to see you. Come right in."

When she was seated opposite him by the kitchen fire, she surveyed him and his surroundings pityingly. Everything had an abject air of forlornness; there was neither tidiness nor comfort. After a few words she rose energetically. "See here, Marcus," said she, "you jest fill up that tea-kettle, and I'm going to slick up here a little for you while I stay."

"Now, Esther, I don't feel as if—"

"Don't you say nothing. Here's the tea-kettle. I might jest as well be doing that as setting still."

He watched her, in a way that made her nervous, as she flew about putting things to rights; but she said to herself that this was easier than sitting still, and gradually leading up to the object for which she had come. She kept wondering if she could ever accomplish it. When the room was in order, finally, she sat down again, with a strained-up look in her face.

"Marcus," said she, "I might as well begin. There was something I wanted to say to you to-night."

He looked at her, and she went on:

"I've been thinking some lately about how matters used to be betwixt you an' me, and it's jest possible—I don't know—but I might have been a little more patient than I was. I don't know as I'd feel the same way now if—"

"Oh, Esther, what do you mean?"

"I ain't going to tell you, Marcus Woodman, if you can't find out. I've said full enough; more'n I ever thought I should."

He was an awkward man, but he rose and threw himself on his knees at her feet with all the grace of complete unconsciousness of action. "Oh, Esther, you don't mean, do you?—you don't mean that you'd be willing to—marry me?"

"No; not if you don't get up. You look ridickerlous."

"Esther, do you mean it?"

"Yes. Now get up."

"You ain't thinking—I can't give up what we had the trouble about, any more now than I could then."

"Ain't I said once that wouldn't make any difference?"

At that he put his head down on her knees and sobbed.

"Do, for mercy sake, stop. Somebody 'll be coming in. 'Tain't as if we was a young couple."

"I ain't going to till I've told you about it, Esther. You ain't never really understood. In the first of it, we was both mad; but we ain't now, and we can talk it over. Oh, Esther, I've had such an awful life! I've looked at you, and—Oh, dear, dear, dear!"

"Marcus, you scare me to death crying so."

"I won't. Esther, look here—it's the gospel truth: I ain't a thing again' Mr. Morton now."

"Then why on earth don't you go into the meeting-house and behave yourself?"

"Don't you suppose I would if I could? I can't, Esther—I can't."

"I don't know what you mean by can't."

"Do you s'pose I've took any comfort sitting there on them steps in the winter snows an' the summer suns? Do you s'pose I've took any comfort not marrying you? Don't you s'pose I'd given all I was worth any time the last ten year to have got up an' walked into the church with the rest of the folks?"

"Well, I'll own, Marcus, I don't see why you couldn't if you wanted to."

"I ain't sure as I see myself, Esther. All I know is I can't make myself give it up. I can't. I ain't made strong enough to."

"As near as I can make out, you've taken to sitting on the church steps the way other men take to smoking and drinking."

"I don't know but you're right, Esther, though I hadn't thought of it in that way before."

"Well, you must try to overcome it."

"I never can, Esther. It ain't right for me to let you think I can."

"Well, we won't talk about it any more to-night. It's time I was going home."

"Esther—did you mean it?"

"Mean what?"

"That you'd marry me any way?"

"Yes, I did. Now do get up. I do hate to see you looking so silly."

Esther had a new pearl-colored silk gown, and a little mantle like it, and a bonnet trimmed with roses and plumes, and she and Marcus were married in June.

The Sunday on which she came out a bride they were late at church; but late as it was, curious people were lingering by the steps to watch them. What would they do? Would Marcus Woodman enter that church door which his awful will had guarded for him so long?

They walked slowly up the steps between the watching people. When they came to the place where he was accustomed to sit, Marcus stopped short and looked down at his wife with an agonized face.

"Oh, Esther, I've—got—to stop."

"Well, we'll both sit down here, then."

"*You?*"

"Yes; I'm willing."

"No; you go in."

"No, Marcus; I sit with you on our wedding Sunday."

Her sharp, middle-aged face as she looked up at him was fairly heroic. This was all that she could do: her last weapon was used. If this failed, she would accept the chances with which she had married, and before the eyes of all these tittering people she would sit down at his side on these church steps. She was determined, and she would not weaken.

He stood for a moment staring into her face. He trembled so that the bystanders noticed it. He actually leaned over towards his old seat as if wire ropes were pulling him down upon it. Then he stood up straight, like a man, and walked through the church door with his wife.

The people followed. Not one of them even smiled. They had felt the pathos in the comedy.

The sitters in the pews watched Marcus wonderingly as he went up the aisle with Esther. He looked strange to them; he had almost the grand mien of a conqueror.

An Independent Thinker

1887

Esther Gay's house was little and square, and mounted on posts like stilts. A stair led up to the door on the left side. Morning-glories climbed up the stair-railing, the front of the house and the other side were covered with them, all the windows but one were curtained with the matted green vines. Esther sat at the uncurtained window, and knitted. She perked her thin, pale nose up in the air, her pointed chin tilted upward too; she held her knitting high, and the needles clicked loud, and shone in the sun. The bell was ringing for church, and a good many people were passing. They could look in on her, and see very plainly what she was doing. Every time a group went by she pursed her thin old lips tighter, and pointed up her nose higher, and knitted more fiercely. Her skinny shoulders jerked. She cast a sharp glance at every one who passed, but no one caught her looking. She knew them all. This was a little village. By and by the bell had stopped tolling, and even the late church-goers had creaked briskly out of sight. The street, which was narrow here, was still and vacant.

Presently a woman appeared in a little flower-garden in front of the opposite house. She was picking a nosegay. She was little and spare, and she bent over the flowers with a stiffness as of stiff wires. It seemed as if it would take mechanical force to spring her up again.

Esther watched her. "It's dretful hard work for her to git around," she muttered to herself.

Finally, she laid down her knitting and called across to her. "Laviny!" said she.

The woman came out to the gate with some marigolds and candytuft in her hand. Her dim blue eyes blinked in the light. She looked over and smiled with a sort of helpless inquiry.

"Come over here a minute."

"I—guess I—can't."

Esther was very deaf. She could not hear a word, but she saw the deprecating shake of the head, and she knew well enough.

"I'd like to know why you can't, a minute. You kin hear your mother the minute she speaks."

The woman glanced back at the house, then she looked over at Esther. Her streaked light hair hung in half-curls over her wide crocheted collar, she had a little, narrow, wrinkled face, but her cheeks were as red as roses.

"I guess I'd better not. It's Sunday, you know," said she. Her soft, timid voice could by no possibility reach those deaf ears across the way.

"What?"

"I—guess I'd better not—as long as it's *Sunday*."

Esther's strained attention caught the last word, and guessed at the rest from a knowledge of the speaker.

"Stuff," said she, with a sniff through her delicate, up-tilted nostrils. "I'd like to know how much worse 'tis for you to step over here a minute, an' tell me how *she* is when I can't hear across the road, than to stop an' talk comin' out o' meetin'; you'd do that quick enough. You're strainin', Laviny Dodge."

Lavinia, as if overwhelmed by the argument, cast one anxious glance back at the house, and came through the gate.

Just then a feeble, tremulous voice, with a wonderful quality of fine sharpness in it, broke forth behind her,

"Laviny, Laviny, where be you goin'? Come back here."

Lavinia, wheeling with such precipitate vigor that it suggested a creak, went up the path.

"I wa'n't goin' anywhere, mother," she called out. "What's the matter?"

"You can't pull the wool over my eyes. I *seed* you a-goin' out the gate."

Lavinia's mother was over ninety and bedridden. That infinitesimal face which had passed through the stages of beauty, commonplaceness, and hideousness, and now arrived at that of the fine grotesqueness which has, as well as beauty, a certain charm of its own, peered out from its great feather pillows. The skin on the pinched face was of a dark-yellow color, the eyes were like black points, the tiny, sunken mouth had a sardonic pucker.

"Esther jest wanted me to come over there a minute. She wanted to ask after you," said Lavinia, standing beside the bed, holding her flowers.

"Hey?"

"She *jest* wanted me to come over an' tell her how you was."

"How I was?"

"Yes."

"Did you tell her I was miser'ble?"

"I didn't go, mother."

"I *seed* you a-goin' out the gate."

"I came back. She couldn't hear 'thout I went way over."

"Hey?"

"It's all right, mother," screamed Lavinia. Then she went about putting the flowers in water.

The old woman's little eyes followed her, with a sharp light like steel.

"I ain't goin' to hev you goin' over to Esther Gay's, Sabbath day," she went on, her thin voice rasping out from her pillows like a file. "She ain't no kind of a girl. Wa'n't she knittin'?"

"Yes."

"Hey?"

"Yes, she was knittin', mother."

"Wa'n't knittin'?"

"Y-e-s, she was."

"I knowed it. Stayin' home from meetin' an' knittin'. I ain't goin' to hev you over thar, Laviny."

Esther Gay, over in her window, held her knitting up higher, and knitted with fury. "H'm, the old lady called her back," said she. "If they want to show out they kin, I'm goin' to do what I think's right."

The morning-glories on the house were beautiful this morning, the purple and white and rosy ones stood out with a soft crispness. Esther Gay's house was not so pretty in winter—there was no paint on it, and some crooked outlines showed. It was a poor little structure, but Esther owned it free of encumbrances. She had also a pension of ninety-six dollars which served her for support. She considered herself well to do. There was not enough for anything besides necessaries, but Esther was one who had always looked upon necessaries as luxuries. Her sharp eyes saw the farthest worth of things. When she bought a half-cord of pine wood with an allotment of her pension-money, she saw in a vision all the warmth and utility which could ever come from it. When it was heaped up in the space under the house which she used for a wood-shed, she used to go and look at it.

"Esther Gay does think so much of her own things," people said.

That little house, which, with its precipitous stair and festoons of morning-glories, had something of a foreign picturesqueness, looked to her like a real palace. She paid a higher tax upon it than she should have done. A lesser one had been levied, and regarded by her as an insult. "My house is worth more'n that," she had told the assessor with an indignant bridle. She paid the increased tax with cheerful pride, and frequently spoke of it. To-day she often glanced from her knitting around the room. There was a certain beauty in it, although it was hardly the one which she recognized. It was full of a lovely, wavering, gold-green light, and there was a fine order and cleanness which gave a sense of peace. But Esther saw mainly her striped rag-carpet, her formally set chairs, her lounge covered with Brussels, and her shining cooking-stove.

Still she looked at nothing with the delight with which she surveyed her granddaughter Hatty, when she returned from church.

"Well, you've got home, ain't you?" she said, when the young, slim girl, with her pale, sharp face, which was like her grandmother's, stood before her. Hatty in her meeting-gown of light-brown delaine, and her white meeting-hat trimmed with light-brown ribbons and blue flowers was not pretty, but the old woman admired her.

"Yes," said Hatty. Then she went into her little bedroom to take off her things. There was a slow shyness about her. She never talked much, even to her grandmother.

"You kin git you somethin' to eat, if you want it," said the old woman. "I don't want to stop myself till I git this heel done. Was Henry to meetin'?"

"Yes."

"His father an' mother?"

"Yes."

Henry was the young man who had been paying attention to Hatty. Her grandmother was proud and pleased; she liked him.

Hatty generally went to church Sunday evenings, and the young man escorted her home, and came in and made a call. To-night the girl did not go to church as usual. Esther was astonished.

"Why, ain't you goin' to meetin'?" said she.

"No; I guess not."

"Why? why not?"

"I thought I wouldn't."

The old woman looked at her sharply. The tea-things were cleared away, and she was at her knitting again, a little lamp at her elbow.

Presently Hatty went out, and sat at the head of the stairs, in the twilight. She sat there by herself until meeting was over, and the people had been straggling by for some time. Then she went down-stairs, and joined a young man who passed at the foot of them. She was gone half an hour.

"Where hev you been?" asked her grandmother, when she returned.

"I went out a little way."

"Who with?"

"Henry."

"Why didn't he come in?"

"He thought he wouldn't."

"I don't see why."

Hatty said nothing. She lit her candle to go to bed. Her little thin face was imperturbable.

She worked in a shop, and earned a little money. Her grandmother would not touch a dollar of it; what she did not need to spend for herself, she made her save. Lately the old woman had been considering the advisability of her taking a sum from the saving's bank to buy a silk dress. She thought she might need it soon.

Monday, she opened upon the subject. "Hatty," said she, "I've been thinkin'—don't you believe it would be a good plan for you to take a little of your money out of the bank an' buy you a nice dress?"

Hatty never answered quickly. She looked at her grandmother, then she kept on with her sewing. It was after supper, her shop-work was done, and she was sitting at the table with her needle. She seemed to be considering her grandmother's remark.

The old woman waited a moment, then she proceeded: "I've been thinkin'—you ain't never had any real nice dress, you know—that it would be a real good plan for you to take some money, now you've got it, an' buy you a silk one. You ain't never had one, an' you're old enough to."

Still Hatty sewed, and said nothing.

"You might want to go somewhar," continued Esther, "an'—well, of course, if anythin' should happen, if Henry—It's jest as well not to hev' to do everythin' all to once, an' it's consider'ble work to make a silk dress— Why don't you say somethin'?"

"I don't want any silk dress."

"I'd like to know why not?"

Hatty made no reply.

"Look here, Hatty, you an' Henry Little ain't had no trouble, hev' you?"

"I don't know as we have."

"What?"

"I don't know as we have."

"Hatty Gay, I know there's somethin' the matter. Now you jest tell me what 'tis. Ain't he comin' here no more?"

Suddenly the girl curved her arm around on the table, and laid her face down on it. She would not speak another word. She did not seem to be crying, but she sat there, hiding her little plain, uncommunicative face.

"Hatty Gay, ain't he comin'? *Why* ain't he comin'?"

Hatty would give the old woman no information. All she got was that obtained from ensuing events. Henry Little did not come; she ascertained that. The weeks went on, and he had never once climbed those vine-wreathed stairs to see Hatty.

Esther fretted and questioned. One day, in the midst of her nervous conjectures, she struck the chord in Hatty which vibrated with information.

"I hope you want too forrard with Henry, Hatty," said the old woman. "You didn't act too anxious arter him, did you? That's apt to turn fellows."

Then Hatty spoke. Some pink spots flared out on her quiet, pale cheeks.

"Grandma," said she, "I'll tell you, if you want to know, what the trouble is. I wasn't goin' to, because I didn't want to make you feel bad; but, if you're goin' to throw out such things as that to me, I don't care. Henry's mother don't like you, there!"

"What?"

"Henry's mother don't like you."

"Don't like me?"

"No."

"Why, what hev I done? I don't see what you mean, Hatty Gay."

"Grace Porter told me. Mrs. Little told her mother. Then I asked him, an' he owned up it was so."

"I'd like to know what she said."

Hatty went on, pitilessly, "She told Grace's mother she didn't want her son to marry into the Gay tribe anyhow. She didn't think much of 'em. She said any girl whose folks didn't keep Sunday, an' stayed away from meetin' an' worked, wouldn't amount to much."

"I don't believe she said it."

"She did. Henry said his mother took on so he was afraid she'd die, if he didn't give it up."

Esther sat up straight. She seemed to bristle out suddenly with points, from her knitting-needles to her sharp elbows and thin chin and nose. "Well, he kin give it up then, if he wants to, for all me. I ain't goin' to give up my principles fir him, nor any of his folks, an' they'll find it out. You kin git somebody else jest as good as he is."

"I don't want anybody else."

"H'm, you needn't have 'em then, ef you ain't got no more sperit. I shouldn't think you'd want your grandmother to give up doin' what's right yourself, Hatty Gay."

"I ain't sure it is right."

"Ain't sure it's right. Then I s'pose you think it would be better for an old woman that's stone deaf, an' can't hear a word of the preachin', to go to meetin' an' set there, doin' nothin' two hours, instead of stayin' to home an' knittin', to airn a leetle money to give to the Lord. All I've got to say is, you kin think so, then. I'm a-goin' to do what's right, no matter what happens."

Hatty said nothing more. She took up her sewing again; her grandmother kept glancing at her. Finally she said, in a mollifying voice, "Why don't you go an' git you a leetle piece of that cake in the cupboard; you didn't eat no supper hardly."

"I don't want any."

"Well, if you want to make yourself sick, an' go without eatin, you kin."

Hatty did go without eating much through the following weeks. She laid awake nights, too, staring pitifully into the darkness, but she did not make herself ill. There was an unflinching strength in that little, meagre body, which lay even back of her own will. It would take long for her lack of spirit to break her down entirely; but her grandmother did not know that. She watched her and worried. Still she had not the least idea of giving in. She knitted more zealously than ever Sundays; indeed, there was, to her possibly distorted perceptions, a religious zeal in it.

She knitted on week-days too. She reeled off a good many pairs of those reliable blue-yarn stockings, and sold them to a dealer in the city. She gave away every cent which she earned, and carefully concealed the direction of her giving. Even Hatty did not know of it.

Six weeks after Hatty's lover left, the old woman across the way died. After the funeral, when measures were taken for the settlement of the estate, it was discovered that all the little property was gone, eaten up by a mortgage and the interest. The two old women had lived upon the small house and the few acres of land for the last ten years, ever since Lavinia's father had died. He had grubbed away in a boot-shop, and earned enough for their frugal support as long as he lived. Lavinia had never been able to work for her own living; she was not now. "Laviny Dodge will have to go to the poorhouse," everybody said.

One noon Hatty spoke of it to her grandmother. She rarely spoke of anything now, but this was uncommon news.

"They say Laviny Dodge has got to go to the poorhouse," said she.

"What?"

"They say Laviny Dodge has got to go to the poorhouse."

"I don't believe a word on't."

"They say it's so."

That afternoon Esther went over to ascertain the truth of the report for herself. She found Lavinia sitting alone in the kitchen crying. Esther went right in, and stood looking at her.

"It's so, ain't it?" said she.

Lavinia started. There was a momentary glimpse of a red, distorted face; then she hid it again, and went on rocking herself to and fro and sobbing. She had seated herself in the rocking-chair to weep. "Yes," she wailed, "it's so! I've got to go. Mr. Barnes come in, an' said I had this mornin'; there ain't no other way. I've—got—to go. Oh, what would mother have said!"

Esther stood still, looking. "A place gits run out afore you know it," she remarked.

"Oh, I didn't s'pose it was quite so near gone. I thought mebbe I could stay—as long as I lived."

"You'd oughter hev kept account."

"I s'pose I hed, but I never knew much 'bout money-matters, an' poor mother, she was too old. Father was real sharp, ef he'd lived. Oh, I've got to go! I never thought it would come to this!"

"I don't think you're fit to do any work."

"No; they say I ain't. My rheumatism has been worse lately. It's been hard work for me to crawl round an' wait on mother. I've got to go. Oh, Esther, it's awful to think I can't die in my own home. Now I've got—to die in the poorhouse! I've—got—to die in the poorhouse!"

"I've got to go now," said Esther.

"Don't go. You ain't but jest come. I ain't got a soul to speak to."

"I'll come in agin arter supper," said Esther, and went out resolutely, with Lavinia wailing after her to come back. At home, she sat down and deliberated. She had a long talk with Hatty when she returned. "I don't care," was all she could get out of the girl, who was more silent than usual. She ate very little supper.

It was eight o'clock when Esther went over to the Dodge house. The windows were all dark. "Land, I believe she's gone to bed," said the old woman, fumbling along through the yard. The door was fast, so she knocked. "Laviny, Laviny, be you gone to bed? Laviny Dodge!"

"Who is it?" said a quavering voice on the other side, presently.

"It's me. You gone to bed?"

"It's you, Mis' Gay, ain't it?"

"Yes. Let me in. I want to see you a minute."

Then Lavinia opened the door and stood there, her old knees knocking together with cold and nervousness. She had got out of bed and put a plaid shawl over her shoulders when she heard Esther.

"I want to come in jest a minute," said Esther. "I hadn't any idee you'd be gone to bed."

The fire had gone out, and it was chilly in the kitchen, where the two women sat down.

"You'll ketch your death of cold in your night-gown," said Esther. "You'd better git somethin' more to put over you."

"I don't keer if I do ketch cold," said Lavinia, with an air of feeble recklessness, which sat oddly upon her.

"Laviny Dodge, don't talk so."

"I don't keer. I'd ruther ketch my death of cold than not; then I shouldn't have to die in the poorhouse." The old head, in its little cotton night-cap, cocked itself sideways, with pitiful bravado.

Esther rose, went into the bedroom, got a quilt and put it over Lavinia's knees. "There," said she, "you hev that over you. There ain't no sense in your talkin' that way. You're jest a-flyin' in the face of Providence, an' Providence don't mind the little flappin' you kin make, any more than a barn does a swaller."

"I can't help it."

"What?"

"I—can't help it."

"Yes, you kin help it, too. Now, I'll tell you what I've come over here for. I've been thinkin' on't all the arternoon, an' I've made up my mind. I want you to come over and live with me."

Lavinia sat feebly staring at her. "Live with you!"

"Yes. I've got my house an' my pension, an' I pick up some with my knittin'. Two won't cost much more'n one. I reckon we kin git along well enough."

Lavinia said nothing, she still sat staring. She looked scared.

Esther began to feel hurt. "Mebbe you don't want to come," she said, stiffly, at last.

Lavinia shivered. "There's jest—one thing—" she commenced.

"What?"

"There's jest one thing—"

"What's that?"

"I dunno what— Mother— You're real good; but—Oh, I don't see how I kin come, Esther!"

"Why not? If there's any reason why you don't want to live with me, I want to know what 'tis."

Lavinia was crying. "I can't tell you," she sobbed; "but, mother— If— you didn't work Sundays. Oh!"

"Then you mean to say you'd ruther go to the poorhouse than come to live with me, Lavinia Dodge?"

"I—can't help it."

"Then, all I've got to say is, you kin go."

Esther went home, and said no more. In a few days she, peering around her curtain, saw poor Lavinia Dodge, a little, trembling, shivering figure, hoisted into the poorhouse covered wagon, and driven off. After the wagon was out of sight, she sat down and cried.

It was early in the afternoon. Hatty had just gone to her work, having scarcely tasted her dinner. Her grandmother had worked hard to get an extra one to-day, too, but she had no heart to eat. Her mournful silence, which seemed almost obstinate, made the old woman at once angry and wretched. Now she wept over Lavinia Dodge and Hatty, and the two causes combined made bitter tears.

"I wish to the land" she cried out loud once—"I wish to the land I could find some excuse; but I ain't goin' to give up what I think's right."

Esther Gay had never been so miserable in her life as she was for the three months after Lavinia Dodge left her home. She thought of her, she watched Hatty, and she knitted. Hatty was at last beginning to show the effects of her long worry. She looked badly, and the neighbors began speaking about it to her grandmother. The old woman seemed to resent it when they did. At times she scolded the girl, at times she tried to pet her, and she knitted constantly, week-days and Sundays.

Lavinia had been in the almshouse three months, when one of the neighbors came in one day and told Esther that she was confined to her bed. Her rheumatism was worse, and she was helpless. Esther dropped her knitting, and stared radiantly at the neighbor. "You said she was an awful sight of trouble, didn't you?" said she.

"Yes; Mis' Marvin said it was worse than takin' care of a baby."

"I should think it would take about all of anybody's time."

"I should. Why, Esther Gay, you look real tickled 'cause she's sick!" cried the woman, bluntly.

Esther colored. "You talk pretty," said she.

"Well, I don't care; you looked so. I don't s'pose you was," said the other, apologetically.

That afternoon Esther Gay made two visits: one at the selectmen's room, in the town-hall, the other at Henry Little's. One of her errands at the selectmen's room was concerning the reduction of her taxes.

"I'm a-payin' too much on that leetle house," said she, standing up, alert and defiant. "It ain't wuth it." There was some dickering, but she gained her point. Poor Esther Gay would never make again her foolish little boast about her large tax. More than all her patient, toilsome knitting was the sacrifice of this bit of harmless vanity.

When she arrived at the Littles', Henry was out in the yard. He was very young; his innocent, awkward face flushed when he saw Esther coming up the path.

"Good arternoon," said she. Henry jerked his head.

"Your mother to home?"

"Ye—s."

Esther advanced and knocked, while Henry stood staring.

Presently Mrs. Little answered the knock. She was a large woman. The astonished young man saw his mother turn red in the face, and rear herself in order of battle, as it were, when she saw who her caller was; then he heard Esther speak.

"I'm a-comin' right to the p'int afore I come in," said she. "I've heard you said you didn't want your son to marry my granddaughter because you didn't like some things about me. Now, I want to know if you said it."

"Yes; I did," replied Mrs. Little, tremulous with agitation, red, and perspiring, but not weakening.

"Then you didn't have nothin' again' Hatty, you nor Henry? 'Twa'n't an excuse?"

"I ain't never had anything against the girl."

"Then I want to come in a minute. I've got somethin' I want to say to you, Mrs. Little."

"Well, you can come in—if you want to."

After Esther had entered, Henry stood looking wistfully at the windows. It seemed to him that he could not wait to know the reason of Esther's visit. He took things more soberly than Hatty; he had not lost his meals nor his sleep; still he had suffered. He was very fond of the girl, and he had a heart which was not easily diverted. It was hardly possible that he would ever die of grief, but it was quite possible that he might live long with a memory, young as he was.

When his mother escorted Esther to the door, as she took leave, there was a marked difference in her manner. "Come again soon, Mis' Gay," he heard her say; "run up any time you feel like it, an' stay to tea. I'd really like to have you."

"Thank ye," said Esther, as she went down the steps. She had an aspect of sweetness about her which did not seem to mix well with herself.

When she reached home she found Hatty lying on the lounge. "How do you feel to-night?" said she, unpinning her shawl.

"Pretty well."

"You'd better go an' brush your hair an' change your dress. I've been over to Henry's an' seen his mother, an' I shouldn't wonder if he was over here to-night."

Hatty sat bolt upright and looked at her grandmother. "What do you mean?"

"What I say. I've been over to Mrs. Little's, an' we've had a talk. I guess she thought she'd been kind of silly to make such a fuss. I reasoned with her, an' I guess she saw I'd been more right about some things than she'd thought for. An' as far as goin' to meetin' an' knittin' Sundays is concerned— Well, I don't s'pose I kin knit any more if I want to. I've been to see about it, an' Laviny Dodge is comin' here Saturday, an' she's so bad

with her rheumatiz that she can't move, an' I guess it'll be all I kin do to
wait on her, without doin' much knittin'. Mebbe I kin git a few minutes
evenin's, but I reckon 'twon't amount to much. Of course I couldn't go to
meetin' if I wanted to. I couldn't leave Laviny."

"Did she say he—was coming?"

"Yes; she said she shouldn't wonder if he was up."

The young man did come that evening, and Esther retired to her little
bedroom early, and lay listening happily to the soft murmur of voices outside. Lavinia Dodge arrived Saturday. The next morning, when Hatty had
gone to church, she called Esther. "I want to speak to you a minute," said
she. "I want to know if— Mr. Winter brought me over, and he married the
Ball girl that's been in the post-office, you know, and somethin' he said—
Esther Gay, I want to know if you're the one that's been sendin' that money
to me and mother all along?"

Esther colored, and turned to go. "I don't see why you think it's me."

"Esther, don't you go. I know 'twas; you can't say 'twa'n't."

"It wa'n't much, anyhow."

"'Twas to us. It kept us goin' a good while longer. We never said anythin'
about it. Mother was awful proud, you know, but I dunno what we should
have done. Esther, how could you do it?"

"Oh, it wa'n't anythin'. It was extra money. I airn'd it."

"Knittin'?"

Esther jerked her head defiantly. The sick woman began to cry. "If I'd ha'
known, I would ha' come. I wouldn't have said a word."

"Yes, you would, too. You was bound to stan' up for what you thought
was right, jest as much as I was. Now, we've both stood up, an' it's all right.
Don't you fret no more about it."

"To think—"

"Land sakes, don't cry. The tea's all steeped, and I'm goin' to bring you
in a cup now."

Henry came that evening. About nine o'clock Esther got a pitcher and
went down to the well to draw some water for the invalid. Her old joints
were so tired and stiff that she could scarcely move. She had had a hard
day. After she had filled her pitcher she stood resting for a moment, staring
up at the bright sitting-room windows. Henry and Hatty were in there: just
a simple, awkward young pair, with nothing beautiful about them, save
the spark of eternal nature, which had its own light. But they sat up stiffly

and timidly in their two chairs, looking at each other with full content. They had glanced solemnly and bashfully at Esther when she passed through the room; she appeared not to see them.

Standing at the well, looking up at the windows, she chuckled softly to herself. "It's all settled right," said she, "an' there don't none of 'em suspect that I'm a-carryin' out my p'int arter all."

A New England Nun

1887

It was late in the afternoon, and the light was waning. There was a difference in the look of the tree shadows out in the yard. Somewhere in the distance cows were lowing and a little bell was tinkling; now and then a farm-wagon tilted by, and the dust flew; some blue-shirted laborers with shovels over their shoulders plodded past; little swarms of flies were dancing up and down before the peoples' faces in the soft air. There seemed to be a gentle stir arising over everything for the mere sake of subsidence—a very premonition of rest and hush and night.

This soft diurnal commotion was over Louisa Ellis also. She had been peacefully sewing at her sitting-room window all the afternoon. Now she quilted her needle carefully into her work, which she folded precisely, and laid in a basket with her thimble and thread and scissors. Louisa Ellis could not remember that ever in her life she had mislaid one of these little feminine appurtenances, which had become, from long use and constant association, a very part of her personality.

Louisa tied a green apron round her waist, and got out a flat straw hat with a green ribbon. Then she went into the garden with a little blue crockery bowl, to pick some currants for her tea. After the currants were picked she sat on the back door-step and stemmed them, collecting the stems carefully in her apron, and afterwards throwing them into the hen-coop. She looked sharply at the grass beside the step to see if any had fallen there.

Louisa was slow and still in her movements; it took her a long time to prepare her tea; but when ready it was set forth with as much grace as if she had been a veritable guest to her own self. The little square table stood exactly in the centre of the kitchen, and was covered with a starched linen cloth whose border pattern of flowers glistened. Louisa had a damask nap-kin on her tea-tray, where were arranged a cut-glass tumbler full of tea-spoons, a silver cream-pitcher, a china sugar-bowl, and one pink china cup and saucer. Louisa used china every day—something which none of her neighbors did. They whispered about it among themselves. Their daily ta-bles were laid with common crockery, their sets of best china stayed in the parlor closet, and Louisa Ellis was no richer nor better bred than they. Still she would use the china. She had for her supper a glass dish full of sugared currants, a plate of little cakes, and one of light white biscuits. Also a leaf or two of lettuce, which she cut up daintily. Louisa was very fond of let-tuce, which she raised to perfection in her little garden. She ate quite heart-ily, though in a delicate, pecking way; it seemed almost surprising that any considerable bulk of the food should vanish.

After tea she filled a plate with nicely baked thin corn-cakes, and carried them out into the back-yard.

"Cæsar!" she called. "Cæsar! Cæsar!"

There was a little rush, and the clank of a chain, and a large yellow-and-white dog appeared at the door of his tiny hut, which was half hidden among the tall grasses and flowers. Louisa patted him and gave him the corn-cakes. Then she returned to the house and washed the tea-things, pol-ishing the china carefully. The twilight had deepened; the chorus of the frogs floated in at the open window wonderfully loud and shrill, and once in a while a long sharp drone from a tree-toad pierced it. Louisa took off her green gingham apron, disclosing a shorter one of pink and white print. She lighted her lamp, and sat down again with her sewing.

In about half an hour Joe Dagget came. She heard his heavy step on the walk, and rose and took off her pink-and-white apron. Under that was still another—white linen with a little cambric edging on the bottom; that was Louisa's company apron. She never wore it without her calico sewing apron over it unless she had a guest. She had barely folded the pink and white one with methodical haste and laid it in a table-drawer when the door opened and Joe Dagget entered.

He seemed to fill up the whole room. A little yellow canary that had been asleep in his green cage at the south window woke up and fluttered wildly, beating his little yellow wings against the wires. He always did so when Joe Dagget came into the room.

"Good-evening," said Louisa. She extended her hand with a kind of sol-emn cordiality.

"Good-evening, Louisa," returned the man, in a loud voice.

She placed a chair for him, and they sat facing each other, with the table between them. He sat bolt-upright, toeing out his heavy feet squarely, glancing with a good-humored uneasiness around the room. She sat gently erect, folding her slender hands in her white-linen lap.

"Been a pleasant day," remarked Dagget.

"Real pleasant," Louisa assented, softly. "Have you been haying?" she asked, after a little while.

"Yes, I've been haying all day, down in the ten-acre lot. Pretty hot work."

"It must be."

"Yes, it's pretty hot work in the sun."

"Is your mother well to-day?"

"Yes, mother's pretty well."

"I suppose Lily Dyer's with her now?"

Dagget colored. "Yes, she's with her," he answered, slowly.

He was not very young, but there was a boyish look about his large face. Louisa was not quite as old as he, her face was fairer and smoother, but she gave people the impression of being older.

"I suppose she's a good deal of help to your mother," she said, further.

"I guess she is; I don't know how mother'd get along without her," said Dagget, with a sort of embarrassed warmth.

"She looks like a real capable girl. She's pretty-looking too," remarked Louisa.

"Yes, she is pretty fair looking."

Presently Dagget began fingering the books on the table. There was a square red autograph album, and a Young Lady's Gift-Book which had belonged to Louisa's mother. He took them up one after the other and opened them; then laid them down again, the album on the Gift-Book.

Louisa kept eying them with mild uneasiness. Finally she rose and changed the position of the books, putting the album underneath. That was the way they had been arranged in the first place.

Dagget gave an awkward little laugh. "Now what difference did it make which book was on top?" said he.

Louisa looked at him with a deprecating smile. "I always keep them that way," murmured she.

"You do beat everything," said Dagget, trying to laugh again. His large face was flushed.

He remained about an hour longer, then rose to take leave. Going out, he stumbled over a rug, and trying to recover himself, hit Louisa's work-basket on the table, and knocked it on the floor.

He looked at Louisa, then at the rolling spools; he ducked himself awkwardly toward them, but she stopped him. "Never mind," said she; "I'll pick them up after you're gone."

She spoke with a mild stiffness. Either she was a little disturbed, or his nervousness affected her, and made her seem constrained in her effort to reassure him.

When Joe Dagget was outside he drew in the sweet evening air with a sigh, and felt much as an innocent and perfectly well-intentioned bear might after his exit from a china shop.

Louisa, on her part, felt much as the kind-hearted, long-suffering owner of the china shop might have done after the exit of the bear.

She tied on the pink, then the green apron, picked up all the scattered treasures and replaced them in her work-basket, and straightened the rug. Then she set the lamp on the floor, and began sharply examining the carpet. She even rubbed her fingers over it, and looked at them.

"He's tracked in a good deal of dust," she murmured. "I thought he must have."

Louisa got a dust-pan and brush, and swept Joe Dagget's track carefully.

If he could have known it, it would have increased his perplexity and uneasiness, although it would not have disturbed his loyalty in the least. He came twice a week to see Louisa Ellis, and every time, sitting there in her delicately sweet room, he felt as if surrounded by a hedge of lace. He was afraid to stir lest he should put a clumsy foot or hand through the fairy web, and he had always the consciousness that Louisa was watching fearfully lest he should.

Still the lace and Louisa commanded perforce his perfect respect and patience and loyalty. They were to be married in a month, after a singular courtship which had lasted for a matter of fifteen years. Four fourteen out of the fifteen years the two had not once seen each other, and they had seldom exchanged letters. Joe had been all those years in Australia, where he had gone to make his fortune, and where he had stayed until he made it. He would have stayed fifty years if it had taken so long, and come home feeble and tottering, or never come home at all, to marry Louisa.

But the fortune had been made in the fourteen years, and he had come home now to marry the woman who had been patiently and unquestioningly waiting for him all that time.

Shortly after they were engaged he had announced to Louisa his determination to strike out into new fields, and secure a competency before they
should be married. She had listened and assented with the sweet serenity
which never failed her, not even when her lover set forth on that long and
uncertain journey. Joe, buoyed up as he was by his sturdy determination,
broke down a little at the last, but Louisa kissed him with a mild blush, and
said good-by.

"It won't be for long," poor Joe had said, huskily; but it was for fourteen
years.

In that length of time much had happened. Louisa's mother and brother
had died, and she was all alone in the world. But greatest happening of
all—a subtle happening which both were too simple to understand—Louisa's feet had turned into a path, smooth maybe under a calm, serene sky,
but so straight and unswerving that it could only meet a check at her grave,
and so narrow that there was no room for any one at her side.

Louisa's first emotion when Joe Dagget came home (he had not apprised
her of his coming) was consternation, although she would not admit it to
herself, and he never dreamed of it. Fifteen years ago she had been in love
with him—at least she considered herself to be. Just at that time, gently ac-
quiescing with and falling into the natural drift of girlhood, she had seen
marriage ahead as a reasonable feature and a probable desirability of life.
She had listened with calm docility to her mother's views upon the subject.
Her mother was remarkable for her cool sense and sweet, even temperament. She talked wisely to her daughter when Joe Dagget presented himself, and Louisa accepted him with no hesitation. He was the first lover she
had ever had.

She had been faithful to him all these years. She had never dreamed of
the possibility of marrying any one else. Her life, especially for the last
seven years, had been full of a pleasant peace, she had never felt discon-
tented nor impatient over her lover's absence; still she had always looked
forward to his return and their marriage as the inevitable conclusion of
things. However, she had fallen into a way of placing it so far in the future
that it was almost equal to placing it over the boundaries of another life.

When Joe came she had been expecting him, and expecting to be married for fourteen years, but she was as much surprised and taken aback as if
she had never thought of it.

Joe's consternation came later. He eyed Louisa with an instant confirmation of his old admiration. She had changed but little. She still kept her

pretty manner and soft grace, and was, he considered, every whit as attractive as ever. As for himself, his stent was done; he had turned his face away from fortune-seeking, and the old winds of romance whistled as loud and sweet as ever through his ears. All the song which he had been wont to hear in them was Louisa; he had for a long time a loyal belief that he heard it still, but finally it seemed to him that although the winds sang always that one song, it had another name. But for Louisa the wind had never more than murmured; now it had gone down, and everything was still. She listened for a little while with half-wistful attention; then she turned quietly away and went to work on her wedding clothes.

Joe had made some extensive and quite magnificent alterations in his house. It was the old homestead; the newly-married couple would live there, for Joe could not desert his mother, who refused to leave her old home. So Louisa must leave hers. Every morning, rising and going about among her neat maidenly possessions, she felt as one looking her last upon the faces of dear friends. It was true that in a measure she could take them with her, but, robbed of their old environments, they would appear in such new guises that they would almost cease to be themselves. Then there were some peculiar features of her happy solitary life which she would probably be obliged to relinquish altogether. Sterner tasks than these graceful but half-needless ones would probably devolve upon her. There would be a large house to care for; there would be company to entertain; there would be Joe's rigorous and feeble old mother to wait upon; and it would be contrary to all thrifty village traditions for her to keep more than one servant. Louisa had a little still, and she used to occupy herself pleasantly in summer weather with distilling the sweet and aromatic essences from roses and peppermint and spearmint. By-and-by her still must be laid away. Her store of essences was already considerable, and there would be no time for her to distil for the mere pleasure of it. Then Joe's mother would think it foolishness; she had already hinted her opinion in the matter. Louisa dearly loved to sew a linen seam, not always for use, but for the simple, mild pleasure which she took in it. She would have been loath to confess how more than once she had ripped a seam for the mere delight of sewing it together again. Sitting at her window during long sweet afternoons, drawing her needle gently through the dainty fabric, she was peace itself. But there was small chance of such foolish comfort in the future. Joe's mother, domineering, shrewd old matron that she was even in her old age, and very likely even Joe himself, with his honest masculine rudeness, would laugh and frown down all these pretty but senseless old maiden ways.

Louisa had almost the enthusiasm of an artist over the mere order and cleanliness of her solitary home. She had throbs of genuine triumph at the sight of the window-panes which she had polished until they shone like jewels. She gloated gently over her orderly bureau-drawers, with their exquisitely folded contents redolent with lavender and sweet clover and very purity. Could she be sure of the endurance of even this? She had visions, so startling that she half repudiated them as indelicate, of coarse masculine belongings strewn about in endless litter; of dust and disorder arising necessarily from a coarse masculine presence in the midst of all this delicate harmony.

Among her forebodings of disturbance, not the least was with regard to Cæsar. Cæsar was a veritable hermit of a dog. For the greater part of his life he had dwelt in his secluded hut, shut out from the society of his kind and all innocent canine joys. Never had Cæsar since his early youth watched at a woodchuck's hole; never had he known the delights of a stray bone at a neighbor's kitchen door. And it was all on account of a sin committed when hardly out of his puppyhood. No one knew the possible depth of remorse of which this mild-visaged, altogether innocent-looking old dog might be capable; but whether or not he had encountered remorse, he had encountered a full measure of righteous retribution. Old Cæsar seldom lifted up his voice in a growl or a bark; he was fat and sleepy; there were yellow rings which looked like spectacles around his dim old eyes; but there was a neighbor who bore on his hand the imprint of several of Cæsar's sharp white youthful teeth, and for that he had lived at the end of a chain, all alone in a little hut, for fourteen years. The neighbor, who was choleric and smarting with the pain of his wound, had demanded either Cæsar's death or complete ostracism. So Louisa's brother, to whom the dog had belonged, had built him his little kennel and tied him up. It was now fourteen years since, in a flood of youthful spirits, he had inflicted that memorable bite, and with the exception of short excursions, always at the end of the chain, under the strict guardianship of his master or Louisa, the old dog had remained a close prisoner. It is doubtful if, with his limited ambition, he took much pride in the fact, but it is certain that he was possessed of considerable cheap fame. He was regarded by all the children in the village and by many adults as a very monster of ferocity. St. George's dragon could hardly have surpassed in evil repute Louisa Ellis's old yellow dog. Mothers charged their children with solemn emphasis not to go too near to him, and the children listened and believed greedily, with a fascinated appetite for terror, and ran by Louisa's house stealthily, with many sidelong and backward glances at the terrible dog. If perchance he sounded a hoarse bark, there was a panic. Wayfarers chancing into Louisa's yard eyed him with respect, and inquired if the chain were stout. Cæsar at large might have seemed a very ordinary dog, and excited no comment whatever; chained, his reputation overshadowed him, so that he lost his own proper outlines and looked darkly vague and enormous. Joe Dagget, however, with his good-humored sense and shrewdness, saw him as he was. He strode valiantly up to him and patted him on the head, in spite of Louisa's soft clamor of warning, and even attempted to set him loose. Louisa grew so alarmed that he desisted, but kept announcing his opinion in the matter quite forcibly at intervals. "There ain't a better-natured dog in town," he would say, "and it's downright cruel to keep him tied up there. Some day I'm going to take him out."

Louisa had very little hope that he would not, one of these days, when their interests and possessions should be more completely fused in one. She pictured to herself Cæsar on the rampage through the quiet and unguarded village. She saw innocent children bleeding in his path. She was herself very fond of the old dog, because he had belonged to her dead brother, and he was always very gentle with her; still she had great faith in his ferocity. She always warned people not to go too near him. She fed him on ascetic fare of corn-mush and cakes, and never fired his dangerous temper with heating and sanguinary diet of flesh and bones. Louisa looked at the old dog munching his simple fare, and thought of her approaching marriage and trembled. Still no anticipation of disorder and confusion in lieu of sweet peace and harmony, no forebodings of Cæsar on the rampage, no wild fluttering of her little yellow canary, were sufficient to turn her a hair's-breadth. Joe Dagget had been fond of her and working for her all these years. It was not for her, whatever came to pass, to prove untrue and break his heart. She put the exquisite little stitches into her wedding-garments, and the time went on until it was only a week before her wedding-day. It was a Tuesday evening, and the wedding was to be a week from Wednesday.

There was a full moon that night. About nine o'clock Louisa strolled down the road a little way. There were harvest-fields on either hand, bordered by low stone walls. Luxuriant clumps of bushes grew beside the wall, and trees—wild cherry and old apple-trees—at intervals. Presently Louisa sat down on the wall and looked about her with mildly sorrowful reflectiveness. Tall shrubs of blueberry and meadow-sweet, all woven together and tangled with blackberry vines and horsebriers, shut her in on either side. She had a little clear space between them. Opposite her, on the other side of the road, was a spreading tree; the moon shone between its boughs, and the leaves twinkled like silver. The road was bespread with a beautiful shifting dapple of silver and shadow; the air was full of a mysterious sweetness. "I wonder if it's wild grapes?" murmured Louisa. She sat there some time. She was just thinking of rising, when she heard footsteps and low voices, and remained quiet. It was a lonely place, and she felt a little timid. She thought she would keep still in the shadow and let the persons, whoever they might be, pass her.

But just before they reached her the voices ceased, and the footsteps. She understood that their owners had also found seats upon the stone wall. She was wondering if she could not steal away unobserved, when the voice broke the stillness. It was Joe Dagget's. She sat still and listened.

The voice was announced by a loud sigh, which was as familiar as itself. "Well," said Dagget, "you've made up your mind, then, I suppose?"

"Yes," returned another voice; "I'm going day after to-morrow."

"That's Lily Dyer," thought Louisa to herself. The voice embodied itself in her mind. She saw a girl tall and full-figured, with a firm, fair face, looking fairer and firmer in the moonlight, her strong yellow hair braided in a close knot. A girl full of a calm rustic strength and bloom, with a masterful way which might have beseemed a princess. Lily Dyer was a favorite with the village folk; she had just the qualities to arouse the admiration. She was good and handsome and smart. Louisa had often heard her praises sounded.

"Well," said Joe Dagget, "I ain't got a word to say."

"I don't know what you could say," returned Lily Dyer.

"Not a word to say," repeated Joe, drawing out the words heavily. Then there was a silence. "I ain't sorry," he began at last, "that that happened yesterday—that we kind of let on how we felt to each other. I guess it's just as well we knew. Of course I can't do anything any different. I'm going right on an' get married next week. I ain't going back on a woman that's waited for me fourteen years, an' break her heart."

"If you should jilt her to-morrow, I wouldn't have you," spoke up the girl, with sudden vehemence.

"Well, I ain't going to give you the chance," said he; "but I don't believe you would, either."

"You'd see I wouldn't. Honor's honor, an' right's right. An' I'd never think anything of any man that went against 'em for me or any other girl; you'd find that out, Joe Dagget."

"Well, you'll find out fast enough that I ain't going against 'em for you or any other girl," returned he. Their voices sounded almost as if they were angry with each other. Louisa was listening eagerly.

"I'm sorry you feel as if you must go away," said Joe, "but I don't know but it's best."

"Of course it's best. I hope you and I have got common-sense."

"Well, I suppose you're right." Suddenly Joe's voice got an undertone of tenderness. "Say, Lily," said he, "I'll get along well enough myself, but I can't bear to think—You don't suppose you're going to fret much over it?"

"I guess you'll find out I sha'n't fret much over a married man."

"Well, I hope you won't—I hope you won't, Lily. God knows I do. And—I hope—one of these days—you'll—come across somebody else—"

"I don't see any reason why I shouldn't." Suddenly her tone changed. She spoke in a sweet, clear voice, so loud that she could have been heard across the street. "No, Joe Dagget," said she, "I'll never marry any other man as long as I live. I've got good sense, an' I ain't going to break my heart nor make a fool of myself; but I'm never going to be married, you can be sure of that. I ain't that sort of a girl to feel this way twice."

Louisa heard an exclamation and a soft commotion behind the bushes; then Lily spoke again—the voice sounded as if she had risen. "This must be put a stop to," said she. "We've stayed here long enough. I'm going home."

Louisa sat there in a daze, listening to their retreating steps. After a while she got up and slunk softly home herself. The next day she did her house-work methodically; that was as much a matter of course as breathing; but she did not sew on her wedding-clothes. She sat at her window and medi-tated. In the evening Joe came. Louisa Ellis had never known that she had any diplomacy in her, but when she came to look for it that night she found it, although meek of its kind, among her little feminine weapons. Even now she could hardly believe that she had heard aright, and that she would not do Joe a terrible injury should she break her troth-plight. She wanted to sound him without betraying too soon her own inclinations in the matter. She did it successfully, and they finally came to an understanding; but it was a difficult thing, for he was as afraid of betraying himself as she.

She never mentioned Lily Dyer. She simply said that while she had no cause of complaint against him, she had lived so long in one way that she shrank from making a change.

"Well, I never shrank, Louisa," said Dagget. "I'm going to be honest enough to say that I think maybe it's better this way; but if you'd wanted to keep on, I'd have stuck to you till my dying day. I hope you know that."

"Yes, I do," said she.

That night she and Joe parted more tenderly than they had done for a long time. Standing in the door, holding each other's hands, a last great wave of regretful memory swept over them.

"Well, this ain't the way we've thought it was all going to end, is it, Louisa?" said Joe.

She shook her head. There was a little quiver on her placid face.

"You let me know if there's ever anything I can do for you," said he. "I ain't ever going to forget you, Louisa." Then he kissed her, and went down the path.

Louisa, all alone by herself that night, wept a little, she hardly knew why; but the next morning, on waking, she felt like a queen who, after fearing lest her domain be wrested away from her, sees it firmly insured in her possession.

Now the tall weeds and grasses might cluster around Cæsar's little hermit hut, the snow might fall on its roof year in and year out, but he never would go on a rampage through the unguarded village. Now the little canary might turn itself into a peaceful yellow ball night after night, and have no need to wake and flutter with wild terror against its bars. Louisa could sew linen seams, and distil roses, and dust and polish and fold away in lavender, as long as she listed. That afternoon she sat with her needle-work at the window, and felt fairly steeped in peace. Lily Dyer, tall and erect and blooming, went past; but she felt no qualm. If Louisa Ellis had sold her birthright she did not know it, the taste of the pottage was so delicious, and had been her sole satisfaction for so long. Serenity and placid narrowness had become to her as the birthright itself. She gazed ahead through a long reach of future days strung together like pearls in a rosary, every one like the others, and all smooth and flawless and innocent, and her heart went up in thankfulness. Outside was the fervid summer afternoon; the air was filled with the sounds of the busy harvest of men and birds and bees; there were halloos, metallic clatterings, sweet calls, and long hummings. Louisa sat, prayerfully numbering her days, like an uncloistered nun.

Christmas Jenny

1888

The day before there had been a rain and a thaw, then in the night the wind had suddenly blown from the north, and it had grown cold. In the morning it was very clear and cold, and there was the hard glitter of ice over everything. The snow-crust had a thin coat of ice, and all the open fields shone and flashed. The tree boughs and trunks, and all the little twigs, were enamelled with ice. The roads were glare and slippery with it, and so were the door-yards. In old Jonas Carey's yard the path that sloped from the door to the well was like a frozen brook.

Quite early in the morning old Jonas Carey came out with a pail, and went down the path to the well. He went slowly and laboriously, shuffling his feet, so he should not fall. He was tall and gaunt, and one side of his body seemed to slant towards the other, he settled so much more heavily upon one foot. He was somewhat stiff and lame from rheumatism.

He reached the well in safety, hung the pail, and began pumping. He pumped with extreme slowness and steadiness; a certain expression of stolid solemnity, which his face wore, never changed.

When he had filled his pail he took it carefully from the pump spout, and started back to the house, shuffling as before. He was two thirds of the way to the door, when he came to an extremely slippery place. Just there some roots from a little cherry-tree crossed the path, and the ice made a dangerous little pitch over them.

Old Jonas lost his footing, and sat down suddenly; the water was all spilled. The house door flew open, and an old woman appeared.

"Oh, Jonas, air you hurt?" she cried, blinking wildly and terrifiedly in the brilliant light.

The old man never said a word. He sat still and looked straight before him, solemnly.

"Oh, Jonas, you ain't broke any bones, hev you?" The old woman gathered up her skirts and began to edge off the door-step, with trembling knees.

Then the old man raised his voice. "Stay where you be," he said, imperatively. "Go back into the house!"

He began to raise himself, one joint at a time, and the old woman went back into the house, and looked out of the window at him.

When old Jonas finally stood upon his feet it seemed as if he had actually constructed himself, so piecemeal his rising had been. He went back to the pump, hung the pail under the spout, and filled it. Then he started on the return with more caution than before. When he reached the dangerous place his feet flew up again, he sat down, and the water was spilled.

The old woman appeared in the door; her dim blue eyes were quite round, her delicate chin was dropped. "Oh, Jonas!"

"Go back!" cried the old man, with an imperative jerk of his head towards her, and she retreated. This time he arose more quickly, and made quite a lively shuffle back to the pump.

But when his pail was filled and he again started on the return, his caution was redoubled. He seemed to scarcely move at all. When he approached the dangerous spot his progress was hardly more perceptible than a scaly leaf-slug's. Repose almost lapped over motion. The old woman in the window watched breathlessly.

The slippery place was almost passed, the shuffle quickened a little—the old man sat down again, and the tin pail struck the ice with a clatter.

The old woman appeared. "Oh, Jonas!"

Jonas did not look at her; he sat perfectly motionless.

"Jonas, air you hurt? Do speak to me for massy sake!" Jonas did not stir.

Then the old woman let herself carefully off the step. She squatted down upon the icy path, and hitched along to Jonas. She caught hold of his arm—"Jonas, you don't feel as if any of your bones were broke, do you?" Her voice was almost sobbing, her small frame was all of a tremble.

"Go back!" said Jonas. That was all he would say. The old woman's tearful entreaties did not move him in the least. Finally she hitched herself back to the house, and took up her station in the window. Once in a while she rapped on the pane, and beckoned piteously.

But old Jonas Carey sat still. His solemn face was inscrutable. Over his head stretched the icy cherry-branches, full of the flicker and dazzle of dia-monds. A woodpecker flew into the tree and began tapping at the trunk, but the ice-enamel was so hard that he could not get any food. Old Jonas sat so still that he did not mind him. A jay flew on the fence within a few feet of him; a sparrow pecked at some weeds piercing the snow-crust be-side the door. Over in the east arose the mountain, covered with frosty fo-liage full of silver and blue and diamond lights. The air was stinging. Old Jonas paid no attention to anything. He sat there.

The old woman ran to the door again. "Oh, Jonas, you'll freeze, settin' there!" she pleaded. "Can't you git up? Your bones ain't broke, air they?" Jonas was silent.

"Oh, Jonas, there's Christmas Jenny comin' down the road—what do you s'pose she'll think?"

Old Jonas Carey was unmoved, but his old wife eagerly watched the woman coming down the road. The woman looked oddly at a distance: like a broad green moving bush; she was dragging something green after her, too. When she came nearer one could see that she was laden with ev-ergreen wreaths—her arms were strung with them; long sprays of ground-pine were wound around her shoulders, she carried a basket trailing with them, and holding also many little bouquets of bright-colored everlasting flowers. She dragged a sled, with a small hemlock-tree bound upon it. She came along sturdily over the slippery road. When she reached the Carey gate she stopped and looked over at Jonas. "Is he hurt?" she sang out to the old woman.

"I dunno—he's fell down three times."

Jenny came through the gate, and proceeded straight to Jonas. She left her sled in the road. She stooped, brought her basket on a level with Jonas's head, and gave him a little push with it. "What's the matter with ye?" Jonas did not wink. "Your bones ain't broke, are they?"

Jenny stood looking at him for a moment. She wore a black hood, her large face was weather-beaten, deeply tanned, and reddened. Her features were strong, but heavily cut. She made one think of those sylvan faces with features composed of bark-wrinkles and knot-holes, that one can fancy looking out of the trunks of trees. She was not an aged woman, but her hair was iron-gray, and crinkled as closely as gray moss.

Finally she turned towards the house. "I'm comin' in a minute," she said to Jonas's wife, and trod confidently up the icy steps.

"Don't you slip," said the old woman, tremulously.

"I ain't afraid of slippin'." When they were in the house she turned around on Mrs. Carey, "Don't you fuss, he ain't hurt."

"No, I don't s'pose he is. It's jest one of his tantrums. But I dunno what I am goin' to do. Oh, dear me suz, I dunno what I am goin' to do with him sometimes!"

"Leave him alone—let him set there."

"Oh, he's tipped all that water over, an' I'm afeard he'll—freeze down. Oh, dear!"

"Let him freeze! Don't you fuss, Betsey."

"I was jest goin' to git breakfast. Mis' Gill she sent us in two sassage-cakes. I was goin' to fry 'em, an' I jest asked him to go out an' draw a pail of water, so's to fill up the tea-kittle. Oh, dear!"

Jenny sat her basket in a chair, strode peremptorily out of the house, picked up the tin pail which lay on its side near Jonas, filled it at the well, and returned. She wholly ignored the old man. When she entered the door his eyes relaxed their solemn stare at vacancy, and darted a swift glance after her.

"Now fill up the kittle, an' fry the sassages," she said to Mrs. Carey.

"Oh, I'm afeard he won't git up, an' they'll be cold! Sometimes his tantrums last a consider'ble while. You see you sot down three times, an' he's awful mad."

"I don't see who he thinks he's spitin'."

"I dunno, 'less it's Providence."

"I reckon Providence don't care much where he sets."

"Oh, Jenny, I'm dreadful afeard he'll freeze down."

"No, he won't. Put on the sassages."

Jonas's wife went about getting out the frying-pan, crooning over her complaint all the time. "He's dreadful fond of sassages," she said, when the odor of the frying sausages became apparent in the room.

"He'll smell 'em an' come in," remarked Jenny, dryly. "He knows there ain't but two cakes, an' he'll be afeard you'll give me one of 'em."

She was right. Before long the two women, taking sly peeps from the window, saw old Jonas lumberingly getting up. "Don't say nothin' to him about it when he comes in," whispered Jenny.

When the old man clumped into the kitchen, neither of the women paid any attention to him. His wife turned the sausages, and Jenny was gathering up her wreaths. Jonas let himself down into a chair, and looked at them uneasily. Jenny laid down her wreaths. "Goin' to stay to breakfast?" said the old man.

"Well, I dunno," replied Jenny. "Them sassages do smell temptin'."

All Jonas's solemnity had vanished, he looked foolish and distressed.

"Do take off your hood, Jenny," urged Betsey. "I ain't very fond of sas-sages myself, an' I'd jest as liv's you'd have my cake as not."

Jenny laughed broadly and good-naturedly, and began gathering up her wreaths again. "Lor', I don't want your sassage-cake," said she. "I've had my breakfast. I'm goin' down to the village to sell my wreaths."

Jonas's face lit up. "Pleasant day, ain't it?" he remarked, affably.

Jenny grew sober. "I don't think it's a very pleasant day; guess you wouldn't if you was a woodpecker or a blue-jay," she replied.

Jonas looked at her with stupid inquiry.

"They can't git no breakfast," said Jenny. "They can't git through the ice on the trees. They'll starve if there ain't a thaw pretty soon. I've got to buy 'em somethin' down to the store. I'm goin' to feed a few of 'em. I ain't goin' to see 'em dyin' in my door-yard if I can help it. I've given 'em all I could spare from my own birds this mornin'."

"It's too bad, ain't it?"

"I think it's too bad. I was goin' to buy me a new caliker dress if this freeze hadn't come, but I can't now. What it would cost will save a good many lives. Well, I've got to hurry along if I'm goin' to git back to-day."

Jenny, surrounded with her trailing masses of green, had to edge herself through the narrow doorway. She went straight to the village and peddled her wares from house to house. She had her regular customers. Every year, the week before Christmas, she came down from the mountain with her evergreens. She was popularly supposed to earn quite a sum of money in that way. In the summer she sold vegetables, but the green Christmas traf-fic was regarded as her legitimate business—it had given her her name among the villagers. However, the fantastic name may have arisen from the popular conception of Jenny's character. She also was considered somewhat fantastic, although there was no doubt of her sanity. In her early youth she had had an unfortunate love affair, that was supposed to have tinctured her whole life with an alien element. "Love-cracked," people called her.

"Christmas Jenny's kind of love-cracked," they said. She was Christmas Jenny in midsummer, when she came down the mountain laden with green peas and string-beans and summer squashes.

She owned a little house and a few acres of cleared land on the moun-tain, and in one way or another she picked up a living from it.

It was noon to-day before she had sold all her evergreens and started up the mountain road for home. She had laid in a small stock of provisions, and she carried them in the basket which had held the little bunches of life-everlasting and amaranth flowers and dried grasses.

The road wound along the base of the mountain. She had to follow it about a mile; then she struck into a cart-path which led up to the clearing where her house was.

After she passed Jonas Carey's there were no houses and no people, but she met many living things that she knew. A little field-mouse, scratching warily from cover to cover, lest his enemies should spy him, had appreciative notice from Jenny Wrayne. She turned her head at the call of a jay, and she caught a glimmer of blue through the dazzling white boughs. She saw with sympathetic eyes a woodpecker drumming on the ice-bound trunk of a tree. Now and then she scattered, with regretful sparseness, some seeds and crumbs from her parcels.

At the point where she left the road for the cart-path there was a gap in the woods, and a clear view of the village below. She stopped and looked back at it. It was quite a large village; over it hung a spraying net-work of frosty branches; the smoke arose straight up from the chimneys. Down in the village street a girl and a young man were walking, talking about her, but she did not know that.

The girl was the minister's daughter. She had just become engaged to the young man, and was walking with him in broad daylight with a kind of shamefaced pride. Whenever they met anybody she blushed, and at the same time held up her head proudly, and swung one arm with an airy motion. She chattered glibly and quite loudly, to cover her embarrassment.

"Yes," she said, in a sweet, crisp voice, "Christmas Jenny has just been to the house, and we've bought some wreaths. We're going to hang them in all the front windows. Mother didn't know as we ought to buy them of her, there's so much talk, but I don't believe a word of it, for my part."

"What talk?" asked the young man. He held himself very stiff and straight, and never turned his head when he shot swift, smiling glances at the girl's pink face.

"Why, don't you know? It's town-talk. They say she's got a lot of birds and rabbits and things shut up in cages, and half starves them; and then that little deaf-and-dumb boy, you know—they say she treats him dreadfully. They're going to look into it. Father and Deacon Little are going up there this week."

"Are they?" said the young man. He was listening to the girl's voice with a sort of rapturous attention, but he had little idea as to what she was saying. As they walked, they faced the mountain.

It was only the next day when the minister and Deacon Little made the visit. They started up a flock of sparrows that were feeding by Jenny's door; but the birds did not fly very far—they settled into a tree and watched. Jenny's house was hardly more than a weather-beaten hut, but there was a grape-vine trained over one end, and the front yard was tidy. Just before the house stood a tall pine-tree. At the rear, and on the right, stretched the remains of Jenny's last summer's garden, full of plough-ridges and glistening corn-stubble.

Jenny was not at home. The minister knocked and got no response. Finally he lifted the latch, and the two men walked in. The room seemed gloomy after the brilliant light outside; they could not see anything at first, but they could hear a loud and demonstrative squeaking and chirping and twittering that their entrance appeared to excite.

At length a small pink-and-white face cleared out of the gloom in the chimney-corner. It surveyed the visitors with no fear nor surprise, but seemingly with an innocent amiability.

"That's the little deaf-and-dumb boy," said the minister, in a subdued voice. The minister was an old man, narrow-shouldered, and clad in long-waisted and wrinkly black. Deacon Little reared himself in his sinewy leanness until his head nearly touched the low ceiling. His face was sallow and severely corrugated, but the features were handsome.

Both stood staring remorselessly at the little deaf-and-dumb boy, who looked up in their faces with an expression of delicate wonder and amusement. The little boy was dressed like a girl, in a long blue gingham pinafore. He sat in the midst of a heap of evergreens, which he had been twining into wreaths; his pretty, soft, fair hair was damp, and lay in a very flat and smooth scallop over his full white forehead.

"He looks as if he was well cared for," said Deacon Little. Both men spoke in hushed tones—it was hard for them to realize that the boy could not hear, the more so because every time their lips moved his smile deepened. He was not in the least afraid.

They moved around the room half guiltily, and surveyed everything. It was unlike any apartment that they had ever entered. It had a curious sylvan air; there were heaps of evergreens here and there, and some small green trees leaned in one corner. All around the room—hung on the walls, standing on rude shelves—were little rough cages and hutches, from which the twittering and chirping sounded. They contained forlorn little birds and rabbits and field-mice. The birds had rough feathers and small, dejected heads, one rabbit had an injured leg, one field-mouse seemed nearly dead. The men eyed them sharply. The minister drew a sigh; the deacon's handsome face looked harder. But they did not say what they thought, on account of the little deaf-and-dumb boy, whose pleasant blue eyes never left their faces. When they had made the circuit of the room, and stood again by the fireplace, he suddenly set up a cry. It was wild and inarticulate, still not wholly dissonant, and it seemed to have a meaning of its own. It united with the cries of the little caged wild creatures, and it was all like a soft clamor of eloquent appeal to the two visitors, but they could not understand it.

They stood solemn and perplexed by the fireplace. "Had we better wait till she comes?" asked the minister.

"I don't know," said Deacon Little.

Back of them arose the tall mantel-shelf. On it were a clock and a candle-stick, and regularly laid bunches of brilliant dried flowers, all ready for Jenny to put in her basket and sell.

Suddenly there was a quick scrape on the crusty snow outside, the door flew open, and Jonas Carey's wife came in. She had her shawl over her head, and she was panting for breath.

She stood before the two men, and a sudden crust of shy formality seemed to form over her. "Good-arternoon," she said, in response to their salutations.

She looked at them for a moment, and tightened her shawl-pin; then the restraint left her. "I knowed you was here," she cried, in her weak, vehement voice; "I knowed it. I've heerd the talk. I knowed somebody was goin' to come up here an' spy her out. I was in Mis' Gregg's the other day, an' her husband came home; he'd been down to the store, an' he said they were talkin' 'bout Jenny, an' sayin' she didn't treat Willy and the birds well, an' the town was goin' to look into it. I knowed you was comin' up here when I seed you go by. I told Jonas so. An' I knowed she wa'n't to home, an' there wa'n't nothin' here that could speak, an' I told Jonas I was comin'. I couldn't stan' it nohow. It's dreadful slippery. I had to go on my hands an' knees in some places, an' I've sot down twice, but I don't care. I ain't goin' to have you comin' up here to spy on Jenny, an' nobody to home that's got any tongue to speak for her."

Mrs. Carey stood before them like a ruffled and defiant bird that was frighting herself as well as them with her temerity. She palpitated all over, but there was a fierce look in her dim blue eyes.

The minister began a deprecating murmur, which the deacon drowned. "You can speak for her all you want to, Mrs. Carey," said he. "We ain't got any objections to hearin' it. An' we didn't know but what she was home. Do you know what she does with these birds and things?"

"Does with 'em? Well, I'll tell you what she does with 'em. She picks 'em up in the woods when they're starvin' an' freezin' an' half dead, an' she brings 'em in here, an' takes care of 'em an' feeds 'em till they git well, an' then she lets 'em go again. That's what she does. You see that rabbit there? Well, he's been in a trap. Somebody wanted to kill the poor little cretur. You see that robin? Somebody fired a gun at him an' broke his wing.

"That's what she does. I dunno but it 'mounts to jest about as much as sendin' money to missionaries. I dunno but what bein' a missionary to robins an' starvin' chippies an' little deaf-an'-dumb children is jest as good as some other kinds, an' that's what she is.

"I ain't afeard to speak; I'm goin' to tell the whole story. I dunno what folks mean by talkin' about her the way they do. There, she took that little dumbie out of the poorhouse. Nobody else wanted him. He don't look as if he was abused very bad, far's I can see. She keeps him jest as nice an' neat as she can, an' he an' the birds has enough to eat, if she don't herself.

"I guess I know 'bout it. Here she is goin' without a new caliker dress, so's to git somethin' for them birds that can't git at the trees, 'cause there's so much ice on 'em.

"You can't tell me nothin'. When Jonas has one of his tantrums she can git him out of it quicker'n anybody I ever see. She ain't goin' to be talked about and spied upon if I can help it. They tell about her bein' love-cracked. H'm, I dunno what they call love-cracked. I know that Anderson fellar went off an' married another girl, when Jenny jest as much expected to have him as could be. He ought to ha' been strung up. But I know one thing—if she did git kind of twisted out of the reg'lar road of lovin', she's in another one, that's full of little dumbies an' starvin' chippies an' lame rabbits, an' she ain't love-cracked no more'n other folks."

Mrs. Carey, carried away by affection and indignation, almost spoke in poetry. Her small face glowed pink, her blue eyes were full of fire, she waved her arms under her shawl. The little meek old woman was a veritable enthusiast.

The two men looked at each other. The deacon's handsome face was as severe and grave as ever, but he waited for the minister to speak. When the minister did speak it was apologetically. He was a gentle old man, and the deacon was his mouthpiece in matters of parish discipline. If he failed him he betrayed how feeble and kindly a pipe was his own. He told Mrs. Carey that he did not doubt everything was as it should be; he apologized for their presence; he praised Christmas Jenny. Then he and the deacon retreated. They were thankful to leave that small, vociferous old woman, who seemed to be pulling herself up by her enthusiasm until she reached the air over their heads, and became so abnormal that she was frightful. Indeed, everything out of the broad, common track was a horror to these men and to many of their village fellows. Strange shadows, that their eyes could not pierce, lay upon such, and they were suspicious. The popular sentiment against Jenny Wrayne was originally the outcome of this characteristic, which was a remnant of the old New England witchcraft superstition. More than anything else, Jenny's eccentricity, her possibly uncanny deviation from the ordinary ways of life, had brought this inquiry upon her. In actual meaning, although not even in self-acknowledgment, it was a witch-hunt that went up the mountain road that December afternoon.

They hardly spoke on the way. Once the minister turned to the deacon. "I rather think there's no occasion for interference," he said, hesitatingly.

"I guess there ain't any need of it," answered the deacon.

The deacon spoke again when they had nearly reached his own house. "I guess I'll send her up a little somethin' Christmas," said he. Deacon Little was a rich man.

"Maybe it would be a good idea," returned the minister. "I'll see what I can do."

Christmas was one week from that day. On Christmas morning old Jonas Carey and his wife, dressed in their best clothes, started up the mountain road to Jenny Wrayne's. Old Jonas wore his great-coat, and had his wife's cashmere scarf wound twice around his neck. Mrs. Carey wore her long shawl and her best bonnet. They walked along quite easily. The ice was all gone now; there had been a light fall of snow the day before, but it was not shoe-deep. The snow was covered with the little tracks of Jenny's friends, the birds and the field-mice and the rabbits, in pretty zigzag lines.

Jonas Carey and his wife walked along comfortably until they reached the cart-path, then the old man's shoestring became loose, and he tripped over it. He stooped and tied it laboriously; then he went on. Pretty soon he stopped again. His wife looked back. "What's the matter?" said she.

"Shoestring untied," replied old Jonas, in a half inarticulate grunt.

"Don't you want me to tie it, Jonas?"

Jonas said nothing more; he tied viciously.

They were in sight of Jenny's house when he stopped again, and sat down on the stone wall beside the path. "Oh, Jonas, what is the matter?"

Jonas made no reply. His wife went up to him, and saw that the shoestring was loose again. "Oh, Jonas, do let me tie it; I'd just as soon as not. Sha'n't I, Jonas?"

Jonas sat there in the midst of the snowy blackberry vines, and looked straight ahead with a stony stare.

His wife began to cry. "Oh, Jonas," she pleaded, "don't you have a tantrum to-day. Sha'n't I tie it? I'll tie it real strong. Oh, Jonas!"

The old woman fluttered around the old man in his great-coat on the wall, like a distressed bird around her mate. Jenny Wrayne opened her door and looked out; then she came down the path. "What's the matter?" she asked.

"Oh, Jenny, I dunno what *to* do. He's got another—tantrum!"

"Has he fell down?"

"No; that ain't it. His shoestring's come untied three times, an' he don't like it, an' he's sot down on the wall. I dunno but he'll set there all day. Oh, dear me suz, when we'd got most to your house, an' I was jest thinkin' we'd come 'long real comfort'ble! I want to tie it for him, but he won't let me, an' I don't darse to when he sets there like that. Oh, Jonas, jest let me tie it, won't you? I'll tie it real nice an' strong, so it won't undo again."

Jenny caught hold of her arm. "Come right into the house," said she, in a hearty voice. She quite turned her back upon the figure on the wall.

"Oh, Jenny, I can't go in an' leave him a-settin' there. I shouldn't wonder if he sot there all day. You don't know nothin' about it. Sometimes I have to stan' an' argue with him for hours afore he'll stir."

"Come right in. The turkey's most done, an' we'll set right down as soon as 'tis. It's 'bout the fattest turkey I ever see. I dunno where Deacon Little could ha' got it. The plum-puddin's all done, an' the vegetables is 'most ready to take up. Come right in, an' we'll have dinner in less than half an hour."

After the two women had entered the house the figure on the wall cast an uneasy glance at it without turning his head. He sniffed a little.

It was quite true that he could smell the roasting turkey, and the turnip and onions, out there.

In the house, Mrs. Carey laid aside her bonnet and shawl, and put them on the bed in Jenny's little bedroom. A Christmas present, a new calico dress, which Jenny had received the night before, lay on the bed also. Jenny showed it with pride. "It's that chocolate color I've always liked," said she. "I don't see what put it into their heads."

"It's real handsome," said Mrs. Carey. She had not told Jenny about her visitors; but she was not used to keeping a secret, and her possession of one gave a curious expression to her face. However, Jenny did not notice it. She hurried about preparing dinner. The stove was covered with steaming pots; the turkey in the oven could be heard sizzling. The little deaf-and-dumb boy sat in his chimney-corner, and took long sniffs. He watched Jenny, and regarded the stove in a rapture, or he examined some treasures that he held in his lap. There were picture-books and cards, and boxes of candy, and oranges. He held them all tightly gathered into his pinafore. The little caged wild things twittered sweetly and pecked at their food. Jenny laid the table with the best table-cloth and her mother's flowered china. The mountain farmers, of whom Jenny sprang, had had their little decencies and comforts, and there were china and a linen table-cloth for a Christmas dinner, poor as the house was.

Mrs. Carey kept peering uneasily out of the window at her husband on the stone wall.

"If you want him to come in you'll keep away from the window," said Jenny; and the old woman settled into a chair near the stove.

Very soon the door opened, and Jonas came in. Jenny was bending over the potato kettle, and she did not look around. "You can put his great-coat on the bed, if you've a mind to, Mrs. Carey," said she.

Jonas got out of his coat, and sat down with sober dignity; he had tied his shoestring very neatly and firmly. After a while he looked over at the little deaf-and-dumb boy, who was smiling at him, and he smiled back again.

The Careys stayed until evening. Jenny set her candle in the window to light them down the cart-path. Down in the village the minister's daughter and her betrothed were out walking to the church, where there was a Christmas-tree. It was quite dark. She clung closely to his arm, and once in a while her pink cheek brushed his sleeve. The stars were out, many of them, and more were coming. One seemed suddenly to flash out on the dark side of the mountain.

"There's Christmas Jenny's candle," said the girl. And it was Christmas Jenny's candle, but it was also something more. Like all common things, it had, and was, its own poem, and that was—a Christmas star.

Life-Everlastin'

1889

"Ain't that your sister goin' 'long the other side of the street, Mis' Ansel?"

Mrs. Ansel peered, scowling—the sun was in her face. "Yes, that's her."

"She's got a basket. I guess she's been somewheres."

"She's been somewheres after life-everlastin' blossoms. They keep forever, you know. She's goin' to make a pillow for old Oliver Weed's asthma; he's real bad off."

"So I've heard. I declare it makes me all out of patience, folks that have got as much money as them Weeds have, not havin' a doctor an' havin' something done. I don't believe his wife amounts to much in sickness either."

"I guess she don't either. I could tell a few things if it wa'n't for talkin' against my neighbors. I tell Luella if she's mind to be such a fool as to slave for folks that's got plenty to do for themselves with, she can. I want to know, now, Mis' Slate, if you think this bonnet is big enough for me. Does it set fur enough onto my head?"

"It sets jest as fur on as the fashion, Mis' Ansel, an' a good deal further on than some. I wish you could see some of 'em."

"Well, I s'pose this ain't a circumstance to some, but it looks dreadful odd to me."

"Of course it looks a little odd at first, you've wore your bonnets so much further forward. You might twist up your hair a little higher if you was a mind to; that would tip it forward a little; but it ain't a mite too fur back for the fashion."

"Land! I can't do my hair any different from what I always do it, bonnet or no bonnet."

"You might friz your hair a little more in front; the hair ought to be real fluffy an' careless with this kind of a bonnet. Let me fix it a little."

Mrs. Ansel stood still before the glass while Mrs. Slate fixed her hair. She smiled a faint, foolish smile, and her homely face had the same expression as a pretty one on seeing itself in a new bonnet. Mrs. Ansel had never known that her face was homely. She was always pleased and satisfied with anything that was her own, and possession was to her the law of beauty.

Mrs. Slate, the milliner, was shorter than she. She stretched up, cocked her head, and twisted her mouth to one side with a superior air while she arranged her customer's thin front locks. Finally they lay tossed loosely over her flat, shiny forehead. "There," said the milliner; "that looks a good deal better. You see what you think."

Mrs. Ansel surveyed herself in the glass; her smile deepened. "Yes, it does look better, I guess."

"It's what I call a real stylish bonnet. You wouldn't be ashamed to wear it to meetin' anywhere, I don't care if it was in Boston or New York. I tell you what 'tis, Mis' Ansel, your sister would look nice in this kind of a bonnet." The milliner's prominent nose sloped her profile out sharply in the centre, like the beak of a bird; her little hands were skinny as claws, and restless; she always smiled, and her voice was subdued.

Mrs. Ansel still looked fondly at herself, but her tone changed; she sighed. "Yes, Luella would look good in it," said she. "I don't know as it would be quite so becomin' to her as it is to me; she never looked so well with anything that set back; but I guess she'd look pretty good in it. But I don't know when Luella's had a new bonnet, Mis' Slate. Of course she don't need any, not goin' to meetin' or anything."

"She don't ever go to meetin', does she?"

"No; she ain't been for twenty-five years. I feel bad 'nough about it. It seems to me sometimes if Luella would jest have a pretty new bonnet, an' go to meetin' Sabbath-days like other folks, I wouldn't ask for anything else."

"It must be a dreadful trial to you, Mis' Ansel."

"You don't know anything about it, Mis' Slate. You think there's bows enough on it, don't you?"

"Oh, plenty. I was speakin' to Jennie the other day about your sister—"

"An' the strings ain't too long?"

"Not a mite. You ain't never had a bonnet that become you any better than this does, Mis' Ansel. To tell the truth, I think you look a little better in it than you did in your summer one."

Mrs. Ansel began taking off the new bonnet, untying the crisp ribbon strings tenderly. "Well, I don't know but it's all right," said she.

"I'll get some paper an' do it up," said the milliner. "I ain't 'fraid but what you'll like it when you get used to it. You've always got to get used to anything new."

When Mrs. Ansel had gone down the street, delicately holding the new bonnet in its soft tissue wrapper, the milliner went into her little back room. There was one window in the room, and a grape-vine hung over it. A girl with fair hair and a delicately severe profile sat sewing by the window, with the grape-vine for a background.

"Well, I'm thankful that woman has gone," said the milliner. "I never saw such a fuss."

The girl said nothing. She nodded a little coldly, that was all.

"Are you puttin' in that linin' full enough?"

"It's all she brought."

"Oh, well, you can't do any better, then, of course. P'rhaps I hadn't ought to speak so about Mis' Ansel; she's a real nice woman; all is, she's kind of tryin' sometimes when anybody feels nervous. It's as hard work to get a bonnet onto her head that suits her as it would be if she was a queen; but after she once gets it she's settled on it, that's one comfort. She's a real nice woman, and I shouldn't want you to repeat what I said, Clara."

"I sha'n't say anything." There was a kind of mild *hauteur* about the girl that made the milliner color and twitch embarrassingly. She took a bonnet off the table and fell to work; but soon some one entered the shop, and she arose again.

Presently she was whispering over the counter to the customer that she had Clara Vinton working for her now; that she was a nice girl, but she'd acted dreadful kind of stiff somehow ever since the minister had been going with her, and she wasn't much company for her; but she didn't want her to say anything about it, for she was a real nice girl.

"I see Mis' Ansel goin' home with her new bonnet," remarked the customer.

"Yes; she jest went out with it."

When she reached home she found her sister, Luella Norcross, sitting on the door-step.

Luella followed her sister into the house. It was quite a smart house. Mrs. Ansel loved to furbish it, and she had a little income of her own. There were no dull colors anywhere; the walls gleamed with gold paper, and the carpets were brilliant.

Luella sat in the sitting-room and waited, while her sister went for a sheet which she had promised her. The mantel-shelf was marble, and there were some tall gilded glass vases on it. The stove shone like a mirror; there was a bright rug before it, and over on the table stood a lamp, whose shade was decorated with roses.

Luella plunged her hand down into the mass of everlasting flowers in her basket; the soft, healing fragrance came up in her face. "They're packed pretty solid," she muttered. "I guess there's enough."

When Mrs. Ansel returned with the sheet she was frowning. "There," said she, "I can't hunt no more to-night. I've had every identical thing out of that red chist, an' that's all I can seem to see. I don't know whether there's any more or not; if there is, you'll have to wait till I ain't jest home from down street, and can hunt better'n I can to-night."

Luella unfolded the sheet and examined it. "Oh, well, this is pretty good; it'll make three, I guess. I'll wait, and maybe you'll come across the others some time."

"You'll have to wait if you have 'em. Did you see the new lamp?"

"Well, no, I didn't notice it, as I know of. That it?"

"You ain't been sittin' right here an' never seen that new lamp?"

"I guess I must have been lookin' at somethin' else."

"I never see such a woman! Anything like that sittin' right there before your face an' eyes, an' you never pay any attention to it! I s'pose if I had Bunker Hill Monument posted up here in the middle of the sittin'-room, you'd set right down under it an' think, an' never notice there was anything uncommon."

"It's a pretty lamp—ain't it?"

"It's real handsome." Luella arose and gathered her shawl about her; she had laid the folded sheet over the top of her basket.

"Wait a minute," said Mrs. Ansel; "you ain't seen my new bonnet."

Luella rested her basket on the chair, and stood patiently while her sister took the bonnet out of the wrapper and adjusted it before the looking-glass.

"There!" said she, turning around, "what do you think of it?"

"I should think it was real pretty."

"You don't think it sets too far back, do you?"

"I shouldn't think it did."

"Shouldn't you rather have this changeable ribbon than plain?"

"Seems to me I should." Luella's voice had unmistakably an abstracted drawl.

Her sister turned on her. "You don't act no more as if you cared anything about my new bonnet than you would if I was the pump with a new tin dipper on the top of it," said she. "If I was you I'd act a little more like other folks, or I'd give up. It's bad enough for you to go 'round lookin' like a scarecrow yourself; you might take a little interest in what your own sister has to wear."

Luella said nothing; she gathered up her basket of everlasting blossoms again.

Her sister paused and eyed her fiercely for a second; then she continued: "For my part, I'm ashamed," said she—"mortified to death. It was only this afternoon that I heard somebody speakin' about it. Here you've been wearin' that old black bonnet, that you had when father died, all these years, an' never goin' to meetin'. If you'd only have a decent new bonnet— I don't know as you'd want one that sets quite so far back as this one—an' go to meetin' like other folks, there'd be some sense in it."

Luella, her basket on her arm, started for the door. Although her shoulders were round, she carried her handsome head in a stately fashion. "We've talked this over times enough," said she.

"Here you are roamin' the woods an' pastures Sabbath-days in that old bonnet, an' jest as likely as not to meet all the folks goin' to meetin'. What do you s'pose I care about havin' a new bonnet if I meet you gettin' along in that old thing—my own sister?"

Luella marched out of the house. When she was nearly out of the yard her sister ran to the door and called after her. "Luella," said she.

The stately figure paused, but did not turn around. "What is it?"

"Look here a minute," said Mrs. Ansel, mysteriously; "I want to tell you something."

Luella stepped back, her sister bent forward—she still had on the new bonnet—"I went into Mis' Plum's on my way down street," said she, "an' she said the minister wanted to marry the Vinton girl, but she won't have him, 'cause there ain't no parsonage, an' she don't think there's 'nough to live on. Mis' Plum says she thinks she shows her sense; he don't have but four hundred a year, an' there'd be a lot of children, the way there always is in poor ministers' families, an' nothin' to keep 'em on. Mis' Plum says she heard he applied to the church to see if they wouldn't give him a parsonage; he didn't know but they'd hire that house of yours that's next to the meetin'-house; but they wouldn't; they say they can't afford it."

"I shouldn't think four hundred dollars was much if preachin' was worth anything," remarked Luella.

"Oh, well, it does very well for you to talk when you don't give anything for preachin'."

Luella again went out of the yard. She was in the street when her sister called her again.

"Look 'round here a minute."

Luella looked.

"Do you think it sets too far back?"

"No, I don't think it does," Luella answered, loudly, then she kept on down the road. She had not far to go. The house where she lived stood at the turn of the road, on a gentle rise of ground; next to it was the large unoccupied cottage which she owned; next to that was the church. Luella lived in the old Norcross homestead; her grandfather had built it. It was one of those old buildings which aped the New England mansion-houses without once approaching their solid state. It settled unevenly down into its place. Its sparse front yard was full of evergreens, lilac bushes, and phlox; its windows, gleaming with green lights, were awry, and all its white clapboards were out of plumb.

Luella went around to the side door: the front one was never used—indeed, it was swollen and would not open—and the front walk was green. The side door opened into a little square entry. On one side was the sitting-room, on the other the kitchen. Luella went into the kitchen, and an old woman rose up from a chair by the stove. She was small as a child, but her muscles were large, her flaxen hair was braided lightly, her round blue eyes were filmy, and she grinned constantly without speaking.

"Got the cleanin' done, 'Liza?" asked Luella. The old woman nodded, and her grin widened. She was called foolish; her humble capabilities could not diffuse themselves, but were strong in only one direction: she could wash and scrub, and in that she took delight. Luella harbored her, fed and clothed her, and let her practise her one little note of work.

After Luella had taken off her bonnet and shawl, she went to work preparing supper. The old woman was not smart enough to do that. She sat watching her. When Luella set the tea-pot on the stove and cut the bread, she fairly crowed like a baby.

"Maria offered me a piece of her new apple-pie an' a piece of sage-cheese," remarked Luella, "but I wouldn't take it. If I'm a mind to stint myself and pay up Joe Perry's rent it's nobody's business, but I ain't goin' to be mean enough to live on other folks to do it."

The old woman grinned as she ate. Luella had fallen into the habit of talking quite confidentially to her, unreciprocative as she was.

After supper Luella put away the tea-things—that was too fine work for the old woman—then she lighted her sitting-room lamp, and sat down there to make the case for the life-everlasting pillow. The old woman crept in after her, and sat by the stove in a little chair, holding her sodden hands in her lap.

"I hope to goodness this pillow will help him some," said Luella. "They're real good for asthma. Mother used to use 'em." She sewed with strong jerks. The old man for whom she was making the pillow was rich in the village sense, and miserly. Ill as he sometimes was, he and his wife would not call in a doctor on account of the expense; they scarcely kept warm and fed themselves. Public opinion was strong against them; very little pity was given to the feeble old man; but Luella viewed it all with a broad charity which was quite past the daily horizon of the village people. "I don't care if they are rich an' able to buy things themselves, we hadn't ought to let 'em suffer," she argued. "Mebbe they can't help bein' close any more'n we can help somethin' we've got. It's a failin', and folks ought to help folks with failin's, I don't care what they are." So Luella Norcross made broth and gruel, and carried them in to old Oliver Weed, and even gave him some of her dry cedar-wood; and people said she was as foolish as old Eliza. All the burly whining tramps, and beseeching pedlars of unsalable wares, who came to the village, flocked to her door, sure of a welcome.

On a summer's day the tramps sat on her door-step, and ate their free lunches, in winter they ate them comfortably by the kitchen fire. Many a time her barn and warm hay-mow harbored them over a cold stormy night.

"Might jest as well stick out a sign, 'Tramps' Tavern,' on the barn, an' done with it," Mrs. Ansel said. "If you don't get set on fire some night by them miserable sneakin' tramps, I miss my guess."

But she never did, and the tramp slouched peaceably out of her yard, late in the frosty morning, after she had given him a good breakfast in the warm kitchen.

There was an old pedlar of essences who came regularly, and she always bought of him, although his essences were poor, and her cake scantily flavored in consequence. Him she often lodged in her nice spare chamber, although she distrusted his cleanliness, and she and old Eliza had much scrubbing to do thereafter.

Luella even traded faithfully with a sly-eyed Italian woman, who went about, bent to one side by a great basket of vases and plaster images. "You'd ought to be ashamed of yourself encouragin' such folks," Mrs. Ansel remonstrated, "she's jest as miserable an' low as she can be."

"I don't care how low she is," said Luella. "She's keepin' one commandment sellin' plaster images to get her livin', an' I'm a-goin' to help her."

And Luella crowded the little plaster flower girls and fruit boys together on the sitting-room shelf, to make room for the new little shepherdess.

This very day she had been visited by an old broken-down minister, who often stood at her door, tall and tremulous in his shiny black broadcloth, with a heavy bag of undesirable books. There were some hanging shelves in Luella's sitting-room which were filled with these books, but to-day she had bought another.

"There ain't room on the shelves for another one, but I s'pose I can stow it away somewhere," she told Eliza, after he had gone. "I've give away all I can seem to. The book ain't very interestin'."

Luella usually lodged the book agent over night, when he came to the village, although he also had his failings. Many a night she was awakened by the creaking of the cellar-stairs, when the old minister crept down stealthily, a lamp balanced unsteadily in his shaking hand, to the cider-barrel. She would listen anxiously until she heard him return to his room, then get up and look about and sniff for fire.

There was not a woman in the village who had so many blessings, worth whatever they might be, offered to her. If she was not in full orthodox flavor among the respectable part of the town, her fame was bright among the poor and maybe lawless element, whom she befriended. They showed it by their shuffling footprints thick in her yard, and the frequency of their petitions at her door. It was the only way in which they could show it. The poor can show their love and gratitude only by the continual out-reaching of their hands.

This evening, while Luella sewed on her life-everlasting pillow, and the old woman sat grinning in the corner, there was a step in the yard. Luella laid down her work, and looked at Eliza, and listened. The step came steadily up the drive; the shoes squeaked. Luella took up her work again.

"I know who 'tis," said she. "It's the book man; his shoes squeak just that way, an' I told him he'd better come back here to-night an' stay over. It saves him payin' for lodgin'."

There came a sharp knock on the side door.

"You go let him in, 'Liza," said Luella.

The old woman patted out of the room. Presently she looked in again, and her grin was a broad laugh. "It's the minister," she chuckled.

Luella arose and went herself. There in the entry stood a young man, short and square-shouldered, with a pleasant boyish face. He looked bravely at Luella, and tried to speak with suave fluency, but his big hands twitched at the ends of his short coat sleeves.

"Good-evening, Miss Norcross, good-evening," said he.

"Oh, it's you, Mr. Sands!" said Luella. "Good-evenin'. Walk in an' be seated."

Luella herself was a little stiff. She pushed forward the big black-covered rocking-chair for the minister, then she sat down herself, and took up her sewing.

"It is a charming evening," remarked the minister.

"I thought it seemed real pleasant when I looked out after supper," said Luella.

She and the minister spoke about the conditions of several of the parish invalids, they spoke about a fire and a funeral which had taken place that week, and all the time there was a constraint in their manners. Finally there was a pause; then the minister burst out. A blush flamed out to the roots of his curly hair. He tried to make his voice casual, but it slipped into his benediction cadences.

"I don't see you at church very often, Miss Norcross," said he.

"You don't see me at all," returned Luella.

The minister tried to smile. "Well, maybe that is a little nearer the truth, Miss Norcross."

Luella sewed a few stitches on her life-everlasting pillow; then she laid it down in her lap, straightened herself, and looked at the minister. Her deep-set blue eyes seemed to see every atom of him; her noble forehead even, from which the gray hair was pulled well back, and which was scarcely lined, seemed to front him with a kind of visual power of its own.

"I may just as well tell you the truth, Mr. Sands," said she, "an' we may just as well come to the point at once. I know what you've come for; my sister told me you was comin' to see about my not going to meetin'. Well, I'll tell you once for all, I've just as much obliged to you, but it won't do any good. I've made up my mind I ain't goin' to meetin', an I've got good reasons."

"Would you mind giving them, Miss Norcross?"

"I ain't going to argue."

"But just giving me a few of your reasons wouldn't be arguing." The young man had now acquired the tone which he wished. He smiled on Luella with an innocent patronage, and crossed his legs. Luella thought he looked very young.

"The fact is," said she, "I'm not a believer, an' I won't be a hypocrite. That's all there is about it."

The minister looked at her. It was the first time he had encountered an outspoken doubter, and it was for a minute to him as if he faced one of the veritable mediæval dragons of the church. This simple and untutored village agnostic filled him with amazement and terror. When he spoke it was not to take up the argument for the doctrine, but to turn its gold side, as it were, towards his opponent, in order to persuade belief. "Your soul's salvation—do you never think of that?" he queried, solemnly. "You know heaven and your soul's salvation depend upon it."

"I ain't never worried much about my soul's salvation," said Luella. "I've had too many other souls to think about. An' it seems to me I'd be dreadful piggish to make goin' to heaven any reason for believin' a thing that ain't reasonable."

The minister made a rally; he remembered one of the things he had planned to say. "But you've read the New Testament, Miss Norcross," said he, "and you must admit that 'never man spake like this man.' When you read the words of Christ you must see that there was never any man like him."

"I know there wa'n't," said Luella, "that's jest the reason why the whole story don't seem sensible."

The minister gave a kind of a gasp. "But you believe in God, don't you, Miss Norcross?" said he.

"I ain't a fool," replied Luella. She arose with a decided air. "Do you like apples, Mr. Sands?" said she.

The minister gasped again, and assented.

"I've got some real nice sweet ones and some Porters," said Luella, in a cheerful tone, "an I'm goin' to get you a plate of 'em, Mr. Sands."

Luella went out and got the plate of apples, and the minister began eating them. He felt uneasily that it was his duty to reopen the argument. "If you believe in God—" he began.

But Luella shook her head at him as if she were his mother. "I'd rather not argue any more," said she. "Try that big Porter; I guess it's meller." And the minister ate his apples with enjoyment. Luella filled his pockets with some when he went home. "He seems like a real good young man," she said to old Eliza after the minister had gone; "an' that Vinton girl would make him jest the kind of a wife he'd ought to have. She's real up an' comin', an' she'd prop him up firm on his feet. I s'pose if I let him have that house he'd be tickled 'most to death. I'd kind of 'lotted on the rent of it, but I s'pose I could get along."

The old woman grinned feebly. She had been asleep in her corner, and her blue eyes looked dimmer than ever. She comprehended not a word; but that did not matter to Luella, who had fallen into the habit of utilizing her as a sort of spiritual lay-figure upon which to drape her own ideas.

The next morning, about nine o'clock, she carried the pillow, which she had finished and stuffed with the life-everlasting blossoms, to old Oliver Weed's. The house stood in a wide field, and there were no other houses very near. The grass was wet with dew, and all the field was sweet in the morning freshness. Luella, carrying her life-everlasting pillow before her, went over the fragrant path to the back door. She noticed as she went that the great barn doors were closed.

"Queer the barn ain't open," she thought to herself. "I wonder what John Gleason's about, late as this in the mornin'?"

John Gleason was old Oliver Weed's hired man. He had been a tramp. Luella herself had fed him, and let him sleep off a drunken debauch in her barn once. People had wondered at Oliver Weed's hiring him, but he had to pay him much less than the regular price for farm hands.

Luella heard the cows low in the barn as she opened the kitchen door. "Where—did all that—blood come from?" said she.

She began to breathe in quick gasps; she stood clutching her pillow, and looking. Then she called: "Mr. Weed! Mr. Weed! Where be you? Mis' Weed! Is anything the matter? Mis' Weed!" The silence seemed to beat against her ears. She went across the kitchen to the bedroom. Here and there she held back her dress. She reached the bedroom door, and looked in.

Luella pressed back across the kitchen into the yard. She went out into the road, and turned towards the village. She still carried the life-everlasting pillow, but she carried it as if her arms and that were all stone. She met a woman whom she knew, and the woman spoke; but Luella did not notice her; she kept on. The woman stopped and looked after her.

Luella went to the house where the sheriff lived, and knocked. The sheriff himself opened the door. He was a large, pleasant man. He began saying something facetious about her being out calling early, but Luella stopped him.

"You'd—better go up to the—Weed house," said she, in a dry voice. "There's some—trouble."

The sheriff started. "Why, what do you mean, Luella?"

"The old man an' his wife are—both killed. I went in there to carry this, an'—I saw them."

"My God!" said the sheriff. He caught up his hat, and started on a run to the barn for his horse.

The sheriff's wife and daughter pressed forward and plied Luella with horrified questions; they urged her to come in and rest, she looked so pale; but she said little, and turned towards home. Flying teams passed her on the road; men rushed up behind her and questioned her. When she reached the Weed house the field seemed black with people. When she got to her own house she went into the sitting-room and sat down. She felt faint. She did not think of lying down; she never did in the daytime. She leaned her head back in her chair and turned her face towards the yard. Everything out there, the trees, the grass, the crowding ranks of daisies, the next house, looked strange, as if another light than that of the sun was on them. But she somehow noticed even then how a blind on the second floor of the house was shut that had been open. "I wonder how that come shut?" she muttered, feebly.

Pretty soon her sister, Mrs. Ansel, came hurrying in. She was wringing her hands. "Oh, ain't it awful? ain't it awful?" she cried. "Good land, Luella, how you look! You'll faint away. I'm goin' to mix you up some peppermint before I do another thing."

Mrs. Ansel made a cup of hot peppermint tea for her, and she drank it.

"Now tell me all about it," said Mrs. Ansel. "What did you see first? What was you goin' in there for?"

"To carry the pillow," said Luella, pointing to it. "I can't talk about it, Maria."

Mrs. Ansel went over to the lounge and took up the pillow. "Mercy sakes! what's that on it?" she cried, in horror.

"I—s'pose I—hit it against the wall somehow," replied Luella. "I can't talk about it, Maria."

Mrs. Ansel could not learn much from her sister. Presently she left, and lingered slowly past the Weed house, to which her curiosity attracted her, but which her terror and horror would not let her approach closely.

The peppermint revived Luella a little. After a while she got up and put on the potatoes for dinner. Old Eliza was scrubbing the floor. When dinner was ready she ate all the potatoes, and Luella sat back and looked at her.

All the afternoon people kept coming to the house and questioning her, and exclaiming with horror. It seemed to Luella that her own horror was beyond exclamations. There was no doubt in the public mind that the murderer was the hired man, John Gleason. He was nowhere to be found; the constables and detectives were searching fiercely for him.

That night when Luella went to bed she stood at her chamber window a minute, looking out. It was bright moonlight. Her window faced the unoccupied house, and she noticed again how the blind was shut.

"It's queer," she thought, "for that blind wouldn't stay shut; the fastenin' wa'n't good." As she looked, the blind swung slowly open. "The wind is jest swingin' it back and forth," she thought. Then she saw distinctly the chamber window open, a dark arm thrust out, and the blind closed again.

"*He's in there*," said Luella. She had put out her lamp. She went downstairs in the dark, and made sure that all the doors and windows were securely fastened. She even put chairs and tables against them. Then she went back to her chamber, dressed herself, and watched the next house. She did not stir until morning. The next day there was a cold rain. The search for John Gleason continued, the whole village was out, and strange officials were driving through the streets. Everybody thought that the murderer had escaped to Canada, taking with him the money which he had stolen from the poor old man's strong-box under his bed.

All the day long Luella watched the next house through the gray drive of the rain. About sunset she packed a basket with food, stole across to the house, and set it in the corner of the door. She got back before a soul passed on the road. She had set Eliza at a task away from the windows.

The moon rose early. After supper Luella sat again in her chamber without any lamp and watched. About nine o'clock she saw the door of the next house swing open a little, and the basket was drawn in.

"*He's in there*," said Luella. She went down and fastened up the house as she had done the night before. Old Eliza went peacefully to bed, and she watched again. She put a coverlid over her shoulders, and sat, all huddled up, peering out. The rain had stopped; the wall of the next house shone like silver in the moonlight. She watched until the moon went down and until daylight came; then she went to bed, and slept an hour.

After breakfast that morning she set old Eliza at a task, and went up to her chamber again. She sank down on her knees beside the bed. "O God," said she, "have I got to give him up—have I? Have I got to give him up to be hung? What's goin' to become of him then? Where'll he go to when he's been so awful wicked? Oh, what shall I do? Here he is a-takin' my vittles, an' comin' to my house, an' a-trustin' me!" Luella lifted her arms; her face was all distorted. She seemed to see the whole crew of her pitiful dependents crowding around her, and pleading for the poor man who had thrown himself upon her mercy. She saw the old drunken essence man, the miserable china women, all the wretched and vicious tramps and drunkards whom she had befriended, pressing up to her, and pleading her to keep faith with their poor brother.

The thought that John Gleason had trusted her, had taken that food when he knew that she might in consequence betray him to the gallows, filled her with a pity that was almost tenderness, and appealed strongly to her loyalty and honor.

On the other hand, she remembered what she had seen in the Weed house. The poor old man and woman seemed calling to her for help. She reflected upon what she had heard the day before: that the detectives were after John Gleason for another murder; this was not the first. She called to mind the danger that other helpless people would be in if this murderer were at large. Would not their blood be upon her hands? She called to mind the horrible details of what she had seen, the useless cruelty, and the horror of it.

Once she arose with a jerk, and got her bonnet out of the closet. Then she put it back, and threw herself down by the bed again. "Oh!" she groaned, "I don't know what to do!"

Luella shut herself in her own room nearly all day. She went down and got the meals, then returned. The sodden old woman did not notice anything unusual. At dusk she watched her chance, and carried over more food, and she watched and saw it taken in again.

This night she did not lock the house. All she fastened was old Eliza's bedroom door; that she locked securely, and hid the key. All the other doors and windows were unfastened, and when she went up-stairs she set the side door partly open. She set her lamp on the bureau, and looked at her face in the glass. It was white and drawn, and there was a desperate look in her deep-set eyes. "Mebbe it's the last time I shall ever see my face," said she. "I don't know but I'm awful wicked to give him the chance to do another murder, but I can't give him up. If he comes in an' kills me, I sha'n't have to, an' maybe he'll jest take the money an' go, an' then I sha'n't have to."

Luella had two or three hundred dollars in an old wallet between her feather-bed and the mattress. She took it out and opened it, spreading the bills. Then she laid it on the bureau. She took a gold ring off her finger, and unfastened her ear-rings and laid them beside it, and a silver watch that had belonged to her father. Down-stairs she had arranged the teaspoons and a little silver cream-jug in full sight on the kitchen table.

After the preparations were all made she blew out her lamp, folded back the bed-spread, lay down in her clothes, and pulled it over her smoothly. She folded her hands and lay there. There was not a bolt or a bar between her and the murderer next door. She closed her eyes and lay still. Every now and then she thought she heard him down-stairs; but the night wore on, and he did not come. At daylight Luella arose. She was so numb and weak that she could scarcely stand. She put away the money and the jewelry, then she went down-stairs and kindled the kitchen fire and got breakfast. The silver was on the table just as she had left it, the door half open, and the cold morning wind coming in. Luella gave one great sob when she shut the door. "He must have seen it," she said, "but he wouldn't do nothin' to hurt me, an' I've got to give him up."

She said no more after that; she was quite calm getting breakfast. After the meal was finished and the dishes cleared away she told old Eliza to put on her other dress and her bonnet and shawl. She had made up her mind to take the old creature with her; she was afraid to leave her alone in the house, with the murderer next door to spy out her own departure.

When the two women were ready they went out of the yard, and Luella felt the eyes of John Gleason upon her. They went down the road to the village, old Eliza keeping a little behind her mistress. Luella aimed straight for the sheriff's house. He drove into the yard as she entered; he had been out all night on a false scent. He stopped when he saw Luella, and she came up to him. "John Gleason is in that vacant house of mine," said she. He caught at the reins, but she stopped him. "You've got to wait long enough to give me time to get home, so I sha'n't be right in the midst of it, if you've got any mercy," said she, in a loud, strained voice. Then she turned and ran. She stopped only long enough to tell old Eliza to follow her straight home and go at once into the house. She ran through the village street like a girl. People came to the windows and stared after her. Every minute she fancied she heard wheels behind her; but the sheriff did not come until after she had been in the house fifteen minutes, and old Eliza also was at home.

Luella was crouching at her chamber window, peering around the curtain, when the sheriff and six men came into the yard and surrounded the next house. She had a wild hope that John Gleason might not be there, that he might have escaped during the night. She watched. The men entered, there was the sound of a scuffle and loud voices, and then she saw John Gleason dragged out.

Presently Luella went down-stairs; she had to keep hold of the banister. Old Eliza was gaping at the kitchen window. "Come away from that window, 'Liza," said Luella, "and wash up the floor right away." Then Luella began cleaning potatoes and beets for dinner.

The next Sunday Luella went to church for the first time in twenty-five years. Old Eliza also went shuffling smilingly up the aisle behind her mistress. Everybody stared. Luella paused at her sister's pew, and her brother-in-law sat a little while looking at her before he arose to let her in.

Mrs. Ansel was quite flushed. She pulled her new bonnet farther on her head; she glanced with agitated hauteur across her sister at old Eliza; then her eyes rolled towards her sister's bonnet.

Presently she touched Luella. "What possessed you to bring her, an' come out lookin' so?" she whispered. "Why didn't you get a new bonnet before you came to meetin'?"

Luella looked at her in a bewildered fashion for a minute, then she set her face towards the pulpit. She listened to the sermon; it had in it some innocent youthful conceits, and also considerable honest belief and ardent feeling. The minister saw Luella, and thought with a flush of pride that his arguments had convinced her. The night before, he had received a note from her tendering him the use of her vacant house. After the service he pressed forward to speak to her. He thanked her for her note, said that he was glad to see her out to meeting, and shook her hand vehemently. Then he joined Clara Vinton quite openly, and the two walked on together. There was quite a little procession passing up the street. The way led between pleasant cottages with the front yards full of autumn flowers—asters and pansies and prince's-feathers. Presently they passed a wide stretch of pasture-land where life-everlasting flowers grew. Luella walked with an old woman with a long, saintly face; old Eliza followed after.

Luella's face looked haggard and composed under her flimsy black crape frillings. She kept her eyes, with a satisfied expression, upon the young minister and the tall girl who walked beside him with a grave, stately air.

"I hear they're goin' to be married," whispered the old woman.

"I guess they are," replied Luella.

Just then Clara turned her face, and her fine, stern profile showed.

"She'll make him a good wife, I guess," said the old woman. She turned to Luella, and her voice had an indescribably shy and caressing tone. "I was real glad to see you to meetin' to-day," she whispered. "I knew you'd feel like comin' some time; I always said you would." She flushed all over her soft old face as she spoke.

Luella also flushed a little, but her voice was resolute. "I ain't got much to say about it, Mis' Alden," said she, "but I'm goin' to say this much—it ain't no more'n right I should, though I don't believe in a lot of palaver about things like this—I've made up my mind that I'm goin' to believe in Jesus Christ. I ain't never, but I'm goin' to now, for"—Luella's voice turned shrill with passion—"*I don't see any other way out of it for John Gleason!*"

A Village Singer

1889

The trees were in full leaf, a heavy south wind was blowing, and there was a loud murmur among the new leaves. The people noticed it, for it was the first time that year that the trees had so murmured in the wind. The spring had come with a rush during the last few days.

The murmur of the trees sounded loud in the village church, where the people sat waiting for the service to begin. The windows were open; it was a very warm Sunday for May.

The church was already filled with this soft sylvan music—the tender harmony of the leaves and the south wind, and the sweet, desultory whistles of birds—when the choir arose and began to sing.

In the centre of the row of women singers stood Alma Way. All the people stared at her, and turned their ears critically. She was the new leading soprano. Candace Whitcomb, the old one, who had sung in the choir for forty years, had lately been given her dismissal. The audience considered that her voice had grown too cracked and uncertain on the upper notes. There had been much complaint, and after long deliberation the church-officers had made known their decision as mildly as possible to the old singer. She had sung for the last time the Sunday before, and Alma Way had been engaged to take her place. With the exception of the organist, the leading soprano was the only paid musician in the large choir. The salary was very modest, still the village people considered it large for a young woman. Alma was from the adjoining village of East Derby; she had quite a local reputation as a singer.

Now she fixed her large solemn blue eyes; her long, delicate face, which had been pretty, turned paler; the blue flowers on her bonnet trembled; her little thin gloved hands, clutching the singing-book, shook perceptibly; but she sang out bravely. That most formidable mountain-height of the world, self-distrust and timidity, arose before her, but her nerves were braced for its ascent. In the midst of the hymn she had a solo; her voice rang out piercingly sweet; the people nodded admiringly at each other; but suddenly there was a stir; all the faces turned toward the windows on the south side of the church. Above the din of the wind and the birds, above Alma Way's sweetly straining tones, arose another female voice, singing another hymn to another tune.

"It's her," the women whispered to each other; they were half aghast, half smiling.

Candace Whitcomb's cottage stood close to the south side of the church. She was playing on her parlor organ, and singing, to drown out the voice of her rival.

Alma caught her breath; she almost stopped; the hymn-book waved like a fan; then she went on. But the long husky drone of the parlor organ and the shrill clamor of the other voice seemed louder than anything else.

When the hymn was finished, Alma sat down. She felt faint; the woman next her slipped a peppermint into her hand. "It ain't worth minding," she whispered, vigorously. Alma tried to smile; down in the audience a young man was watching her with a kind of fierce pity.

In the last hymn Alma had another solo. Again the parlor organ droned above the carefully delicate accompaniment of the church organ, and again Candace Whitcomb's voice clamored forth in another tune.

After the benediction, the other singers pressed around Alma. She did not say much in return for their expressions of indignation and sympathy. She wiped her eyes furtively once or twice, and tried to smile. William Emmons, the choir leader, elderly, stout, and smooth-faced, stood over her, and raised his voice. He was the old musical dignitary of the village, the leader of the choral club and the singing-schools. "A most outrageous proceeding," he said. People had coupled his name with Candace Whitcomb's. The old bachelor tenor and old maiden soprano had been wont to walk together to her home next door after the Saturday night rehearsals, and they had sung duets to the parlor organ. People had watched sharply her old face, on which the blushes of youth sat pitifully, when William Emmons entered the singing-seats. They wondered if he would ever ask her to marry him.

And now he said further to Alma Way that Candace Whitcomb's voice had failed utterly of late, that she sang shockingly, and ought to have had sense enough to know it.

When Alma went down into the audience-room, in the midst of the chattering singers, who seemed to have descended, like birds, from song flights to chirps, the minister approached her. He had been waiting to speak to her. He was a steady-faced, fleshy old man, who had preached from that one pulpit over forty years. He told Alma, in his slow way, how much he regretted the annoyance to which she had been subjected, and intimated that he would endeavor to prevent a recurrence of it. "Miss Whitcomb— must be—reasoned with," said he; he had a slight hesitation of speech, not an impediment. It was as if his thoughts did not slide readily into his words, although both were present. He walked down the aisle with Alma, and bade her good-morning when he saw Wilson Ford waiting for her in the doorway. Everybody knew that Wilson Ford and Alma were lovers; they had been for the last ten years.

Alma colored softly, and made a little imperceptible motion with her head; her silk dress and the lace on her mantle fluttered, but she did not speak. Neither did Wilson, although they had not met before that day. They did not look at each other's faces—they seemed to see each other without that—and they walked along side by side.

They reached the gate before Candace Whitcomb's little house. Wilson looked past the front yard, full of pink and white spikes on flowering bushes, at the lace-curtained windows; a thin white profile, stiffly inclined, apparently over a book, was visible at one of them. Wilson gave his head a shake. He was a stout man, with features so strong that they overcame his flesh. "I'm going up home with you, Alma," said he; "and then—I'm just coming back, to give Aunt Candace one blowing up."

"Oh, don't, Wilson."

"Yes, I shall. If you want to stand this kind of a thing you may; I sha'n't."

"There's no need of you talking to her. Mr. Pollard's going to."

"Did he say he was?"

"Yes. I think he's going in before the afternoon meeting, from what he said."

"Well, there's one thing about it, if she does that thing again this afternoon, I'll go in there and break that old organ up into kindling-wood." Wilson set his mouth hard, and shook his head again.

Alma gave little side glances up at him, her tone was deprecatory, but her face was full of soft smiles. "I suppose she does feel dreadfully about it," said she. "I can't help feeling kind of guilty, taking her place."

"I don't see how you're to blame. It's outrageous, her acting so."

"The choir gave her a photograph album last week, didn't they?"

"Yes. They went there last Thursday night, and gave her an album and a surprise-party. She ought to behave herself."

"Well, she's sung there so long, I suppose it must be dreadful hard for her to give it up."

Other people going home from church were very near Wilson and Alma. She spoke softly that they might not hear; he did not lower his voice in the least. Presently Alma stopped before a gate.

"What are you stopping here for?" asked Wilson.

"Minnie Lansing wanted me to come and stay with her this noon."

"You're going home with me."

"I'm afraid I'll put your mother out."

"Put mother out! I told her you were coming, this morning. She's got all ready for you. Come along; don't stand here."

He did not tell Alma of the pugnacious spirit with which his mother had received the announcement of her coming, and how she had stayed at home to prepare the dinner, and make a parade of her hard work and her injury.

Wilson's mother was the reason why he did not marry Alma. He would not take his wife home to live with her, and was unable to support separate establishments. Alma was willing enough to be married and put up with Wilson's mother, but she did not complain of his decision. Her delicate blond features grew sharper, and her blue eyes more hollow. She had had a certain fine prettiness, but now she was losing it, and beginning to look old, and there was a prim, angular, old maiden carriage about her narrow shoulders.

Wilson never noticed it, and never thought of Alma as not possessed of eternal youth, or capable of losing or regretting it.

"Come along, Alma," said he; and she followed meekly after him down the street.

Soon after they passed Candace Whitcomb's house, the minister went up the front walk and rang the bell. The pale profile at the window had never stirred as he opened the gate and came up the walk. However, the door was promptly opened, in response to his ring. "Good-morning, Miss Whitcomb," said the minister.

"*Good*-morning." Candace gave a sweeping toss of her head as she spoke. There was a fierce upward curl to her thin nostrils and her lips, as if she scented an adversary. Her black eyes had two tiny cold sparks of fury in them, like an enraged bird's. She did not ask the minister to enter, but he stepped lumberingly into the entry, and she retreated rather than led the way into her little parlor. He settled into the great rocking-chair and wiped his face. Candace sat down again in her old place by the window. She was a tall woman, but very slender and full of pliable motions, like a blade of grass.

"It's a—very pleasant day," said the minister.

Candace made no reply. She sat still, with her head drooping. The wind stirred the looped lace-curtains; a tall rose-tree outside the window waved; soft shadows floated through the room. Candace's parlor organ stood in front of an open window that faced the church; on the corner was a pitcher with a bunch of white lilacs. The whole room was scented with them. Presently the minister looked over at them and sniffed pleasantly.

"You have—some beautiful—lilacs there."

Candace did not speak. Every line of her slender figure looked flexible, but it was a flexibility more resistant than rigor.

The minister looked at her. He filled up the great rocking-chair; his arms in his shiny black coat-sleeves rested squarely and comfortably upon the hair-cloth arms of the chair.

"Well, Miss Whitcomb, I suppose I—may as well come to—the point. There was—a little—matter I wished to speak to you about. I don't suppose you were—at least I can't suppose you were—aware of it, but—this morning, during the singing by the choir, you played and—sung a little too—loud. That is, with—the windows open. It—disturbed us—a little. I hope you won't feel hurt—my dear Miss Candace, but I knew you would rather I would speak of it, for I knew—you would be more disturbed than anybody else at the idea of such a thing."

Candace did not raise her eyes; she looked as if his words might sway her through the window. "I ain't disturbed at it," said she. "I did it on purpose; I meant to."

The minister looked at her.

"You needn't look at me. I know jest what I'm about. I sung the way I did on purpose, an' I'm goin' to do it again, an' I'd like to see you stop me. I guess I've got a right to set down to my own organ, an' sing a psalm tune on a Sabbath day, 'f I want to; an' there ain't no amount of talkin' an' palav-

erin' a-goin' to stop me. See there!" Candace swung aside her skirts a little.
"Look at that!"

The minister looked. Candace's feet were resting on a large red-plush
photograph album.

"Makes a nice footstool, don't it?" said she.

The minister looked at the album, then at her; there was a slowly gathering alarm in his face; he began to think she was losing her reason.

Candace had her eyes full upon him now, and her head up. She laughed,
and her laugh was almost a snarl. "Yes; I thought it would make a beautiful
footstool," said she. "I've been wantin' one for some time." Her tone was
full of vicious irony.

"Why, miss—" began the minister; but she interrupted him:

"I know what you're a-goin' to say, Mr. Pollard, an' now I'm goin' to
have my say; I'm a-goin' to speak. I want to know what you think of folks
that pretend to be Christians treatin' anybody the way they've treated me?
Here I've sung in those singin'-seats forty years. I 'ain't never missed a Sunday, except when I've been sick, an' I've gone an' sung a good many times
when I'd better been in bed, an' now I'm turned out without a word of
warnin'. My voice is jest as good as ever 'twas; there can't anybody say it
ain't. It wa'n't ever quite so high-pitched as that Way girl's, mebbe; but she
flats the whole durin' time. My voice is as good an' high to-day as it was
twenty year ago; an' if it wa'n't, I'd like to know where the Christianity
comes in. I'd like to know if it wouldn't be more to the credit of folks in a
church to keep an old singer an' an old minister, if they didn't sing an' hold
forth quite so smart as they used to, ruther than turn 'em off an' hurt their
feelin's. I guess it would be full as much to the glory of God. S'pose the
singin' an' the preachin' wa'n't quite so good, what difference would it
make? Salvation don't hang on anybody's hittin' a high note, that I ever
heard of. Folks are gettin' as high-steppin' an' fussy in a meetin'-house as
they are in a tavern, nowadays. S'pose they should turn you off, Mr. Pollard, come an' give you a photograph album, an' tell you to clear out,
how'd you like it? I ain't findin' any fault with your preachin'; it was always good enough to suit me; but it don't stand to reason folks 'll be as
took up with your sermons as when you was a young man. You can't expect it. S'pose they should turn you out in your old age, an' call in some
young bob squirt, how'd you feel? There's William Emmons, too; he's
three years older'n I am, if he does lead the choir an' run all the singin' in
town. If my voice has gi'en out, it stan's to reason his has. It ain't, though.

William Emmons sings jest as well as he ever did. Why don't they turn him out the way they have me, an' give him a photograph album? I dun know but it would be a good idea to send everybody, as soon as they get a little old an' gone by, an' young folks begin to push, onto some desert island, an' give 'em each a photograph album. Then they can sit down an' look at pictures the rest of their days. Mebbe government 'll take it up.

"There they come here last week Thursday, all the choir, jest about eight o'clock in the evenin', an' pretended they'd come to give me a nice little surprise. Surprise! h'm! Brought cake an' oranges, an' was jest as nice as they could be, an' I was real tickled. I never had a surprise-party before in my life. Jenny Carr she played, an' they wanted me to sing alone, an' I never suspected a thing. I've been mad ever since to think what a fool I was, an' how they must have laughed in their sleeves.

"When they'd gone I found this photograph album on the table, all done up as nice as you please, an' directed to Miss Candace Whitcomb from her many friends, an' I opened it, an' there was the letter inside givin' me notice to quit.

"If they'd gone about it any decent way, told me right out honest that they'd got tired of me, an' wanted Alma Way to sing instead of me, I wouldn't minded so much; I should have been hurt 'nough, for I'd felt as if some that had pretended to be my friends wa'n't; but it wouldn't have been as bad as this. They said in the letter that they'd always set great value on my services, an' it wa'n't from any lack of appreciation that they turned me off, but they thought the duty was gettin' a little too arduous for me. H'm! I hadn't complained. If they'd turned me right out fair an' square, showed me the door, an' said, 'Here, you get out,' but to go an' spill molasses, as it were, all over the threshold, tryin' to make me think it's all nice an' sweet—

"I'd sent that photograph album back quick's I could pack it, but I didn't know who started it, so I've used it for a footstool. It's all it's good for, 'cordin' to my way of thinkin'. An' I ain't been particular to get the dust off my shoes before I used it neither."

Mr. Pollard, the minister, sat staring. He did not look at Candace; his eyes were fastened upon a point straight ahead. He had a look of helpless solidity, like a block of granite. This country minister, with his steady, even temperament, treading with heavy precision his one track for over forty years, having nothing new in his life except the new sameness of the seasons, and desiring nothing new, was incapable of understanding a woman like this, who had lived as quietly as he, and all the time held within herself the elements of revolution. He could not account for such violence, such extremes, except in a loss of reason. He had a conviction that Candace was getting beyond herself. He himself was not a typical New-Englander; the national elements of character were not pronounced in him. He was aghast and bewildered at this outbreak, which was tropical, and more than tropical, for a New England nature has a floodgate, and the power which it releases is an accumulation. Candace Whitcomb had been a quiet woman, so delicately resolute that the quality had been scarcely noticed in her, and her ambition had been unsuspected. Now the resolution and the ambition appeared raging over her whole self.

She began to talk again. "I've made up my mind that I'm goin' to sing Sundays the way I did this mornin', an' I don't care what folks say," said she. "I've made up my mind that I'm goin' to take matters into my own hands. I'm goin' to let folks see that I ain't trod down quite flat, that there's a little rise left in me. I ain't goin' to give up beat yet a while; an I'd like to see anybody stop me. If I ain't got a right to play a psalm tune on my organ an' sing, I'd like to know. If you don't like it, you can move the meetin'-house."

Candace had had an inborn reverence for clergymen. She had always treated Mr. Pollard with the utmost deference. Indeed, her manner toward all men had been marked by a certain delicate stiffness and dignity. Now she was talking to the old minister with the homely freedom with which she might have addressed a female gossip over the back fence. He could not say much in return. He did not feel competent to make headway against any such tide of passion; all he could do was to let it beat against him. He made a few expostulations, which increased Candace's vehemence; he expressed his regret over the whole affair, and suggested that they should kneel and ask the guidance of the Lord in the matter, that she might be led to see it all in a different light.

Candace refused flatly. "I don't see any use prayin' about it," said she. "I don't think the Lord's got much to do with it, anyhow."

It was almost time for the afternoon service when the minister left. He had missed his comfortable noontide rest, through this encounter with his revolutionary parishioner. After the minister had gone, Candace sat by the window and waited. The bell rang, and she watched the people file past. When her nephew Wilson Ford with Alma appeared, she grunted to herself. "She's thin as a rail," said she; "guess there won't be much left of her by the time Wilson gets her. Little soft-spoken nippin' thing, she wouldn't make him no kind of a wife, anyway. Guess it's jest as well."

When the bell had stopped tolling, and all the people entered the church, Candace went over to her organ and seated herself. She arranged a singing-book before her, and sat still, waiting. Her thin, colorless neck and temples were full of beating pulses; her black eyes were bright and eager; she leaned stiffly over toward the music-rack, to hear better. When the church organ sounded out she straightened herself; her long skinny fingers pressed her own organ-keys with nervous energy. She worked the pedals with all her strength; all her slender body was in motion. When the first notes of Alma's solo began, Candace sang. She had really possessed a fine voice, and it was wonderful how little she had lost it. Straining her throat with jealous fury, her notes were still for the main part true. Her voice filled the whole room; she sang with wonderful fire and expression. That, at least, mild little Alma Way could never emulate. She was full of steadfastness and unquestioning constancy, but there were in her no smouldering fires of ambition and resolution. Music was not to her what it had been to her older rival. To this obscure woman, kept relentlessly by circumstances in a narrow track, singing in the village choir had been as much as Italy was to Napoleon—and now on her island of exile she was still showing fight.

After the church service was done, Candace left the organ and went over to her old chair by the window. Her knees felt weak, and shook under her. She sat down, and leaned back her head. There were red spots on her cheeks. Pretty soon she heard a quick slam of her gate, and an impetuous tread on the gravel-walk. She looked up, and there was her nephew Wilson Ford hurrying up to the door. She cringed a little, then she settled herself more firmly in her chair.

Wilson came into the room with a rush. He left the door open, and the wind slammed it to after him.

"Aunt Candace, where are you?" he called out, in a loud voice.

She made no reply. He looked around fiercely, and his eyes seemed to pounce upon her.

"Look here, Aunt Candace," said he, "are you crazy?" Candace said nothing. "Aunt Candace!" She did not seem to see him. "If you don't answer me," said Wilson, "I'll just go over there and pitch that old organ out of the window!"

"Wilson Ford!" said Candace, in a voice that was almost a scream.

"Well, what say! What have you got to say for yourself, acting the way you have? I tell you what 'tis, Aunt Candace, I won't stand it."

"I'd like to see you help yourself."

"I will help myself. I'll pitch that old organ out of the window, and then I'll board up the window on that side of your house. Then we'll see."

"It ain't your house, and it won't never be."

"Who said it was my house? You're my aunt, and I've got a little lookout for the credit of the family. Aunt Candace, what are you doing this way for?"

"It don't make no odds what I'm doin' so for. I ain't bound to give my reasons to a young fellar like you, if you do act so mighty toppin'. But I'll tell you one thing, Wilson Ford, after the way you've spoke to-day, you sha'n't never have one cent of my money, an' you can't never marry that Way girl if you don't have it. You can't never take her home to live with your mother, an' this house would have been mighty nice an' convenient for you some day. Now you won't get it. I'm goin' to make another will. I'd made one, if you did but know it. Now you won't get a cent of my money, you nor your mother neither. An' I ain't goin' to live a dreadful while longer, neither. Now I wish you'd go home; I want to lay down. I'm 'bout sick."

Wilson could not get another word from his aunt. His indignation had not in the least cooled. Her threat of disinheriting him did not cow him at all; he had too much rough independence, and indeed his aunt Candace's house had always been too much of an air-castle for him to contemplate seriously. Wilson, with his burly frame and his headlong common-sense, could have little to do with air-castles, had he been hard enough to build them over graves. Still, he had not admitted that he never could marry Alma. All his hopes were based upon a rise in his own fortunes, not by some sudden convulsion, but by his own long and steady labor. Some time, he thought, he should have saved enough for the two homes.

He went out of his aunt's house still storming. She arose after the door had shut behind him, and got out into the kitchen. She thought that she would start a fire and make a cup of tea. She had not eaten anything all day. She put some kindling-wood into the stove and touched a match to it; then she went back to the sitting-room, and settled down again into the chair by the window. The fire in the kitchen-stove roared, and the light wood was soon burned out. She thought no more about it. She had not put on the tea-kettle. Her head ached, and once in a while she shivered. She sat at the window while the afternoon waned and the dusk came on. At seven o'clock the meeting bell rang again, and the people flocked by. This time she did not stir. She had shut her parlor organ. She did not need to out-sing her rival this evening; there was only congregational singing at the Sunday-night prayer-meeting.

She sat still until it was nearly time for meeting to be done; her head ached harder and harder, and she shivered more. Finally she rose. "Guess I'll go to bed," she muttered. She went about the house, bent over and shaking, to lock the doors. She stood a minute in the back door, looking over the fields to the woods. There was a red light over there. "The woods are on fire," said Candace. She watched with a dull interest the flames roll up, withering and destroying the tender green spring foliage. The air was full of smoke, although the fire was half a mile away.

Candace locked the door and went in. The trees with their delicate garlands of new leaves, with the new nests of song birds, might fall, she was in the roar of an intenser fire; the growths of all her springs and the delicate wontedness of her whole life were going down in it. Candace went to bed in her little room off the parlor, but she could not sleep. She lay awake all night. In the morning she crawled to the door and hailed a little boy who was passing. She bade him go for the doctor as quickly as he could, then to Mrs. Ford's, and ask her to come over. She held on to the door while she was talking. The boy stood staring wonderingly at her. The spring wind fanned her face. She had drawn on a dress skirt and put her shawl over her shoulders, and her gray hair was blowing over her red cheeks.

She shut the door and went back to her bed. She never arose from it again. The doctor and Mrs. Ford came and looked after her, and she lived a week. Nobody but herself thought until the very last that she would die; the doctor called her illness merely a light run of fever; she had her senses fully.

But Candace gave up at the first. "It's my last sickness," she said to Mrs. Ford that morning when she first entered; and Mrs. Ford had laughed at the notion; but the sick woman held to it. She did not seem to suffer much physical pain; she only grew weaker and weaker, but she was distressed mentally. She did not talk much, but her eyes followed everybody with an agonized expression.

On Wednesday William Emmons came to inquire for her. Candace heard him out in the parlor. She tried to raise herself on one elbow that she might listen better to his voice.

"William Emmons come in to ask how you was," Mrs. Ford said, after he was gone.

"I—heard him," replied Candace. Presently she spoke again. "Nancy," said she, "where's that photograph album?"

"On the table," replied her sister, hesitatingly.

"Mebbe—you'd better—brush it up a little."

"Well."

Sunday morning Candace wished that the minister should be asked to come in at the noon intermission. She had refused to see him before. He came and prayed with her, and she asked his forgiveness for the way she had spoken the Sunday before. "I—hadn't ought to—spoke so," said she. "I was—dreadful wrought up."

"Perhaps it was your sickness coming on," said the minister, soothingly.

Candace shook her head. "No—it wa'n't. I hope the Lord will—forgive me."

After the minister had gone, Candace still appeared unhappy. Her pitiful eyes followed her sister everywhere with the mechanical persistency of a portrait.

"What is it you want, Candace?" Mrs. Ford said at last. She had nursed her sister faithfully, but once in a while her impatience showed itself.

"Nancy!"

"What say?"

"I wish—you'd go out when—meetin's done, an'—head off Alma an' Wilson, an'—ask 'em to come in. I feel as if—I'd like to—hear her sing."

Mrs. Ford stared. "Well," said she.

The meeting was now in session. The windows were all open, for it was another warm Sunday. Candace lay listening to the music when it began, and a look of peace came over her face. Her sister had smoothed her hair back, and put on a clean cap. The white curtain in the bedroom window waved in the wind like a white sail. Candace almost felt as if she were better, but the thought of death seemed easy.

Mrs. Ford at the parlor window watched for the meeting to be out. When the people appeared, she ran down the walk and waited for Alma and Wilson. When they came she told them what Candace wanted, and they all went in together.

"Here's Alma an' Wilson, Candace," said Mrs. Ford, leading them to the bedroom door.

Candace smiled. "Come in," she said, feebly. And Alma and Wilson entered and stood beside the bed. Candace continued to look at them, the smile straining her lips.

"Wilson!"

"What is it, Aunt Candace?"

"I ain't altered that—will. You an' Alma can—come here an'—live—

when I'm—gone. Your mother won't mind livin' alone. Alma can have—all—my things."

"Don't, Aunt Candace." Tears were running over Wilson's cheeks, and Alma's delicate face was all of a quiver.

"I thought—maybe—Alma 'd be willin' to—sing for me," said Candace.

"What do you want me to sing?" Alma asked, in a trembling voice.

"'Jesus, lover of my soul.'"

Alma, standing there beside Wilson, began to sing. At first she could hardly control her voice, then she sang sweetly and clearly.

Candace lay and listened. Her face had a holy and radiant expression. When Alma stopped singing it did not disappear, but she looked up and spoke, and it was like a secondary glimpse of the old shape of a forest tree through the smoke and flame of the transfiguring fire the instant before it falls. "You flatted a little on—soul," said Candace.

A Church Mouse

1889

"I never heard of a woman's bein' saxton."

"I dun' know what difference that makes; I don't see why they shouldn't have women saxtons as well as men saxtons, for my part, nor nobody else neither. They'd keep dusted 'nough sight cleaner. I've seen the dust layin' on my pew thick enough to write my name in a good many times, an' ain't said nothin' about it. An' I ain't goin' to say nothin' now again Joe Sowen, now he's dead an' gone. He did jest as well as most men do. Men git in a good many places where they don't belong, an' where they set as awkward as a cow on a hen-roost, jest because they push in ahead of women. I ain't blamin' 'em; I s'pose if I could push in I should, jest the same way. But there ain't no reason that I can see, nor nobody else neither, why a woman shouldn't be saxton."

Hetty Fifield stood in the rowen hay-field before Caleb Gale. He was a deacon, the chairman of the selectmen, and the rich and influential man of the village. One looking at him would not have guessed it. There was nothing imposing about his lumbering figure in his calico shirt and baggy trousers. However, his large face, red and moist with perspiration, scanned the distant horizon with a stiff and reserved air; he did not look at Hetty.

"How'd you go to work to ring the bell?" said he. "It would have to be tolled, too, if anybody died."

"I'd jest as lief ring that little meetin'-house bell as to stan' out here an' jingle a cow bell," said Hetty; "an' as for tollin', I'd jest as soon toll the bell for Methusaleh, if he was livin' here! I'd laugh if I ain't got strength 'nough for that."

"It takes a kind of a knack."

"If I ain't got as much knack as old Joe Sowen ever had, I'll give up the ship."

"You couldn't tend the fires."

"Couldn't tend the fires—when I've cut an' carried in all the wood I've burned for forty year! Couldn't keep the fires a-goin' in them two little wood-stoves!"

"It's consider'ble work to sweep the meetin'-house."

"I guess I've done 'bout as much work as to sweep that little meetin'-house, I ruther guess I have."

"There's one thing you ain't thought of."

"What's that?"

"Where'd you live? All old Sowen got for bein' saxton was twenty dollar a year, an' we couldn't pay a woman so much as that. You wouldn't have enough to pay for your livin' anywheres."

"Where am I goin' to live whether I'm saxton or not?"

Caleb Gale was silent.

There was a wind blowing, the rowen hay drifted round Hetty like a brown-green sea touched with ripples of blue and gold by the asters and golden-rod. She stood in the midst of it like a May-weed that had gathered a slender toughness through the long summer; her brown cotton gown clung about her like a wilting leaf, outlining her harsh little form. She was as sallow as a squaw, and she had pretty black eyes; they were bright, although she was old. She kept them fixed upon Caleb. Suddenly she raised herself upon her toes; the wind caught her dress and made it blow out; her eyes flashed. "I'll tell you where I'm goin' to live," said she. "*I'm goin' to live in the meetin'-house.*"

Caleb looked at her. "*Goin' to live in the meetin'-house!*"

"Yes, I be."

"Live in the meetin'-house!"

"I'd like to know why not."

"Why—you couldn't—live in the meetin'-house. You're crazy."

Caleb flung out the rake which he was holding, and drew it in full of rowen. Hetty moved around in front of him, he raked imperturbably; she moved again right in the path of the rake, then he stopped. "There ain't no sense in such talk."

"All I want is jest the east corner of the back gall'ry, where the chimbly goes up. I'll set up my cookin'-stove there, an' my bed, an' I'll curtain it off with my sunflower quilt, to keep off the wind."

"A cookin'-stove an' a bed in the meetin'-house!"

"Mis' Grout she give me that cookin'-stove, an' that bed I've allers slept on, before she died. She give 'em to me before Mary Anne Thomas, an' I moved 'em out. They air settin' out in the yard now, an' if it rains that stove an' that bed will be spoilt. It looks some like rain now. I guess you'd better give me the meetin'-housekey right off."

"You don't think you can move that cookin'-stove an' that bed into the meetin'-house—I ain't goin' to stop to hear such talk."

"My worsted-work, all my mottoes I've done, an' my wool flowers, air out there in the yard."

Caleb raked. Hetty kept standing herself about until he was forced to stop, or gather her in with the rowen hay. He looked straight at her, and scowled; the perspiration trickled down his cheeks. "If I go up to the house can Mis' Gale git me the key to the meetin'-house?" said Hetty.

"No, she can't."

"Be you goin' up before long?"

"No, I ain't." Suddenly Caleb's voice changed: it had been full of stubborn vexation, now it was blandly argumentative. "Don't you see it ain't no use talkin' such nonsense, Hetty? You'd better go right along, an' make up your mind it ain't to be thought of."

"Where be I goin' to-night, then?"

"To-night?"

"Yes; where be I a-goin'?"

"Ain't you got any place to go to?"

"Where do you s'pose I've got any place? Them folks air movin' into Mis' Grout's house, an' they as good as told me to clear out. I ain't got no folks to take me in. I dun' know where I'm goin'; mebbe I can go to your house?"

Caleb gave a start. "We've got company to home," said he, hastily. "I'm 'fraid Mis' Gale wouldn't think it was convenient."

Hetty laughed. "Most everybody in the town has got company," said she.

Caleb dug his rake into the ground as if it were a hoe, then he leaned on it, and stared at the horizon. There was a fringe of yellow birches on the edge of the hay-field; beyond them was a low range of misty blue hills. "You ain't got no place to go to, then?"

"I dun' know of any. There ain't no poor-house here, an' I ain't got no folks."

Caleb stood like a statue. Some crows flew cawing over the field. Hetty waited. "I s'pose that key is where Mis' Gale can find it?" she said, finally.

Caleb turned and threw out his rake with a jerk. "She knows where 'tis; it's hangin' up behind the settin'-room door. I s'pose you can stay there to-night, as long as you ain't got no other place. We shall have to see what can be done."

Hetty scuttled off across the field. "You mustn't take no stove nor bed into the meetin'-house," Caleb called after her; "we can't have that, nohow."

Hetty went on as if she did not hear.

The golden-rod at the sides of the road was turning brown; the asters were in their prime, blue and white ones; here and there were rows of thistles with white tops. The dust was thick; Hetty, when she emerged from Caleb's house, trotted along in a cloud of it. She did not look to the right or left, she kept her small eager face fixed straight ahead, and moved forward like some little animal with the purpose to which it was born strong within it.

Presently she came to a large cottage-house on the right of the road; there she stopped. The front yard was full of furniture, tables and chairs standing among the dahlias and clumps of marigolds. Hetty leaned over the fence at one corner of the yard, and inspected a little knot of household goods set aside from the others. There were a small cooking-stove, a hair trunk, a yellow bedstead stacked up against the fence, and a pile of bedding. Some children in the yard stood in a group and eyed Hetty. A woman appeared in the door—she was small, there was a black smutch on her face, which was haggard with fatigue, and she scowled in the sun as she looked over at Hetty. "Well, got a place to stay in?" said she, in an unexpectedly deep voice.

"Yes, I guess so," replied Hetty.

"I dun' know how in the world I can have you. All the beds will be full— I expect his mother some to-night, an' I'm dreadful stirred up anyhow."

"Everybody's havin' company; I never see anything like it." Hetty's voice was inscrutable. The other woman looked sharply at her.

"You've got a place, ain't you?" she asked, doubtfully.

"Yes, I have."

At the left of this house, quite back from the road, was a little unpainted cottage, hardly more than a hut. There was smoke coming out of the chimney, and a tall youth lounged in the door. Hetty, with the woman and children staring after her, struck out across the field in the little foot-path towards the cottage. "I wonder if she's goin' to stay there?" the woman muttered, meditating.

The youth did not see Hetty until she was quite near him, then he aroused suddenly as if from sleep, and tried to slink off around the cottage. But Hetty called after him. "Sammy," she cried, "Sammy, come back here, I want you!"

"What d'ye want?"

"Come back here!"

The youth lounged back sulkily, and a tall woman came to the door. She bent out of it anxiously to hear Hetty.

"I want you to come an' help me move my stove an' things," said Hetty.

"Where to?"

"Into the meetin'-house."

"The meetin'-house?"

"Yes, the meetin'-house."

The woman in the door had sodden hands; behind her arose the steam of a wash-tub. She and the youth stared at Hetty, but surprise was too strong an emotion for them to grasp firmly.

"I want Sammy to come right over an' help me," said Hetty.

"He ain't strong enough to move a stove," said the woman.

"Ain't strong enough!"

"He's apt to git lame."

"Most folks are. Guess I've got lame. Come right along, Sammy!"

"He ain't able to lift much."

"I s'pose he's able to be lifted, ain't he?"

"I dun' know what you mean."

"The stove don't weigh nothin'," said Hetty; "I could carry it myself if I could git hold of it. Come, Sammy!"

Hetty turned down the path, and the youth moved a little way after her, as if perforce. Then he stopped, and cast an appealing glance back at his mother. Her face was distressed. "Oh, Sammy, I'm afraid you'll git sick," said she.

"No, he ain't goin' to git sick," said Hetty. "Come, Sammy." And Sammy followed her down the path.

It was four o'clock then. At dusk Hetty had her gay sunflower quilt curtaining off the chimney-corner of the church gallery; her stove and little bedstead were set up, and she had entered upon a life which endured successfully for three months. All that time a storm brewed; then it broke; but Hetty sailed in her own course for the three months.

It was on a Saturday that she took up her habitation in the meeting-house. The next morning, when the boy who had been supplying the dead sexton's place came and shook the door, Hetty was prompt on the other side. "Deacon Gale said for you to let me in so I could ring the bell," called the boy.

"Go away," responded Hetty. "I'm going to ring the bell; I'm saxton."

Hetty rang the bell with vigor, but she made a wild, irregular jangle at first; at the last it was better. The village people said to each other that a new hand was ringing. Only a few knew that Hetty was in the meeting-house. When the congregation had assembled, and saw that gaudy tent pitched in the house of the Lord, and the resolute little pilgrim at the door of it, there was a commotion. The farmers and their wives were stirred out of their Sabbath decorum. After the service was over, Hetty, sitting in a pew corner of the gallery, her little face dark and watchful against the flaming background of her quilt, saw the people below gathering in groups, whispering, and looking at her.

Presently the minister, Caleb Gale, and the other deacon came up the gallery stairs. Hetty sat stiffly erect. Caleb Gale went up to the sunflower quilt, slipped it aside, and looked in. He turned to Hetty with a frown. Today his dignity was supported by important witnesses. "Did you bring that stove an' bedstead here?"

Hetty nodded.

"What made you do such a thing?"

"What was I goin' to do if I didn't? How's a woman as old as me goin' to sleep in a pew, an' go without a cup of tea?"

The men looked at each other. They withdrew to another corner of the gallery and conferred in low tones; then they went down-stairs and out of the church. Hetty smiled when she heard the door shut. When one is hard pressed, one, however simple, gets wisdom as to vantage-points. Hetty comprehended hers perfectly. She was the propounder of a problem; as long as it was unguessed, she was sure of her foothold as propounder. This little village in which she had lived all her life had removed the shelter from her head; she being penniless, it was beholden to provide her another; she asked it what. When the old woman with whom she had lived died, the town promptly seized the estate for taxes—none had been paid for years. Hetty had not laid up a cent; indeed, for the most of the time she had received no wages. There had been no money in the house; all she had gotten for her labor for a sickly, impecunious old woman was a frugal board. When the old woman died, Hetty gathered in the few household articles for which she had stipulated, and made no complaint. She walked out of the house when the new tenants came in; all she asked was, "What are you going to do with me?" This little settlement of narrow-minded, prosperous farmers, however hard a task charity might be to them, could not turn an old woman out into the fields and high-ways to seek for food as they would a Jersey cow. They had their Puritan consciences, and her note of distress would sound louder in their ears than the Jersey's bell echoing down the valley in the stillest night. But the question as to Hetty Fifield's disposal was a hard one to answer. There was no almshouse in the village, and no private family was willing to take her in. Hetty was strong and capable; although she was old, she could well have paid for her food and shelter by her labor; but this could not secure her an entrance even among this hard-working and thrifty people, who would ordinarily grasp quickly enough at service without wage in dollars and cents. Hetty had somehow gotten for herself an unfortunate name in the village. She was held in the light of a long-thorned brier among the beanpoles, or a fierce little animal with claws and teeth bared. People were afraid to take her into their families; she had the reputation of always taking her own way, and never heeding the voice of authority. "I'd take her in an' have her give me a lift with the work," said one sickly farmer's wife; "but, near's I can find out, I couldn't never be sure that I'd get molasses in the beans, nor saleratus in my sour-milk cakes, if she took a notion not to put it in. I don't dare to risk it."

Stories were about concerning Hetty's authority over the old woman with whom she had lived. "Old Mis' Grout never dared to say her soul was her own," people said. Then Hetty's sharp, sarcastic sayings were repeated; the justice of them made them sting. People did not want a tongue like that in their homes.

Hetty as a church sexton was directly opposed to all their ideas of church decorum and propriety in general; her pitching her tent in the Lord's house was almost sacrilege; but what could they do? Hetty jangled the Sabbath bells for the three months; once she tolled the bell for an old man, and it seemed by the sound of the bell as if his long, calm years had swung by in a weak delirium; but people bore it. She swept and dusted the little meeting-house, and she garnished the walls with her treasures of worsted-work. The neatness and the garniture went far to quiet the dissatisfaction of the people. They had a crude taste. Hetty's skill in fancy-work was quite celebrated. Her wool flowers were much talked of, and young girls tried to copy them. So these wreaths and clusters of red and blue and yellow wool roses and lilies hung as acceptably between the meeting-house windows as pictures of saints in a cathedral.

Hetty hung a worsted motto over the pulpit; on it she set her chiefest treasure of art, a white wax cross with an ivy vine trailing over it, all covered with silver frost-work. Hetty always surveyed this cross with a species of awe; she felt the irresponsibility and amazement of a genius at his own work.

When she set it on the pulpit, no queen casting her rich robes and her jewels upon a shrine could have surpassed her in generous enthusiasm. "I guess when they see that they won't say no more," she said.

But the people, although they shared Hetty's admiration for the cross, were doubtful. They, looking at it, had a double vision of a little wax Virgin upon an altar. They wondered if it savored of popery. But the cross remained, and the minister was mindful not to jostle it in his gestures.

It was three months from the time Hetty took up her abode in the church, and a week before Christmas, when the problem was solved. Hetty herself precipitated the solution. She prepared a boiled dish in the meeting-house, upon a Saturday, and the next day the odors of turnip and cabbage were strong in the senses of the worshippers. They sniffed and looked at one another. This superseding the legitimate savor of the sanctuary, the fragrance of pepper-mint lozenges and wintergreen, the breath of Sunday clothes, by the homely week-day odors of kitchen vegetables, was too much for the sensibilities of the people. They looked indignantly around at Hetty, sitting before her sunflower hanging, comfortable from her good dinner of the day before, radiant with the consciousness of a great plateful of cold vegetables in her tent for her Sabbath dinner.

Poor Hetty had not many comfortable dinners. The selectmen doled out a small weekly sum to her, which she took with dignity as being her hire; then she had a mild forage in the neighbors' cellars and kitchens, of poor apples and stale bread and pie, paying for it in teaching her art of worsted-work to the daughters. Her Saturday's dinner had been a banquet to her: she had actually bought a piece of pork to boil with the vegetables; somebody had given her a nice little cabbage and some turnips, without a thought of the limitations of her housekeeping. Hetty herself had not a thought. She made the fires as usual that Sunday morning; the meeting-house was very clean, there was not a speck of dust anywhere, the wax cross on the pulpit glistened in a sunbeam slanting through the house. Hetty, sitting in the gallery, thought innocently how nice it looked.

After the meeting, Caleb Gale approached the other deacon. "Somethin's got to be done," said he. And the other deacon nodded. He had not smelt the cabbage until his wife nudged him and mentioned it; neither had Caleb Gale.

In the afternoon of the next Thursday, Caleb and the other two selectmen waited upon Hetty in her tabernacle. They stumped up the gallery stairs, and Hetty emerged from behind the quilt and stood looking at them scared and defiant. The three men nodded stiffly; there was a pause; Caleb Gale motioned meaningly to one of the others, who shook his head; finally he himself had to speak. "I'm 'fraid you find it pretty cold here, don't you, Hetty?" said he.

"No, thank ye; it's very comfortable," replied Hetty, polite and wary.

"It ain't very convenient for you to do your cookin' here, I guess."

"It's jest as convenient as I want. I don't find no fault."

"I guess it's rayther lonesome here nights, ain't it?"

"I'd 'nough sight ruther be alone than have comp'ny, any day."

"It ain't fit for an old woman like you to be livin' alone here this way."

"Well, I dun' know of anything that's any fitter; mebbe you do."

Caleb looked appealingly at his companions; they stood stiff and irresponsive. Hetty's eyes were sharp and watchful upon them all.

"Well, Hetty," said Caleb, "we've found a nice, comfortable place for you, an' I guess you'd better pack up your things, an' I'll carry you right over there." Caleb stepped back a little closer to the other men. Hetty, small and trembling and helpless before them, looked vicious. She was like a little animal driven from its cover, for whom there is nothing left but desperate warfare and death.

"Where to?" asked Hetty. Her voice shrilled up into a squeak.

Caleb hesitated. He looked again at the other selectmen. There was a solemn, far-away expression upon their faces. "Well," said he, "Mis' Radway wants to git somebody, an'—"

"You ain't goin' to take me to that woman's!"

"You'd be real comfortable—"

"I ain't goin'."

"Now, why not, I'd like to know?"

"I don't like Susan Radway, hain't never liked her, an' I ain't goin' to live with her."

"Mis' Radway's a good Christian woman. You hadn't ought to speak that way about her."

"You know what Susan Radway is, jest as well's I do; an' everybody else does too. I ain't goin' a step, an' you might jest as well make up your mind to it."

Then Hetty seated herself in the corner of the pew nearest her tent, and folded her hands in her lap. She looked over at the pulpit as if she were listening to preaching. She panted, and her eyes glittered, but she had an immovable air.

"Now, Hetty, you've got sense enough to know you can't stay here," said Caleb. "You'd better put on your bonnet, an' come right along before dark. You'll have a nice ride."

Hetty made no response.

The three men stood looking at her. "Come, Hetty," said Caleb, feebly; and another selectman spoke. "Yes, you'd better come," he said, in a mild voice.

Hetty continued to stare at the pulpit.

The three men withdrew a little and conferred. They did not know how to act. This was a new emergency in their simple, even lives. They were not constables; these three steady, sober old men did not want to drag an old woman by main force out of the meeting-house, and thrust her into Caleb Gale's buggy as if it were a police wagon.

Finally Caleb brightened. "I'll go over an' git mother," said he. He started with a brisk air, and went down the gallery stairs; the others followed. They took up their stand in the meeting-house yard, and Caleb got into his buggy and gathered up the reins. The wind blew cold over the hill. "Hadn't you better go inside and wait out of the wind?" said Caleb.

"I guess we'll wait out here," replied one; and the other nodded.

"Well, I sha'n't be gone long," said Caleb. "Mother'll know how to manage her." He drove carefully down the hill; his buggy wings rattled in the wind. The other men pulled up their coat collars, and met the blast stubbornly.

"Pretty ticklish piece of business to tackle," said one, in a low grunt.

"That's so," assented the other. Then they were silent, and waited for Caleb. Once in a while they stamped their feet and slapped their mittened hands. They did not hear Hetty slip the bolt and turn the key of the meet-ing-house door, nor see her peeping at them from a gallery window.

Caleb returned in twenty minutes; he had not far to go. His wife, stout and handsome and full of vigor, sat beside him in the buggy. Her face was red with the cold wind; her thick cashmere shawl was pinned tightly over her broad bosom. "Has she come down yet?" she called out, in an imperi-ous way.

The two selectmen shook their heads. Caleb kept the horse quiet while his wife got heavily and briskly out of the buggy. She went up the meeting-house steps, and reached out confidently to open the door. Then she drew back and looked around. "Why," said she, "the door's locked; she's locked the door. I call this pretty work!"

She turned again quite fiercely, and began beating on the door. "Hetty!" she called; "Hetty, Hetty Fifield! Let me in! What have you locked this door for?"

She stopped and turned to her husband.

"Don't you s'pose the barn key would unlock it?" she asked.

"I don't b'lieve 'twould."

"Well, you'd better go home and fetch it."

Caleb again drove down the hill, and the other men searched their pockets for keys. One had the key of his corn-house, and produced it hope-fully; but it would not unlock the meeting-house door.

A crowd seldom gathered in the little village for anything short of a fire; but to-day in a short time quite a number of people stood on the meeting-house hill, and more kept coming. When Caleb Gale returned with the barn key his daughter, a tall, pretty young girl, sat beside him, her little face alert and smiling in her red hood. The other selectmen's wives toiled ea-gerly up the hill, with a young daughter of one of them speeding on ahead. Then the two young girls stood close to each other and watched the pro-ceedings. Key after key was tried; men brought all the large keys they could find, running importantly up the hill, but none would unlock the meeting-house door. After Caleb had tried the last available key, stooping and screwing it anxiously, he turned around. "There ain't no use in it, any way," said he; "most likely the door's bolted."

"You don't mean there's a bolt on that door?" cried his wife.

"Yes, there is."

"Then you might jest as well have tore 'round for hen's feathers as keys.

Of course she's bolted it if she's got any wit, an' I guess she's got most as much as some of you men that have been bringin' keys. Try the windows."

But the windows were fast. Hetty had made her sacred castle impregnable except to violence. Either the door would have to be forced or a window broken to gain an entrance.

The people conferred with one another. Some were for retreating, and leaving Hetty in peaceful possession until time drove her to capitulate. "She'll open it to-morrow," they said. Others were for extreme measures, and their impetuosity gave them the lead. The project of forcing the door was urged; one man started for a crow-bar.

"They are a parcel of fools to do such a thing," said Caleb Gale's wife to another woman. "Spoil that good door! They'd better leave the poor thing alone till to-morrow. I dun' know what's goin' to be done with her when they git in. I ain't goin' to have father draggin' her over to Mis' Radway's by the hair of her head."

"That's jest what I say," returned the other woman.

Mrs. Gale went up to Caleb and nudged him. "Don't you let them break that door down, father," said she.

"Well, well, we'll see," Caleb replied. He moved away a little; his wife's voice had been drowned out lately by a masculine clamor, and he took advantage of it.

All the people talked at once; the wind was keen, and all their garments fluttered; the two young girls had their arms around each other under their shawls; the man with the crow-bar came stalking up the hill.

"Don't you let them break down that door, father," said Mrs. Gale.

"Well, well," grunted Caleb.

Regardless of remonstrances, the man set the crow-bar against the door; suddenly there was a cry, "There she is!" Everybody looked up. There was Hetty looking out of a gallery window.

Everybody was still. Hetty began to speak. Her dark old face, peering out of the window, looked ghastly; the wind blew her poor gray locks over it. She extended her little wrinkled hands. "Jest let me say one word," said she; "jest one word." Her voice shook. All her coolness was gone. The magnitude of her last act of defiance had caused it to react upon herself like an overloaded gun.

"Say all you want to, Hetty, an' don't be afraid," Mrs. Gale called out.

"I jest want to say a word," repeated Hetty. "Can't I stay here, nohow? It don't seem as if I could go to Mis' Radway's. I ain't nothin' again' her. I s'pose she's a good woman, but she's used to havin' her own way, and I've been livin' all my life with them that was, an' I've had to fight to keep a footin' on the earth, an' now I'm gittin' too old for't. If I can jest stay here in the meetin'-house, I won't ask for nothin' any better. I sha'n't need much to keep me, I wa'n't never a hefty eater; an' I'll keep the meetin'-house jest as clean as I know how. An' I'll make some more of them wool flowers. I'll make a wreath to go the whole length of the gallery, if I can git wool 'nough. Won't you let me stay? I ain't complainin', but I've always had a dretful hard time; seems as if now I might take a little comfort the last of it, if I could stay here. I can't go to Mis' Radway's nohow." Hetty covered her face with her hands; her words ended in a weak wail.

Mrs. Gale's voice rang out clear and strong and irrepressible. "Of course you can stay in the meetin'-house," said she; "I should laugh if you couldn't. Don't you worry another mite about it. You sha'n't go one step to Mis' Radway's; you couldn't live a day with her. You can stay jest where you are; you've kept the meetin'-house enough sight cleaner than I've ever seen it. Don't you worry another mite, Hetty."

Mrs. Gale stood majestically, and looked defiantly around, tears were in her eyes. Another woman edged up to her. "Why couldn't she have that little room side of the pulpit, where the minister hangs his hat?" she whispered. "He could hang it somewhere else."

"Course she could," responded Mrs. Gale, with alacrity, "jest as well as not. The minister can have a hook in the entry for his hat. She can have her stove an' her bed in there, an' be jest as comfortable as can be. I should laugh if she couldn't. Don't you worry, Hetty."

The crowd gradually dispersed, sending out stragglers down the hill until it was all gone. Mrs. Gale waited until the last, sitting in the buggy in state. When her husband gathered up the reins, she called back to Hetty: "Don't you worry one mite more about it, Hetty. I'm comin' up to see you in the mornin'!"

It was almost dusk when Caleb drove down the hill; he was the last of the besiegers, and the feeble garrison was left triumphant.

The next day but one was Christmas, the next night Christmas Eve. On Christmas Eve Hetty had reached what to her was the flood-tide of peace and prosperity. Established in that small, lofty room, with her bed and her stove, with gifts of a rocking-chair and table, and a goodly store of food, with no one to molest or disturb her, she had nothing to wish for on earth. All her small desires were satisfied. No happy girl could have a merrier

Christmas than this old woman with her little measure full of gifts. That Christmas Eve Hetty lay down under her sunflower quilt, and all her old hardships looked dim in the distance, like far-away hills, while her new joys came out like stars.

She was a light sleeper; the next morning she was up early. She opened the meeting-house door and stood looking out. The smoke from the village chimneys had not yet begun to rise blue and rosy in the clear frosty air. There was no snow, but over all the hill there was a silver rime of frost; the bare branches of the trees glistened. Hetty stood looking. "Why, it's Christmas mornin'," she said, suddenly. Christmas had never been a gala-day to this old woman. Christmas had not been kept at all in this New England village when she was young. She was led to think of it now only in connection with the dinner Mrs. Gale had promised to bring her to-day.

Mrs. Gale had told her she should have some of her Christmas dinner, some turkey and plum-pudding. She called it to mind now with a thrill of delight. Her face grew momentarily more radiant. There was a certain beauty in it. A finer morning light than that which lit up the wintry earth seemed to shine over the furrows of her old face. "I'm goin' to have turkey an' plum-puddin' to-day," said she; "it's Christmas." Suddenly she started, and went into the meeting-house, straight up the gallery stairs. There in a clear space hung the bell-rope. Hetty grasped it. Never before had a Christmas bell been rung in this village; Hetty had probably never heard of Christmas bells. She was prompted by pure artless enthusiasm and grateful happiness. Her old arms pulled on the rope with a will, the bell sounded peal on peal. Down in the village, curtains rolled up, letting in the morning light, happy faces looked out of the windows. Hetty had awakened the whole village to Christmas Day.

A Poetess

1890

The garden-patch at the right of the house was all a gay spangle with sweet-peas and red-flowering beans, and flanked with feathery asparagus. A woman in blue was moving about there. Another woman, in a black bonnet, stood at the front door of the house. She knocked and waited. She could not see from where she stood the blue-clad woman in the garden. The house was very close to the road, from which a tall evergreen hedge separated it, and the view to the side was in a measure cut off.

The front door was open; the woman had to reach to knock on it, as it swung into the entry. She was a small woman and quite young, with a bright alertness about her which had almost the effect of prettiness. It was to her what greenness and crispness are to a plant. She poked her little face forward, and her sharp pretty eyes took in the entry and a room at the left, of which the door stood open. The entry was small and square and unfurnished, except for a well-rubbed old card-table against the back wall. The room was full of green light from the tall hedge, and bristling with grasses and flowers and asparagus stalks.

"Betsey, you there?" called the woman. When she spoke, a yellow canary, whose cage hung beside the front door, began to chirp and twitter.

"Betsey, you there?" the woman called again. The bird's chirps came in a quick volley; then he began to trill and sing.

"She ain't there," said the woman. She turned and went out of the yard through the gap in the hedge; then she looked around. She caught sight of the blue figure in the garden. "There she is," said she.

She went around the house to the garden. She wore a gay cashmere-patterned calico dress with her mourning bonnet, and she held it carefully away from the dewy grass and vines.

The other woman did not notice her until she was close to her and said, "Good-mornin', Betsey." Then she started and turned around.

"Why, Mis' Caxton! That you?" said she.

"Yes. I've been standin' at your door for the last half-hour. I was jest goin' away when I caught sight of you out here."

In spite of her brisk speech her manner was subdued. She drew down the corners of her mouth sadly.

"I declare I'm dreadful sorry you had to stan' there so long!" said the other woman.

She set a pan partly filled with beans on the ground, wiped her hands, which were damp and green from the wet vines, on her apron, then extended her right one with a solemn and sympathetic air.

"It don't make much odds, Betsey," replied Mrs. Caxton. "I ain't got much to take up my time nowadays." She sighed heavily as she shook hands, and the other echoed her.

"We'll go right in now. I'm dreadful sorry you stood there so long," said Betsey.

"You'd better finish pickin' your beans."

"No; I wa'n't goin' to pick any more. I was jest goin' in."

"I declare, Betsey Dole, I shouldn't think you'd got enough for a cat!" said Mrs. Caxton, eying the pan.

"I've got pretty near all there is. I guess I've got more flowerin' beans than eatin' ones, anyway."

"I should think you had," said Mrs. Caxton, surveying the row of bean-poles topped with swarms of delicate red flowers. "I should think they were pretty near all flowerin' ones. Had any peas?"

"I didn't have more'n three or four messes. I guess I planted sweet-peas mostly. I don't know hardly how I happened to."

"Had any summer squash?"

"Two or three. There's some more set, if they ever get ripe. I planted some gourds. I think they look real pretty on the kitchen shelf in the winter."

"I should think you'd got a sage bed big enough for the whole town."

"Well, I have got a pretty good-sized one. I always like them blue sage-blows. You'd better hold up your dress real careful goin' through here, Mis' Caxton, or you'll get it wet."

The two women picked their way through the dewy grass, around a corner of the hedge, and Betsey ushered her visitor into the house.

"Set right down in the rockin-chair," said she. "I'll jest carry these beans out into the kitchen."

"I should think you'd better get another pan and string 'em, or you won't get 'em done for dinner."

"Well, mebbe I will, if you'll excuse it, Mis' Caxton. The beans had ought to boil quite a while; they're pretty old."

Betsey went into the kitchen and returned with a pan and an old knife. She seated herself opposite Mrs. Caxton, and began to string and cut the beans.

"If I was in your place I shouldn't feel as if I'd got enough to boil a kettle for," said Mrs. Caxton, eying the beans. "I should 'most have thought when you didn't have any more room for a garden than you've got that you'd planted more real beans and peas instead of so many flowerin' ones. I'd rather have a good mess of green peas boiled with a piece of salt pork than all the sweet-peas you could give me. I like flowers well enough, but I never set up for a butterfly, an' I want something else to live on." She looked at Betsey with pensive superiority.

Betsey was near-sighted; she had to bend low over the beans in order to string them. She was fifty years old, but she wore her streaky light hair in curls like a young girl. The curls hung over her faded cheeks and almost concealed them. Once in a while she flung them back with a childish gesture which sat strangely upon her.

"I dare say you're in the right of it," she said, meekly.

"I know I am. You folks that write poetry wouldn't have a single thing to eat growin' if they were left alone. And that brings to mind what I come for. I've been thinkin' about it ever since—our—little Willie—left us." Mrs. Caxton's manner was suddenly full of shamefaced dramatic fervor, her eyes reddened with tears.

Betsey looked up inquiringly, throwing back her curls. Her face took on unconsciously lines of grief so like the other woman's that she looked like her for the minute.

"I thought maybe," Mrs. Caxton went on, tremulously, "you'd be willin' to—write a few lines."

"Of course I will, Mis' Caxton. I'll be glad to, if I can do 'em to suit you," Betsey said, tearfully.

"I thought jest a few—lines. You could mention how—handsome he was, and good, and I never had to punish him but once in his life, and how pleased he was with his little new suit, and what a sufferer he was, and—how we hope he is at rest—in a better land."

"I'll try, Mis' Caxton, I'll try," sobbed Betsey. The two women wept together for a few minutes.

"It seems as if—I couldn't have it so sometimes," Mrs. Caxton said, brokenly. "I keep thinkin' he's in the other—room. Every time I go back home when I've been away it's like—losin' him again. Oh, it don't seem as if I could go home and not find him there—it don't, it don't! Oh, you don't know anything about it, Betsey. You never had any children!"

"I don't s'pose I do, Mis' Caxton; I don't s'pose I do."

Presently Mrs. Caxton wiped her eyes. "I've been thinkin'," said she, keeping her mouth steady with an effort, "that it would be real pretty to have—some lines printed on some sheets of white paper with a neat black border. I'd like to send some to my folks, and one to the Perkinses in Brigham, and there's a good many others I thought would value 'em."

"I'll do jest the best I can, Mis' Caxton, an' be glad to. It's little enough anybody can do at such times."

Mrs. Caxton broke out weeping again. "Oh, it's true, it's true, Betsey!" she sobbed. "Nobody can do anything, and nothin' amounts to anything—poetry or anything else—when he's *gone*. Nothin' can bring him back. Oh, what shall I do, what shall I do?"

Mrs. Caxton dried her tears again, and arose to take leave. "Well, I must be goin', or Wilson won't have any dinner," she said, with an effort at self-control.

"Well, I'll do jest the best I can with the poetry," said Betsey. "I'll write it this afternoon." She had set down her pan of beans and was standing beside Mrs. Caxton. She reached up and straightened her black bonnet, which had slipped backward.

"I've got to get a pin," said Mrs. Caxton, tearfully. "I can't keep it anywheres. It drags right off my head, the veil is so heavy."

Betsey went to the door with her visitor. "It's dreadful dusty, ain't it?" she remarked, in that sad, contemptuous tone with which one speaks of discomforts in the presence of affliction.

"Terrible," replied Mrs. Caxton. "I wouldn't wear my black dress in it nohow; a black bonnet is bad enough. This dress is 'most too good. It's enough to spoil everything. Well, I'm much obliged to you, Betsey, for bein' willin' to do that."

"I'll do jest the best I can, Mis' Caxton."

After Betsey had watched her visitor out of the yard she returned to the sitting-room and took up the pan of beans. She looked doubtfully at the handful of beans all nicely strung and cut up. "I declare I don't know what to do," said she. "Seems as if I should kind of relish these, but it's goin' to take some time to cook 'em, tendin' the fire an' everything, an' I'd ought to go to work on that poetry. Then, there's another thing, if I have 'em to-day, I can't to-morrow. Mebbe I shall take more comfort thinkin' about 'em. I guess I'll leave 'em over till to-morrow."

Betsey carried the pan of beans out into the kitchen and set them away in the pantry. She stood scrutinizing the shelves like a veritable Mother Hubbard. There was a plate containing three or four potatoes and a slice of cold boiled pork, and a spoonful of red jelly in a tumbler; that was all the food in sight. Betsey stooped and lifted the lid from an earthen jar on the floor. She took out two slices of bread. "There!" said she. "I'll have this bread and that jelly this noon, an' to-night I'll have a kind of dinner-supper with them potatoes warmed up with the pork. An' then I can sit right down an' go to work on that poetry."

It was scarcely eleven o'clock, and not time for dinner. Betsey returned to the sitting-room, got an old black portfolio and pen and ink out of the chimney cupboard, and seated herself to work. She meditated, and wrote one line, then another. Now and then she read aloud what she had written with a solemn intonation. She sat there thinking and writing, and the time went on. The twelve-o'clock bell rang, but she never noticed it; she had quite forgotten the bread and jelly. The long curls drooped over her cheeks; her thin yellow hand, cramped around the pen, moved slowly and fitfully over the paper. The light in the room was dim and green, like the light in an arbor, from the tall hedge before the windows. Great plumy bunches of asparagus waved over the tops of the looking-glass; a framed sampler, a steel engraving of a female head taken from some old magazine, and sheaves of dried grasses hung on or were fastened to the walls; vases and tumblers of flowers stood on the shelf and table. The air was heavy and sweet.

Betsey in this room, bending over her portfolio, looked like the very genius of gentle, old-fashioned, sentimental poetry. It seemed as if one, given the premises of herself and the room, could easily deduce what she would write, and read without seeing those lines wherein flowers rhymed sweetly with vernal bowers, home with beyond the tomb, and heaven with even.

The summer afternoon wore on. It grew warmer and closer; the air was full of the rasping babble of insects, with the cicadas shrilling over them; now and then a team passed, and a dust cloud floated over the top of the hedge; the canary at the door chirped and trilled, and Betsey wrote poor little Willie Caxton's obituary poetry.

Tears stood in her pale blue eyes; occasionally they rolled down her cheeks, and she wiped them away. She kept her handkerchief in her lap with her portfolio. When she looked away from the paper she seemed to see two childish forms in the room—one purely human, a boy clad in his little girl petticoats, with a fair chubby face; the other in a little straight white night-gown, with long, shining wings, and the same face. Betsey had not enough imagination to change the face. Little Willie Caxton's angel was still himself to her, although decked in the paraphernalia of the resurrection.

"I s'pose I can't feel about it nor write about it anything the way I could if I'd had any children of my own an' lost 'em. I s'pose it *would* have come home to me different," Betsey murmured once, sniffing. A soft color flamed up under her curls at the thought. For a second the room seemed all aslant with white wings, and smiling with the faces of children that had never been. Betsey straightened herself as if she were trying to be dignified to her inner consciousness. "That's one trouble I've been clear of, anyhow," said she; "an' I guess I can enter into her feelin's considerable."

She glanced at a great pink shell on the shelf, and remembered how she had often given it to the dead child to play with when he had been in with his mother, and how he had put it to his ear to hear the sea.

"Dear little fellow!" she sobbed, and sat awhile with her handkerchief at her face.

Betsey wrote her poem upon backs of old letters and odd scraps of paper. She found it difficult to procure enough paper for fair copies of her poems when composed; she was forced to be very economical with the first draft. Her portfolio was piled with a loose litter of written papers when she at length arose and stretched her stiff limbs. It was near sunset; men with dinner-pails were tramping past the gate, going home from their work.

Betsey laid the portfolio on the table. "There! I've wrote sixteen verses," said she, "an' I guess I've got everything in. I guess she'll think that's enough. I can copy it off nice to-morrow. I can't see to-night to do it, anyhow."

There were red spots on Betsey's cheeks; her knees were unsteady when she walked. She went into the kitchen and made a fire, and set on the teakettle. "I guess I won't warm up them potatoes to-night," said she; "I'll have the bread an' jelly, an' save 'em for breakfast. Somehow I don't seem to feel so much like 'em as I did, an' fried potatoes is apt to lay heavy at night."

When the kettle boiled, Betsey drank her cup of tea and soaked her slice of bread in it; then she put away her cup and saucer and plate, and went out to water her garden. The weather was so dry and hot it had to be watered every night. Betsey had to carry the water from a neighbor's well; her own was dry. Back and forth she went in the deepening twilight, her slender body strained to one side with the heavy water-pail, until the garden-mould looked dark and wet. Then she took in the canary-bird, locked up her house, and soon her light went out. Often on these summer nights Betsey went to bed without lighting a lamp at all. There was no moon, but it was a beautiful starlight night. She lay awake nearly all night, thinking of her poem. She altered several lines in her mind.

She arose early, made herself a cup of tea, and warmed over the potatoes, then sat down to copy the poem. She wrote it out on both sides of note-paper, in a neat, cramped hand. It was the middle of the afternoon before it was finished. She had been obliged to stop work and cook the beans for dinner, although she begrudged the time. When the poem was fairly copied, she rolled it neatly and tied it with a bit of black ribbon; then she made herself ready to carry it to Mrs. Caxton's.

It was a hot afternoon. Betsey went down the street in her thinnest dress—an old delaine, with delicate bunches of faded flowers on a faded green ground. There was a narrow green belt ribbon around her long waist. She wore a green barège bonnet, stiffened with rattans, scooping over her face, with her curls pushed forward over her thin cheeks in two bunches, and she carried a small green parasol with a jointed handle. Her costume was obsolete, even in the little country village where she lived. She had worn it every summer for the last twenty years. She made no more change in her attire than the old perennials in her garden. She had no money with which to buy new clothes, and the old satisfied her. She had come to regard them as being as unalterably a part of herself as her body.

Betsey went on, setting her slim, cloth-gaitered feet daintily in the hot sand of the road. She carried her roll of poetry in a black-mitted hand. She walked rather slowly. She was not very strong; there was a limp feeling in her knees; her face, under the green shade of her bonnet, was pale and moist with the heat.

She was glad to reach Mrs. Caxton's and sit down in her parlor, damp and cool and dark as twilight, for the blinds and curtains had been drawn all day. Not a breath of the fervid out-door air had penetrated it.

"Come right in this way; it's cooler than the sittin'-room," Mrs. Caxton said; and Betsey sank into the hair-cloth rocker and waved a palm-leaf fan.

Mrs. Caxton sat close to the window in the dim light, and read the poem. She took out her handkerchief and wiped her eyes as she read. "It's beautiful, beautiful," she said, tearfully, when she had finished. "It's jest as comfortin' as it can be, and you worked that in about his new suit so nice. I feel real obliged to you, Betsey, and you shall have one of the printed ones when they're done. I'm going' to see to it right off."

Betsey flushed and smiled. It was to her as if her poem had been approved and accepted by one of the great magazines. She had the pride and self-wonderment of recognized genius. She went home buoyantly, under the wilting sun, after her call was done. When she reached home there was no one to whom she could tell her triumph, but the hot spicy breath of the evergreen hedge and the fervent sweetness of the sweet-peas seemed to greet her like the voices of friends.

She could scarcely wait for the printed poem. Mrs. Caxton brought it, and she inspected it, neatly printed in its black border. She was quite overcome with innocent pride.

"Well, I don't know but it does read pretty well," said she.

"It's beautiful," said Mrs. Caxton, fervently. "Mr. White said he never read anything any more touchin', when I carried it to him to print. I think folks are goin' to think a good deal of havin' it. I've had two dozen printed."

It was to Betsey like a large edition of a book. She had written obituary poems before, but never one had been printed in this sumptuous fashion. "I declare I think it would look pretty framed!" said she.

"Well, I don't know but it would," said Mrs. Caxton. "Anybody might have a neat little black frame, and it would look real appropriate."

"I wonder how much it would cost?" said Betsey.

After Mrs. Caxton had gone, she sat long, staring admiringly at the poem, and speculating as to the cost of a frame. "There ain't no use; I can't have it nohow, not if it don't cost more'n a quarter of a dollar," said she.

Then she put the poem away and got her supper. Nobody knew how frugal Betsey Dole's suppers and breakfasts and dinners were. Nearly all her food in the summer came from the scanty vegetables which flourished between the flowers in her garden. She ate scarcely more than her canary-bird, and sang as assiduously. Her income was almost infinitesimal: the interest at a low per cent of a tiny sum in the village savings-bank, the remnant of her father's little hoard after his funeral expenses had been paid. Betsey had lived upon it for twenty years, and considered herself well-to-do. She had never received a cent for her poems; she had not thought of such a thing as possible. The appearance of this last in such shape was worth more to her than its words represented in as many dollars.

Betsey kept the poem pinned on the wall under the looking-glass; if any one came in, she tried with delicate hints to call attention to it. It was two weeks after she received it that the downfall of her innocent pride came.

One afternoon Mrs. Caxton called. It was raining hard. Betsey could scarcely believe it was she when she went to the door and found her standing there.

"Why, Mis' Caxton!" said she. "Ain't you wet to your skin?"

"Yes, I guess I be, pretty near. I s'pose I hadn't ought to come 'way down here in such a soak; but I went into Sarah Rogers's a minute after dinner, and something she said made me so mad, I made up my mind I'd come down here and tell you about it if I got drowned." Mrs. Caxton was out of breath; rain-drops trickled from her hair over her face; she stood in the door and shut her umbrella with a vicious shake to scatter the water from it. "I don't know what you're goin' to do with this," said she; "it's drippin'."

"I'll take it out an' put it in the kitchen sink."

"Well, I'll take off my shawl here too, and you can hang it out in the kitchen. I spread this shawl out. I thought it would keep the rain off me some. I know one thing, I'm goin' to have a waterproof if I live."

When the two women were seated in the sitting-room, Mrs. Caxton was quiet for a moment. There was a hesitating look on her face, fresh with the moist wind, with strands of wet hair clinging to the temples.

"I don't know as I had ought to tell you," she said, doubtfully.

"Why hadn't you ought to?"

"Well, I don't care; I'm goin' to, anyhow. I think you'd ought to know, an' it ain't so bad for you as it is for me. It don't begin to be. I put considerable money into 'em. I think Mr. White was pretty high, myself."

Betsey looked scared. "What is it?" she asked, in a weak voice.

"Sarah Rogers says that the minister told her Ida that that poetry you wrote was jest as poor as it could be, an' it was in dreadful bad taste to have it printed an' sent round that way. What do you think of that?"

Betsey did not reply. She sat looking at Mrs. Caxton as a victim whom the first blow had not killed might look at her executioner. Her face was like a pale wedge of ice between her curls.

Mrs. Caxton went on. "Yes, she said that right to my face, word for word. An' there was something else. She said the minister said that you had never wrote anything that could be called poetry, an' it was a dreadful waste of time. I don't s'pose he thought 'twas comin' back to you. You know he goes with Ida Rogers, an' I s'pose he said it to her kind of confidential when she showed him the poetry. There! I gave Sarah Rogers one of them nice printed ones, an' she acted glad enough to have it. Bad taste! H'm! If anybody wants to say anything against that beautiful poetry, printed with that nice black border, they can. I don't care if it's the minister, or who it is. I don't care if he does write poetry himself, an' has had some printed in a magazine. Maybe his ain't quite so fine as he thinks 'tis. Maybe them magazine folks jest took his for lack of something better. I'd like to have you send that poetry there. Bad taste! I jest got right up. 'Sarah Rogers,' says I, 'I hope you won't never do anything yourself in any worse taste.' I trembled so I could hardly speak, and I made up my mind I'd come right straight over here."

Mrs. Caxton went on and on. Betsey sat listening, and saying nothing. She looked ghastly. Just before Mrs. Caxton went home she noticed it. "Why, Betsey Dole," she cried, "you look as white as a sheet. You ain't takin' it to heart as much as all that comes to, I hope. Goodness, I wish I hadn't told you!"

"I'd a good deal ruther you told me," replied Betsey, with a certain dignity. She looked at Mrs. Caxton. Her back was as stiff as if she were bound to a stake.

"Well, I thought you would," said Mrs. Caxton, uneasily; "and you're dreadful silly if you take it to heart, Betsey, that's all I've got to say. Goodness, I guess I don't, and it's full as hard on me as 'tis on you!"

Mrs. Caxton arose to go. Betsey brought her shawl and umbrella from the kitchen, and helped her off. Mrs. Caxton turned on the door-step and looked back at Betsey's white face. "Now don't go to thinkin' about it any more," said she. "I ain't goin' to. It ain't worth mindin'. Everybody knows what Sarah Rogers is. Good-by."

"Good-by, Mis' Caxton," said Betsey. She went back into the sitting-room. It was a cold rain, and the room was gloomy and chilly. She stood looking out of the window, watching the rain pelt on the hedge. The bird-cage hung at the other window. The bird watched her with his head on one side; then he begun to chirp.

Suddenly Betsey faced about and began talking. It was not as if she were talking to herself; it seemed as if she recognized some other presence in the room. "I'd like to know if it's fair," said she. "I'd like to know if you think it's fair. Had I ought to have been born with the wantin' to write poetry if I couldn't write it—had I? Had I ought to have been let to write all my life, an' not know before there wa'n't any use in it? Would it be fair if that ca-nary-bird there, that ain't never done anything but sing, should turn out not to be singin'? Would it, I'd like to know? S'pose them sweet-peas shouldn't be smellin' the right way? I ain't been dealt with as fair as they have, I'd like to know if I have."

The bird trilled and trilled. It was as if the golden down on his throat bubbled. Betsey went across the room to a cupboard beside the chimney. On the shelves were neatly stacked newspapers and little white rolls of writing-paper. Betsey began clearing the shelves. She took out the news-papers first, got the scissors, and cut a poem neatly out of the corner of each. Then she took up the clipped poems and the white rolls in her apron, and carried them into the kitchen. She cleaned out the stove carefully, re-moving every trace of ashes; then she put in the papers, and set them on fire. She stood watching them as their edges curled and blackened, then leaped into flame. Her face twisted as if the fire were curling over it also. Other women might have burned their lovers' letters in agony of heart. Betsey had never had any lover, but she was burning all the love-letters that had passed between her and life. When the flames died out she got a blue china sugar-bowl from the pantry and dipped the ashes into it with one of her thin silver teaspoons; then she put on the cover and set it away in the sitting-room cupboard.

The bird, who had been silent while she was out, began chirping again. Betsey went back to the pantry and got a lump of sugar, which she stuck between the cage wires. She looked at the clock on the kitchen shelf as she went by. It was after six. "I guess I don't want any supper to-night," she muttered.

She sat down by the window again. The bird pecked at his sugar. Betsey shivered and coughed. She had coughed more or less for years. People said she had the old-fashioned consumption. She sat at the window until it was quite dark; then she went to bed in her little bedroom out of the sitting-room. She shivered so she could not hold herself upright crossing the room. She coughed a great deal in the night.

Betsey was always an early riser. She was up at five the next morning. The sun shown, but it was very cold for the season. The leaves showed white in a north wind, and the flowers looked brighter than usual, though they were bent with the rain of the day before. Betsey went out in the garden to straighten her sweet-peas.

Coming back, a neighbor passing in the street eyed her curiously. "Why, Betsey, you sick?" said she.

"No; I'm kinder chilly, that's all," replied Betsey.

But the woman went home and reported that Betsey Dole looked dreadfully, and she didn't believe she'd ever see another summer.

It was now late August. Before October it was quite generally recognized that Betsey Dole's life was nearly over. She had no relatives, and hired nurses were rare in this little village. Mrs. Caxton came voluntarily and took care of her, only going home to prepare her husband's meals. Betsey's bed was moved into the sitting-room, and the neighbors came every day to see her, and brought little delicacies. Betsey had talked very little all her life; she talked less now, and there was a reticence about her which somewhat intimidated the other women. They would look pityingly and solemnly at her, and whisper in the entry when they went out.

Betsey never complained; but she kept asking if the minister had got home. He had been called away by his mother's illness, and returned only a week before Betsey died.

He came over at once to see her. Mrs. Caxton ushered him in one afternoon.

"Here's Mr. Lang come to see you, Betsey," said she, in the tone she would have used towards a little child. She placed the rocking-chair for the minister, and was about to seat herself, when Betsey spoke:

"Would you mind goin' out in the kitchen jest a few minutes, Mis' Caxton?" said she.

Mrs. Caxton arose, and went out with an embarrassed trot. Then there was silence. The minister was a young man—a country boy who had worked his way through a country college. He was gaunt and awkward, but sturdy in his loose clothes. He had a homely, impetuous face, with a good forehead.

He looked at Betsey's gentle, wasted face, sunken in the pillow, framed by its clusters of curls; finally he began to speak in the stilted fashion, yet with a certain force by reason of his unpolished honesty, about her spiritual welfare. Betsey listened quietly; now and then she assented. She had been a church member for years. It seemed now to the young man that this elderly maiden, drawing near the end of her simple, innocent life, had indeed her lamp, which no strong winds of temptation had ever met, well trimmed and burning.

When he paused, Betsey spoke. "Will you go to the cupboard side of the chimney and bring me the blue sugar-bowl on the top shelf?" said she, feebly.

The young man stared at her a minute; then he went to the cupboard, and brought the sugar-bowl to her. He held it, and Betsey took off the lid with her weak hand. "Do you see what's in there?" said she.

"It looks like ashes."

"It's—the ashes of all—the poetry I—ever wrote."

"Why, what made you burn it, Miss Dole?"

"I found out it wa'n't worth nothin'."

The minister looked at her in a bewildered way. He began to question if she were not wandering in her mind. He did not once suspect his own connection with the matter.

Betsey fastened her eager, sunken eyes upon his face. "What I want to know is—if you'll 'tend to—havin' this—buried with me."

The minister recoiled. He thought to himself that she certainly was wandering.

"No, I ain't out of my head," said Betsey. "I know what I'm sayin'. Maybe it's queer soundin', but it's a notion I've took. If you'll—'tend to it, I shall be—much obliged. I don't know anybody else I can ask."

"Well, I'll attend to it, if you wish me to, Miss Dole," said the minister, in a serious, perplexed manner. She replaced the lid on the sugar-bowl, and left it in his hands.

"Well, I shall be much obliged if you will 'tend to it; an' now there's something else," said she.

"What is it, Miss Dole?"

She hesitated a moment. "You write poetry, don't you?"

The ministered colored. "Why, yes; a little sometimes."

"It's good poetry, ain't it? They printed some in a magazine."

The minister laughed confusedly. "Well, Miss Dole. I don't know how good poetry it may be, but they did print some in a magazine."

Betsey lay looking at him. "I never wrote none that was—good," she whispered, presently; "but I've been thinkin'—if you would jest write a few—lines about me—afterward— I've been thinkin' that—mebbe my—dyin' was goin' to make me—a good subject for—poetry, if I never wrote none. If you would jest write a few lines."

The minister stood holding the sugar-bowl; he was quite pale with bewilderment and sympathy. "I'll—do the best I can, Miss Dole," he stammered.

"I'll be much obliged," said Betsey, as if the sense of grateful obligation was immortal like herself. She smiled, and the sweetness of the smile was as evident through the drawn lines of her mouth as the old red in the leaves of a withered rose. The sun was setting; a red beam flashed softly over the top of the hedge and lay along the opposite wall; then the bird in his cage began to chirp. He chirped faster and faster until he trilled into a triumphant song.

The Revolt of "Mother"

1890

"Father!"

"What is it?"

"What are them men diggin' over there in the field for?"

There was a sudden dropping and enlarging of the lower part of the old man's face, as if some heavy weight had settled therein; he shut his mouth tight, and went on harnessing the great bay mare. He hustled the collar on to her neck with a jerk.

"Father!"

The old man slapped the saddle upon the mare's back.

"Look here, father, I want to know what them men are diggin' over in the field for, an' I'm goin' to know."

"I wish you'd go into the house, mother, an' 'tend to your own affairs," the old man said then. He ran his words together, and his speech was almost as inarticulate as a growl.

But the woman understood; it was her most native tongue. "I ain't goin' into the house till you tell me what them men are doin' over there in the field," said she.

Then she stood waiting. She was a small woman, short and straight-waisted like a child in her brown cotton gown. Her forehead was mild and benevolent between the smooth curves of gray hair; there were meek downward lines about her nose and mouth; but her eyes, fixed upon the old man, looked as if the meekness had been the result of her own will, never of the will of another.

They were in the barn, standing before the wide open doors. The spring air, full of the smell of growing grass and unseen blossoms, came in their faces. The deep yard in front was littered with farm wagons and piles of wood; on the edges, close to the fence and the house, the grass was a vivid green, and there were some dandelions.

The old man glanced doggedly at his wife as he tightened the last buckles on the harness. She looked as immovable to him as one of the rocks in his pasture-land, bound to the earth with generations of blackberry vines. He slapped the reins over the horse, and started forth from the barn.

"*Father!*" said she.

The old man pulled up. "What is it?"

"I want to know what them men are diggin' over there in that field for."

"They're diggin' a cellar, I s'pose, if you've got to know."

"A cellar for what?"

"A barn."

"A barn? You ain't goin' to build a barn over there where we was goin' to have a house, father?"

The old man said not another word. He hurried the horse into the farm wagon, and clattered out of the yard, jouncing as sturdily on his seat as a boy.

The woman stood a moment looking after him, then she went out of the barn across a corner of the yard to the house. The house, standing at right angles with the great barn and a long reach of sheds and out-buildings, was infinitesimal compared with them. It was scarcely as commodious for people as the little boxes under the barn eaves were for doves.

A pretty girl's face, pink and delicate as a flower, was looking out of one of the house windows. She was watching three men who were digging over in the field which bounded the yard near the road line. She turned quietly when the woman entered.

"What are they digging for, mother?" said she. "Did he tell you?"

"They're diggin' for—a cellar for a new barn."

"Oh, mother, he ain't going to build another barn?"

"That's what he says."

A boy stood before the kitchen glass combing his hair. He combed slowly and painstakingly, arranging his brown hair in a smooth hillock over his forehead. He did not seem to pay any attention to the conversation.

"Sammy, did you know father was going to build a new barn?" asked the girl.

The boy combed assiduously.

"Sammy!"

He turned, and showed a face like his father's under his smooth crest of hair. "Yes, I s'pose I did," he said, reluctantly.

"How long have you known it?" asked his mother.

"'Bout three months, I guess."

"Why didn't you tell of it?"

"Didn't think 'twould do no good."

"I don't see what father wants another barn for," said the girl, in her sweet, slow voice. She turned again to the window, and stared out at the digging men in the field. Her tender, sweet face was full of a gentle distress. Her forehead was as bald and innocent as a baby's, with the light hair strained back from it in a row of curl-papers. She was quite large, but her soft curves did not look as if they covered muscles.

Her mother looked sternly at the boy. "Is he goin' to buy more cows?" said she.

The boy did not reply; he was tying his shoes.

"Sammy, I want you to tell me if he's goin' to buy more cows."

"I s'pose he is."

"How many?"

"Four, I guess."

His mother said nothing more. She went into the pantry and there was a clatter of dishes. The boy got his cap from a nail behind the door, took an old arithmetic from the shelf, and started for school. He was lightly built, but clumsy. He went out of the yard with a curious spring in the hips, that made his loose home-made jacket tilt up in the rear.

The girl went to the sink, and began to wash the dishes that were piled up there. Her mother came promptly out of the pantry, and shoved her aside. "You wipe 'em," said she; "I'll wash. There's a good many this mornin'."

The mother plunged her hands vigorously into the water, the girl wiped the plates slowly and dreamily. "Mother," said she, "don't you think it's too bad father's going to build that new barn, much as we need a decent house to live in?"

Her mother scrubbed a dish fiercely. "You ain't found out yet we're women-folks, Nanny Penn," said she. "You ain't seen enough of men-folks yet to. One of these days you'll find it out, an' then you'll know that we know only what men-folks think we do, so far as any use of it goes, an' how we'd ought to reckon men-folks in with Providence, an' not complain of what they do any more than we do of the weather."

"I don't care; I don't believe George is anything like that, anyhow," said Nanny. Her delicate face flushed pink, her lips pouted softly, as if she were going to cry.

"You wait an' see. I guess George Eastman ain't no better than other men. You hadn't ought to judge father, though. He can't help it, 'cause he don't look at things jest the way we do. An' we've been pretty comfortable here, after all. The roof don't leak—ain't never but once—that's one thing. Father's kept it shingled right up."

"I do wish we had a parlor."

"I guess it won't hurt George Eastman any to come to see you in a nice clean kitchen. I guess a good many girls don't have as good a place as this. Nobody's ever heard me complain."

"I ain't complained either, mother."

"Well, I don't think you'd better, a good father an' a good home as you've got. S'pose your father made you go out an' work for your livin'? Lots of girls have to that ain't no stronger an' better able to than you be."

Sarah Penn washed the frying-pan with a conclusive air. She scrubbed the outside of it as faithfully as the inside. She was a masterly keeper of her box of a house. Her one living-room never seemed to have in it any of the dust which the friction of life with inanimate matter produces. She swept, and there seemed to be no dirt to go before the broom; she cleaned, and one could see no difference. She was like an artist so perfect that he has apparently no art. To-day she got out a mixing bowl and a board, and rolled some pies, and there was no more flour upon her than upon her daughter who was doing finer work. Nanny was to be married in the fall, and she was sewing on some white cambric and embroidery. She sewed industriously while her mother cooked, her soft milk-white hands and wrists showed whiter than her delicate work.

"We must have the stove moved out in the shed before long," said Mrs. Penn. "Talk about not havin' things, it's been a real blessin' to be able to put a stove up in that shed in hot weather. Father did one good thing when he fixed that stove-pipe out there."

Sarah Penn's face as she rolled her pies had that expression of meek vigor which might have characterized one of the New Testament saints. She was making mince-pies. Her husband, Adoniram Penn, liked them better than any other kind. She baked twice a week. Adoniram often liked a piece of pie between meals. She hurried this morning. It had been later than usual when she began, and she wanted to have a pie baked for dinner. However deep a resentment she might be forced to hold against her husband, she would never fail in sedulous attention to his wants.

Nobility of character manifests itself at loop-holes when it is not provided with large doors. Sarah Penn's showed itself to-day in flaky dishes of pastry. So she made the pies faithfully, while across the table she could see, when she glanced up from her work, the sight that rankled in her patient and steadfast soul—the digging of the cellar of the new barn in the place where Adoniram forty years ago had promised her their new house should stand.

The pies were done for dinner. Adoniram and Sammy were home a few minutes after twelve o'clock. The dinner was eaten with serious haste. There was never much conversation at the table in the Penn family. Adoniram asked a blessing, and they ate promptly, then rose up and went about their work.

Sammy went back to school, taking soft sly lopes out of the yard like a rabbit. He wanted a game of marbles before school, and feared his father would give him some chores to do. Adoniram hastened to the door and called after him, but he was out of sight.

"I don't see what you let him go for, mother," said he. "I wanted him to help me unload that wood."

Adoniram went to work out in the yard unloading wood from the wagon. Sarah put away the dinner dishes, while Nanny took down her curl-papers and changed her dress. She was going down to the store to buy some more embroidery and thread.

When Nanny was gone, Mrs. Penn went to the door. "Father!" she called.

"Well, what is it!"

"I want to see you jest a minute, father."

"I can't leave this wood nohow. I've got to git it unloaded an' go for a load of gravel afore two o'clock. Sammy had ought to helped me. You hadn't ought to let him go to school so early."

"I want to see you jest a minute."

"I tell ye I can't, nohow, mother."

"Father, you come here." Sarah Penn stood in the door like a queen; she held her head as if it bore a crown; there was that patience which makes authority royal in her voice. Adoniram went.

Mrs. Penn led the way into the kitchen, and pointed to a chair. "Sit down, father," said she; "I've got somethin' I want to say to you."

He sat down heavily; his face was quite stolid, but he looked at her with restive eyes. "Well, what is it, mother?"

"I want to know what you're buildin' that new barn for, father?"

"I ain't got nothin' to say about it."

"It can't be you think you need another barn?"

"I tell ye I ain't got nothin' to say about it, mother; an' I ain't goin' to say nothin'."

"Be you goin' to buy more cows?"

Adoniram did not reply; he shut his mouth tight.

"I know you be, as well as I want to. Now, father, look here"—Sarah Penn had not sat down; she stood before her husband in the humble fashion of a Scripture woman—"I'm goin' to talk real plain to you; I never have sence I married you, but I'm goin' to now. I ain't never complained, an' I ain't goin' to complain now, but I'm goin' to talk plain. You see this room here, father; you look at it well. You see there ain't no carpet on the floor, an' you see the paper is all dirty, an' droppin' off the walls. We ain't had no new paper on it for ten year, an' then I put it on myself an' it didn't cost but ninepence a roll. You see this room, father; it's all the one I've had to work in an' eat in an' sit in since we was married. There ain't another woman in the whole town whose husband ain't got half the means you have but what's got better. It's all the room Nanny's got to have her company in; an' there ain't one of her mates but what's got better, an' their fathers not so able as hers is. It's all the room she'll have to be married in. What would you have thought, father, if we had had our weddin' in a room no better than this? I was married in my mother's parlor, with a carpet on the floor, an' stuffed furniture, an' a mahogany card-table. An' this is all the room my daughter will have to be married in. Look here, father!"

Sarah Penn went across the room as though it were a tragic stage. She flung open a door and disclosed a tiny bedroom, only large enough for a bed and bureau, with a path between. "There, father," said she—"there's all the room I've had to sleep in forty year. All my children were born there—the two that died, an' the two that's livin'. I was sick with a fever there."

She stepped to another door and opened it. It led into the small, ill-lighted pantry. "Here," said she, "is all the buttery I've got—every place

I've got for my dishes, to set away my victuals in, an' to keep my milk-pans in. Father, I've been takin' care of the milk of six cows in this place, an' now you're goin' to build a new barn, an' keep more cows, an' give me more to do in it."

She threw open another door. A narrow crooked flight of stairs wound upward from it. "There, father," said she, "I want you to look at the stairs that go up to them two unfinished chambers that are all the places our son an' daughter have had to sleep in all their lives. There ain't a prettier girl in town nor a more ladylike one than Nanny, an' that's the place she has to sleep in. It ain't so good as your horse's stall; it ain't so warm an' tight."

Sarah Penn went back and stood before her husband. "Now, father," said she, "I want to know if you think you're doin' right an' accordin' to what you profess. Here, when we was married, forty year ago, you promised me faithful that we should have a new house built in that lot over in the field before the year was out. You said you had money enough, an' you wouldn't ask me to live in no such place as this. It is forty year now, an' you've been makin' more money, an' I've been savin' of it for you ever since, an' you ain't built no house yet. You've built sheds an' cow-houses an' one new barn, an' now you're goin' to build another. Father, I want to know if you think it's right. You're lodgin' your dumb beasts better than you are your own flesh an' blood. I want to know if you think it's right."

"I ain't got nothin' to say."

"You can't say nothin' without ownin' it ain't right, father. An' there's another thing—I ain't complained; I've got along forty year, an' I s'pose I should forty more, if it wa'n't for that—if we don't have another house. Nanny she can't live with us after she's married. She'll have to go somewheres else to live away from us, an' it don't seem as if I could have it so, noways, father. She wa'n't ever strong. She's got considerable color, but there wa'n't never any backbone to her. I've always took the heft of everything off her, an' she ain't fit to keep house an' do everything herself. She'll be all worn out inside of a year. Think of her doin' all the washin' an' ironin' an' bakin' with them soft white hands an' arms, an' sweepin'! I can't have it so, noways, father."

Mrs. Penn's face was burning; her mild eyes gleamed. She had pleaded her little cause like a Webster; she had ranged from severity to pathos; but her opponent employed that obstinate silence which makes eloquence futile with mocking echoes. Adoniram arose clumsily.

"Father, ain't you got nothin' to say?" said Mrs. Penn.

"I've got to go off after that load of gravel. I can't stan' here talkin' all day."

"Father, won't you think it over, an' have a house built there instead of a barn?"

"I ain't got nothin' to say."

Adoniram shuffled out. Mrs. Penn went into her bedroom. When she came out, her eyes were red. She had a roll of unbleached cotton cloth. She spread it out on the kitchen table, and began cutting out some shirts for her husband. The men over in the field had a team to help them this afternoon; she could hear their halloos. She had a scanty pattern for the shirts; she had to plan and piece the sleeves.

Nanny came home with her embroidery, and sat down with her needle-work. She had taken down her curl-papers, and there was a soft roll of fair hair like an aureole over her forehead; her face was as delicately fine and clear as porcelain. Suddenly she looked up, and the tender red flamed all over her face and neck. "Mother," said she.

"What say?"

"I've been thinking—I don't see how we're goin' to have any—wedding in this room. I'd be ashamed to have his folks come if we didn't have any-body else."

"Mebbe we can have some new paper before then; I can put it on. I guess you won't have no call to be ashamed of your belongin's."

"We might have the wedding in the new barn," said Nanny, with gentle pettishness. "Why, mother, what makes you look so?"

Mrs. Penn had started, and was staring at her with a curious expression. She turned again to her work, and spread out a pattern carefully on the cloth. "Nothin'," said she.

Presently Adoniram clattered out of the yard in his two-wheeled dump cart, standing as proudly upright as a Roman charioteer. Mrs. Penn opened the door and stood there a minute looking out; the halloos of the men sounded louder.

It seemed to her all through the spring months that she heard nothing but the halloos and the noises of saws and hammers. The new barn grew fast. It was a fine edifice for this little village. Men came on pleasant Sundays, in their meeting suits and clean shirt bosoms, and stood around it admiringly. Mrs. Penn did not speak of it, and Adoniram did not mention it to her, although sometimes, upon a return from inspecting it, he bore himself with injured dignity.

"It's a strange thing how your mother feels about the new barn," he said, confidentially, to Sammy one day.

Sammy only grunted after an odd fashion for a boy; he had learned it from his father.

The barn was all completed ready for use by the third week in July. Adoniram had planned to move his stock in on Wednesday; on Tuesday he received a letter which changed his plans. He came in with it early in the morning. "Sammy's been to the post-office," said he, "an' I've got a letter from Hiram." Hiram was Mrs. Penn's brother, who lived in Vermont.

"Well," said Mrs. Penn, "what does he say about the folks?"

"I guess they're all right. He says he thinks if I come up country right off there's a chance to buy jest the kind of a horse I want." He stared reflectively out of the window at the new barn.

Mrs. Penn was making pies. She went on clapping the rolling-pin into the crust, although she was very pale, and her heart beat loudly.

"I dun' know but what I'd better go," said Adoniram. "I hate to go off jest now, right in the midst of hayin', but the ten-acre lot's cut, an' I guess Rufus an' the others can git along without me three or four days. I can't get a horse round here to suit me, nohow, an' I've got to have another for all that wood-haulin' in the fall. I told Hiram to watch out, an' if he got wind of a good horse to let me know. I guess I'd better go."

"I'll get out your clean shirt an' collar," said Mrs. Penn calmly.

She laid out Adoniram's Sunday suit and his clean clothes on the bed in the little bedroom. She got his shaving-water and razor ready. At last she buttoned on his collar and fastened his black cravat.

Adoniram never wore his collar and cravat except on extra occasions. He held his head high, with a rasped dignity. When he was all ready, with his coat and hat brushed, and a lunch of pie and cheese in a paper bag, he hesitated on the threshold of the door. He looked at his wife, and his manner was defiantly apologetic. "If them cows come to-day, Sammy can drive 'em into the new barn," said he; "an' when they bring the hay up, they can pitch it in there."

"Well," replied Mrs. Penn.

Adoniram set his shaven face ahead and started. When he had cleared the door-step, he turned and looked back with a kind of nervous solemnity. "I shall be back by Saturday if nothin' happens," said he.

"Do be careful, father," returned his wife.

She stood in the door with Nanny at her elbow and watched him out of sight. Her eyes had a strange, doubtful expression in them; her peaceful forehead was contracted. She went in, and about her baking again. Nanny sat sewing. Her wedding-day was drawing nearer, and she was getting pale and thin with her steady sewing. Her mother kept glancing at her.

"Have you got that pain in your side this mornin'?" she asked.

"A little."

Mrs. Penn's face, as she worked, changed, her perplexed forehead smoothed, her eyes were steady, her lips firmly set. She formed a maxim for herself, although incoherently with her unlettered thoughts. "Unsolicited opportunities are the guide-posts of the Lord to the new roads of life," she repeated in effect, and she made up her mind to her course of action.

"S'posin' I *had* wrote to Hiram," she muttered once, when she was in the pantry—"s'posin' I had wrote, an' asked him if he knew of any horse? But I didn't, an' father's goin' wa'n't none of my doin'. It looks like a providence." Her voice rang out quite loud at the last.

"What you talkin' about, mother?" called Nanny.

"Nothin'."

Mrs. Penn hurried her baking; at eleven o'clock it was all done. The load of hay from the west field came slowly down the cart track, and drew up at the new barn. Mrs. Penn ran out. "Stop!" she screamed—"stop!"

The men stopped and looked; Sammy upreared from the top of the load, and stared at his mother.

"Stop!" she cried out again. "Don't you put the hay in that barn; put it in the old one."

"Why, he said to put it in here," returned one of the hay-makers, wonderingly. He was a young man, a neighbor's son, whom Adoniram hired by the year to help on the farm.

"Don't you put the hay in the new barn; there's room enough in the old one, ain't there?" said Mrs. Penn.

"Room enough," returned the hired man, in his thick, rustic tones. "Didn't need the new barn, nohow, far as room's concerned. Well, I s'pose he changed his mind." He took hold of the horses' bridles.

Mrs. Penn went back to the house. Soon the kitchen windows were darkened, and a fragrance like warm honey came into the room.

Nanny laid down her work. "I thought father wanted them to put the hay into the new barn?" she said, wonderingly.

"It's all right," replied her mother.

Sammy slid down from the load of hay, and came in to see if dinner was ready.

"I ain't goin' to get a regular dinner to-day, as long as father's gone," said his mother. "I've let the fire go out. You can have some bread an' milk an' pie. I thought we could get along." She set out some bowls of milk, some bread, and a pie on the kitchen table. "You'd better eat your dinner now," said she. "You might jest as well get through with it. I want you to help me afterward."

Nanny and Sammy stared at each other. There was something strange in their mother's manner. Mrs. Penn did not eat anything herself. She went into the pantry, and they heard her moving dishes while they ate. Presently she came out with a pile of plates. She got the clothes-basket out of the shed, and packed them in it. Nanny and Sammy watched. She brought out cups and saucers, and put them in with the plates.

"What you goin' to do, mother?" inquired Nanny, in a timid voice. A sense of something unusual made her tremble, as if it were a ghost. Sammy rolled his eyes over his pie.

"You'll see what I'm goin' to do," replied Mrs. Penn. "If you're through, Nanny, I want you to go up-stairs an' pack up your things; an' I want you, Sammy, to help me take down the bed in the bedroom."

"Oh, mother, what for?" gasped Nanny.

"You'll see."

During the next few hours a feat was performed by this simple, pious New England mother which was equal in its way to Wolfe's storming of the Heights of Abraham. It took no more genius and audacity of bravery for Wolfe to cheer his wondering soldiers up those steep precipices, under the sleeping eyes of the enemy, than for Sarah Penn, at the head of her children, to move all their little household goods into the new barn while her husband was away.

Nanny and Sammy followed their mother's instructions without a murmur; indeed, they were overawed. There is a certain uncanny and superhuman quality about all such purely original undertakings as their mother's was to them. Nanny went back and forth with her light loads, and Sammy tugged with sober energy.

At five o'clock in the afternoon the little house in which the Penns had lived for forty years had emptied itself into the new barn.

Every builder builds somewhat for unknown purposes, and is in a measure of prophet. The architect of Adoniram Penn's barn, while he designed it for the comfort of four-footed animals, had planned better than he knew for the comfort of humans. Sarah Penn saw at a glance its possibilities. Those great box-stalls, with quilts hung before them, would make better bedrooms than the one she had occupied for forty years, and there was a tight carriage-room. The harness-room, with its chimney and shelves, would make a kitchen of her dreams. The great middle space would make a parlor, by-and-by, fit for a palace. Up stairs there was as much room as down. With partitions and windows, what a house would there be! Sarah looked at the row of stanchions before the allotted space for cows, and reflected that she would have her front entry there.

At six o'clock the stove was up in the harness-room, the kettle was boiling, and the table set for tea. It looked almost as home-like as the abandoned house across the yard had ever done. The young hired man milked, and Sarah directed him calmly to bring the milk to the new barn. He came gaping, dropping little blots of foam from the brimming pails on the grass. Before the next morning he had spread the story of Adoniram Penn's wife moving into the new barn all over the little village. Men assembled in the store and talked it over, women with shawls over their heads scuttled into each other's houses before their work was done. Any deviation from the ordinary course of life in this quiet town was enough to stop all progress in it. Everybody paused to look at the staid, independent figure on the side track. There was a difference of opinion with regard to her. Some held her to be insane; some, of a lawless and rebellious spirit.

Friday the minister went to see her. It was in the forenoon, and she was at the barn door shelling pease for dinner. She looked up and returned his salutation with dignity, then she went on with her work. She did not invite him in. The saintly expression of her face remained fixed, but there was an angry flush over it.

The minister stood awkwardly before her, and talked. She handled the pease as if they were bullets. At last she looked up, and her eyes showed the spirit that her meek front had covered for a lifetime.

"There ain't no use talkin', Mr. Hersey," said she. "I've thought it all over an' over, an' I believe I'm doin' what's right. I've made it the subject of prayer, an' it's betwixt me an' the Lord an' Adoniram. There ain't no call for nobody else to worry about it."

"Well, of course, if you have brought it to the Lord in prayer, and feel satisfied that you are doing right, Mrs. Penn," said the minister, helplessly.

His thin gray-bearded face was pathetic. He was a sickly man; his youthful confidence had cooled; he had to scourge himself up to some of his pastoral duties as relentlessly as a Catholic ascetic, and then he was prostrated by the smart.

"I think it's right jest as much as I think it was right for our forefathers to come over from the old country 'cause they didn't have what belonged to 'em," said Mrs. Penn. She arose. The barn threshold might have been Plymouth Rock from her bearing. "I don't doubt you mean well, Mr. Hersey," said she, "but there are things people hadn't ought to interfere with. I've been a member of the church for over forty year. I've got my own mind an' my own feet, an' I'm goin' to think my own thoughts an' go my own ways, an' nobody but the Lord is goin' to dictate to me unless I've a mind to have him. Won't you come in an' set down? How is Mis' Hersey?"

"She is well, I thank you," replied the minister. He added some more perplexed apologetic remarks; then he retreated.

He could expound the intricacies of every character study in the Scriptures, he was competent to grasp the Pilgrim Fathers and all historical innovators, but Sarah Penn was beyond him. He could deal with primal cases, but parallel ones worsted him. But, after all, although it was aside from his province, he wondered more how Adoniram Penn would deal with his wife than how the Lord would. Everybody shared the wonder. When Adoniram's four new cows arrived, Sarah ordered three to be put in the old barn, the other in the house shed where the cooking-stove had stood. That added to the excitement. It was whispered that all four cows were domiciled in the house.

Towards sunset on Saturday, when Adoniram was expected home, there was a knot of men in the road near the new barn. The hired man had milked, but he still hung around the premises. Sarah Penn had supper all ready. There were brown-bread and baked beans and a custard pie; it was the supper that Adoniram loved on a Saturday night. She had on a clean calico, and she bore herself imperturbably. Nanny and Sammy kept close at her heels. Their eyes were large, and Nanny was full of nervous tremors. Still there was to them more pleasant excitement than anything else. An inborn confidence in their mother over their father asserted itself.

Sammy looked out of the harness-room window. "There he is," he announced, in an awed whisper. He and Nanny peeped around the casing. Mrs. Penn kept on about her work. The children watched Adoniram leave the new horse standing in the drive while he went to the house door. It was fastened. Then he went around to the shed. That door was seldom locked, even when the family was away. The thought how her father would be confronted by the cow flashed upon Nanny. There was a hysterical sob in her throat. Adoniram emerged from the shed and stood looking about in a dazed fashion. His lips moved; he was saying something, but they could not hear what it was. The hired man was peeping around a corner of the old barn, but nobody saw him.

Adoniram took the new horse by the bridle and led him across the yard to the new barn. Nanny and Sammy slunk close to their mother. The barn doors rolled back, and there stood Adoniram, with the long mild face of the great Canadian farm horse looking over his shoulder.

Nanny kept behind her mother, but Sammy stepped suddenly forward, and stood in front of her.

Adoniram stared at the group. "What on airth you all down here for?" said he. "What's the matter over to the house?"

"We've come here to live, father," said Sammy. His shrill voice quavered out bravely.

"What"—Adoniram sniffed—"what is it smells like cookin?" said he. He stepped forward and looked in the open door of the harness-room. Then he turned to his wife. His old bristling face was pale and frightened. "What on airth does this mean, mother?" he gasped.

"You come in here, father," said Sarah. She led the way into the harness-room and shut the door. "Now, father," said she, "you needn't be scared. I ain't crazy. There ain't nothin' to be upset over. But we've come here to live, an' we're goin' to live here. We've got jest as good a right here as new horses an' cows. The house wa'n't fit for us to live in any longer, an' I made up my mind I wa'n't goin' to stay there. I've done my duty by you forty year, an' I'm goin' to do it now; but I'm goin' to live here. You've got to put in some windows and partitions; an' you'll have to buy some furniture."

"Why, mother!" the old man gasped.

"You'd better take your coat off an' get washed—there's the wash-basin—an' then we'll have supper."

"Why, mother!"

Sammy went past the window, leading the new horse to the old barn. The old man saw him, and shook his head speechlessly. He tried to take off his coat, but his arms seemed to lack the power. His wife helped him. She poured some water into the tin basin, and put in a piece of soap. She got the comb and brush, and smoothed his thin gray hair after he had washed. Then she put the beans, hot bread, and tea on the table. Sammy came in, and the family drew up. Adoniram sat looking dazedly at his plate, and they waited.

"Ain't you goin' to ask a blessin', father?" said Sarah.

And the old man bent his head and mumbled.

All through the meal he stopped eating at intervals, and stared furtively at his wife; but he ate well. The home food tasted good to him, and his old frame was too sturdily healthy to be affected by his mind. But after supper he went out, and sat down on the step of the smaller door at the right of the barn, through which he had meant his Jerseys to pass in stately file, but which Sarah designed for her front house door, and he leaned his head on his hands.

After the supper dishes were cleared away and the milk-pans washed, Sarah went out to him. The twilight was deepening. There was a clear green glow in the sky. Before them stretched the smooth level of field; in the distance was a cluster of hay-stacks like the huts of a village; the air was very cool and calm and sweet. The landscape might have been an ideal one of peace.

Sarah bent over and touched her husband on one of his thin, sinewy shoulders. "Father!"

The old man's shoulders heaved: he was weeping.

"Why, don't do so, father," said Sarah.

"I'll—put up the—partitions, an'—everything you—want, mother."

Sarah put her apron up to her face; she was overcome by her own triumph.

Adoniram was like a fortress whose walls had no active resistance, and went down the instant the right besieging tools were used. "Why, mother," he said, hoarsely, "I hadn't no idee you was so set on't as all this comes to."

Louisa

1890

"I don't see what kind of ideas you've got in your head, for my part." Mrs. Britton looked sharply at her daughter Louisa, but she got no response.

Louisa sat in one of the kitchen chairs close to the door. She had dropped into it when she first entered. Her hands were all brown and grimy with garden-mould; it clung to the bottom of her old dress and her coarse shoes.

Mrs. Britton, sitting opposite by the window, waited, looking at her. Suddenly Louisa's silence seemed to strike her mother's will with an electric shock; she recoiled, with an angry jerk of her head. "You don't know nothin' about it. You'd like him well enough after you was married to him," said she, as if in answer to an argument.

Louisa's face looked fairly dull; her obstinacy seemed to cast a film over it. Her eyelids were cast down; she leaned her head back against the wall.

"Sit there like a stick if you want to!" cried her mother.

Louisa got up. As she stirred, a faint earthy odor diffused itself through the room. It was like a breath from a ploughed field.

Mrs. Britton's little sallow face contracted more forcibly. "I s'pose now you're goin' back to your potater patch," said she. "Plantin' potaters out there jest like a man, for all the neighbors to see. Pretty sight, I call it."

"If they don't like it, they needn't look," returned Louisa. She spoke quite evenly. Her young back was stiff with bending over the potatoes, but she straightened it rigorously. She pulled her old hat farther over her eyes.

There was a shuffling sound outside the door and a fumble at the latch. It opened, and an old man came in, scraping his feet heavily over the threshold. He carried an old basket.

"What you got in that basket, father?" asked Mrs. Britton.

The old man looked at her. His old face had the round outlines and naïve grin of a child.

"Father, what you got in that basket?"

Louisa peered apprehensively into the basket. "Where did you get those potatoes, grandfather?" said she.

"Digged 'em." The old man's grin deepened. He chuckled hoarsely.

"Well, I'll give up if he ain't been an' dug up all them potaters you've been plantin'!" said Mrs. Britton.

"Yes, he has," said Louisa. "Oh, grandfather, didn't you know I'd jest planted those potatoes?"

The old man fastened his bleared blue eyes on her face, and still grinned.

"Didn't you know better, grandfather?" she asked again.

But the old man only chuckled. He was so old that he had come back into the mystery of childhood. His motives were hidden and inscrutable; his amalgamation with the human race was so much weaker.

"Land sakes! don't waste no more time talkin' to him," said Mrs. Britton. "You can't make out whether he knows what he's doin' or not. I've give it up. Father, you jest set them pertaters down, an' you come over here an' set down in the rockin'-chair; you've done about 'nough work to-day."

The old man shook his head with slow mutiny.

"Come right over here."

Louisa pulled at the basket of potatoes. "Let me have 'em, grandfather," said she. "I've got to have 'em."

The old man resisted. His grin disappeared, and he set his mouth. Mrs. Britton got up, with a determined air, and went over to him. She was a sickly, frail-looking woman, but the voice came firm, with deep bass tones, from her little lean throat.

"Now, father," said she, "you jest give her that basket, an' you walk across the room, and you set down in that rockin'-chair."

The old man looked down into her little, pale, wedge-shaped face. His grasp on the basket weakened. Louisa pulled it away, and pushed past out of the door, and the old man followed his daughter sullenly across the room to the rocking-chair.

The Brittons did not have a large potato field; they had only an acre of land in all. Louisa had planted two thirds of her potatoes; now she had to plant them all over again. She had gone to the house for a drink of water; her mother had detained her, and in the meantime the old man had undone her work. She began putting the cut potatoes back in the ground. She was careful and laborious about it. A strong wind, full of moisture, was blowing from the east. The smell of the sea was in it, although this was some miles inland. Louisa's brown calico skirt blew out in it like a sail. It beat her in the face when she raised her head.

"I've got to get these in to-day somehow," she muttered. "It 'll rain to-morrow."

She worked as fast as she could, and the afternoon wore on. About five o'clock she happened to glance at the road—the potato field lay beside it—and she saw Jonathan Nye driving past with his gray horse and buggy. She turned her back to the road quickly, and listened until the rattle of the wheels died away. At six o'clock her mother looked out of the kitchen window and called her to supper.

"I'm comin' in a minute," Louisa shouted back. Then she worked faster than ever. At half-past six she went into the house, and the potatoes were all in the ground.

"Why didn't you come when I called you?" asked her mother.

"I had to get the potatoes in."

"I guess you wa'n't bound to get 'em all in to-night. It's kind of discouragin' when you work, an' get supper all ready, to have it stan' an hour, I call it. An' you've worked 'bout long enough for one day out in this damp wind, I should say."

Louisa washed her hands and face at the kitchen sink, and smoothed her hair at the little glass over it. She had wet her hair too, and made it look darker: it was quite a light brown. She brushed it in smooth straight lines back from her temples. Her whole face had a clear bright look from being exposed to the moist wind. She noticed it herself, and gave her head a little conscious turn.

When she sat down to the table her mother looked at her with admiration, which she veiled with disapproval.

"Jest look at your face," said she; "red as a beet. You'll be a pretty-lookin' sight before the summer's out, at this rate."

Louisa thought to herself that the light was not very strong, and the glass must have flattered her. She could not look as well as she had imagined. She spread some butter on her bread very sparsely. There was nothing for supper but some bread and butter and weak tea, though the old man had his dish of Indian-meal porridge. He could not eat much solid food. The porridge was covered with milk and molasses. He bent low over it, and ate large spoonfuls with loud noises. His daughter had tied a towel around his neck as she would have tied a pinafore on a child. She had also spread a towel over the table-cloth in front of him, and she watched him sharply lest he should spill his food.

"I wish I could have somethin' to eat that I could relish the way he does that porridge and molasses," said she. She had scarcely tasted anything. She sipped her weak tea laboriously.

Louisa looked across at her mother's meagre little figure in its neat old dress, at her poor small head bending over the tea-cup, showing the wide parting in the thin hair.

"Why don't you toast your bread, mother?" said she. "I'll toast it for you."

"No, I don't want it. I'd jest as soon have it this way as any. I don't want no bread, nohow. I want somethin' to relish—a herrin', or a little mite of cold meat, or somethin'. I s'pose I could eat as well as anybody if I had as much as some folks have. Mis' Mitchell was sayin' the other day that she didn't believe but what they had butcher's meat up to Mis' Nye's every day in the week. She said Jonathan he went to Wolfsborough and brought home great pieces in a market-basket every week. I guess they have everything."

Louisa was not eating much herself, but now she took another slice of bread with a resolute air. "I guess some folks would be thankful to get this," said she.

"Yes, I s'pose we'd ought to be thankful for enough to keep us alive, anybody takes so much comfort livin'," returned her mother, with a tragic bitterness that sat oddly upon her, as she was so small and feeble. Her face worked and strained under the stress of emotion; her eyes were full of tears; she sipped her tea fiercely.

"There's some sugar," said Louisa. "We might have had a little cake."

The old man caught the word. "Cake?" he mumbled, with pleased inquiry, looking up, and extending his grasping old hand.

"I guess we ain't got no sugar to waste in cake," returned Mrs. Britton. "Eat your porridge, father, an' stop teasin'. There ain't no cake."

After supper Louisa cleared away the dishes; then she put on her shawl and hat.

"Where you goin'?" asked her mother.

"Down to the store."

"What for?"

"The oil's out. There wasn't enough to fill the lamps this mornin'. I ain't had a chance to get it before."

It was nearly dark. The mist was so heavy it was almost rain. Louisa went swiftly down the road with the oil-can. It was a half-mile to the store where the few staples were kept that sufficed the simple folk in this little settlement. She was gone a half-hour. When she returned, she had besides the oil-can a package under her arm. She went into the kitchen and set them down. The old man was asleep in the rocking-chair. She heard voices in the adjoining room. She frowned, and stood still, listening.

"Louisa!" called her mother. Her voice was sweet, and higher pitched than usual. She sounded the *i* in Louisa long.

"What say?"

"Come in here after you've taken your things off."

Louisa knew that Jonathan Nye was in the sitting-room. She flung off her hat and shawl. Her old dress was damp, and had still some earth stains on it; her hair was roughened by the wind, but she would not look again in the glass; she went into the sitting-room just as she was.

"It's Mr. Nye, Louisa," said her mother, with effusion.

"Good-evenin', Mr. Nye," said Louisa.

Jonathan Nye half arose and extended his hand, but she did not notice it. She sat down peremptorily in a chair at the other side of the room. Jonathan had the one rocking-chair; Mrs. Britton's frail little body was poised anxiously on the hard rounded top of the carpet-covered lounge. She looked at Louisa's dress and hair, and her eyes were stony with disapproval, but her lips still smirked, and she kept her voice sweet. She pointed to a glass dish on the table.

"See what Mr. Nye has brought us over, Louisa," said she.

Louisa looked indifferently at the dish.

"It's honey," said her mother; "some of his own bees made it. Don't you want to get a dish an' taste of it? One of them little glass sauce dishes."

"No, I guess not," replied Louisa. "I never cared much about honey. Grandfather 'll like it."

The smile vanished momentarily from Mrs. Britton's lips, but she recovered herself. She arose and went across the room to the china closet. Her set of china dishes was on the top shelves, the lower were filled with books and papers. "I've got somethin' to show you, Mr. Nye," said she.

This was scarcely more than a hamlet, but it was incorporated, and had its town books. She brought forth a pile of them, and laid them on the table beside Jonathan Nye. "There," said she, "I thought mebbe you'd like to look at these." She opened one and pointed to the school report. This mother could not display her daughter's accomplishments to attract a suitor, for she had none. Louisa did not own a piano or organ; she could not paint; but she had taught school acceptably for eight years—ever since she was sixteen—and in every one of the town books was testimonial to that effect, intermixed with glowing eulogy. Jonathan Nye looked soberly through the books; he was a slow reader. He was a few years older than Louisa, tall and clumsy, long-featured and long-necked. His face was a deep red with embarrassment, and it contrasted oddly with his stiff dignity of demeanor.

Mrs. Britton drew a chair close to him while he read. "You see, Louisa taught that school for eight year," said she; "an' she'd be teachin' it now if Mr. Mosely's daughter hadn't grown up an' wanted somethin' to do, an' he put her in. He was committee, you know. I dun' know as I'd ought to say so, an' I wouldn't want you to repeat it, but they do say Ida Mosely don't give very good satisfaction, an' I guess she won't have no reports like these in the town books unless her father writes 'em. See this one."

Jonathan Nye pondered over the fulsome testimony to Louisa's capability, general worth, and amiability, while she sat in sulky silence at the farther corner of the room. Once in a while her mother, after a furtive glance at Jonathan, engrossed in a town book, would look at her and gesticulate fiercely for her to come over, but she did not stir. Her eyes were dull and quiet, her mouth closely shut; she looked homely. Louisa was very pretty when pleased and animated, at other times she had a look like a closed flower. One could see no prettiness in her.

Jonathan Nye read all the school reports; then he arose heavily. "They're real good," said he. He glanced at Louisa and tried to smile; his blushes deepened.

"Now don't be in a hurry," said Mrs. Britton.

"I guess I'd better be goin'; mother's alone."

"She won't be afraid; it's jest on the edge of the evenin'."

"I don't know as she will. But I guess I'd better be goin'." He looked hesitatingly at Louisa.

She arose and stood with an indifferent air.

"You'd better set down again," said Mrs. Britton.

"No; I guess I'd better be goin'." Jonathan turned towards Louisa. "Good-evenin'," said he.

"Good-evenin'."

Mrs. Britton followed him to the door. She looked back and beckoned imperiously to Louisa, but she stood still. "Now come again, do," Mrs. Britton said to the departing caller. "Run in any time; we're real lonesome evenin's. Father he sets an' sleeps in his chair, an' Louisa an' me often wish somebody'd drop in; folks around here ain't none too neighborly. Come in any time you happen to feel like it, an' we'll both of us be glad to see you. Tell your mother I'll send home that dish to-morrer, an' we shall have a real feast off that beautiful honey."

When Mrs. Britton had fairly shut the outer door upon Jonathan Nye, she came back into the sitting-room as if her anger had a propelling power like steam upon her body.

"Now, Louisa Britton," said she, "you'd ought to be ashamed of yourself—ashamed of yourself! You've treated him like a—hog!"

"I couldn't help it."

"Couldn't help it! I guess you could treat anybody decent if you tried. I never saw such actions! I guess you needn't be afraid of him. I guess he ain't so set on you that he means to ketch you up an' run off. There's other girls in town full as good as you an' better-lookin'. Why didn't you go an' put on your other dress? Comin' into the room with that old thing on, an' your hair all in a frowse! I guess he won't want to come again."

"I hope he won't," said Louisa, under her breath. She was trembling all over.

"What say?"

"Nothin'."

"I shouldn't think you'd want to say anything, treatin' him that way, when he came over and brought all that beautiful honey! He was all dressed up, too. He had on a real nice coat—cloth jest as fine as it could be, an' it was kinder damp when he come in. Then he dressed all up to come over here this rainy night an' bring this honey." Mrs. Britton snatched the dish of honey and scudded into the kitchen with it. "Sayin' you didn't like honey after he took all that pains to bring it over!" said she. "I'd said I liked it if I'd lied up hill and down." She set the dish in the pantry. "What in creation smells so kinder strong an' smoky in here?" said she, sharply.

"I guess it's the herrin'. I got two or three down to the store."

"I'd like to know what you got herrin' for?"

"I thought maybe you'd relish 'em."

"I don't want no herrin's, now we've got this honey. But I don't know that you've got money to throw away." She shook the old man by the stove into partial wakefulness, and steered him into his little bedroom off the kitchen. She herself slept in one off the sitting-room; Louisa's room was up-stairs.

Louisa lighted her candle and went to bed, her mother's scolding voice pursuing her like a wrathful spirit. She cried when she was in bed in the dark, but she soon went to sleep. She was too healthfully tired with her out-door work not to. All her young bones ached with the strain of manual labor as they had ached many a time this last year since she had lost her school.

The Brittons had been and were in sore straits. All they had in the world was this little house with the acre of land. Louisa's meagre school money had bought their food and clothing since her father died. Now it was almost starvation for them. Louisa was struggling to wrest a little sustenance from their stony acre of land, toiling like a European peasant woman, sacrificing her New England dignity. Lately she had herself split up a cord of wood which she had bought of a neighbor, paying for it in instalments with work for his wife.

"Think of a school-teacher goin' into Mis' Mitchell's house to help clean!" said her mother.

She, although she had been of poor, hard-working people all her life, with the humblest surroundings, was a born aristocrat, with that fiercest and most bigoted aristocracy which sometimes arises from independent poverty. She had the feeling of a queen for a princess of the blood about her school-teacher daughter; her working in a neighbor's kitchen was as galling and terrible to her. The projected marriage with Jonathan Nye was like a royal alliance for the good of the state. Jonathan Nye was the only eligible young man in the place; he was the largest land-owner; he had the best house. There were only himself and his mother; after her death the property would all be his. Mrs. Nye was an older woman than Mrs. Britton, who forgot her own frailty in calculating their chances of life.

"Mis' Nye is considerable over seventy," she said often to herself; "an' then Jonathan will have it all."

She saw herself installed in that large white house as reigning dowager. All the obstacle was Louisa's obstinacy, which her mother could not understand. She could see no fault in Jonathan Nye. So far as absolute approval went, she herself was in love with him. There was no more sense, to her mind, in Louisa's refusing him than there would have been in a princess refusing the fairy prince and spoiling the story.

"I'd like to know what you've got against him," she said often to Louisa.
"I ain't got anything against him."

"Why don't you treat him different, then, I want to know?"

"I don't like him." Louisa said "like" shamefacedly, for she meant love,
and dared not say it.

"*Like!* Well, I don't know nothin' about such likin's as some pretend to,
an' I don't want to. If I see anybody is good an' worthy, I like 'em, an' that's
all there is about it."

"I don't—believe that's the way you felt about—father," said Louisa,
softly, her young face flushed red.

"Yes, it was. I had some common sense about it."

And Mrs. Britton believed it. Many hard middle-aged years lay between
her and her own love-time, and nothing is so changed by distance as the re-
alities of youth. She believed herself to have been actuated by the same
calm reason in marrying young John Britton, who had had fair prospects,
which she thought should actuate her daughter in marrying Jonathan Nye.

Louisa got no sympathy from her, but she persisted in her refusal. She
worked harder and harder. She did not spare herself in doors or out. As the
summer wore on her face grew as sunburnt as a boy's, her hands were hard
and brown. When she put on her white dress to go to meeting on a Sunday
there was a white ring around her neck where the sun had not touched it.
Above it her face and neck showed browner. Her sleeves were rather short,
and there were also white rings above her brown wrists.

"You look as if you were turnin' Injun by inches," said her mother.

Louisa, when she sat in the meeting-house, tried slyly to pull her sleeves
down to the brown on her wrists; she gave a little twitch to the ruffle
around her neck. Then she glanced across, and Jonathan Nye was looking
at her. She thrust her hands, in their short-wristed, loose cotton gloves, as
far out of the sleeves as she could; her brown wrists showed conspicuously
on her white lap. She had never heard of the princess who destroyed her
beauty that she might not be forced to wed the man whom she did not love,
but she had something of the same feeling, although she did not have it for
the sake of any tangible lover. Louisa had never seen anybody whom she
would have preferred to Jonathan Nye. There was no other marriageable
young man in the place. She had only her dreams, which she had in common with other girls.

That Sunday evening before she went to meeting her mother took some
old wide lace out of her bureau drawer. "There," said she, "I'm goin' to

sew this in your neck an' sleeves before you put your dress on. It'll cover up a little; it's wider than the ruffle."

"I don't want it in," said Louisa.

"I'd like to know why not? You look like a fright. I was ashamed of you this mornin'."

Louisa thrust her arms into the white dress sleeves peremptorily. Her mother did not speak to her all the way to meeting. After meeting, Jonathan Nye walked home with them, and Louisa kept on the other side of her mother. He went into the house and stayed an hour. Mrs. Britton entertained him, while Louisa sat silent. When he had gone, she looked at her daughter as if she could have used bodily force, but she said nothing. She shot the bolt of the kitchen door noisily. Louisa lighted her candle. The old man's loud breathing sounded from his room; he had been put to bed for safety before they went to meeting; through the open windows sounded the loud murmur of the summer night, as if that, too, slept heavily.

"Good-night, mother," said Louisa, as she went up-stairs; but her mother did not answer.

The next day was very warm. This was an exceptionally hot summer. Louisa went out early; her mother would not ask her where she was going. She did not come home until noon. Her face was burning; her wet dress clung to her arms and shoulders.

"Where have you been?" asked her mother.

"Oh, I've been out in the field."

"What field?"

"Mr. Mitchell's."

"What have you been doin' out there?"

"Rakin' hay."

"Rakin' hay with the men?"

"There wasn't anybody but Mr. Mitchell and Johnny. Don't, mother!"

Mrs. Britton had turned white. She sank into a chair. "I can't stan' it nohow," she moaned. "All the daughter I've got."

"Don't, mother! I ain't done any harm. What harm is it? Why can't I rake hay as well as a man? Lots of women do such things, if nobody round here does. He's goin' to pay me right off, and we need the money. Don't, mother!" Louisa got a tumbler of water. "Here, mother, drink this."

Mrs. Britton pushed it away. Louisa stood looking anxiously at her. Lately her mother had grown thinner than ever; she looked scarcely bigger than a child. Presently she got up and went to the stove.

"Don't try to do anything, mother; let me finish getting dinner," pleaded Louisa. She tried to take the pan of biscuits out of her mother's hands, but she jerked it away.

The old man was sitting on the door-step, huddled up loosely in the sun, like an old dog.

"Come, father," Mrs. Britton called, in a dry voice, "dinner's ready— what there is of it!"

The old man shuffled in, smiling.

There was nothing for dinner but the hot biscuits and tea. The fare was daily becoming more meagre. All Louisa's little hoard of school money was gone, and her earnings were very uncertain and slender. Their chief dependence for food through the summer was their garden, but that had failed them in some respects.

One day the old man had come in radiant, with his shaking hands full of potato blossoms; his old eyes twinkled over them like a mischievous child's. Reproaches were useless; the little potato crop was sadly damaged. Lately, in spite of close watching, he had picked the squash blossoms, piling them in a yellow mass beside the kitchen door. Still, it was nearly time for the pease and beans and beets; they would keep them from starvation while they lasted.

But when they came, and Louisa could pick plenty of green food every morning, there was still a difficulty: Mrs. Britton's appetite and digestion were poor; she could not live upon a green-vegetable diet; and the old man missed his porridge, for the meal was all gone.

One morning in August he cried at the breakfast-table like a baby, because he wanted his porridge, and Mrs. Britton pushed away her own plate with a despairing gesture.

"There ain't no use," said she. "I can't eat no more garden-sauce nohow. I don't blame poor father a mite. You ain't got no feelin' at all."

"I don't know what I can do; I've worked as hard as I can," said Louisa, miserably.

"I know what you can do, and so do you."

"No, I don't, mother," returned Louisa, with alacrity. "He ain't been here for two weeks now, and I saw him with my own eyes yesterday carryin' a dish into the Moselys', and I knew 'twas honey. I think he's after Ida."

"Carryin' honey into the Moselys'? I don't believe it."

"He was; I saw him."

"Well, I don't care if he was. If you're a mind to act decent now, you can bring him around again. He was dead set on you, an' I don't believe he's changed round to that Mosely girl as quick as this."

"You don't want me to ask him to come back here, do you?"

"I want you to act decent. You can go to meetin' to-night, if you're a mind to—I sha'n't go; I ain't got strength 'nough—an' 'twouldn't hurt you none to hang back a little after meetin', and kind of edge round his way. 'Twouldn't take more'n a look."

"Mother!"

"Well, I don't care. 'Twouldn't hurt you none. It's the way more'n one girl does, whether you believe it or not. Men don't do all the courtin'—not by a long shot. 'Twon't hurt you none. You needn't look so scart."

Mrs. Britton's own face was a burning red. She looked angrily away from her daughter's honest, indignant eyes.

"I wouldn't do such a thing as that for a man I liked," said Louisa; "and I certainly sha'n't for a man I don't like."

"Then me an' your grandfather 'll starve," said her mother; "that's all there is about it. We can't neither of us stan' it much longer."

"We could—"

"Could what?"

"Put a—little mortgage on the house."

Mrs. Britton faced her daughter. She trembled in every inch of her weak frame. "Put a mortgage on this house, an' by-an'-by not have a roof to cover us! Are you crazy? I tell you what 'tis, Louisa Britton, we may starve, your grandfather an' me, an' you can follow us to the graveyard over there, but there's only one way I'll ever put a mortgage on this house. If you have Jonathan Nye, I'll ask him to take a little one to tide us along an' get your weddin' things."

"Mother, I'll tell you what I'm goin' to do."

"What?"

"I am goin' to ask Uncle Solomon."

"I guess when Solomon Mears does anythin' for us you'll know it. He never forgave your father about that wood lot, an' he's hated the whole of us ever since. When I went to his wife's funeral he never answered when I spoke to him. I guess if you go to him you'll take it out in goin'."

Louisa said nothing more. She began clearing away the breakfast dishes and setting the house to rights. Her mother was actually so weak that she could scarcely stand, and she recognized it. She had settled into the rocking-chair, and leaned her head back. Her face looked pale and sharp against the dark calico cover.

When the house was in order, Louisa stole up-stairs to her own chamber. She put on her clean old blue muslin and her hat, then she went slyly down and out the front way.

It was seven miles to her uncle Solomon Mears's, and she had made up her mind to walk them. She walked quite swiftly until the house windows were out of sight, then she slackened her pace a little. It was one of the fiercest dog-days. A damp heat settled heavily down upon the earth; the sun scalded.

At the foot of the hill Louisa passed a house where one of her girl acquaintances lived. She was going in the gate with a pan of early apples. "Hullo, Louisa," she called.

"Hullo, Vinnie."

"Where you goin'?"

"Oh, I'm goin' a little way."

"Ain't it awful hot? Say, Louisa, do you know Ida Mosely's cuttin' you out?"

"She's welcome."

The other girl, who was larger and stouter than Louisa, with a sallow, unhealthy face, looked at her curiously. "I don't see why you wouldn't have him," said she. "I should have thought you'd jumped at the chance."

"Should you if you didn't like him, I'd like to know?"

"I'd like him if he had such a nice house and as much money as Jonathan Nye," returned the other girl.

She offered Louisa some apples, and she went along the road eating them. She herself had scarcely tasted food that day.

It was about nine o'clock; she had risen early. She calculated how many hours it would take her to walk the seven miles. She walked as fast as she could to hold out. The heat seemed to increase as the sun stood higher. She had walked about three miles when she heard wheels behind her. Presently a team stopped at her side.

"Good-mornin'," said an embarrassed voice.

She looked around. It was Jonathan Nye, with his gray horse and light wagon.

"Good-mornin'," said she.

"Goin' far?"

"A little ways."

"Won't you—ride?"

"No, thank you. I guess I'd rather walk."

Jonathan Nye nodded, made an inarticulate noise in his throat, and drove on. Louisa watched the wagon bowling lightly along. The dust flew back. She took out her handkerchief and wiped her dripping face.

It was about noon when she came in sight of her uncle Solomon Mears's house in Wolfsborough. It stood far back from the road, behind a green expanse of untrodden yard. The blinds on the great square front were all closed; it looked as if everybody were away. Louisa went around to the side door. It stood wide open. There was a thin blue cloud of tobacco smoke issuing from it. Solomon Mears sat there in the large old kitchen smoking his pipe. On the table near him was an empty bowl; he had just eaten his dinner of bread and milk. He got his own dinner, for he had lived alone since his wife died. He looked at Louisa. Evidently he did not recognize her.

"How do you do, Uncle Solomon?" said Louisa.

"Oh, it's John Britton's daughter! How d'ye do?"

He took his pipe out of his mouth long enough to speak, then replaced it. His eyes, sharp under their shaggy brows, were fixed on Louisa; his broad bristling face had a look of stolid rebuff like an ox; his stout figure, in his soiled farmer dress, surged over his chair. He sat full in the doorway. Louisa standing before him, the perspiration trickling over her burning face, set forth her case with a certain dignity. This old man was her mother's nearest relative. He had property and to spare. Should she survive him, it would be hers, unless willed away. She, with her unsophisticated sense of justice, had a feeling that he ought to help her.

The old man listened. When she stopped speaking he took the pipe out of his mouth slowly, and stared gloomily past her at his hay field, where the grass was now a green stubble.

"I ain't got no money I can spare jest now," said he. "I s'pose you know your father cheated me out of consider'ble once?"

"We don't care so much about money, if you have got something you could spare to—eat. We ain't got anything but garden-stuff."

Solomon Mears still frowned past her at the hay field. Presently he arose slowly and went across the kitchen. Louisa sat down on the door-step and waited. Her uncle was gone quite a while. She, too, stared over at the field, which seemed to undulate like a lake in the hot light.

"Here's some things you can take, if you want 'em," said her uncle, at her back.

She got up quickly. He pointed grimly to the kitchen table. He was a deacon, an orthodox believer; he recognized the claims of the poor, but he gave alms as a soldier might yield up his sword. Benevolence was the result of warfare with his own conscience.

On the table lay a ham, a bag of meal, one of flour, and a basket of eggs.

"I'm afraid I can't carry 'em all," said Louisa.

"Leave what you can't then." Solomon caught up his hat and went out. He muttered something about not spending any more time as he went.

Louisa stood looking at the packages. It was utterly impossible for her to carry them all at once. She heard her uncle shout to some oxen he was turning out of the barn. She took up the bag of meal and the basket of eggs and carried them out to the gate; then she returned, got the flour and ham, and went with them to a point beyond. Then she returned for the meal and eggs, and carried them past the others. In that way she traversed the seven miles home. The heat increased. She had eaten nothing since morning but the apples that her friend had given her. Her head was swimming, but she kept on. Her resolution was as immovable under the power of the sun as a rock. Once in a while she rested for a moment under a tree, but she soon arose and went on. It was like a pilgrimage, and the Mecca at the end of the burning, desert-like road was her own maiden independence.

It was after eight o'clock when she reached home. Her mother stood in the doorway watching for her, straining her eyes in the dusk.

"For goodness sake, Louisa Britton! where have you been?" she began; but Louisa laid the meal and eggs down on the step.

"I've got to go back a little ways," she panted.

When she returned with the flour and ham, she could hardly get into the house. She laid them on the kitchen table, where her mother had put the other parcels, and sank into a chair.

"Is this the way you've brought all these things home?" asked her mother.

Louisa nodded.

"All the way from Uncle Solomon's?"

"Yes."

Her mother went to her and took her hat off. "It's a mercy if you ain't got a sunstroke," said she, with a sharp tenderness. "I've got somethin' to tell you. What do you s'pose has happened? Mr. Mosely has been here, an' he wants you to take the school again when it opens next week. He says Ida ain't very well, but I guess that ain't it. They think she's goin' to get somebody. Mis' Mitchell says so. She's been in. She says he's carryin' things over there the whole time, but she don't b'lieve there's anything settled yet. She says they feel so sure of it they're goin' to have Ida give the school up. I told her I thought Ida would make him a good wife, an' she was easier suited than some girls. What do you s'pose Mis' Mitchell says? She says old Mis' Nye told her that there was one thing about it: if Jonathan had you, he wa'n't goin' to have me an' father hitched on to him; he'd look out for that. I told Mis' Mitchell that I guess there wa'n't none of us willin' to hitch, you nor anybody else. I hope she'll tell Mis' Nye. Now I'm a-goin' to turn you out a tumbler of milk—Mis' Mitchell she brought over a whole pitcherful; says she's got more'n they can use—they ain't got no pig now—an' then you go an' lay down on the sittin'-room lounge, an' cool off; an' I'll stir up some porridge for supper, an' boil some eggs. Father 'll be tickled to death. Go right in there. I'm dreadful afraid you'll be sick. I never heard of anybody doin' such a thing as you have."

Louisa drank the milk and crept into the sitting-room. It was warm and close there, so she opened the front door and sat down on the step. The twilight was deep, but there was a clear yellow glow in the west. One great star had come out in the midst of it. A dewy coolness was spreading over everything. The air was full of bird calls and children's voices. Now and then there was a shout of laughter. Louisa leaned her head against the doorpost.

The house was quite near the road. Some one passed—a man carrying a basket. Louisa glanced at him, and recognized Jonathan Nye by his gait. He kept on down the road toward the Moselys', and Louisa turned again from him to her sweet, mysterious, girlish dreams.

Part Two

Stories from
Silence (1898)
The Love of Parson Lord (1900)
Understudies (1901)
Six Trees (1903)
The Wind in the Rose-Bush (1903)

Evelina's Garden

1896

On the south a high arbor-vitæ hedge separated Evelina's garden from the road. The hedge was so high that when the school-children lagged by, and the secrets behind it fired them with more curiosity than those between their battered book covers, the tallest of them by stretching up on tiptoe could not peer over. And so they were driven to childish engineering feats, and would set to work and pick away sprigs of the arbor-vitæ with their little fingers, and make peep-holes—but small ones, that Evelina might not discern them. Then they would thrust their pink faces into the hedge, and the enduring fragrance of it would come to their nostrils like a gust of aromatic breath from the mouth of the northern woods, and peer into Evelina's garden as through the green tubes of vernal telescopes.

Then suddenly hollyhocks, blooming in rank and file, seemed to be marching upon them like platoons of soldiers, with detonations of color that dazzled their peeping eyes; and, indeed, the whole garden seemed charging with its mass of riotous bloom upon the hedge. They could scarcely take in details of marigold and phlox and pinks and London-pride and cock's-combs, and prince's-feathers waving overhead like standards.

Sometimes also there was the purple flutter of Evelina's gown; and Evelina's face, delicately faded, hung about with softly drooping gray curls, appeared suddenly among the flowers, like another flower uncannily instinct with nervous melancholy.

Then the children would fall back from their peep-holes, and huddle off together with scared giggles. They were afraid of Evelina. There was a shade of mystery about her which stimulated their childish fancies when they heard her discussed by their elders. They might easily have conceived her to be some baleful fairy intrenched in her green stronghold, withheld from leaving it by the fear of some dire penalty for magical sins. Summer and winter, spring and fall, Evelina Adams never was seen outside her own domain of old mansion-house and garden, and she had not set her slim lady feet in the public highway for nearly forty years, if the stories were true.

People differed as to the reason why. Some said she had had an unfortunate love affair, that her heart had been broken, and she had taken upon herself a vow of seclusion from the world, but nobody could point to the unworthy lover who had done her this harm. When Evelina was a girl, not one of the young men of the village had dared address her. She had been set apart by birth and training, and also by a certain exclusiveness of manner, if not of nature. Her father, old Squire Adams, had been the one man of wealth and college learning in the village. He had owned the one fine old mansion-house, with its white front propped on great Corinthian pillars, overlooking the village like a broad brow of superiority.

He had owned the only coach and four. His wife during her short life had gone dressed in rich brocades and satins that rustled loud in the ears of the village women, and her nodding plumes had dazzled the eyes under their modest hoods. Hardly a woman in the village but could tell—for it had been handed down like a folk-lore song from mother to daughter— just what Squire Adams's wife wore when she walked out first as bride to meeting. She had been clad all in blue.

"Squire Adams's wife, when she walked out bride, she wore a blue satin brocade gown, all wrought with blue flowers of a darker blue, cut low neck and short sleeves. She wore long blue silk mitts wrought with blue, blue satin shoes, and blue silk clocked stockings. And she wore a blue crape mantle that was brought from overseas, and a blue velvet hat, with a long blue ostrich feather curled over it—it was so long it reached her shoulder, and waved when she walked; and she carried a little blue crape fan with ivory sticks." So the women and girls told each other when the Squire's bride had been dead nearly seventy years.

The blue bride attire was said to be still in existence, packed away in a cedar chest, as the Squire had ordered after his wife's death. "He stood over the woman that took care of his wife whilst she packed the things away, and he never shed a tear, but she used to hear him a-goin' up to the north chamber nights, when he couldn't sleep, to look at 'em," the women told.

People had thought the Squire would marry again. They said Evelina, who was only four years old, needed a mother, and they selected one and another of the good village girls. But the Squire never married. He had a single woman, who dressed in black silk, and wore always a black wrought veil over the side of her bonnet, come to live with them, to take charge of Evelina. She was said to be a distant relative of the Squire's wife, and was much looked up to by the village people, although she never did more than interlace, as it were, the fringes of her garments with theirs. "She's stuck up," they said, and felt, curiously enough, a certain pride in the fact when they met her in the street and she ducked her long chin stiffly into the folds of her black shawl by way of salutation.

When Evelina was fifteen years old this single woman died, and the village women went to her funeral, and bent over her lying in a last helpless dignity in her coffin, and stared with awed freedom at her cold face. After that Evelina was sent away to school, and did not return, except for a yearly vacation, for six years to come. Then she returned, and settled down in her old home to live out her life, and end her days in a perfect semblance of peace, if it were not peace.

Evelina never had any young school friend to visit her; she had never, so far as any one knew, a friend of her own age. She lived alone with her father and three old servants. She went to meeting, and drove with the Squire in his chaise. The coach was never used after his wife's death, except to carry Evelina to and from school. She and the Squire also took long walks, but they never exchanged aught but the merest civilities of good-days and nods with the neighbors whom they met, unless indeed the Squire had some matter of business to discuss. Then Evelina stood aside and waited, her fair face drooping gravely aloof. She was very pretty, with a gentle high-bred prettiness that impressed the village folk, although they looked at it somewhat askance.

Evelina's figure was tall, and had a fine slenderness; her silken skirts hung straight from the narrow silk ribbon that girt her slim waist; there was a languidly graceful bend in her long white throat; her long delicate hands hung inertly at her sides among her skirt folds, and were never seen to clasp anything; her softly clustering fair curls hung over her thin blooming cheeks, and her face could scarce be seen, unless, as she seldom did, she turned and looked full upon one. Then her dark blue eyes, with a little nervous frown between them, shone out radiantly; her thin lips showed a warm red, and her beauty startled one.

Everybody wondered why she did not have a lover, why some fine young man had not been smitten by her while she had been away at school. They did not know that the school had been situated in another little village, the counterpart of the one in which she had been born, wherein a fitting mate for a bird of her feather could hardly be found. The simple young men of the country-side were at once attracted and intimidated by her. They cast fond sly glances across the meeting-house at her lovely face, but they were confused before her when they jostled her in the doorway and the rose and lavender scent of her lady garments came in their faces. Not one of them dared accost her, much less march boldly upon the great Corinthian-pillared house, raise the brass knocker, and declare himself a suitor for the Squire's daughter.

One young man there was, indeed, who treasured in his heart an experience so subtle and so slight that he could scarcely believe in it himself. He never recounted it to mortal soul, but kept it as a secret sacred between himself and his own nature, but something to be scoffed at and set aside by others.

It had happened one Sabbath day in summer, when Evelina had not been many years home from school, as she sat in the meeting-house in her Sabbath array of rose-colored satin gown, and white bonnet trimmed with a long white feather and a little wreath of feathery green, that of a sudden she raised her head and turned her face, and her blue eyes met this young man's full upon hers, with all his heart in them, and it was for a second as if her own heart leaped to the surface, and he saw it, although afterwards he scarce believed it to be true.

Then a pallor crept over Evelina's delicately brilliant face. She turned it away, and her curls falling softly from under the green wreath on her bonnet brim hid it. The young man's cheeks were a hot red, and his heart beat loudly in his ears when he met her in the doorway after the sermon was done. His eager, timorous eyes sought her face, but she never looked his way. She laid her slim hand in its cream-colored silk mitt on the Squire's arm; her satin gown rustled softly as she passed before him, shrinking against the wall to give her room, and a faint fragrance which seemed like the very breath of the unknown delicacy and exclusiveness of life came to his bewildered senses.

Many a time he cast furtive glances across the meeting-house at Evelina, but she never looked his way again. If his timid boy-eyes could have seen her cheek behind its veil of curls, he might have discovered that the color came and went before his glances, although it was strange how she could have been conscious of them; but he never knew.

And he also never knew how, when he walked past the Squire's house of a Sunday evening, dressed in his best, with his shoulders thrust consciously back, and the windows in the westering sun looked full of blank gold to his furtive eyes, Evelina was always peeping at him from behind a shutter, and he never dared go in. His intuitions were not like hers, and so nothing happened that might have, and he never fairly knew what he knew. But that he never told, even to his wife when he married; for his hot young blood grew weary and impatient with this vain courtship, and he turned to one of his villagemates, who met him fairly half way, and married her within a year.

On the Sunday when he and his bride first appeared in the meeting-house Evelina went up the aisle behind her father in an array of flowered brocade, stiff with threads of silver, so wonderful that people all turned their heads to stare at her. She wore also a new bonnet of rose-colored satin, and her curls were caught back a little, and her face showed as clear and beautiful as an angel's.

The young bridegroom glanced at her once across the meeting-house, then he looked at his bride in her gay wedding finery with a faithful look.

When Evelina met them in the doorway, after meeting was done, she bowed with a sweet cold grace to the bride, who courtesied blushingly in return, with an awkward sweep of her foot in the bridal satin shoe. The bridegroom did not look at Evelina at all. He held his chin well down in his stock with solemn embarrassment, and passed out stiffly, his bride on his arm.

Evelina, shining in the sun like a silver lily, went up the street, her father stalking beside her with stately swings of his cane, and that was the last time she was ever seen at meeting. Nobody knew why.

When Evelina was a little over thirty her father died. There was not much active grief for him in the village; he had really figured therein more as a stately monument of his own grandeur than anything else. He had been a man of little force of character, and that little had seemed to degenerate since his wife died. An inborn dignity of manner might have served to disguise his weakness with any others than these shrewd New-Englanders, but they read him rightly. "The Squire wa'n't ever one to set the river a-fire," they said. Then, moreover, he left none of his property to the village to build a new meeting-house or a town-house. It all went to Evelina.

People expected that Evelina would surely show herself in her mourning at meeting the Sunday after the Squire died, but she did not. Moreover, it began to be gradually discovered that she never went out in the village street nor crossed the boundaries of her own domains after her father's death. She lived in the great house with her three servants—a man and his wife, and the woman who had been with her mother when she died. Then it was that Evelina's garden began. There had always been a garden at the back of the Squire's house, but not like this, and only a low fence had separated it from the road. Now one morning in the autumn the people saw Evelina's man-servant, John Darby, setting out the arbor-vitæ hedge, and in the spring after that there were ploughing and seed-sowing extending over a full half-acre, which later blossomed out in glory.

Before the hedge grew so high Evelina could be seen at work in her garden. She was often stooping over the flower-beds in the early morning when the village was first astir, and she moved among them with her watering-pot in the twilight—a shadowy figure that might, from her grace and her constancy to the flowers, have been Flora herself.

As the years went on, the arbor-vitæ hedge got each season a new growth and waxed taller, until Evelina could no longer be seen above it. That was an annoyance to people, because the quiet mystery of her life kept their curiosity alive, until it was in a constant struggle, as it were, with the green luxuriance of the hedge.

"John Darby had ought to trim that hedge," they said. They accosted him in the street: "John, if ye don't cut that hedge down a little it 'll all die out."

But he only made a surly grunting response, intelligible to himself alone, and passed on. He was an Englishman, and had lived in the Squire's family since he was a boy.

He had a nature capable of only one simple line of force, with no radiations or parallels, and that had early resolved itself into the service of the Squire and his house. After the Squire's death he married a woman who lived in the family. She was much older than himself, and had a high temper, but was a good servant, and he married her to keep her to her allegiance to Evelina. Then he bent her, without her knowledge, to take his own attitude towards his mistress. No more could be gotten out of John Darby's wife than out of John Darby concerning the doings at the Squire's house. She met curiosity with a flash of hot temper, and he with surly taciturnity, and both intimidated.

The third of Evelina's servants was the woman who had nursed her mother, and she was naturally subdued and undemonstrative, and rendered still more so by a ceaseless monotony of life. She never went to meeting, and was seldom seen outside the house. A passing vision of a long white-capped face at a window was about all the neighbors ever saw of this woman.

So Evelina's gentle privacy was well guarded by her own household, as by a faithful system of domestic police. She grew old peacefully behind her green hedge, shielded effectually from all rough bristles of curiosity. Every new spring her own bloom showed paler beside the new bloom of her flowers, but people could not see it.

Some thirty years after the Squire's death the man John Darby died; his wife, a year later. That left Evelina alone with the old woman who had nursed her mother. She was very old, but not feeble, and quite able to perform the simple household tasks for herself and Evelina. An old man, who saved himself from the almshouse in such ways, came daily to do the rougher part of the garden-work in John Darby's stead. He was aged and decrepit; his muscles seemed able to perform their appointed tasks only through the accumulated inertia of a patiently toilsome life in the same tracks. Apparently they would have collapsed had he tried to force them to aught else than the holding of the ploughshare, the pulling of weeds, the digging around the roots of flowers, and the planting of seeds.

Every autumn he seemed about to totter to his fall among the fading flowers; every spring it was like Death himself urging on the resurrection; but he lived on year after year, and tended well Evelina's garden, and the gardens of other maiden-women and widows in the village. He was taciturn, grubbing among his green beds as silently as a worm, but now and then he warmed a little under a fire of questions concerning Evelina's garden. "Never see none sech flowers in nobody's garden in this town, not sence I knowed 'nough to tell a pink from a piny," he would mumble. His speech was thick; his words were all uncouthly slurred; the expression of his whole life had come more through his old knotted hands of labor than through his tongue. But he would wipe his forehead with his shirt-sleeve and lean a second on his spade, and his face would change at the mention of the garden. Its wealth of bloom illumined his old mind, and the roses and honeysuckles and pinks seemed for a second to be reflected in his bleared old eyes.

There had never been in the village such a garden as this of Evelina Adams's. All the old blooms which had come over the seas with the early colonists, and started as it were their own colony of flora in the new country, flourished there. The naturalized pinks and phlox and hollyhocks and the rest, changed a little in color and fragrance by the conditions of a new climate and soil, were all in Evelina's garden, and no one dreamed what they meant to Evelina; and she did not dream herself, for her heart was always veiled to her own eyes, like the face of a nun. The roses and pinks, the poppies and heart's-ease, were to this maiden-woman, who had innocently and helplessly outgrown her maiden heart, in the place of all the loves of life which she had missed. Her affections had forced an outlet in roses; they exhaled sweetness in pinks, and twined and clung in honeysuckle-vines. The daffodils, when they came up in the spring, comforted her like the smiles of children; when she saw the first rose, her heart leaped as at the face of a lover.

She had lost the one way of human affection, but her feet had found a little single side-track of love, which gave her still a zest in the journey of life. Even in the winter Evelina had her flowers, for she kept those that would bear transplanting in pots, and all the sunny windows in her house were gay with them. She would also not let a rose leaf fall and waste in the garden soil, or a sprig of lavender or thyme. She gathered them all, and stored them away in chests and drawers and old china bowls—the whole house seemed laid away in rose leaves and lavender. Evelina's clothes gave out at every motion that fragrance of dead flowers which is like the fragrance of the past, and has a sweetness like that of sweet memories. Even the cedar chest where Evelina's mother's blue bridal array was stored had its till heaped with rose leaves and lavender.

When Evelina was nearly seventy years old the old nurse who had lived with her her whole life died. People wondered then what she would do. "She can't live all alone in that great house," they said. But she did live there alone six months, until spring, and people used to watch her evening lamp when it was put out, and the morning smoke from her kitchen chimney. "It ain't safe for her to be there alone in that great house," they said.

But early in April a young girl appeared one Sunday in the old Squire's pew. Nobody had seen her come to town, and nobody knew who she was or where she came from, but the old people said she looked just as Evelina Adams used to when she was young, and she must be some relation. The old man who had used to look across the meeting-house at Evelina, over forty years ago, looked across now at this young girl, and gave a great start, and his face paled under his gray beard stubble. His old wife gave an anxious, wondering glance at him, and crammed a peppermint into his hand. "Anything the matter, father?" she whispered; but he only gave his head a half-surly shake, and then fastened his eyes straight ahead upon the pulpit. He had reason to that day, for his only son, Thomas, was going to preach his first sermon therein as a candidate. His wife ascribed his nervousness to that. She put a peppermint in her own mouth and sucked it comfortably. "That's all 'tis," she thought to herself. "Father always was easy worked up," and she looked proudly up at her son sitting on the hair-cloth sofa in the pulpit, leaning his handsome young head on his hand, as he had seen old divines do. She never dreamed that her old husband sitting beside her was possessed of an inner life so strange to her that she would not have known him had she met him in the spirit. And, indeed, it had been so always, and she had never dreamed of it. Although he had been faithful to his wife, the image of Evelina Adams in her youth, and that one love-look which she had given him, had never left his soul, but had given it a guise and complexion of which his nearest and dearest knew nothing.

It was strange; but now, as he looked up at his own son as he arose in the pulpit, he could seem to see a look of that fair young Evelina, who had never had a son to inherit her beauty. He had certainly a delicate brilliancy of complexion, which he could have gotten directly from neither father nor mother; and whence came that little nervous frown between his dark blue eyes? His mother had blue eyes, but not like his; they flashed over the great pulpit Bible with a sweet fire that matched the memory in his father's heart.

But the old man put the fancy away from him in a minute; it was one which his stern common-sense always overcame. It was impossible that Thomas Merriam should resemble Evelina Adams; indeed, people always called him the very image of his father.

The father tried to fix his mind upon his son's sermon, but presently he glanced involuntarily across the meeting-house at the young girl, and again his heart leaped and his face paled; but he turned his eyes gravely back to the pulpit, and his wife did not notice. Now and then she thrust a sharp elbow in his side to call his attention to a grand point in their son's discourse. The odor of peppermint was strong in his nostrils, but through it all he seemed to perceive the rose and lavender scent of Evelina Adams's youthful garments. Whether it was with him simply the memory of an odor, which affected him like the odor itself, or not, those in the vicinity of the Squire's pew were plainly aware of it. The gown which the strange young girl wore was, as many an old woman discovered to her neighbor with loud whispers, one of Evelina's, which had been laid away in a sweet-smelling chest since her old girlhood. It had been somewhat altered to suit the fashion of a later day, but the eyes which had fastened keenly upon it when Evelina first wore it up the meeting-house aisle could not mistake it. "It's Evelina Adams's lavender satin made over," one whispered, with a sharp hiss of breath, in the other's ear.

The lavender satin, deepening into purple in the folds, swept in a rich circle over the knees of the young girl in the Squire's pew. She folded her little hands, which were encased in Evelina's cream-colored silk mitts, over it, and looked up at the young minister, and listened to his sermon with a grave and innocent dignity, as Evelina had done before her. Perhaps the resemblance between this young girl and the young girl of the past was more one of mien than aught else, although the type of face was the same. This girl had the same fine sharpness of feature and delicately bright color, and she also wore her hair in curls, although they were tied back from her face with a black velvet ribbon, and did not veil it when she drooped her head, as Evelina's used to do.

The people divided their attention between her and the new minister. Their curiosity goaded them in equal measure with their spiritual zeal. "I can't wait to find out who that girl is," one woman whispered to another.

The girl herself had no thought of the commotion which she awakened. When the service was over, and she walked with a gentle maiden stateliness, which seemed a very copy of Evelina's own, out of the meeting-house, down the street to the Squire's house, and entered it, passing under the stately Corinthian pillars, with a last purple gleam of her satin skirts, she never dreamed of the eager attention that followed her.

It was several days before the village people discovered who she was. The information had to be obtained, by a process like mental thumb-screwing, from the old man who tended Evelina's garden, but at last they knew. She was the daughter of a cousin of Evelina's on the father's side. Her name was Evelina Leonard; she had been named for her father's cousin. She had been finely brought up, and had attended a Boston school for young ladies. Her mother had been dead many years, and her father had died some two years ago, leaving her with only a very little money, which was now all gone, and Evelina Adams had invited her to live with her. Evelina Adams had herself told the old gardener, seeing his scant curiosity was somewhat awakened by the sight of the strange young lady in the garden, but he seemed to have almost forgotten it when the people questioned him.

"She'll leave her all her money, most likely," they said, and they looked at this new Evelina in the old Evelina's perfumed gowns with awe.

However, in the space of a few months the opinion upon this matter was divided. Another cousin of Evelina Adams's came to town, and this time an own cousin—a widow in fine black bombazine, portly and florid, walking with a majestic swell, and, moreover, having with her two daughters, girls of her own type, not so far advanced. This woman hired one of the village cottages, and it was rumored that Evelina Adams paid the rent. Still, it was considered that she was not very intimate with these last relatives. The neighbors watched, and saw, many a time, Mrs. Martha Loomis and her girls try the doors of the Adams house, scudding around angrily from front, to side and back, and knock and knock again, but with no admittance. "Evelina she won't let none of 'em in more'n once a week," the neighbors said. It was odd that, although they had deeply resented Evelina's seclusion on their own accounts, they were rather on her side in this matter, and felt a certain delight when they witnessed a crestfallen retreat of the widow and her daughters. "I don't s'pose she wants them Loomises marchin' in on her every minute," they said.

The new Evelina was not seen much with the other cousins, and she made no acquaintances in the village. Whether she was to inherit all the Adams property or not, she seemed, at any rate, heiress to all the elder Evelina's habits of life. She worked with her in the garden, and wore her old girlish gowns, and kept almost as close at home as she. She often, however, walked abroad in the early dusk, stepping along in a grave and stately fashion, as the elder Evelina had used to do, holding her skirts away from the dewy road-side weeds, her face showing out in the twilight like a white flower, as if it had a pale light of its own.

Nobody spoke to her; people turned furtively after she had passed and stared after her, but they never spoke. This young Evelina did not seem to expect it. She passed along with the lids cast down over her blue eyes, and the rose and lavender scent of her garments came back in their faces.

But one night when she was walking slowly along, a full half-mile from home, she heard rapid footsteps behind, and the young minister, Thomas Merriam, came up beside her and spoke.

"Good-evening," said he, and his voice was a little hoarse through nervousness.

Evelina started, and turned her fair face up towards his. "Good-evening," she responded, and courtesied as she had been taught at school, and stood close to the wall, that he might pass; but Thomas Merriam paused also.

"I—" he began, but his voice broke. He cleared his throat angrily, and went on. "I have seen you in meeting," he said, with a kind of defiance, more of himself than of her. After all, was he not the minister, and had he not the right to speak to everybody in the congregation? Why should he embarrass himself?

"Yes, sir," replied Evelina. She stood drooping her head before him, and yet there was a certain delicate hauteur about her. Thomas was afraid to speak again. They both stood silent for a moment, and then Evelina stirred softly, as if to pass on, and Thomas spoke out bravely. "Is your cousin, Miss Adams, well?" said he.

"She is pretty well, I thank you, sir."

"I have been wanting to—call," he began; then he hesitated again. His handsome young face was blushing crimson.

Evelina's own color deepened. She turned her face away. "Cousin Evelina never sees callers," she said, with grave courtesy; "perhaps you did not know. She has not for a great many years."

"Yes, I did know it," returned Thomas Merriam; "that's the reason I haven't called."

"Cousin Evelina is not strong," remarked the young girl, and there was a savor of apology in her tone.

"But—" stammered Thomas; then he stopped again. "May I—has she any objections to—anybody's coming to see you?"

Evelina started. "I am afraid Cousin Evelina would not approve," she answered, primly. Then she looked up in his face, and a girlish piteousness came into her own. "I am very sorry," she said, and there was a catch in her voice.

Thomas bent over her impetuously. All his ministerial state fell from him like an outer garment of the soul. He was young, and he had seen this girl Sunday after Sunday. He had written all his sermons with her image before his eyes, he had preached to her, and her only, and she had come between his heart and all the nations of the earth in his prayers. "Oh," he stammered out, "I am afraid you can't be very happy living there the way you do. Tell me—"

Evelina turned her face away with sudden haughtiness. "My cousin Evelina is very kind to me, sir," she said.

"But—you must be lonesome with nobody—of your own age—to speak to," persisted Thomas, confusedly.

"I never cared much for youthful company. It is getting dark; I must be going," said Evelina. "I wish you good-evening, sir."

"Sha'n't I—walk home with you?" asked Thomas, falteringly.

"It isn't necessary, thank you, and I don't think Cousin Evelina would approve," she replied, primly; and her light dress fluttered away into the dusk and out of sight like the pale wing of a moth.

Poor Thomas Merriam walked on with his head in a turmoil. His heart beat loud in his ears. "I've made her mad with me," he said to himself, using the old rustic school-boy vernacular, from which he did not always depart in his thoughts, although his ministerial dignity guarded his conversations. Thomas Merriam came of a simple homely stock, whose speech came from the emotions of the heart, all unregulated by the usages of the schools. He was the first for generations who had aspired to college learning and a profession, and had trained his tongue by the models of the educated and polite. He could not help, at times, the relapse of his thoughts, and their speaking to himself in the dialect of his family and his ancestors. "She's 'way above me, and I ought to ha' known it," he further said, with the meekness of an humble but fiercely independent race, which is meek to itself alone. He would have maintained his equality with his last breath to an opponent; in his heart of hearts he felt himself below the scion of the one old gentle family of his native village.

This young Evelina, by the fine dignity which had been born with her and not acquired by precept and example, by the sweetly formal diction which seemed her native tongue, had filled him with awe. Now, when he thought she was angered with him, he felt beneath her lady-feet, his nostrils choked with a spiritual dust of humiliation.

He went forward blindly. The dusk had deepened; from either side of the road, from the mysterious gloom of the bushes, came the twangs of the katydids, like some coarse rustic quarrellers, each striving for the last word in a dispute not even dignified by excess of passion.

Suddenly somebody jostled him to his own side of the path. "That you, Thomas? Where you been?" said a voice in his ear.

"That you, father? Down to the post-office."

"Who was that you was talkin' with back there?"

"Miss Evelina Leonard."

"That girl that's stayin' there—to the old Squire's?"

"Yes." The son tried to move on, but his father stood before him dumbly for a minute.

"I must be going, father. I've got to work on my sermon," Thomas said, impatiently.

"Wait a minute," said his father. "I've got something to say to ye, Thomas, an' this is as good a time to say it as any. There ain't anybody 'round. I don't know as ye'll thank me for it—but mother said the other day that she thought you'd kind of an idea—she said you asked her if she thought it would be anything out of the way for you to go up to the Squire's to make a call. Mother she thinks you can step in anywheres, but I don't know. I know your book-learnin' and your bein' a minister has set you up a good deal higher than your mother and me and any of our folks, and I feel as if you were good enough for anybody, as far as that goes; but that ain't all. Some folks have different startin'-points in this world, and they see things different; and when they do, it ain't much use tryin' to make them walk alongside and see things alike. Their eyes have got different cants, and they ain't able to help it. Now this girl she's related to the old Squire, and she's been brought up different, and she started ahead, even if her father did lose all his property. She 'ain't never eat in the kitchen, nor been scart to set down in the parlor, and satin and velvet, and silver spoons, and cream-pots 'ain't never looked anything out of the common to her, and they always will to you. No matter how many such things you may live to have, they'll always get a little the better of ye. She'll be 'way above 'em; and you won't, no matter how hard you try. Some ideas can't never mix; and when ideas can't mix, folks can't."

"I never said they could," returned Thomas, shortly. "I can't stop to talk any longer, father. I must go home."

"No, you wait a minute, Thomas. I'm goin' to say out what I started to, and then I sha'n't ever bring it up again. What I was comin' at was this: I wanted to warn ye a little. You musn't set too much store by little things that you think mean consider'ble when they don't. Looks don't count for much, and I want you to remember it, and not be upset by 'em."

Thomas gave a great start, and colored high. "I'd like to know what you mean, father," he cried, sharply.

"Nothin'. I don't mean nothin', only I'm older 'n you, and it's come in my way to know some things, and it's fittin you should profit by it. A young woman's looks at you don't count for much. I don't s'pose she knows why she gives 'em herself half the time; they ain't like us. It's best you should make up your mind to it; if you don't, you may find it out by the hardest. That's all. I ain't never goin' to bring this up again."

"I'd like to know what you mean, father." Thomas's voice shook with embarrassment and anger.

"I ain't goin' to say anything more about it," replied the old man. "Mary Ann Pease and Arabella Mann are both in the settin'-room with your mother. I thought I'd tell ye, in case ye didn't want to see 'em, and wanted to go to work on your sermon."

Thomas made an impatient ejaculation as he strode off. When he reached the large white house where he lived he skirted it carefully. The chirping treble of girlish voices came from the open sitting-room window, and he caught a glimpse of a smooth brown head and a high shell comb in front of the candle-light. The young minister tiptoed in the back door and across the kitchen to the back stairs. The sitting-room door was open, and the candle-light streamed out, and the treble voices rose high. Thomas, advancing through the dusky kitchen with cautious steps, encountered suddenly a chair in the dark corner by the stairs, and just saved himself from falling. There was a startled outcry from the sitting-room, and his mother came running into the kitchen with a candle.

"Who is it?" she demanded, valiantly. Then she started and gasped as her son confronted her. He shook a furious warning fist at the sitting-room door and his mother, and edged towards the stairs. She followed him close. "Hadn't you better jest step in a minute?" she whispered. "Them girls have been here an hour, and I know they're waitin' to see you." Thomas shook his head fiercely, and swung himself around the corner into the dark crook of the back stairs. His mother thrust the candle into his hand. "Take this, or you'll break your neck on them stairs," she whispered.

Thomas, stealing up the stairs like a cat, heard one of the girls call to his mother—"Is it robbers, Mis' Merriam? Want us to come an' help tackle 'em?"—and he fairly shuddered; for Evelina's gentle-lady speech was still in his ears, and this rude girlish call seemed to jar upon his sensibilities.

"The idea of any girl screeching out like that," he muttered. And if he had carried speech as far as his thought, he would have added, "when Evelina is a girl!"

He was so angry that he did not laugh when he heard his mother answer back, in those conclusive tones of hers that were wont to silence all argument: "It ain't anything. Don't be scared. I'm coming right back." Mrs. Merriam scorned subterfuges. She took always a silent stand in a difficulty, and let people infer what they would. When Mary Ann Pease inquired if it was the cat that had made the noise, she asked if her mother had finished her blue and white counterpane.

The two girls waited a half-hour longer, then they went home. "What do you s'pose made that noise out in the kitchen?" asked Arabella Mann of Mary Ann Pease, the minute they were out-of-doors.

"I don't know," replied Mary Ann Pease. She was a broad-backed young girl, and looked like a matron as she hurried along in the dusk.

"Well, I know what I think it was," said Arabella Mann, moving ahead with sharp jerks of her little dark body.

"What?"

"It was him."

"You don't mean—"

"I think it was Thomas Merriam, and he was tryin' to get up the back stairs unbeknownst to anybody, and he run into something."

"What for?"

"Because he didn't want to see *us*."

"Now, Arabella Mann, I don't believe it! He's always real pleasant to me."

"Well, I do believe it, and I guess he'll know it when I set foot in that house again. I guess he'll find out I didn't go there to see him! He needn't feel so fine, if he is the minister; his folks ain't any better than mine, an' we've got 'nough sight handsomer furniture in our parlor."

"Did you see how the tallow had all run down over the candles?"

"Yes, I did. She gave that candle she carried out in the kitchen to him, too. Mother says she wasn't never any kind of a housekeeper."

"Hush! Arabella: here he is coming now."

But it was not Thomas; it was his father, advancing through the evening with his son's gait and carriage. When the two girls discovered that, one tittered out quite audibly, and they scuttled past. They were not rivals; they simply walked faithfully side by side in pursuit of the young minister, giving him as it were an impartial choice. There were even no heart-burnings between them; one always confided in the other when she supposed herself to have found some slight favor in Thomas's sight; and, indeed, the young minister could scarcely bow to one upon the street unless she flew to the other with the news.

Thomas Merriam himself was aware of all this devotion on the part of the young women of his flock, and it filled him with a sort of angry shame.

He could not have told why, but he despised himself for being the object of their attention more than he despised them. His heart sank at the idea of Evelina's discovering it. What would she think of him if she knew all those young women haunted his house and lagged after meeting on the chance of getting a word upon him? Suppose she should see their eyes upon his face in meeting time, and decipher their half-unconscious boldness, as he had done against his will. Once Evelina had looked at him, even as the older Evelina had looked at his father, and all other looks of maidens seemed to him like profanations of that, even although he doubted afterwards that he had rightly interpreted it. Full it had seemed to him of that tender maiden surprise and wonder, of that love that knows not itself, and sees its own splendor for the first time in another's face, and flees at the sight. It had happened once when he was coming down the aisle after the sermon and Evelina had met him at the door of her pew. But she had turned her head quickly, and her soft curls flowed over her red cheek, and he doubted ever after if he had read the look aright. When he had gotten the courage to speak to her, and she had met him with the gentle coldness which she had learned of her lady aunt and her teacher in Boston, his doubt was strong upon him. The next Sunday he looked not her way at all. He even tried faithfully from day to day to drive her image from his mind with prayer and religious thoughts, but in spite of himself he would lapse into dreams about her, as if borne by a current of nature too strong to be resisted. And sometimes, upon being awakened from them, as he sat over his sermon with the ink drying on his quill, by the sudden outburst of treble voices in his mother's sitting-room below, the fancy would seize him that possibly these other young damsels took fond liberties with him in their dreams, as he with Evelina, and he resented it with a fierce maidenliness of spirit, although he was a man. The thought that possibly they, over their spinning or their quilting, had in their hearts the image of himself with fond words upon his lips and fond looks in his eyes, filled him with shame and rage, although he took the same liberty with the delicately haughty maiden Evelina.

But Thomas Merriam was not given to undue appreciation of his own fascination, as was proved by his ready discouragement in the case of Evelina. He had the knowledge of his conquests forced upon his understanding until he could no longer evade it. Every day were offerings laid upon his shrine, of pound-cakes and flaky pies, and loaves of white bread, and cups of jelly, whereby the culinary skill of his devotees might be proved. Silken

purses and beautiful socks knitted with fancy stitches, and holy book-
marks for his Bible, and even a wonderful bedquilt, and a fine linen shirt
with hem-stitched bands, poured in upon him. He burned with angry
blushes when his mother, smiling meaningly, passed them over to him.
"Put them away, mother; I don't want them," he would growl out, in a distress that was half comic and half pathetic. He would never taste of the
tempting viands which were brought to him. "How you act, Thomas!" his
mother would say. She was secretly elated by these feminine libations upon
the altar of her son. They did not grate upon her sensibilities, which were
not delicate. She even tried to assist two or three of the young women in
their designs; she would often praise them and their handiwork to her
son—and in this she was aided by an old woman aunt of hers who lived
with the family. "Nancy Winslow is as handsome a girl as ever I set eyes on,
an' I never see any nicer sewin'," Mrs. Merriam said, after the advent of the
linen shirt, and she held it up to the light admiringly. "Jest look at that hemstitchin'!" she said.

"I guess whoever made that shirt calkilated 'twould do for a weddin'
one," said old Aunt Betty Green, and Thomas made an exclamation and
went out of the room, tingling all over with shame and disgust.

"Thomas don't act nateral," said the old woman, glancing after him
through her iron-bound spectacles.

"I dun'no' what's got into him," returned his mother.

"Mebbe they foller him up a leetle too close," said Aunt Betty. "I dun'no'
as I should have ventured on a shirt when I was a gal. I made a satin vest
once for Joshua, but that don't seem quite as p'inted as a shirt. It didn't
scare Joshua, nohow. He asked me to have him the next week."

"Well, I dun'no'," said Mrs. Merriam again. "I kind of wish Thomas
would settle on somebody, for I'm pestered most to death with 'em, an' I
feel as if 'twas kind of mean takin' all these things into the house."

"They've 'bout kept ye in sweet cake, 'ain't they, lately?"

"Yes; but I don't feel as if it was jest right for us to eat it up, when 'twas
brought for Thomas. But he won't touch it. I can't see as he has the least
idee of any one of them. I don't believe Thomas has ever seen anybody he
wanted for a wife."

"Well, he's got the pick of 'em, a-settin' their caps right in his face," said
Aunt Betty.

Neither of them dreamed how the young man, sleeping and eating and
living under the same roof, beloved of them since he entered the world,

holding himself coldly aloof from this crowd of half-innocently, half-boldly ardent young women, had set up for himself his own divinity of love, before whom he consumed himself in vain worship. His father suspected, and that was all, and he never mentioned the matter again to his son.

After Thomas had spoken to Evelina the weeks went on, and they never exchanged another word, and their eyes never met. But they dwelt constantly within each other's thoughts, and were ever present to each other's spiritual vision. Always as the young minister bent over his sermon-paper, laboriously tracing out with sputtering quill his application of the articles of the orthodox faith, Evelina's blue eyes seemed to look out at him between the stern doctrines like the eyes of an angel. And he could not turn the pages of the Holy Writ unless he found some passage therein which to his mind treated directly of her, setting forth her graces like a prophecy. "The fairest among women," read Thomas Merriam, and nodded his head, while his heart leaped with the satisfied delight of all its fancies, at the image of his love's fair and gentle face. "Her price is far above rubies," read Thomas Merriam, and he nodded his head again, and saw Evelina shining as with gold and pearls, more precious than all the jewels of the earth. In spite of all his efforts, when Thomas Merriam studied the Scriptures in those days he was more nearly touched by those old human hearts which throbbed down to his through the ages, welding the memories of their old loves to his living one until they seemed to prove its eternity, than by the Messianic prophecies. Often he spent hours upon his knees, but arose with Evelina's face before his very soul in spite of all.

And as for Evelina, she tended the flowers in the elder Evelina's garden with her poor cousin, whose own love-dreams had been illustrated as it were by the pinks and lilies blooming around them when they had all gone out of her heart, and Thomas Merriam's half-bold, half-imploring eyes looked up at her out of every flower and stung her heart like bees. Poor young Evelina feared much lest she had offended Thomas, and yet her own maiden decorum had been offended by him, and she had offended it herself, and she was faint with shame and distress when she thought of it. How had she been so bold and shameless as to give him that look in the meeting-house? and how had he been so cruel as to accost her afterwards? She told herself she had done right for the maintenance of her own maiden dignity, and yet she feared lest she had angered him and hurt him. "Suppose he had been fretted by her coolness?" she thought, and then a great wave of tender pity went over her heart, and she would almost have spoken to him of her own accord. But then she would reflect how he continued to write such beautiful sermons, and prove so clearly and logically the tenets of the faith; and how could he do that with a mind in distress? Scarcely could she herself tend the flower-beds as she should, nor set her embroidery stitches finely and evenly, she was so ill at ease. It must be that Thomas had not given the matter an hour's worry, since he continued to do his work so faithfully and well. And then her own heart would be sorer than ever with the belief that his was happy and at rest, although she would chide herself for it.

And yet this young Evelina was a philosopher and an analyst of human nature in a small way, and she got some slight comfort out of a shrewd suspicion that the heart of a man might love and suffer on a somewhat different principle from the heart of a woman. "It may be," thought Evelina, sitting idle over her embroidery with far-away blue eyes, "that a man's heart can always turn a while from love to other things as weighty and serious, although he be just as fond, while a woman's heart is always fixed one way by loving, and cannot be turned unless it breaks. And it may be wise," thought young Evelina, "else how could the state be maintained and governed, battles for independence be fought, and even souls be saved, and the gospel carried to the heathen, if men could not turn from the concerns of their own hearts more easily than women? Women should be patient," thought Evelina, "and consider that if they suffer 'tis due to the lot which a wise Providence has given them." And yet tears welled up in her earnest blue eyes and fell over her fair cheeks and wet the embroidery—when the elder Evelina was not looking, as she seldom was. The elder Evelina was kind to her young cousin, but there were days when she seemed to dwell alone in her own thoughts, apart from the whole world, and she seldom spoke either to Evelina or her old servant-man.

Young Evelina, trying to atone for her former indiscretion and establish herself again on her height of maiden reserve in Thomas Merriam's eyes, sat resolutely in the meeting-house of a Sabbath day, with her eyes cast down, and after service she glided swiftly down the aisle and was out of the door before the young minister could much more than descend the pulpit stairs, unless he ran an indecorous race.

And young Evelina never at twilight strolled up the road in the direction of Thomas Merriam's home, where she might quite reasonably hope to

meet him, since he was wont to go to the store when the evening stage-
coach came in with the mail from Boston.

Instead she paced the garden paths, or, when there was not too heavy a
dew, rambled across the fields; and there was also a lane where she loved to
walk. Whether or not Thomas Merriam suspected this, or had ever seen, as
he passed the mouth of the lane, the flutter of maidenly draperies in the distance, it so happened that one evening he also went a-walking there, and
met Evelina. He had entered the lane from the highway, and she from the
fields at the head. So he saw her first afar off, and could not tell fairly
whether her light muslin skirt might not be only a white flowering bush.
For, since his outlook upon life had been so full of Evelina, he had found
that often the most common and familiar things would wear for a second a
look of her to startle him. And many a time his heart had leaped at the sight
of a white bush ahead stirring softly in the evening wind, and he had
thought it might be she. Now he said to himself impatiently that this was
only another fancy; but soon he saw that it was indeed Evelina, in a light
muslin gown, with a little lace kerchief on her head. His handsome young
face was white; his lips twitched nervously; but he reached out and pulled
a spray of white flowers from a bush, and swung it airily to hide his agitation as he advanced.

As for Evelina, when she first espied Thomas she started and half turned,
as if to go back; then she held up her white kerchiefed head with gentle
pride and kept on. When she came up to Thomas she walked so far to one
side that her muslin skirt was in danger of catching and tearing on the
bushes, and she never raised her eyes, and not a flicker of recognition
stirred her sweet pale face as she passed him.

But Thomas started as if she had struck him, and dropped his spray of
white flowers, and could not help a smothered cry that was half a sob, as he
went on, knocking blindly against the bushes. He went a little way, then
he stopped and looked back with his piteous hurt eyes. And Evelina had
stopped also, and she had the spray of white flowers which he had dropped,
in her hand, and her eyes met his. Then she let the flowers fall again, and
clapped both her little hands to her face to cover it, and turned to run; but
Thomas was at her side, and he put out his hand and held her softly by her
white arm.

"Oh," he panted, "I—did not mean to be—too presuming, and offend
you. I—crave your pardon—"

Evelina had recovered herself. She stood with her little hands clasped, and her eyes cast down before him; but not a quiver stirred her pale face, which seemed turned to marble by this last effort of her maiden pride. "I have nothing to pardon," said she. "It was I, whose bold behavior, unbecoming a modest and well-trained young woman, gave rise to what seemed like presumption on your part." The sense of justice was strong within her, but she made her speech haughtily and primly, as if she had learned it by rote from some maiden school-mistress, and pulled her arm away and turned to go; but Thomas's words stopped her.

"Not—unbecoming if it came—from the heart," said he, brokenly, scarcely daring to speak, and yet not daring to be silent.

Then Evelina turned on him, with a sudden strange pride that lay beneath all other pride, and was of a noble and truer sort. "Do you think I would have given you the look that I did if it had not come from my heart?" she demanded. "What did you take me to be—false and a jilt? I may be a forward young woman, who has overstepped the bounds of maidenly decorum, and I shall never get over the shame of it, but I am truthful, and I am no jilt." The brilliant color flamed out on Evelina's cheeks. Her blue eyes met Thomas's with that courage of innocence and nature which dares all shame. But it was only for a second; the tears sprung into them. "I beg you to let me go home," she said, pitifully; but Thomas caught her in his arms, and pressed her troubled maiden face against his breast.

"Oh, I love you so!" he whispered—"I love you so, Evelina, and I was afraid you were angry with me for it."

"And I was afraid," she faltered, half weeping and half shrinking from him, "lest you were angry with me for betraying the state of my feelings, when you could not return them." And even then she used that gentle formality of expression with which she had been taught by her maiden preceptors to veil decorously her most ardent emotions. And, in truth, her training stood her in good stead in other ways; for she presently commanded, with that mild dignity of hers which allowed of no remonstrance, that Thomas should take away his arm from her waist, and give her no more kisses for that time.

"It is not becoming for any one," said she, "and much less for a minister of the gospel. And as for myself, I know not what Mistress Perkins would say to me. She has a mind much above me, I fear."

"Mistress Perkins is enjoying her mind in Boston," said Thomas Merriam, with the laugh of a triumphant young lover.

But Evelina did not laugh. "It might be well for both you and me if she were here," said she, seriously. However, she tempered a little her decorous following of Mistress Perkins's precepts, and she and Thomas went hand in hand up the lane and across the fields.

There was no dew that night, and the moon was full. It was after nine o'clock when Thomas left her at the gate in the fence which separated Evelina Adams's garden from the field, and watched her disappear between the flowers. The moon shone full on the garden. Evelina walked as it were over a silver dapple, which her light gown seemed to brush away and dispel for a moment. The bushes stood in sweet mysterious clumps of shadow.

Evelina had almost reached the house, and was close to the great althea bush, which cast a wide circle of shadow, when it seemed suddenly to separate and move into life.

The elder Evelina stepped out from the shadow of the bush. "Is that you, Evelina?" she said, in her soft melancholy voice, which had in it a nervous vibration.

"Yes, Cousin Evelina."

The elder Evelina's pale face, drooped about with gray curls, had an unfamiliar, almost uncanny, look in the moonlight, and might have been the sorrowful visage of some marble nymph, lovelorn, with unceasing grace. "Who—was with you?" she asked.

"The minister," replied young Evelina.

"Did he meet you?"

"He met me in the lane, Cousin Evelina."

"And he walked home with you across the field?"

"Yes, Cousin Evelina."

Then the two entered the house, and nothing more was said about the matter. Young Evelina and Thomas Merriam agreed that their affection was to be kept a secret for a while. "For," said young Evelina, "I cannot leave Cousin Evelina yet a while, and I cannot have her pestered with thinking about it, at least before another spring, when she has the garden fairly growing again."

"That is nearly a whole year; it is August now," said Thomas, half reproachfully, and he tightened his clasp of Evelina's slender fingers.

"I cannot help that," replied Evelina. "It is for you to show Christian patience more than I, Thomas. If you could have seen poor Cousin Evelina, as I have seen her, through the long winter days, when her garden is dead, and she has only the few plants in her window left! When she is not watering and tending them she sits all day in the window and looks out over the garden and the naked bushes and the withered flower-stalks. She used not to be so, but would read her Bible and good books, and busy herself somewhat over fine needle-work, and at one time she was compiling a little floral book, giving a list of the flowers, and poetical selections and sentiments appropriate to each. That was her pastime for three winters, and it is now nearly done; but she has given that up, and all the rest, and sits there in the window and grows older and feebler until spring. It is only I who can divert her mind, by reading aloud to her and singing; and sometimes I paint the flowers she loves the best on card-board with water-colors. I have a poor skill in it, but Cousin Evelina can tell which flower I have tried to represent, and it pleases her greatly. I have even seen her smile. No, I cannot leave her, nor even pester her with telling her before another spring, and you must wait, Thomas," said young Evelina.

And Thomas agreed, as he was likely to do to all which she proposed which touched not his own sense of right and honor. Young Evelina gave Thomas one more kiss for his earnest pleading, and that night wrote out the tale in her journal. "It may be that I overstepped the bounds of maidenly decorum," wrote Evelina, "but my heart did so entreat me," and no blame whatever did she lay upon Thomas.

Young Evelina opened her heart only to her journal, and her cousin was told nothing, and had little cause for suspicion. Thomas Merriam never came to the house to see his sweetheart; he never walked home with her from meeting. Both were anxious to avoid village gossip, until the elder Evelina could be told.

Often in the summer evenings the lovers met, and strolled hand in hand across the fields, and parted at the garden gate with the one kiss which Evelina allowed, and that was all.

Sometimes when young Evelina came in with her lover's kiss still warm upon her lips the elder Evelina looked at her wistfully, with a strange retrospective expression in her blue eyes, as if she were striving to remember something that the girl's face called to mind. And yet she could have had nothing to remember except dreams.

And once, when young Evelina sat sewing through a long summer afternoon and thinking about her lover, the elder Evelina, who was storing rose leaves mixed with sweet spices in a jar, said, suddenly, "He looks as his father used to."

Young Evelina started. "Whom do you mean, Cousin Evelina?" she asked, wonderingly; for the elder Evelina had not glanced at her, nor even seemed to address her at all.

"Nothing," said the elder Evelina, and a soft flush stole over her withered face and neck, and she sprinkled more cassia on the rose leaves in the jar.

Young Evelina said no more; but she wondered, partly because Thomas was always in her mind, and it seemed to her naturally that nearly everything must have a savor of meaning of him, if her cousin Evelina could possibly have referred to him and his likeness to his father. For it was commonly said that Thomas looked very like his father, although his figure was different. The young man was taller and more firmly built, and he had not the meek forward curve of shoulder which had grown upon his father of late years.

When the frosty nights came Thomas and Evelina could not meet and walk hand in hand over the fields behind the Squire's house, and they very seldom could speak to each other. It was nothing except a "good-day" on the street, and a stolen glance, which set them both a-trembling lest all the congregation had noticed, in the meeting-house. When the winter set fairly in they met no more, for the elder Evelina was taken ill, and her young cousin did not leave her even to go to meeting. People said they guessed it was Evelina Adams's last sickness, and they furthermore guessed that she would divide her property between her cousin Martha Loomis and her two girls and Evelina Leonard, and that Evelina would have the house as her share.

Thomas Merriam heard this last with a satisfaction which he did not try to disguise from himself, because he never dreamed of there being any selfish element in it. It was all for Evelina. Many a time he had looked about the humble house where he had been born, and where he would have to take Evelina after he had married her, and striven to see its poor features with her eyes—not with his, for which familiarity had tempered them. Often, as he sat with his parents in the old sitting-room, in which he had kept so far an unquestioning belief, as in a friend of his childhood, the scales of his own personality would fall suddenly from his eyes. Then he would see, as Evelina, the poor, worn, humble face of his home, and his heart would sink. "I don't see how I ever can bring her here," he thought. He began to save, a few cents at a time out of his pitiful salary, to at least beautify his own chamber a little when Evelina should come. He made up his mind that she should have a little dressing-table, with an oval mirror, and a white muslin frill around it, like one he had seen in Boston. "She shall have that to sit before while she combs her hair," he thought, with defiant tenderness, when he stowed away another shilling in a little box in his trunk. It was money which he ordinarily bestowed upon foreign missions; but his Evelina had come between him and the heathen. To procure some dainty furnishings for her bridal-chamber he took away a good half of his tithes for the spread of the gospel in the dark lands. Now and then his conscience smote him, he felt shamefaced before his deacons, but Evelina kept her first claim. He resolved that another year he would hire a piece of land, and combine farming with his ministerial work, and so try to eke out his salary, and get a little more money to beautify his poor home for his bride.

Now if Evelina Adams had come to the appointed time for the closing of her solitary life, and if her young cousin should inherit a share of her goodly property and the fine old mansion-house, all necessity for anxiety of this kind was over. Young Evelina would not need to be taken away, for the sake of her love, from all these comforts and luxuries. Thomas Merriam rejoiced innocently, without a thought for himself.

In the course of the winter he confided in his father; he couldn't keep it to himself any longer. Then there was another reason. Seeing Evelina so little made him at times almost doubt the reality of it all. There were days when he was depressed, and inclined to ask himself if he had not dreamed it. Telling somebody gave it substance.

His father listened soberly when he told him; he had grown old of late.

"Well," said he, "she 'ain't been used to living the way you have, though you have had advantages that none of your folks ever had; but if she likes you, that's all there is to it, I s'pose."

The old man sighed wearily. He sat in his arm-chair at the kitchen fireplace; his wife had gone in to one of the neighbors, and the two were alone.

"Of course," said Thomas, simply, "if Evelina Adams shouldn't live, the chances are that I shouldn't have to bring her here. She wouldn't have to give up anything on my account—you know that, father."

Then the young man started, for his father turned suddenly on him with a pale, wrathful face. "You ain't countin' on that!" he shouted. "You ain't countin' on that—a son of mine countin' on anything like that!"

Thomas colored. "Why, father," he stammered, "you don't think—you know, it's all for *her*—and they say she can't live anyway. I had never thought of such a thing before. I was wondering how I could make it comfortable for Evelina here."

But his father did not seem to listen. "Countin' on that!" he repeated. "Countin' on a poor old soul, that 'ain't ever had anything to set her heart on but a few posies, dyin' to make room for other folks to have what she's been cheated out on. Countin' on that!" The old man's voice broke into a hoarse sob; he got up, and went hurriedly out of the room.

"Why, father!" his son called after him, in alarm. He got up to follow him, but his father waved him back and shut the door hard.

"Father must be getting childish," Thomas thought, wonderingly. He did not bring up the subject to him again.

Evelina Adams died in March. One morning the bell tolled seventy long melancholy tones before people had eaten their breakfasts. They ran to their doors and counted. "It's her," they said, nodding, when they had waited a little after the seventieth stroke. Directly Mrs. Martha Loomis and her two girls were seen hustling importantly down the road, with their shawls over their heads, to the Squire's house. "Mis' Loomis can lay her out," they said. "It ain't likely that young Evelina knows anything about such things. Guess she'll be thankful she's got somebody to call on now, if she 'ain't mixed much with the Loomises." Then they wondered when the funeral would be, and the women furbished up their black gowns and bonnets, and even in a few cases drove to the next town and borrowed from relatives; but there was a great disappointment in store for them.

Evelina Adams died on a Saturday. The next day it was announced from the pulpit that the funeral would be private, by the particular request of the deceased. Evelina Adams had carried her delicate seclusion beyond death, to the very borders of the grave. Nobody, outside the family, was bidden to the funeral, except the doctor, the minister, and the two deacons of the church. They were to be the bearers. The burial also was to be private, in the Squire's family burial-lot, at the north of the house. The bearers would carry the coffin across the yard, and there would not only be no funeral, but no funeral procession, and no hearse. "It don't seem scarcely decent," the women whispered to each other; "and more than all that, she ain't goin' to be *seen*." The deacon's wives were especially disturbed by this last, as they might otherwise have gained many interesting particulars by proxy.

Monday was the day set for the burial. Early in the morning old Thomas Merriam walked feebly up the road to the Squire's house. People noticed him as he passed. "How terrible fast he's grown old lately!" they said. He opened the gate which led into the Squire's front yard with fumbling fingers, and went up the walk to the front door, under the Corinthian pillars, and raised the brass knocker.

Evelina opened the door, and started and blushed when she saw him. She had been crying; there were red rings around her blue eyes, and her pretty lips were swollen. She tried to smile at Thomas's father, and she held out her hand with shy welcome.

"I want to see her," the old man said, abruptly.

Evelina started, and looked at him wonderingly. "I—don't believe—I know who you mean," said she. "Do you want to see Mrs. Loomis?"

"No; I want to see her."

"Her?"

"Yes, her."

Evelina turned pale as she stared at him. There was something strange about his face. "But—Cousin Evelina," she faltered—"she—didn't want— Perhaps you don't know: she left special directions that nobody was to look at her."

"I *want* to see her," said the old man, and Evelina gave way. She stood aside for him to enter, and led him into the great north parlor, where Evelina Adams lay in her mournful state. The shutters were closed, and one on entering could distinguish nothing but that long black shadow in the middle of the room. Young Evelina opened a shutter a little way, and a slanting shaft of spring sunlight came in and shot athwart the coffin. The old man tiptoed up and leaned over and looked at the dead woman. Evelina Adams had left further instructions about her funeral, which no one understood, but which were faithfully carried out. She wished, she had said, to be attired for her long sleep in a certain rose-colored gown, laid away in rose leaves and lavender in a certain chest in a certain chamber. There were also silken hose and satin shoes with it, and these were to be put on, and a wrought lace tucker fastened with a pearl brooch.

It was the costume she had worn one Sabbath day back in her youth, when she had looked across the meeting-house and her eyes had met young Thomas Merriam's; but nobody knew nor remembered; even young Evelina thought it was simply a vagary of her dead cousin's.

"It don't seem to me decent to lay away anybody dressed so," said Mrs. Martha Loomis; "but of course last wishes must be respected."

The two Loomis girls said they were thankful nobody was to see the departed in her rose-colored shroud.

Even old Thomas Merriam, leaning over poor Evelina, cold and dead in the garb of her youth, did not remember it, and saw no meaning in it. He looked at her long. The beautiful color was all faded out of the yellow-white face; the sweet full lips were set and thin; the closed blue eyes sunken in dark hollows; the yellow hair showed a line of gray at the edge of her old woman's cap, and thin gray curls lay against the hollow cheeks. But old Thomas Merriam drew a long breath when he looked at her. It was like a gasp of admiration and wonder; a strange rapture came into his dim eyes; his lips moved as if he whispered to her, but young Evelina could not hear a sound. She watched him, half frightened, but finally he turned to her. "I 'ain't seen her—fairly," said he, hoarsely—"I 'ain't seen her, savin' a glimpse of her at the window, for over forty year, and she 'ain't changed, not a look. I'd have known her anywheres. She's the same as she was when she was a girl. It's wonderful—wonderful!"

Young Evelina shrank a little. "We think she looks natural," she said, hesitatingly.

"She looks jest as she did when she was a girl and used to come into the meetin'-house. She *is* jest the same," the old man repeated, in his eager, hoarse voice. Then he bent over the coffin, and his lips moved again. Young Evelina would have called Mrs. Loomis, for she was frightened, had he not been Thomas's father, and had it not been for her vague feeling that there might be some old story to explain this which she had never heard. "Maybe he was in love with poor Cousin Evelina, as Thomas is with me," thought young Evelina, using her own leaping-pole of love to land straight at the truth. But she never told her surmise to any one except Thomas, and that was long afterwards, when the old man was dead. Now she watched him with her blue dilated eyes. But soon he turned away from the coffin and made his way straight out of the room, without a word. Evelina followed him through the entry and opened the outer door. He turned on the threshold and looked back at her, his face working.

"Don't ye go to lottin' too much on what ye're goin' to get through folks that have died an' not had anything," he said; and he shook his head almost fiercely at her.

"No, I won't. I don't think I understand what you mean, sir," stammered Evelina.

The old man stood looking at her a moment. Suddenly she saw the tears rolling over his old cheeks. "I'm much obliged to ye for lettin' of me see her," he said, hoarsely, and crept feebly down the steps.

Evelina went back trembling to the room where her dead cousin lay, and covered her face, and closed the shutter again. Then she went about her household duties, wondering. She could not understand what it all meant; but one thing she understood—that in some way this old dead woman, Evelina Adams, had gotten immortal youth and beauty in one human heart. "She looked to him just as she did when she was a girl," Evelina kept thinking to herself with awe. She said nothing about it to Mrs. Martha Loomis or her daughters. They had been in the back part of the house, and had not heard old Thomas Merriam come in, and they never knew about it.

Mrs. Loomis and the two girls stayed in the house day and night until after the funeral. They confidently expected to live there in the future. "It isn't likely that Evelina Adams thought a young woman no older than Evelina Leonard could live here alone in this great house with nobody but that old Sarah Judd. It would not be proper nor becoming," said Martha Loomis to her two daughters; and they agreed, and brought over many of their possessions under cover of night to the Squire's house during the interval before the funeral.

But after the funeral and the reading of the will the Loomises made sundry trips after dusk back to their old home, with their best petticoats and cloaks over their arms, and their bonnets dangling by their strings at their sides. For Evelina Adams's last will and testament had been read, and therein provision was made for the continuance of the annuity heretofore paid them for their support, with the condition affixed that not one night should they spend after the reading of the will in the house known as the Squire Adams house. The annuity was an ample one, and would provide the widow Martha Loomis and her daughters, as it had done before, with all the needfuls of life; but upon hearing the will they stiffened their double chins into their kerchiefs with indignation, for they had looked for more.

Evelina Adams's will was a will of conditions, for unto it she had affixed two more, and those affected her beloved cousin Evelina Leonard. It was notable that "beloved" had not preceded her cousin Martha Loomis's name in the will. No pretence of love, when she felt none, had she ever made in her life. The entire property of Evelina Adams, spinster, deceased, with the exception of Widow Martha Loomis's provision, fell to this beloved young Evelina Leonard, subject to two conditions—firstly, she was never to enter into matrimony, with any person whomsoever, at any time whatsoever; secondly, she was never to let the said spinster Evelina Adams's garden, situated at the rear and southward of the house known as the Squire Adams house, die through any neglect of hers. Due allowance was to be made for the dispensations of Providence: for hail and withering frost and long-continued drought, and for times wherein the said Evelina Adams might, by reason of being confined to the house by sickness, be prevented from attending to the needs of the growing plants, and the verdict in such cases was to rest with the minister and the deacons of the church. But should this beloved Evelina love and wed, or should she let, through any wilful neglect, that garden perish in the season of flowers, all that goodly property would she forfeit to a person unknown, whose name, enclosed in a sealed envelope, was to be held meantime in the hands of the executor, who had also drawn up the will, Lawyer Joshua Lang.

There was great excitement in the village over this strange and unwonted will. Some were there who held that Evelina Adams had not been of sound mind, and it should be contested. It was even rumored that Widow Martha Loomis had visited Lawyer Joshua Lang and broached the subject, but he had dismissed the matter peremptorily by telling her that Evelina Adams, spinster, deceased, had been as much in her right mind at the time of drawing the will as anybody of his acquaintance.

"Not setting store by relations, and not wanting to have them under your roof, doesn't go far in law nor common-sense to send folks to the madhouse," old Lawyer Lang, who was famed for his sharp tongue, was reported to have said. However, Mrs. Martha Loomis was somewhat comforted by her firm belief that either her own name or that of one of her daughters was in that sealed envelope kept by Lawyer Joshua Lang in his strong-box, and by her firm purpose to watch carefully lest Evelina prove derelict in fulfilling the two conditions whereby she held the property.

Larger peep-holes were soon cut away mysteriously in the high arborvitæ hedge, and therein were often set for a few moments, when they passed that way, the eager eyes of Mrs. Martha or her daughter Flora or Fidelia Loomis. Frequent calls they also made upon Evelina, living alone with the old woman Sarah Judd, who had been called in during her cousin's illness, and they strolled into the garden, spying anxiously for withered leaves or dry stalks. They at every opportunity interviewed the old man who assisted Evelina in her care of the garden concerning its welfare. But small progress they made with him, standing digging at the earth with his spade while they talked, as if in truth his wits had gone therein before his body and he would uncover them.

Moreover, Mrs. Martha Loomis talked much slyly to mothers of young men, and sometimes with bold insinuations to the young men themselves, of the sad lot of poor young Evelina, condemned to a solitary and loveless life, and of her sweetness and beauty and desirability in herself, although she could not bring the old Squire's money to her husband. And once, but no more than that, she touched lightly upon the subject to the young minister, Thomas Merriam, when he was making a pastoral call.

"My heart bleeds for the poor child living all alone in that great house," said she. And she looked down mournfully, and did not see how white the young minister's face turned. "It seems almost a pity," said she, furthermore—"Evelina is a good housekeeper, and has rare qualities in herself, and so many get poor wives nowadays—that some godly young man should not court her in spite of the will. I doubt, too, if she would not have a happier lot than growing old over that garden, as poor Cousin Evelina did before her, even if she has a fine house to live in and a goodly sum in the bank. She looks pindling enough lately. I'll warrant she has lost a good ten pound since poor Evelina was laid away, and—"

But Thomas Merriam cut her short. "I see no profit in discussing matters which do not concern us," said he, and only his ministerial estate saved him from the charge of impertinence.

As it was, Martha Loomis colored high. "I'll warrant he'll look out which side his bread is buttered on; ministers always do," she said to her daughters after he had gone. She never dreamed how her talk had cut him to the heart.

Had he not seen more plainly than any one else, Sunday after Sunday, when he glanced down at her once or twice cautiously from his pulpit, how weary-looking and thin she was growing? And her bright color was well-nigh gone, and there were pitiful downward lines at the corners of her sweet mouth. Poor young Evelina was fading like one of her own flowers, as if some celestial gardener had failed in his care of her. And Thomas saw it, and in his heart of hearts he knew the reason, and yet he would not yield. Not once had he entered the old Squire's house since he attended the dead Evelina's funeral, and stood praying and eulogizing, with her coffin between him and the living Evelina, with her pale face shrouded in black bombazine. He had never spoken to her since, nor entered the house; but he had written her a letter, in which all the fierce passion and anguish of his heart was cramped and held down by formal words and phrases, and poor young Evelina did not see beneath them. When her lover wrote her that he felt it inconsistent with his Christian duty and the higher aims of his existence to take any further steps toward a matrimonial alliance, she felt merely that Thomas either cared no more for her, or had come to consider, upon due reflection, that she was not fit to undertake the responsible position of a minister's wife. "It may be that in some way I failed in my attendance upon Cousin Evelina," thought poor young Evelina, "or it may be that he thinks I have not enough dignity of character to inspire respect among the older women in the church." And sometimes, with a sharp thrust of misery that shook her out of her enforced patience and meekness, she wondered if indeed her own loving freedom with him had turned him against her, and led him in his later and sober judgment to consider her too light-minded for a minister's wife. "It may be that I was guilty of great indecorum, and almost indeed forfeited my claim to respect for maidenly modesty, inasmuch as I suffered him to give me kisses, and did almost bring myself to return them in kind. But my heart did so entreat me, and in truth it seemed almost like a lack of sincerity for me to wholly withstand it," wrote poor young Evelina in her journal at that time; and she further wrote: "It is indeed hard for one who has so little knowledge to be fully certain of what is or is not becoming and a Christian duty in matters of this kind; but if I have in any manner, through my ignorance or unwarrantable affection, failed, and so lost the love and respect of a good man, and the opportunity to become his helpmeet during life, I pray that I may be forgiven—for I sinned not wilfully—that the lesson may be sanctified unto me, and that I may live as the Lord order, in Christian patience and meekness, and not repining." It never occurred to young Evelina that possibly Thomas Merriam's sense of duty might be strengthened by the loss of all her cousin's property should she marry him, and neither did she dream that he might hesitate to take her from affluence into poverty for her own sake. For herself the property, as put in the balance beside her love, was lighter than air itself. It was so light that it had no place in her consciousness. She simply had thought, upon hearing the will, of Martha Loomis and her daughters in possession of the property, and herself with Thomas, with perfect acquiescence and rapture.

Evelina Adams's disapprobation of her marriage, which was supposedly expressed in the will, had indeed, without reference to the property, somewhat troubled her tender heart, but she told herself that Cousin Evelina had not known she had promised to marry Thomas; that she would not wish her to break her solemn promise. And furthermore, it seemed to her quite reasonable that the condition had been inserted in the will mainly through concern for the beloved garden.

"Cousin Evelina might have thought perhaps I would let the flowers die when I had a husband and children to take care of," said Evelina. And so she had disposed of all the considerations which had disturbed her, and had thought of no others.

She did not answer Thomas's letter. It was so worded that it seemed to require no reply, and she felt that he must be sure of her acquiescence in whatever he thought best. She laid the letter away in a little rosewood box, in which she had always kept her dearest treasures since her school-days. Sometimes she took it out and read it, and it seemed to her that the pain in her heart would put an end to her in spite of all her prayers for Christian fortitude; and yet she could not help reading it again.

It was seldom that she stole a look at her old lover as he stood in the pulpit in the meeting-house, but when she did she thought with an anxious pang that he looked worn and ill, and that night she prayed that the Lord would restore his health to him for the sake of his people.

It was four months after Evelina Adams's death, and her garden was in the full glory of midsummer, when one evening, towards dusk, young Evelina went slowly down the street. She seldom walked abroad now, but kept herself almost as secluded as her cousin had done before her. But that night a great restlessness was upon her, and she put a little black silk shawl over her shoulders and went out. It was quite cool, although it was midsummer. The dusk was deepening fast; the katydids called back and forth from the wayside bushes. Evelina met nobody for some distance. Then she saw a man coming towards her, and her heart stood still, and she was about to turn back, for she thought for a minute it was the young minister. Then she saw it was his father, and she went on slowly, with her eyes downcast. When she met him she looked up and said good-evening, gravely, and would have passed on, but he stood in her way.

"I've got a word to say to ye, if ye'll listen," he said.

Evelina looked at him tremblingly. There was something strained and solemn in his manner.

"I'll hear whatever you have to say, sir," she said.

The old man leaned his pale face over her and raised a shaking forefinger. "I've made up my mind to say something," said he. "I don't know as I've got any right to, and maybe my son will blame me, but I'm goin' to see that you have a chance. It's been borne in upon me that women folks don't always have a fair chance. It's jest this I'm goin' to say: I don't know whether you know how my son feels about it or not. I don't know how open he's been with you. Do you know jest why he quit you?"

Evelina shook her head. "No," she panted—"I don't—I never knew. He said it was his duty."

"Duty can get to be an idol of wood and stone, an' I don't know but Thomas's is," said the old man. "Well, I'll tell you. He don't think it's right for him to marry you, and make you leave that big house, and lose all that money. He don't care anything about it for himself, but it's for you. Did you know that?"

Evelina grasped the old man's arm hard with her little fingers.

"You don't mean that—was why he did it!" she gasped.

"Yes, that was why."

Evelina drew away from him. She was ashamed to have Thomas's father see the joy in her face. "Thank you, sir," she said. "I did not understand. I—will write to him."

"Maybe my son will think I have done wrong coming betwixt him and his idees of duty," said old Thomas Merriam, "but sometimes there's a good deal lost for lack of a word, and I wanted you to have a fair chance an' a fair say. It's been borne in upon me that women folks don't always have it. Now you can do jest as you think best, but you must remember one thing—riches ain't all. A little likin' for you that's goin' to last, and keep honest and faithful to you as long as you live, is worth more; an' it's worth more to women folks than 'tis to men, an' it's worth enough to them. My son's poorly. His mother and I are worried about him. He don't eat nor sleep—walks his chamber nights. His mother don't know what the matter is, but he let on to me some time since."

"I'll write a letter to him," gasped Evelina again. "Good-night, sir." She pulled her little black silk shawl over her head and hastened home, and all night long her candle burned, while her weary little fingers toiled over pages of foolscap-paper to convince Thomas Merriam fully, and yet in terms not exceeding maidenly reserve, that the love of his heart and the companionship of his life were worth more to her than all the silver and gold in the world. Then the next morning she despatched it, all neatly folded and sealed, and waited.

It was strange that a letter like that could not have moved Thomas Merriam, when his heart too pleaded with him so hard to be moved. But that might have been the very reason why he could withstand her, and why the consciousness of his own weakness gave him strength. Thomas Merriam was one, when he had once fairly laid hold of duty, to grasp it hard, although it might be to his own pain and death, and maybe to that of others. He wrote to poor young Evelina another letter, in which he emphasized and repeated his strict adherence to what he believed the line of duty in their separation, and ended it with a prayer for her welfare and happiness, in which, indeed, for a second, the passionate heart of the man showed forth. Then he locked himself in his chamber, and nobody ever knew what he suffered there. But one pang he did not suffer which Evelina would have suffered in his place. He mourned not over nor realized the grief of her tender heart when she should read his letter, otherwise he could not have sent it. He writhed under his own pain alone, and his duty hugged him hard, like the iron maiden of the old tortures, but he would not yield.

As for Evelina, when she got his letter, and had read it through, she sat still and white for a long time, and did not seem to hear when old Sarah Judd spoke to her. But at last she rose and went to her chamber, and knelt down, and prayed for a long time; and then she went out in the garden and cut all the most beautiful flowers, and tied them in wreaths and bouquets, and carried them out to the north side of the house, where her cousin Evelina was buried, and covered her grave with them. And then she knelt down there and hid her face among them, and said, in a low voice, as if in a listening ear, "I pray you, Cousin Evelina, forgive me for what I am about to do."

And then she returned to the house, and sat at her needle-work as usual; but the old woman kept looking at her, and asking if she were sick, for there was a strange look in her face.

She and old Sarah Judd had always their tea at five o'clock, and put the candles out at nine, and this night they did as they were wont. But at one o'clock in the morning young Evelina stole softly down the stairs with her lighted candle, and passed through into the kitchen; and a half-hour after she came forth into the garden, which lay in full moonlight, and she had in her hand a steaming teakettle, and she passed around among the shrubs and watered them, and a white cloud of steam rose around them. Back and forth she went to the kitchen; for she had heated the great copper wash-kettle full of water; and she watered all the shrubs in the garden, moving amid curling white wreaths of steam, until the water was gone. And then she set to work and tore up by the roots with her little hands and trampled with her little feet all the beautiful tender flower-beds; all the time weeping, and moaning softly: "Poor Cousin Evelina! poor Cousin Evelina! Oh, forgive me, poor Cousin Evelina!"

And at dawn the garden lay in ruin, for all the tender plants she had torn up by the roots and trampled down, and all the stronger-rooted shrubs she had striven to kill with boiling water and salt.

Then Evelina went into the house, and made herself tidy as well as she could when she trembled so, and put her little shawl over her head, and went down the road to the Merriams' house. It was so early the village was scarcely astir, but there was smoke coming out of the kitchen chimney at the Merriams'; and when she knocked, Mrs. Merriam opened the door at once, and stared at her.

"Is Sarah Judd dead?" she cried; for her first thought was that something must have happened when she saw the girl standing there with her wild pale face.

"I want to see the minister," said Evelina, faintly, and she looked at Thomas's mother with piteous eyes.

"Be you sick?" asked Mrs. Merriam. She laid a hard hand on the girl's arm, and led her into the sitting-room, and put her into the rocking-chair with the feather cushion. "You look real poorly," said she. "Sha'n't I get you a little of my elderberry wine?"

"I want to see him," said Evelina, and she almost sobbed.

"I'll go right and speak to him," said Mrs. Merriam. "He's up, I guess. He gets up early to write. But hadn't I better get you something to take first? You do look sick."

But Evelina only shook her head. She had her face covered with her hands, and was weeping softly. Mrs. Merriam left the room, with a long backward glance at her. Presently the door opened and Thomas came in. Evelina stood up before him. Her pale face was all wet with tears, but there was an air of strange triumph about her.

"The garden is dead," said she.

"What do you mean?" he cried out, staring at her, for indeed he thought for a minute that her wits had left her.

"The garden is dead," said she. "Last night I watered the roses with boiling water and salt, and I pulled the other flowers up by their roots. The garden is dead, and I have lost all Cousin Evelina's money, and it need not come between us any longer." She said that, and looked up in his face with her blue eyes, through which the love of the whole race of loving women from which she had sprung, as well as her own, seemed to look, and held out her little hands; but even then Thomas Merriam could not understand, and stood looking at her.

"Why—did you do it?" he stammered.

"Because you would have me no other way, and—I couldn't bear that anything like that should come between us," she said, and her voice shook like a harp-string, and her pale face went red, then pale again.

But Thomas still stood staring at her. Then her heart failed her. She thought that he did not care, and she had been mistaken. She felt as if it were the hour of her death, and turned to go. And then he caught her in his arms.

"Oh," he cried, with a great sob, "the Lord make me worthy of thee, Evelina!"

There had never been so much excitement in the village as when the fact of the ruined garden came to light. Flora Loomis, peeping through the hedge on her way to the store, had spied it first. Then she had run home for her mother, who had in turn sought Lawyer Lang, panting bonnetless down the road. But before the lawyer had started for the scene of disaster, the minister, Thomas Merriam, had appeared, and asked for a word in private with him. Nobody ever knew just what that word was, but the lawyer was singularly uncommunicative and reticent as to the ruined garden.

"Do you think the young woman is out of her mind?" one of the deacons asked him, in a whisper.

"I wish all the young women were as much in their minds; we'd have a better world," said the lawyer, gruffly.

"When do you think we can begin to move in here?" asked Mrs. Martha Loomis, her wide skirts sweeping a bed of uprooted verbenas.

"When your claim is established," returned the lawyer, shortly, and turned on his heel and went away, his dry old face scanning the ground like a dog on a scent. That afternoon he opened the sealed document in the presence of witnesses, and the name of the heir to whom the property fell was disclosed. It was "Thomas Merriam, the beloved and esteemed minister of this parish," and young Evelina would gain her wealth instead of losing it by her marriage. And furthermore, after the declaration of the name of the heir was this added: "This do I in the hope and belief that neither the greed of riches nor the fear of them shall prevent that which is good and wise in the sight of the Lord, and with the surety that a love which shall triumph over so much in its way shall endure, and shall be a blessing and not a curse to my beloved cousin, Evelina Leonard."

Thomas Merriam and Evelina were married before the leaves fell in that same year, by the minister of the next village, who rode over in his chaise, and brought his wife, who was also a bride, and wore her wedding-dress of a pink and pearl shot silk. But young Evelina wore the blue bridal array which had been worn by old Squire Adams's bride, all remodelled daintily to suit the fashion of the times; and as she moved, the fragrances of roses and lavender of the old summers during which it had been laid away were evident, like sweet memories.

One Good Time

1897

Richard Stone was nearly seventy-five years old when he died, his wife was over sixty, and his daughter Narcissa past middle age. Narcissa Stone had been very pretty, and would have been pretty still had it not been for those lines, as distinctly garrulous of discontent and worry as any words of mouth, which come so easily in the face of a nervous, delicate-skinned woman. They were around Narcissa's blue eyes, her firmly closed lips, her thin nose; a frown like a crying repetition of some old anxiety and indecision was on her forehead; and she had turned her long neck so much to look over her shoulder for new troubles on her track that the lines of fearful expectation had settled there. Narcissa had yet her beautiful thick hair, which the people in the village had never quite liked because it was red, her cheeks were still pink, and she stooped only a little from her slender height when she walked. Some people said that Narcissa Stone would be quite good-looking now if she had a decent dress and bonnet. Neither she nor her mother had any clothes which were not deemed shabby, even by the humbly attired women in the little mountain village. "Mis' Richard Stone, she 'ain't had a new silk dress since Narcissa was born," they said; "and as for Narcissa, she 'ain't never had anything that looked fit to wear to meeting."

When Richard Stone died, people wondered if his widow and Narcissa would not have something new. Mrs. Nathan Wheat, who was a third cousin to Richard Stone, went, the day before the funeral, a half-mile down the brook road to see Hannah Turbin, the dressmaker. The road was little travelled; she walked through an undergrowth of late autumn flowers, and when she reached the Turbins' house her black thibet gown was gold-powdered and white-flecked to the knees with pollen and winged seeds of passed flowers.

Hannah Turbin's arm, brown and wrinkled like a monkey's, in its woollen sleeve, described arcs of jerky energy past the window, and never ceased when Mrs. Wheat came up the path and entered the house. Hannah herself scarcely raised her seamy brown face from her work.

"Good-afternoon," said Mrs. Wheat.

Hannah nodded. "Good-afternoon," she responded then, as if words were an afterthought.

Mrs. Wheat shook her black skirts vigorously. "I'm all over dust from them yaller weeds," said she. "Well, I don't care about this old thibet." She pulled a rocking-chair forward and seated herself. "Warm for this time of year," said she.

Hannah drew her thread through her work. "Yes, 'tis," she returned, with a certain pucker of scorn, as if the utter foolishness of allusions to obvious conditions of nature struck her. Hannah Turbin was not a favorite in the village, but she was credited with having much common-sense, and people held her in somewhat distant respect.

"Guess it's Injun summer," remarked Mrs. Wheat.

Hannah Turbin said nothing at all to that. Mrs. Wheat cast furtive glances around the room as she swayed in her rocking-chair. Everything was very tidy, and there were few indications of its owner's calling. A number of fashion papers were neatly piled on a bureau in the corner, and some nicely folded breadths of silk lay beside them. There was not a scrap or shred of cloth upon the floor; not a thread, even. Hannah was basting a brown silk basque. Mrs. Wheat could see nowhere the slightest evidence of what she had come to ascertain, so was finally driven to inquiry, still, however, by devious windings.

"Seems sad about Richard," she said.

"Yes," returned Hannah, with a sudden contraction of her brown face, which seemed to flash a light over a recollection in Mrs. Wheat's mind. She remembered that there was a time, years ago, when Richard Stone had paid some attention to Hannah Turbin, and people had thought he might marry her instead of Jane Basset. However, it had happened so long ago that she did not really believe that Hannah dwelt upon it, and it faded immediately from her own mind.

"Well," said she, with a sigh, "it is a happy release, after all, he's been such a sufferer so long. It's better for him, and it's better for Jane and Narcissa. He's left 'em comfortable; they've got the farm, and his life's insured, you know. Besides, I suppose Narcissa 'll marry William Crane now. Most likely they'll rent the farm, and Jane will go and live with Narcissa when she's married. I want to know—"

Hannah Turbin sewed.

"I was wondering," continued Mrs. Wheat, "if Jane and Narcissa wasn't going to have some new black dresses for the funeral. They 'ain't got a thing that's fit to wear, I know. I don't suppose they've got much money on hand now except what little Richard saved up for his funeral expenses. I know he had a little for that because he told me so, but the life-insurance is coming in, and anybody would trust them. There's a nice piece of black cashmere down to the store, a dollar a yard. I didn't know but they'd get dresses off it; but Jane she never tells me anything—anybody 'd think she might, seeing as I was poor Richard's cousin; and as for Narcissa, she's as close as her mother."

Hannah Turbin sewed.

"'Ain't Jane and Narcissa said anything to you about making them any new black dresses to wear to the funeral?" asked Mrs. Wheat, with desperate directness.

"No, they 'ain't," replied Hannah Turbin.

"Well, then, all I've got to say is they'd ought to be ashamed of themselves. There they've got fourteen if not fifteen hundred dollars coming in from poor Richard's insurance money, and they ain't even going to get decent clothes to wear to his funeral out of it. They 'ain't made any plans for new bonnets, I know. It ain't showing proper respect to the poor man. Don't you say so?"

"I suppose folks are their own best judges," said Hannah Turbin, in her conclusive, half-surly fashion, which intimidated most of her neighbors. Mrs. Wheat did not stay much longer. When she went home through the ghostly weeds and grasses of the country road she was almost as indignant with Hannah Turbin as with Jane Stone and Narcissa. "Never saw anybody so close in my life," said she to herself. "Needn't talk if she don't want to. Dun'no' as thar's any harm in my wanting to know if my own third cousin is going to have mourning wore for him."

Mrs. Wheat, when she reached home, got a black shawl which had belonged to her mother out of the chest, where it had lain in camphor, and hung it on the clothesline to air. She also removed a spray of bright velvet flowers from her bonnet, and sewed in its place a black ostrich feather. She found an old crape veil too, and steamed it into stiffness. "I'm going to go to that funeral looking decent, if his own wife and daughter ain't," she told her husband.

"If I wa'n't along, folks would take you for the widder," said Nathan Wheat, with a chuckle. Nathan Wheat was rather inclined to be facetious with his wife.

However, Mrs. Wheat was not the only person who attended poor Richard Stone's funeral in suitable attire. Hannah Turbin was black from head to foot; the material, it is true, was not of the conventional mourning kind, but the color was. She wore a black silk gown, a black ladies'-cloth mantle, a black velvet bonnet trimmed with black flowers, and a black lace veil.

"Hannah Turbin looked as if she was dressed in second mourning," Mrs. Wheat said to her husband after the funeral. "I should have thought she'd most have worn some color, seeing as some folks might remember she was disappointed about Richard Stone; but, anyway, it was better than to go looking the way Jane and Narcissa did. There was Jane in that old brown dress, and Narcissa in her green, with a blue flower in her bonnet. I think it was dreadful, and poor Richard leaving them all that money through his dying, too."

In truth, all the village was scandalized at the strange attire of the widow and daughter of Richard Stone at his funeral, except William Crane. He could not have told what Mrs. Stone wore, through scarcely admitting her in any guise into his inmost consciousness, and as for Narcissa, he admitted her so fully that he could not see her robes at all in such a dazzlement of vision.

"William Crane never took his eyes off Narcissa Stone all through the funeral; shouldn't be surprised if he married her in a month or six weeks," people said.

William Crane took Jane and Narcissa to the grave in his covered wagon, keeping his old white horse at a decorous jog behind the hearse in the little funeral procession, and people noted that. They wondered if he would go over to the Stones' that evening, and watched, but he did not. He left the mother and daughter to their close communion of grief that night, but the next the neighbors saw him in his best suit going down the road before dark. "Must have done up his chores early to get started soon as this," they said.

William Crane was about Narcissa's age but he looked older. His gait was shuffling, his hair scanty and gray, and, moreover, he had that expression of patience which comes only from long abiding, both of body and soul. He went through the south yard to the side door of the house, stepping between the rocks. The yard abounded in mossy slopes of half-sunken rocks, as did the entire farm. Folks often remarked of Richard Stone's place, as well as himself, "Stone by name, and stone by nature." Underneath nearly all his fields, cropping plentifully to the surface, were rock ledges. The grass could be mown only by hand. As for this south yard, it required skilful manœuvring to drive a team through it. When William Crane knocked that evening, Narcissa opened the door. "Oh, it's you!" she said. "How do you do?"

"How do you do, Narcissa?" William responded, and walked in. He could have kissed his old love in the gloom of the little entry, but he did not think of that. He looked at her anxiously with his soft, patient eyes. "How are you gettin' on?" he asked.

"Well as can be expected," replied Narcissa.

"How's your mother?"

"She's well as can be expected."

William followed Narcissa, who led the way, not into the parlor, as he had hoped, but into the kitchen. The kitchen's great interior of smoky gloom was very familiar to him, but to-night it looked strange. For one thing, the arm-chair to which Richard Stone had been bound with his rheumatism for the last fifteen years was vacant, and pushed away into a corner. William looked at it, and it seemed to him that he must see the crooked, stern old figure in it, and hear again the peremptory tap of the stick which he kept always at his side to summon assistance. After his first involuntary glance at the dead man's chair, William saw his widow coming forward out of her bedroom with a great quilt over her arm.

"Good-evenin', William," she said, with faint melancholy, then lapsed into feeble weeping.

"Now, mother, you said you wouldn't; you know it don't do any good, and you'll be sick," Narcissa cried out, impatiently.

"I know it, Narcissa, but I can't help it, I can't. I'm dreadful upset! Oh, William, I'm dreadful upset! It ain't his death alone—it's—"

"Mother, I'd rather tell him myself," interrupted Narcissa. She took the quilt from her mother, and drew the rocking-chair towards her. "Do sit down and keep calm, mother," said she.

But it was not easy for the older woman, in her bewilderment of grief and change, to keep calm.

"Oh, William, do you know what we're goin' to do?" she wailed, yet seating herself obediently in the rocking-chair. "We're goin' to New York. Narcissa says so. We're goin' to take the insurance money, when we get it, an' we're goin' to New York. I tell her we hadn't ought to, but she won't listen to it! There's the trunk. Look at there, William! She dragged it down from the garret this forenoon. Look at there, William!"

William's startled eyes followed the direction of Mrs. Stone's wavering index finger, and saw a great ancient trunk lined with blue and white wallpaper, standing open against the opposite wall.

"She dragged it down from the garret this forenoon," continued Mrs. Stone, in the same tone of unfaltering tragedy, while Narcissa, her delicate lips pursed tightly, folded up the bedquilt which her mother had brought. "It bumped so hard on those garret stairs I thought she'd break it, or fall herself, but she wouldn't let me help her. Then she cleaned it, an' made some paste, an' lined it with some of the parlor paper. There ain't any key to it— I never remember none. The trunk was in this house when I come here. Richard had it when he went West before we were married. Narcissa she says she is goin' to tie it up with the clothes-line. William, can't you talk to her? Seems to me I can't go to New York nohow."

William turned then to Narcissa, who was laying the folded bedquilt in the trunk. He looked pale and bewildered, and his voice trembled when he spoke. "This ain't true, is it, Narcissa?" he said.

"Yes, it is," she replied, shortly, still bending over the trunk.

"We ain't goin' for a month," interposed her mother again; "we can't get the insurance money before then, Lawyer Maxham says; but she says she's goin' to have the trunk standin' there, an' put things in when she thinks of it, so she won't forget nothin'. She says we'd better take one bedquilt with us, in case they don't have 'nough clothes on the bed. We've got to stay to a hotel. Oh, William, can't you say anything to stop her?"

"This ain't true, Narcissa?" William repeated, helplessly.

Narcissa raised herself and faced him. Her cheeks were red, her blue eyes glowing, her hair tossing over her temples in loose waves. She looked as she had when he first courted her. "Yes, it is, William Crane," she cried. "Yes, it is."

William looked at her so strangely and piteously that she softened a little. "I've got my reasons," said she. "Maybe I owe it to you to tell them. I suppose you were expecting something different." She hesitated a minute, looking at her mother, who cried out again:

"Oh, William, say somethin' to stop her! Can't you say somethin' to stop her?"

Then Narcissa motioned to him resolutely. "Come into the parlor, William," said she, and he followed her out across the entry. The parlor was chilly; the chairs stood as they had done at the funeral, primly against the walls glimmering faintly in the dusk with blue and white paper like the trunk lining. Narcissa stood before William and talked with feverish haste. "I'm going," said she—"I'm going to take that money and go with mother to New York, and you mustn't try to stop me, William. I know what you've been expecting. I know, now father's gone, you think there ain't anything to hinder our getting married; you think we'll rent this house, and mother and me will settle down in yours for the rest of our lives. I know you ain't counting on that insurance money; it ain't like you."

"The Lord knows it ain't, Narcissa," William broke out with pathetic pride.

"I know that as well as you do. You thought we'd put it in the bank for a rainy day, in case mother got feeble, or anything, and that is all you did think. Maybe I'd ought to. I s'pose I had, but I ain't going to. I 'ain't never done anything my whole life that I thought I ought not to do, but now I'm going to. I'm going to if it's wicked. I've made up my mind. I 'ain't never had one good time in my whole life, and now I'm going to, even if I have to suffer for it afterwards.

"I 'ain't never had anything like other women. I've never had any clothes nor gone anywhere. I've just stayed at home here and drudged. I've done a man's work on the farm. I've milked and made butter and cheese; I've waited on father; I've got up early and gone to bed late. I've just drudged, drudged, ever since I can remember. I don't know anything about the world nor life. I don't know anything but my own old tracks, and—I'm going to get out of them for a while, whether or no."

"How long are you calculating to stay?"

"I don't know."

"I've been thinking," said William, "I'd have some new gilt paper on the sitting-room at my house, and a new stove in the kitchen. I thought—"

"I know what you thought," interrupted Narcissa, still trembling and glowing with nervous fervor. "And you're real good, William. It ain't many men would have waited for me as you've done, when father wouldn't let me get married as long as he lived. I know by good rights I hadn't ought to keep you waiting, but I'm going to, and it ain't because I don't think enough of you—it ain't that; I can't help it. If you give up having me at all, if you think you'd rather marry somebody else, I can't help it; I won't blame you—"

"Maybe you want me to, Narcissa," said William, with a sad dignity. "If you do, if you want to get rid of me, if that's it—"

Narcissa started. "That ain't it," said she. She hesitated, and added, with formal embarrassment—she had the usual reticence of a New England village woman about expressions of affection, and had never even told her lover in actual words that she loved him—"My feelings towards you are the same as they have always been, William."

It was almost dark in the parlor. They could see only each other's faces gleaming as with pale light. "It would be a blow to me if I thought they wa'n't, Narcissa," William returned, simply.

"They are."

William put his arm around her waist, and they stood close together for a moment. He stroked back her tumbled red hair with clumsy tenderness. "You have had a hard time, Narcissa," he whispered, brokenly. "If you want to go, I ain't going to say anything against it. I ain't going to deny I'm kind of disappointed. I've been living alone so long, and I feel kind of sore sometimes with waitin', but—"

"I shouldn't make you any kind of a wife if I married you now, without waiting," Narcissa said, in a voice at once stern and tender. She stood apart from him, and put up her hand with a sort of involuntary maiden primness to smooth her hair where his had stroked it awry. "If," she went on, "I had to settle down in your house, as I have done in father's, and see the years stretching ahead like a long road without any turn, and nothing but the same old dog-trot of washing and ironing and scrubbing and cooking and sewing and washing dishes till I drop into my grave, I should hate you, William Crane."

"I could fetch an' carry all the water for the washin', Narcissa, and I could wash the dishes," said William, with humble beseeching.

"It ain't that. I know you'd do all you could. It's— Oh, William! I've got to have a break; I've got to have one good time. I—like you, and—I liked father; but love ain't enough sometimes when it ties anybody. Everybody has got their own feet and their own wanting to use 'em, and sometimes when love comes in the way of that, it ain't anything but a dead wall. Once we had a black heifer that would jump all the walls; we had to sell her. She always made me think of myself. I tell you, William, I've got to jump my wall, and I've got to have one good time."

William Crane nodded his gray head in patient acquiescence. His forehead was knitted helplessly; he could not in the least understand what his sweetheart meant; in her present mood she was in altogether a foreign language for him, but still the unintelligible sound of her was sweet as a song to his ears. This poor village lover had at least gained the crown of absolute faith through his weary years of waiting; the woman he loved was still a star, and her rays not yet resolved into human reachings and graspings.

"How long do you calculate to be gone, Narcissa?" he asked again.

"I don't know," she replied. "Fifteen hundred dollars is a good deal of money. I s'pose it'll take us quite a while to spend it, even if we ain't very saving."

"You ain't goin' to spend it all, Narcissa!" William gave a little dismayed gasp in spite of himself.

"Land, no! we couldn't, unless we stayed three years, an' I ain't calculating to be gone as long as that. I'm going to bring home what we don't want, and put it in the bank; but—I shouldn't be surprised if it took 'most a year to spend what I've laid out to."

"'Most a year!"

"Yes; I've got to buy us both new clothes for one thing. We 'ain't neither of us got anything fit to wear, and 'ain't had for years. We didn't go to the funeral lookin' decent, and I know folks talked. Mother felt bad about it, but I couldn't help it. I wa'n't goin' to lay out money foolish and get things here when I was going to New York and could have others the way they ought to be. I'm going to buy us some jewelry too; I 'ain't never had a good breastpin even; and as for mother, father never even bought her a ring when they were married. I ain't saying anything against him; it wa'n't the fashion so much in those days."

"I was calculatin'—" William stammered, blushing. "I always meant to, Narcissa."

"Yes, I know you have; but you mustn't lay out too much on it, and I don't care anything about a stone ring—just a plain gold one. There's another thing I'm going to have, too, an' that's a gold watch. I've wanted one all my life."

"Mebbe—" began William, painfully.

"No!" cried Narcissa, peremptorily. "I don't want you to buy me one. I 'ain't ever thought of it. I'm going to buy it myself. I'm going to buy mother a real cashmere shawl, too, like the one that New York lady had that came to visit Lawyer Maxham's wife. I've got a list of things written down on paper. I guess I'll have to buy another trunk in New York to put them in."

"Well," said William, with a great sigh, "I guess I'd better be goin'. I hope you'll have as good a time as you're countin' on, Narcissa."

"It's the first good time I ever did count on, and I'd ought to," said Narcissa. "I'm going to take mother to the theatre, too. I don't know but it's wicked, but I'm going to." Narcissa fluttered out of the parlor and William shuffled after her. He would not go into the kitchen again.

"Well, good-night," said Narcissa, and William also said good-night, with another heavy sigh. "Look out for them rocks going out of the yard, an' don't tumble over 'em," she called after him.

"I'm used to 'em," he answered back, sadly, from the darkness.

Narcissa shut and bolted the door. "He don't like it; he feels real bad about it; but I can't help it—I'm going."

Through the next few weeks Narcissa Stone's face looked strange to those who had known her from childhood. While the features were the same, her soul informed them with a new purpose, which overlighted all the old ones of her life, and even the simple village folks saw the effect, though with no understanding. Soon the news that Narcissa and her mother were going to New York was abroad. On the morning they started, in the three-seated open wagon which served as stage to connect the little village with the railroad ten miles away, all the windows were set with furtively peering faces.

"There they go," the women told one another. "Narcissa an' her mother an' the trunk. Wonder if Narcissa's got that money put away safe? They're wearin' the same old clothes. S'pose we sha'n't know 'em when they get back. Heard they was goin' to stay a year. Guess old Mr. Stone would rise up in his grave if he knew it. Lizzy saw William Crane a-helpin' Narcissa h'ist the trunk out ready for the stage. I wouldn't stan' it if I was him. Ten chances to one Narcissa 'll pick up somebody down to New York, with all that money. She's good-lookin', and she looks better since her father died."

Narcissa, riding out of her native village to those unknown fields in which her imagination had laid the scene of the one good time of her life, regarded nothing around her. She sat straight, her slender body resisting stiffly the jolt of the stage. She said not a word, but looked ahead with shining eyes. Her mother wept, a fold of her old shawl before her face. Now and then she lamented aloud, but softly, lest the driver hear. "Goin' away from the place where I was born an' married, an' have lived ever since I knew anything, to stay a year. I can't stan' it, I can't."

"Hush, mother! You'll have a real good time."

"No, I sha'n't, I sha'n't. Goin'—to stay a whole—year. I—can't, nohow."

"S'pose we sha'n't see you back in these parts for some time," the stage-driver said, when he helped them out at the railroad station. He was an old man, and had known Narcissa since her childhood.

"Most likely not," she replied. Her mother's face was quite stiff with repressed emotion when the stage-driver lifted her out. She did not want him to report in the village that she was crying when she started for New York. She had some pride in spite of her distress.

"Well, I'll be on the lookout for ye a year from to-day," said the stage-driver, with a jocular twist of his face. There were no passengers for his village on the in-coming train, so he had to drive home alone through the melancholy autumn woods. The sky hung low with pale, freezing clouds; over everything was that strange hush which prevails before snow. The stage-driver, holding the reins loosely over his tramping team, settled forward with elbows on his knees, and old brows bent with aimless brooding. Over and over again his brain worked the thought, like a peaceful cud of contemplation. "They're goin' to be gone a year. Narcissa Stone an' her mother are goin' to be gone a year, afore I'll drive 'em home."

So little imagination had the routine of his life fostered that he speculated not, even upon the possible weather of that far-off day, or the chances of his living to see it. It was simply, "They're goin' to be gone a year afore I'll drive 'em home."

So fixed was his mind upon that one outcome of the situation that when Narcissa and her mother reappeared in less than one week—in six days— he could not for a moment bring his mind intelligently to bear upon it. The old stage-driver may have grown something like his own horses through his long sojourn in their company, and his intelligence, like theirs, been given to only the halts and gaits of its first breaking.

For a second he had a bewildered feeling that time had flown fast, that a week was a year. Everybody in the village had said the travellers would not return for a year. He hoisted the ancient paper-lined trunk into his stage, then a fine new one, nailed and clamped with shining brass, then a number of packages, all the time with puzzled eyes askant upon Narcissa and her mother. He would scarcely have known them, as far as their dress was concerned. Mrs. Stone wore a fine black satin gown; her perturbed old face looked out of luxurious environments of fur and lace and rich black plumage. As for Narcissa, she was almost regal. The old stage-driver backed and ducked awkwardly, as if she were a stranger, when she approached. Her fine skirts flared imposingly, and rustled with unseen silk; her slender shoulders were made shapely by the graceful spread of rich fur, her red hair shone under a hat fit for a princess, and there was about her a faint perfume of violets which made the stage-driver gaze confusedly at the snowy ground under the trees when they had started on the homeward road. "Seems as if I smelt posies, but I know there ain't none hereabouts this time of year," he remarked, finally, in a tone of mild ingratiation, as if more to himself than to his passengers.

"It's some perfumery Narcissa's got on her pocket-handkerchief that she bought in New York," said Mrs. Stone, with a sort of sad pride. She looked worn and bewildered, ready to weep at the sight of familiar things, and yet distinctly superior to all such weakness. As for Narcissa, she looked like a child thrilled with scared triumph at getting its own way, who rejoices even in the midst of correction at its own assertion of freedom.

"That so?" said the stage-driver, admiringly. Then he added, doubtfully, bringing one white-browed eye to bear over his shoulder, "Didn't stay quite so long as you calculated on?"

"No, we didn't," replied Narcissa, calmly. She nudged her mother with a stealthy, firm elbow, and her mother understood well that she was to maintain silence.

"I ain't going to tell a living soul about it but William Crane; I owe it to him," Narcissa had said to her mother before they started on their homeward journey. "The other folks sha'n't know. They can guess and surmise all they want to, but they sha'n't know. I sha'n't tell; and William, he's as close-mouthed as a rock; and as for you, mother, you always did know enough to hold your tongue when you made up your mind to it."

Mrs. Stone had compressed her mouth until it looked like her daughter's. She nodded. "Yes," said she; "I know some things that I 'ain't never told you, Narcissa."

The stage passed William Crane's house. He was shuffling around to the side door from the barn, with a milk-pail in each hand, when they reached it.

"Stop a minute," Narcissa said to the driver. She beckoned to William, who stared, standing stock-still, holding his pails. Narcissa beckoned

again imperatively. Then William set the pails down on the snowy ground
and came to the fence. He looked over it, quite pale, and gaping.

"We've got home," said Narcissa.

William nodded; he could not speak.

"Come over by-and-by," said Narcissa.

William nodded.

"I'm ready to go now," Narcissa said to the stage-driver. "That's all."

That evening, when William Crane reached his sweetheart's house, a
bright light shone on the road from the parlor windows. Narcissa opened
the door. He stared at her open-mouthed. She wore a gown the like of
which he had never seen before—soft lengths of blue silk and lace trailed
about her, blue ribbons fluttered.

"How do you do?" said she.

William nodded solemnly.

"Come in."

William followed her into the parlor, with a wary eye upon his feet, lest
they trample her trailing draperies. Narcissa settled gracefully into the
rocking-chair; William sat opposite and looked at her. Narcissa was a little
pale, still her face wore that look of insistent triumph.

"Home quicker 'n you expected," William said, at length.

"Yes," said Narcissa. There was a wonderful twist on her red hair, and
she wore a high shell comb. William's dazzled eyes noted something spar-
kling in the laces at her throat; she moved her hand, and something on that
flashed like a point of white flame. William remembered vaguely how, often in the summer-time when he had opened his house-door in the sunny
morning, the dewdrops on the grass had flashed in his eyes. He had never
seen diamonds.

"What started you home so much sooner than you expected?" he asked,
after a little.

"I spent—all the money—"

"All—that money?"

"Yes."

"Fifteen hundred dollars in less 'n a week?"

"I spent more 'n that."

"More 'n that?" William could scarcely bring out the words. He was
very white.

"Yes," said Narcissa. She was paler than when he had entered, but she
spoke quite decidedly. "I'm going to tell you all about it, William. I ain't

going to make a long story of it. If after you've heard it you think you'd rather not marry me, I sha'n't blame you. I sha'n't have anything to say against it. I'm going to tell you just what I've been doing; then you can make up your mind.

"To-day's Tuesday, and we went away last Thursday. We've been gone just six days. Mother an' me got to New York Thursday night, an' when we got out of the cars the men come round hollering this hotel an' that hotel. I picked out a man that looked as if he didn't drink and would drive straight, an' he took us to an elegant carriage, an' mother an' me got in. Then we waited till he got the trunk an' put it up on the seat with him where he drove. Mother she hollered to him not to let it fall off.

"We went to a beautiful hotel. There was a parlor with a red velvet carpet and red stuffed furniture, and a green sitting-room, and a blue one. The ceilin' had pictures on it. There was a handsome young gentleman downstairs at a counter in the room where we went first, and mother asked him, before I could stop her, if the folks in the hotel was all honest. She'd been worrying all the way for fear somebody 'd steal the money.

"The gentleman said—he was real polite—if we had any money or valuables, we had better leave them with him, and he would put them in the safe. So we did. Then a young man with brass buttons on his coat took us to the elevator and showed us our rooms. We had a parlor with a velvet carpet an' stuffed furniture and a gilt clock on the mantel-shelf, two bedrooms, and a bath-room. There ain't anything in town equal to it. Lawyer Maxham ain't got anything to come up to it. The young man offered to untie the rope on the trunk, so I let him. He seemed real kind about it.

"Soon 's the young man went I says to mother, 'We ain't going down to get any tea to-night.'

"'Why not?' says she.

"'I ain't going down a step in this old dress,' says I, 'an' you ain't going in yours.'

"Mother didn't like it very well. She said she was faint to her stomach, and wanted some tea, but I made her eat some gingerbread we'd brought from home, an' get along. The young man with the brass buttons come again after a while an' asked if there was anything we wanted, but I thanked him an' told him there wasn't.

"I would have asked him to bring up mother some tea and a hot biscuit, but I didn't know but what it would put 'em out; it was after seven o'clock then. So we got along till morning.

"The next morning mother an' me went out real early, an' went into a bakery an' bought some cookies. We ate 'em as we went down the street, just to stay our stomachs; then we went to buying. I'd taken some of the money in my purse, an' I got mother an' me, first of all, two handsome black silk dresses, and we put 'em on as soon as we got back to the hotel, and went down to breakfast.

"You never see anythin' like the dining-room, and the kinds of things to eat. We couldn't begin to eat 'em all. There were men standin' behind our chairs to wait on us all the time.

"Right after breakfast mother an' me put our rooms to rights; then we went out again and bought things at the stores. Everybody was buying Christmas presents, an' the stores were all trimmed with evergreen—you never see anything like it. Mother an' me never had any Christmas presents, an' I told her we'd begin, an' buy 'em for each other. When the money I'd taken with us was gone, I sent things to the hotel for the gentleman at the counter to pay, the way he'd told me to. That day we bought our breast-pins and this ring, an' mother's and my gold watch, an'—I got one for you too, William. Don't you say anything—it's your Christmas present. That afternoon we went to Central Park, an' that evenin' we went to the theatre. The next day we went to the stores again, an' I bought mother a black satin dress, and me a green one. I got this I've got on, too. It's what they call a tea-gown. I always wore it to tea in the hotel after I got it. I got a hat, too, an' mother a bonnet; an' I got a fur cape, and mother a cloak with fur on the neck an' all around it. That evening mother an' me went to the opera; we sat in something they call a box. I wore my new green silk and breastpin, an' mother wore her black satin. We both of us took our bonnets off. The music was splendid; but I wouldn't have young folks go to it much.

"The next day was Sunday. Mother an' me went to meeting in a splendid church, and wore our new black silks. They gave us seats way up in front, an' there was a real good sermon, though mother thought it wa'n't very practical, an' folks got up an' sat down more'n we do. Mother an' me set still, for fear we'd get up an' down in the wrong place. That evening we went to a sacred concert. Everywhere we went we rode in a carriage. They invited us to at the hotel, an' I s'posed it was free, but it wa'n't, I found out afterwards.

"The next day was Monday—that's yesterday. Mother an' me went out to the stores again. I bought a silk bed-quilt, an' some handsome vases, an' some green an' gilt teacups setting in a tray to match. I've got 'em home without breaking. We got some silk stockings, too, an' some shoes, an' some gold-bowed spectacles for mother, an' two more silk dresses, an' mother a real cashmere shawl. Then we went to see some wax-works, and the pictures and curiosities in the Art Museum; then in the afternoon we went to ride again, and we were goin' to the theatre in the evening; but the gentleman at the counter called out to me when I was going past an' said he wanted to speak to me a minute.

"Then I found out we'd spent all that fifteen hundred dollars, an' more too. We owed 'em 'most ten dollars at the hotel; an' that wa'n't the worst of it—we didn't have enough money to take us home.

"Mother she broke right down an' cried, an' said it was all we had in the world besides the farm, an' it was poor father's insurance money, an' we couldn't get home, an' we'd have to go to prison.

"Folks come crowding around, an' I couldn't stop her. I don't know what I did do myself; I felt kind of dizzy, an' things looked dark. A lady come an' held a smelling-bottle to my nose, an' the gentleman at the counter sent a man with brass buttons for some wine.

"After I felt better an' could talk steady they questioned me up pretty sharp, an' I told 'em the whole story—about father an' his rheumatism, an' everything, just how I was situated, an' I must say they treated us like Christian folks, though, after all, I don't know as we were much beholden to 'em. We never begun to eat all there was on the list, an' we were real careful of the furniture; we didn't really get our money's worth after all was said. But they said the rest of our bill to them was no matter, an' they gave us our tickets to come home."

There was a pause. William looked at Narcissa in her blue gown as if she were a riddle whose answer was lost in his memory. His honest eyes were fairly pitiful from excess of questioning.

"Well," said Narcissa, "I've come back, an' I've spent all that money. I've been wasteful an' extravagant an'— There was a gentleman beautifully dressed who sat at our table, an' he talked real pleasant about the weather, an'—I got to thinking about him a little. Of course I didn't like him as well as you, William, for what comes first comes last with all our folks, but somehow he seemed to be kind of a part of the good time. I sha'n't never see him again, an' all there was betwixt us was his saying twice it was a pleasant day, an' once it was cold, an' me saying yes; but I'm going to tell you the whole. I've been an' wasted fifteen hundred dollars; I've let my thoughts wander from you; an' that ain't all. I've had a good time, an' I can't say I 'ain't. I've had one good time, an'—I ain't sorry. You can—do just what you think best, William, an'—I won't blame you."

William Crane went over to the window. When he turned round and looked at Narcissa his eyes were full of tears and his wide mouth was trembling. "Do you think you can be contented to—stay on my side of the wall now, Narcissa?" he said, with a sweet and pathetic dignity.

Narcissa in her blue robes went over to him, and put, for the first time of her own accord, an arm around his faithful neck. "I wouldn't go out again if the bars were down," said she.

The Parrot

1900

The parrot was a superb bird—a vociferous symmetry of green and gold and ruby red, with eyes like jewels, with their identical irresponsibility of fire, with a cling, not of loving dependence, but of ruthless insistence, to his mistress's hand, or the wires of his cage, and a beak of such a fine curve of cruelty as was never excelled.

The parrot's mistress was a New England woman, with the influence of a stern training strong upon her, and yet with a rampant force of individuality constantly at war with it. She lived alone, except for the parrot, in a sharply angled village house, looking upon the world with a clean, repellent glare of windows and white broadside of wall, in a yard whose grass seemed as if combed always by one wind, so evenly slanted was it. There was a decorously trimmed rose-bush on either side of the front door, and one elm-tree at the gate which leaned decidedly to the south with all its green sweep of branches, and always in consequence gave the woman a vague and unreasoning sense of immorality.

Inside, the house showed stiff parallelograms of white curtains, and dull carpets threadbare with cleanliness, and little pools of reflected light from the polished surfaces of old tables and desks, and one glass-doored bookcase filled with works on divinity bound uniformly in rusty black.

The woman's father had been a Congregational clergyman, and this was his old library. She had read every book over and over with a painful concentration, and afterwards admitted her crime of light-mindedness, and prayed to be forgiven, and have her soul so wrought upon by grace that she might truthfully enjoy these godly publications. She had never read a novel; she looked upon cards as wiles of the devil; once, and once only, had she been to a concert of strictly secular music in the town-hall, and had felt thereby contaminated for days, having a temperament which was strangely wrought upon by music, and yet a total ignorance of it. She felt guilty under the influence of all harmonies which did not, through being linked to spiritual words, turn her soul to thoughts of heaven; and yet sometimes, to her sore bewilderment, the tunes which she heard in church did not so sway her wayward fancy; and then she accused herself of being perverted in her comprehension of good through the influence of that worldly concert.

This woman went nowhere except to church, to prayer-meeting, to the village store, and once a month to the missionary sewing-circle, and to the supper and sociable in the evening. She dressed always in black, her face was delicately spare, her lips were a compressed line of red, and yet she was pretty, with a prettiness almost of youth, from that undiminished fire of the spirit which dwelt within her, as securely caged by her training and narrowness of life as was the parrot by the strong wires of his house.

The parrot was the one bright thing in the woman's life; he was the link with that which was outside her, and yet with that which was of her truest inwardness of self. This tropical thing, screaming and laughing, and shrieking out dissonant words, and oftentimes speeches, with a seemingly diabolical comprehension of the situation, was the one note of utter freedom and irresponsibility in her life. She adored him, but always with a sense of guilt upon her. Often she said to herself that some judgment would come upon her for so loving such a bird, for there was in truth about him as much utter gracelessness as can be conceived of in one of the lower creation. He swore such oaths that his mistress would fairly fly out of the door with hands to her ears. Always, when she saw a caller coming, she would remove his cage to a distant room and shut all the doors between. She felt that if any one heard him sending forth those profane shrieks, possibly to his spiritual contamination, she might be driven by her sense of duty to have the bird put to death. She knew, as she believed, that she risked her own soul by listening and yet loving, but that she had no courage to forego.

As for the parrot, he loved his mistress, if he loved anything. He would extend an ingratiating but deceitful claw towards her between his cage wires whenever she approached. If ever she had a torn finger in consequence, she made light of it, like any wound of love. He would take morsels of food from between her thin lips.

When she talked to him with that language of love which every soul knows by instinct, and which is intelligible to all who are not too deadened and deafened with self, he would cock his glittering head and look at her with that inscrutable jewel-eye of his. Then he would thrust out a claw towards her with that insistence which was ruthless, and yet not more ruthless than the insistence of love, and often say something which confounded her with its apparent wisdom of sequence, and then the doubt and the conviction which at once tormented and enraptured her would seize upon her.

She tried to conceal it from herself, she held it as the rankest atheism, she thought vaguely of the idols of wood and stone in the hymn-book, of Baal, and the golden calf, and the witch of Endor, and every forbidden thing which is the antithesis of holiness, and yet she could not be sure that her parrot had not a soul. Sometimes she wondered if she ought to speak of her state of mind to the minister, and ask his advice, but she shrank from doing that, both because of her natural reserve and because he was unmarried, and she knew that people had coupled his name with hers. He was of suitable age, and it was urged that a match for him with the solitary daughter of the former minister would be eminently appropriate.

The woman had never considered the possibility of such a thing, although she had heard of the plan of the parish from many a female friend. She had had her stifled dreams in her early youth, but she had not been one to attract lovers, being perchance bound as to her true graces somewhat too much after the fashion of her father's old divinity books. No man in her whole life had ever looked at her with a look of love, and she had never heard the involuntary break of it in his voice. Sometimes on summer evenings, she, sitting by her open window, saw village lovers going past with covert arms of affection around slim, girlish waists. One night she saw, half shrinking from the sight, a fond pair standing in the shadow of the elm-tree at her gate, and clasped in each other's arms, and saw the girl's face raised to the young man's for his eager kisses, the while a murmur of love, like a song in an unknown tongue, came to her ears.

It was a warm night, and the parrot's cage was slung for coolness on a peg over the window, and he shrieked out with his seemingly unholy apprehension of things, "What is that? What is that? Do you know what that is, Martha?" Then ended his query with such a wild clamor of laughter that the lovers at the gate fled, and his mistress, Martha, rose and took the bird in.

She set him on the sitting-room table along with the Bible and the Concordance, and a neat little pile of religious papers, while she lighted a lamp.

Then she looked half affrightedly, half with loving admiration, at the gorgeous thing, swinging himself frantically on the ring in his cage.

Then, swifter than lightning, down on his perch he dropped, cast a knowing eye like a golden spark at the solitary woman, and shrieked out again:

"What was that? What was that, Martha? Martha, Martha, Martha, Martha. Polly don't want a cracker; Polly don't want a cracker; Polly will be damned if she eats a cracker. You don't want a cracker, do you, Martha? Martha, Martha, Martha, want a cracker? What was that, Martha? Martha, want a cracker? Martha will be damned if she eats a cracker. Martha, Martha, Martha!"

Then the bird was off in such another explosion of laughs, thrusting a claw through his wires at his mistress, that the house rang with them. Martha took the extended claw tenderly; she put her pretty, delicate, faded face to that treacherous beak; she murmured fond words. Then ceased suddenly as she heard a step on the walk, and the parrot cried out, with a cry of sharpest and most sardonic exultation:

"He's coming, he's coming, Martha!"

Then, to Martha's utter horror, before she had time to remove the bird, a knock came on her front door, which stood open, and there was the minister.

He had called upon her before, in accordance with his pastoral duty, but seldom, and always with his mother, who kept his house with him. This time he was alone, and there was something new in his manner.

He was a handsome man, no younger than she, but looking younger, with a dash of manner which many considered unministerial. He would not allow Martha to remove the parrot, though she strove tremblingly to do so, and laughed with a loud peal like a boy when the parrot shrieked, to his mistress's sore discomfiture:

"He's come, Martha, damned if he ain't. Martha, Martha, where in hell is that old cracker?"

Martha felt as if her hour of retribution had come, and she was vaguely and guiltily pleased and relieved when the minister not only did not seem shocked with the free speaking of her bird, but was apparently amused.

She watched him touch the parrot caressingly, and heard him talk persuasively, coaxing him to further speech, and for the first time in her life a complete sense of human comradeship came to her.

After a while the parrot resolved himself into a gorgeous plumy ball of slumber on his perch, then his mistress sat an hour in the moonlight with the minister.

She had put out the lamp at his request, timidly, and yet with a conviction that such a course must be strictly proper, since it was proposed by the minister.

The two sat near each other at the open window, and the soft sweetness of the summer night came in, and the influence of the moonlight was over them both. The lovers continued to stroll past the gate, and a rule of sequence holds good in all things. Presently, for the first time in her life, this solitary woman felt a man's hand clasping her own little slender one in her black cashmere lap. The minister made no declaration of love in words, but the tones of his voice were enough.

When he spoke of exchanging with a neighboring clergyman in two weeks, the speech was set to the melody of a love-song, and there was no cheating ears which were attuned to it, no matter if it had been long in coming.

When the minister took his leave, and Martha lighted her lamp again, the parrot stirred and woke, and brought that round golden eye of his to bear upon her face flushed like a girl's, and cried out:

"Why, Martha! why, Martha! what is the matter?"

Then Martha dropped on her knees beside the cage, and touched the bird's head with a finger of tenderest caressing.

"Oh, you darling, you darling, you precious!" she murmured, and began to weep. And the parrot did not laugh, but continued to eye her.

"He has come, hasn't he, Martha?" said he.

Then Martha was more than ever inclined to think that the bird had a soul; still she doubted, because of the unorthodoxy of it, and the remembrance of man and man alone being made in God's own image.

Still, through having no friend in whom to confide her new hope and happiness, the parrot became doubly dear to her. Curiously enough, in the succeeding weeks he was not so boisterous, he did not swear so much, but would sit watching his mistress as she sat dreaming, and now and then he said something which seemed inconceivable to her simple mind, unless he had a full understanding of the situation.

The minister came oftener and oftener; he stayed longer. He came home on Sunday nights with her after meeting. He kissed her at the door. He always held her little hand, which yielded to his with an indescribably gentle and innocent maidenliness, while he talked about the mission work in foreign lands, and always his lightest speech was set to that love-melody.

Martha began to expect to marry him. She overlooked her supply of linen. Visions of a new silk for a wedding-dress, brown instead of black, flashed before her eyes. She talked more than usual to the parrot in those days, using the words and tone which she might have used towards the minister, had not the restraints of her New England birth and training enclosed her like the wires of a cage, and the parrot eyed her with wise attentiveness which grew upon him, only now and then uttering one of his favorite oaths.

Then suddenly the disillusion of the poor soul as to her first gospel of love came. She went to the sewing-circle one Wednesday in early spring, after the minister had been to see her for nearly a year, and she wore her best black silk, thinking he would be there, and she had crimped her hair and looked as radiant as a girl when she entered the low vestry filled with the discordant gabble of sewing-women.

Then she heard the news. It was told her with some protest and friendly preparation, for everybody had thought that the match between herself and the minister was as good as made. There was a whispered discussion among groups of women, with sly eyes upon her face; then one, who was a leader among them, a woman of affectionate glibness, approached her, after Martha had heard a feminine voice lingering in the outskirts of a sudden hush say:

"And she's got on her best silk, too, poor thing."

Martha now looked up, and her radiant face paled slowly as the woman began to talk to her. The news seemed to smite her like some hammer of fate, her brain reeled, and her ears rang with it.

The minister was engaged, and had, in fact, gone to be married. He would bring his bride home the next week; another minister was to occupy his pulpit the next Sunday. He was to marry a woman to whom he had been attached for years, but the marriage had been delayed.

Martha listened, then suddenly the color flashed back into her white cheeks—she had stanch blood in her.

"Well, I am glad to hear it," she said, and lied with no compunction for the first time in her life, and never repented it. "I have always thought it was much better for a minister to be married," she said. "I have always thought that his usefulness would be much enhanced. Father used to say so." Then she took out her needle and thread and went to work with the others.

The women eyed her furtively, but she made no sign of noticing it. When one said to her that she had kind of thought that maybe the minister was shining up to her, she only laughed, and said gently that they were very goods friends, but there had never been a word of anything else between them.

She overheard one woman whisper to another that, "if Martha was cut up, she would deceive the very elect," and the other reply, "that maybe he had told Martha all about the woman he was going to marry."

Martha stayed as usual to the supper and the entertainment. A young couple sat on a settee in front of her while some singing was going on, and at a tender passage she saw the boy furtively press the girl's hand, and she set her lips hard.

But at last she was free to go home, and when she had unlocked the door and entered her lonely house, down upon the floor in her sitting-room she flung herself, with all the floodgates of her New England nature open at last. She wept and wailed her grief and anger aloud like a Southern woman.

Then in the midst of it all came a wild wailing cry from the parrot, a cry of uncanny sympathy and pain and tenderness outside the pale of humanity.

"Why, Martha! why, Martha! what's the matter?"

Then the woman rose and went to cage, her delicate face and lips so swollen with grief that she was appalling; she had even trailed her best black silk in the mud on her way home. She was past the bounds of decency in her frenzy of misery. She opened the cage door, and the parrot flew out and to her slender shoulder, and she sobbed out her grief to him amid his protesting cries.

"Poor Martha, why, poor Martha," he said, and she felt almost certain that he had a soul, and she no longer felt so shocked by her leaning towards that belief, but was comforted.

But all of a sudden the parrot on her shoulder gave a tweak at her hair, and shrieked out:

"That was a damned cracker, Martha," and her belief wavered.

She put him back in his cage and locked up her house for the night, and put out her lamp and went to bed, but she could not go to sleep, for the loss of her old dream of love gave the whole world and all life such a hollowness and emptiness that it was like thunder in her ears, and forced its waking realization upon her.

All during the next week, if it had not been for the parrot, she felt that she would have gone mad. She went out in her small daily tracks to the village store, and the prayer-meetings, and on Sunday to church, her agony of concern being that no one should know that she was fretting over the minister's desertion of her.

She talked about the engagement and marriage with her gentle stateliness of manner, which never failed her, but when she got home to her parrot, and the healing solitariness of her own house, she felt like one who had a cooling lotion applied to a burn.

And she wondered more and more if the parrot had not verily a soul, and could not approach her with a sympathy which was better than any human sympathy, since it was so beyond all human laws, but she was not fully convinced of it until the minister brought his new wife to call upon her a few weeks after his marriage.

She had wondered vaguely if he would do it, if he could do it, but he came in with all his dashing grace of manner, and his bride was smiling at his side, in her wedding silks, and Martha greeted them with no disturbance of her New England calm and stiffness, but inwardly her very soul stormed and protested; and as they were sitting in the parlor there came of a sudden from the next room, where he had been at large, the parrot, like a very whirlwind of feathered rage, and, with a wild shriek, he dashed upon the bridal bonnet, plucking furiously at roses and plumes.

Then there was a frightened and flurried exit, with confusion and apologies, and screams of baffled wrath, and rueful smoothing of torn finery.

And after the minister and his bride had gone, Martha looked at her parrot, and his golden eyes met hers, and she recognized in the fierce bird a comradeship and an equality, for he had given vent to an emotion of her own nature, and she knew forevermore that the parrot had a soul.

Arethusa

1900

In whatever month Arethusa, the nymph of Elis, fled from her lover Alpheus, the river god, her namesake the flower, pursued and overtaken by her destiny of life, arrived in May. She paused on the border of the marsh, tremulous in the soft spring wind, clad in her single leaf-gown of green, drooping delicately her lovely head, exhaling her sweet breath deeply, like one who pants after running, until it might well have betrayed her presence. But it is seldom that any man sees the flower arethusa, for she comes rarely to secluded places, and blooms to herself. Of all the spring flowers, arethusa is one of the rarest and the most beautiful of the great wild orchid family to which she belongs; she is the maiden. In that great orchid family are many flowers in semblances of strange and uncanny things, of fiends, and elves, and dragons, and unclassed beings, but arethusa comes in the likeness of a fair and delicate nymph. There is about her no horror of the grotesque and unnatural, only tender, timid bloom, and maybe a gentle dread of love and a repellent curve of her rosy lip.

Every spring when arethusa appeared there came another maiden to visit her in her shy fastness. She belonged to a family living on the country road, a mile across the fields. It was a rough way to travel, but the girl trod it with the zeal of one friend hastening to see another for the first time after a long absence. She was small and spare, with a thin, rosy-cheeked face, and a close-braided cap of silky dark hair. Everything about the girl except her hair seemed fluttering and blowing. She wore ruffled garments of thin fabrics, and she walked swiftly with a curious movement of her delicate shoulder-blades, almost as if they were propelling her like wings. Her eyes had an intent expression of joyful anticipation and unrestrained impulse of motion. She wore gay-colored gowns—blues, and pinks, and greens—and she was exquisitely dainty. She was an only daughter, and her mother's chief delight was to adorn her with fine needle-work. This needle-work seemed the only fully opened gate between the mother and the daughter, for their two natures were so widely at variance that even love could only cramp them painfully together. The mother was a farmer's widow, carrying on a great farm with a staff of hired men and a farmer. She was shrewd and emulative, with a steady eye and ready elbow for her place in the ranks. The only fineness of detail about her was her love for dainty needle-work and her delight in applying it to the decoration of love. Through the long summer afternoons the mother used to sit beside her window, plying her needle on fine cambrics, and linens, and muslins, and felt vaguely that by so doing she kept herself more nearly abreast with the object of her love and adoration. Sometimes she used to sigh in a bewildered fashion when she saw the girl, whose name was Lucy, fluttering away across the field, for she was to her incomprehensibly fond of long solitary walks; then she would turn for a solace to the fine hem of her frock, and so seem to follow at a little distance. As for the girl, when she danced away across the fields, a curious sense of flight from she knew not what was always over her. Her heart beat fast. She half amused, half terrified herself with the sound of imaginary footsteps behind her. When she reached the green marsh, she felt safe, both from real and imaginary pursuers.

Arethusa stood on the border of the marsh, else the girl could not have penetrated to her hiding-place. Once there, she stooped and looked at her. She bent over her and inhaled her fragrant breath, which seemed to her like a kiss of welcome. She never picked the flower. She never quite knew why she did not.

"There is such a beautiful flower in the swamp now," she told her mother.

"Where is it?" asked her mother.

"Oh, in the swamp."

"Didn't you pick it?"

"Oh no."

"Why didn't you?"

"I don't know."

"Well, Edson will go after supper and get it for you; maybe there are more," said her mother.

"Oh no, no!" the girl cried out, in terror, "I wouldn't have it picked for anything, mother. It would die then, and it is such a beautiful flower!"

"You are a queer child," her mother said, adoringly but wonderingly. "Let me try on your new dress now; I can't sew the sleeves in till I do."

When Lucy slipped her thin girlish arms into the ruffled muslin, she cried out with delight. "Why, that is just the color of the flower!" she said.

"You ought to have it to wear with it to the party to-morrow night, then," said her mother.

"Oh, mother, I wouldn't have it picked for anything!" cried Lucy. Lucy did not want to go to the party, though she would not tell her mother so. She was gently acquiescent towards all wishes of others. Indeed, the girl herself seemed but a mild acquiescence towards existence and the general scheme thereof. She had no more vital interest in the ordering of daily village and domestic life than the flower arethusa over in the swamp. With her feet of a necessity in the mould, her head seemed thrust well outside the garden-pale of common life.

She had no real mates among girls of her age. Her mother was anxious that she should have, and had made little parties for her, but from the first, even when she was a child, Lucy had never come out of her corner of gentle aloofness.

When it came to lovers, the girl's beauty and sweetness and prospective property had lured many, but one after another withdrew, strangely discomfited. They might as well have sat on a meadow-stone and wooed a violet as this girl. She was unfailingly sweet, but utterly unresponsive. The village young men began to say that Lucy Greenleaf wasn't as smart as some. They could explain in no other way her lack of comprehension of that untaught but self-evident language of love and passion in which they had addressed her.

However, when Edson Abbot came, he was persistent, both because he was incredulous as to any girl being unlike other girls, and because he always seized with a grip, which made his own fate, upon anything which seemed about to elude him.

"I wish she would fancy you, Edson, but I'm afraid it isn't any use," Mrs. Greenleaf told him.

"A girl's fancy depends mostly upon a man's," he replied, "and I can hold my fancy to the wheel longer than some men. I shouldn't have given up like Willy Slosum."

"It isn't so much because she won't as because she neither won't nor will," said her mother, with a sigh of bewilderment. This woman, who had been insensibly trained by all her circumstances of life to regard a husband like rain in its season, or war, or a full harvest, or an epidemic, something to be accepted without question if offered, whether good or bad, as sent by the will of the Lord, and who had herself promptly accepted a man with whom she was not in love, without the least hesitation, and lived as happily as it was in her nature to live ever after, could not possibly comprehend the nature of her own daughter.

She was, moreover, with that passionate protectiveness which was the strongest feature of her mother-love, anxious to see this little ewe lamb of hers well settled in life with some one to shield her from its storms before she herself was taken from her. Edson Abbot, the young man who took charge of the farm and lived with them, entirely filled her ideal of what Lucy's husband should be. He was handsome, with a strong masculine description of good looks which appealed to her powerfully. He came of a fine family, but treated the tillage of the earth from a scientific stand-point. He had books and papers about, which were as Greek to Mrs. Greenleaf, but which impressed her still more with his unusual ability to take care of her darling.

"I don't want to hurry you, Lucy," she said to her daughter one day. "I know you ain't very strong, but Edson is one man in a thousand, and it doesn't seem right for you to let him slip through your fingers, just for want of a kind word. You don't pay any more attention to him than you do to that strange bush at the gate."

Lucy looked at her mother, then at the syringa-bush standing, all clothed in white like a bride, at the gate.

"What do you want me to do, mother?" she asked.

"Do, child? Why, treat Edson Abbot the way any other girl in this town would treat him, and give all her old shoes for the chance."

The soft red mounted slowly over the girl's face, as she still looked at her mother.

"Do you mean for me to kiss him?" whispered she. "I don't feel as if I could."

A swift blush came over the older woman's face. She laughed, half in embarrassment, half in dismay. "I never saw such a baby in my life as you be," said she; "will you never be anything but a baby, Lucy? It scares me to think of leavin' you some day, if you ain't different. *You* ain't fit to take care of yourself, and Edson is a good man, and he thinks a heap of you, and mother wants to make sure you're taken care of—that's all. Don't you feel as if you might be willing to marry Edson some time if he asked you, Lucy?"

The girl shook and trembled, and eyed her mother with a strange intentness as of fascinated fear. "Oh, mother, I don't want to," she said. "I don't want to marry anybody. I don't like men. I am afraid of them. I want to stay with you."

"You can stay with me. You can go right on living with me, dear child. You shall never leave mother as long as she lives, and she will never leave you."

"I want to just live with you," said Lucy; "I don't like men."

"Girls are apt to feel that way," said her mother, "but you'd come to feel different after a while. It's the way people were meant to do; to be married and given in marriage. You know what it says in the Bible. And then you would be sure to have somebody to take care of you as long as you live."

"Wouldn't I have God?" asked Lucy, with an indescribably innocent rounding of her soft eyes at her mother.

"God sends people to take care of folks," replied her mother, judicially. "He can't come down to earth and see to it that your fires are kindled, and your paths shovelled out, and your wood chopped, and all the heavy things of life lifted off your shoulders. Think of the way Susan Dagget lives."

Lucy was unconvinced and unmoved by all this reasoning. She was much more convinced by the steady broadside of a strong masculine will brought skilfully to bear upon her at all times and seasons. Edson Abbot was a most able young man, of great strength of character, and even some talent. He was something of a diplomat in his wooing. He never frightened this fine, timid creature, who never looked at him without the impulse of flight in her eyes, like a rabbit or a bird. He was exceedingly gentle, but she was made to feel always his firm, unrelaxing will towards her, and his demand for her obedience. Whenever he saw that his presence was awakening beyond control the wild impulses which always underlie timidity, he pressed her no further; he withdrew, but when she needed him he was always there.

Insensibly, she began to depend upon him for services which had always come from her mother. Then he had a ready skill to invent some of his own. It was Edson who conceived the idea of a wild garden for her in a corner of the field, who had a miniature pond of lilies made for her for a birthday surprise. Lucy acquired the habit of looking at him as she had always looked at her mother for confirmation and encouragement. He humored her in all her little idiosyncrasies. When her mother feared to have her take a long, solitary ramble, since a tramp had been seen in the neighborhood, he took her part and bade her go, and himself followed, unseen, at a distance to protect her. She came gradually to think of him as always on her side, even against her own mother. When one day he again asked her to marry him, though she still looked at him with flight in her eyes, she listened. He pleaded well, for, although he wondered at himself, he loved this slight, frail girl, who, in comparison with others of her age and time, seemed either to have scarcely arrived upon the same level or to have passed it.

Edson got no answer to his suit that night, but the next, coming home from the village, he saw a white flutter at the gate, and Lucy came slowly down the road to meet him. It was the first time such a thing had happened. It was full moonlight, and he could see her face quite plainly when she reached him and paused. It expressed the utmost gentleness and docile assent; only her body, which still shrank away from him, and her little hands, which she kept behind her like a child who will not yield up some sweet, betrayed anything of her old alarm. "I will," she said, tremulously; "I will, Edson. Mother says I ought to, and I will."

It was not a very flattering acceptance of a lover's suit, but if the grasp of possession be strong enough it precludes the realization of any lack of pressure on the other hand. Edson found no fault with it. His heart seemed fairly to leap forward and encompass the girl, but he no more dared touch her than he would have touched a butterfly which had settled upon his hand. He could always keep a straight course on the road to his own desires. "You shall never regret it, darling," he said, and so controlled his voice, even then, that only a look of startled wonder came into the girl's eyes. Then she walked home with him contentedly enough, fluttering along at his side. There was undoubtedly something about the love and tenderness of this handsome, strong fellow which pleased her after a fashion. She had something in common with others of her sex. She might be cold, if such a negative state could be called cold, but she loved, or she had not dwelt on the earth at all. It was only when he pursued her too ardently that she rebelled.

Edson and Lucy went in to the girl's mother, who began to cry when she saw them coming. "Oh, you dear child; mother is so glad," she said, and held Lucy closely and kissed her.

After Mrs. Greenleaf had gone to bed, the young man and the girl sat side by side on the door-step in the moonlight. Her little hands were folded in her lap. He looked longingly at them.

Suddenly Lucy spoke, fixing her child-like eyes fully upon his face.

"I found that beautiful flower, for the first time this year, to-day in the swamp," said she.

"What flower, sweet?" Edson asked, and took advantage of the unwariness of her thoughts to lay his hand over hers, which fluttered a little.

"Ought I to let you hold my hand because you are going to marry me?" said she.

"Of course. Go on. What was the flower, darling?"

"That beautiful flower that comes every spring, you know."

"Did you bring it home?"

"Bring it home! No, I wouldn't pick it for anything in the world."

"I'll get you some to-morrow; I guess I know the flower you mean. The swamp is too wet for you to go far. I will find a whole bouquet of those flowers for you."

Lucy pulled her hand away fiercely.

"If—if you do that, if you pick that flower, I—I will never marry you, Edson Abbot."

The young man laughed, though a little uneasily. For the first time a doubt as to the actual normal mental state of the girl came into his mind, then he dismissed it. She was simply, as he had told himself a hundred times, poetical and ultra-imaginative, a fine elusive moonlight sort of nature, grafted into the shrewd, practical New England stock. She was like a maiden out of a midsummer-night dream, but she was only the more precious for that. "Darling," he said, "I would no more pick that flower, if you did not want me to do so, than I would hurt you."

The marriage was fixed for a year later. Mrs. Greenleaf herself pleaded for time. "She is young, and not strong, Edson," she said. "I think she ought to have time to get used to the idea. Then, too, I want to make her outfit."

Edson yielded easily enough. He himself had doubts as to the wisdom of swift proceeding with Lucy. Then, too, he was ambitious. He was putting in some hot-houses, and he wished to be sure of a larger income before settling himself in matrimony. He had put in some money, and was to work the farm on shares. Mrs. Greenleaf grew prouder than ever of her prospective son-in-law. She was thoroughly happy. She stitched away on Lucy's dainty garments, and every stitch seemed one towards the completion of her own wedding attire. She had never been in love herself, and now that came to her for the first time, through her loving imagination over her daughter. Edson Abbot was the sort of man whom she might herself have loved, and she, being so bound up in unselfish love for the girl, could in a measure grasp all her happiness, and so, in a sense, she grasped her lover.

As for Lucy, she did not seem unhappy. She was peaceful and docile. She sewed a little on her wedding clothes, she went walking and driving with Edson, she sat with him sometimes a little while after her mother had gone to bed; she always smiled readily at him with her sweet, evasive sort of smile. She acquiesced, with the greatest docility, in her mother's suggestion that she should learn something more of house-wifery than she had hitherto known. She spent hours cooking and setting the house in order. She had not done much of that, being delicate, and always shielded by her strong mother; and that had been one of the grounds of complaint against her in the neighborhood. Now, however, she surprised everybody. "She's taken hold as well as anybody I ever see," reported the extra help whom Mrs. Greenleaf had hired Thanksgiving week. "She's real smart. She made as good a plum-puddin' as I ever eat."

Indeed, there seemed to come to the girl an awakening either of latent cleverness or inherited instincts. She seemed to take a certain pleasure in her new tasks, and she thrived under them. She grew stouter; her cheeks had a more fixed color. Abbot was triumphant. He realized less and less than anything was wanting to the sum of his happiness. Such was the force of his own will that, once on the turn towards possession, he comprehended no other counter-current. The wedding-day was fixed in the month of May. The ceremony was to take place at eight o'clock in the evening. When that hour came all the guests were assembled, the bridegroom, bridesmaids, and minister were waiting, but the bride had disappeared. Her wedding-gown lay on her bed with her veil; her little white shoes stood prettily toed out side by side, but the bride was gone. Her mother and Edson conferred in Lucy's chamber.

"They mustn't know it, if we can find her without it," said Mrs. Greenleaf. Her face was white and set; she jerked her black-silk elbow towards the floor, indicating the company assembled below. Edson looked palely at her. "Where do you think she is?" he said.

"I don't know. I've looked everywhere. She ain't in the house."

For once Edson Abbot seemed dazed. He stared at Mrs. Greenleaf. "You don't think—" he began.

"I don't know but we've made a mistake," said the woman, brokenly. "I don't know as Lucy ought to have had anybody but her mother."

Then the young man made an impatient exclamation. "It is too late to talk about that now," he said. "I'm going to find her."

He strode out of the chamber and down the back stairs, lest the company see him. The sound of their voices floated after him as he slipped out of the house. He did not know where to begin his search, but some instinct took him into the field behind the house. He hastened across it, a handsome, stalwart figure in his wedding-suit. His face was pale, his brows bent; he felt as if he had met a wall of gossamer with a shock of alabaster. The utter docility and gentleness of the girl made this frightful. He felt no alarm for her safety. He seemed to understand that she had set herself against him in a last assertion of her maiden freedom.

The sun was low in an ineffable rosy sky, with dregs of violet at the horizon line. One great star was burning through the paling radiance. A fragrant, damp coolness was rising from the earth; a silvery film of dew was over all the grass. He heard in the distance the sound of a cow-bell and a boy whistling. All these familiar sights and sounds served to enrage this man whose feet were set so firmly in the regular tracks of life still further with this savor of the irregular and the unusual which had come to him. He felt for the first time a fierce impulse to bend forcibly this other will which had come into contact with his own. He thought, with a sort of fury, of all those waiting people. Then he saw coming towards him across the field, with her singular half-flying motion of the shoulders and arms, the girl whom he was seeking.

He strode forward rapidly to meet her, and grasped her roughly by her slender arm. "Lucy, what does this mean?" he asked, frowning down at her sternly.

She looked at him with such terror that it intimidated him more than any defiance could have done. He weakened, for, after all, he loved her.

"Lucy," he said, gently, "you should not have gone off like this. Don't you know what time it is?"

"Is it eight yet?" she gasped.

"Of course it is, and after."

"I thought I had time," she faltered.

"Time for what?"

"To see if that flower had come. I thought if it had, it would be gone before we get back. I thought I had time, Edson."

"You ought to have picked that flower just this once to wear to your wedding, you think so much of it," said Mrs. Greenleaf.

"Oh, mother!" said Lucy.

"You are a queer child," her mother said, laughing in an odd, embarrassed fashion. Along with her great tenderness towards this little ewe lamb of hers, she felt that night a singular awe and shame and wonder, almost as if she herself stood in her place.

When Lucy, in her bridal array, went downstairs, people drew long breaths.

"She looks like an angel," one woman whispered, so loud that many heard her. There was, in fact, that about the girl's beauty, as she floated among them in her bridal white, which made her seem more than human. She apparently did not realize that the eyes of all the company were upon her. She stood beside her bridegroom before the minister as unconscious as arethusa over yonder in the swamp. A color as purely fine as the flower's was in her cheeks; in her eyes were as mysterious depths of sweetness.

"She looked as handsome as a picture," the neighbors said, going home when the wedding was over and the bridal pair had departed. "But she don't look quite right, somehow. Wonder what made her so late?" They further mentioned this and that girl who, in their estimation, would have made a more reliable helpmeet than Lucy Greenleaf.

However, Lucy seemed, as time went on, to prove them mistaken. She filled her place as wife and mother well to all appearances. There were two handsome children, with Edson's sturdy beauty. They bore not the slightest resemblance to their mother. "They are all Edson's," Mrs. Greenleaf used to say. Lucy loved them, and they loved her, yet they went from the first more naturally to their father and grandmother.

"They act more like your children than your daughter's," the neighbors said. "Lucy takes good care of them," her mother returned, jealously. That was quite true. Lucy neglected nothing and nobody. She performed all her duties with a fine precision. She seemed happy, yet always she had that look of her youth, the look of one who, with her feet on the common earth, can see past common horizons. And every spring she went by herself, when she could, stealing away unnoticed, to see that great orchid in bloom in the swamp for the first time that year. She never allowed her children to follow her; if the little things tried to do so, she sent them back. Her husband also forbade them, indulging, as he had always done, his wife in what he considered a harmless idiosyncrasy, not dreaming that it had its root in the very depths of her nature, and that she perhaps sought this fair neutral ground of the flower kingdom as a refuge from the exigency of life. In his full tide of triumphant possession he was as far from the realization of the truth as was Alpheus, the fabled river god, after he had overtaken the nymph Arethusa, whom, changed into a fountain to elude his pursuit, he had followed under the sea, and never knew that, while forever his, even in his embrace, she was forever her own.

Every spring this woman, growing old as to her fair, faded face, went to see arethusa, coming upon her standing on the border of the marsh, clad in her green leaf, drooping delicately her beautiful purplish-pink head, with the same rapture as of old. This soul, bound fast to life with fleshly bonds, yet forever maiden, anomalous and rare among her kind, greeted the rare and anomalous flower with unending comfort and delight. It was to her as if she had come upon a fair rhyme to her little halting verse of life.

The Balsam Fir

1901

Martha Elder had lived alone for years on Amesboro road, a mile from the nearest neighbor, three miles from the village. She lived in the low cottage which her grandfather had built. It was painted white, and there was a green trellis over the front door shaded by a beautiful rose-vine. Martha had very little money, but somehow she always managed to keep her house in good order, though she had never had any blinds. It had always been the dream of Martha's life to have blinds; her mild blue eyes were very sensitive to the glare of strong sunlight, and the house faced west. Sometimes of a summer afternoon Martha waxed fairly rebellious because of her lack of green blinds to soften the ardent glare. She had green curtains, but they flapped in the wind and made her nervous, and she could not have them drawn.

Blinds were not the only things which aroused in Martha Elder a no less strong, though unexpressed, spirit of rebellion against the smallness of her dole of the good things of life. Nobody had ever heard this tall, fair, gentle woman utter one word of complaint. She spoke and moved with mild grace. The sweetest acquiescence seemed evident in her every attitude of body and tone of voice. People said that Martha Elder was an old maid, that she was all alone in the world, that she had a hard time to get along and keep out of the poor-house, but that she was perfectly contented and happy. But people did not know; she had her closets of passionate solitude to which they did not penetrate. When her sister Adeline, ten years after her father's death, had married the man who everybody had thought would marry Martha, she had made a pretty wedding for her, and people had said Martha did not care, after all; that she was cut out for an old maid; that she did not want to marry. Nobody knew, not her sister, not even the man himself, who had really given her reason to blame him, how she felt. She was encased in an armor of womanly pride as impenetrable as a coat of mail; it was proof against everything except the arrows of agony of her own secret longings.

Martha had been a very pretty girl, much prettier than her younger sister Adeline; it was strange that she had not been preferred; it was strange that she had not had suitors in plenty; but there may have been something about the very fineness of her femininity and its perfection which made it repellent. Adeline, with her coarse bloom and loud laugh and ready stare, had always had admirers by the score, while Martha, who was really exquisite, used to go to bed and lie awake listening to the murmur of voices under the green trellis of the front door, until the man who married her sister came. Then for a brief space his affections did verge towards Martha; he said various things to her in a voice whose cadences ever after made her music of life; he looked at her with an expression which became photographed, as by some law of love instead of light, on her heart. Then Adeline, exuberant with passion, incredulous that he could turn to her sister instead of herself, won him away by her strong pull upon the earthy part of him. Martha had not dreamed of contesting the matter, of making a fight for the man whom she loved. She yielded at once with her pride so exquisite that it seemed like meekness.

When Adeline went away, she settled down at once into her solitary old-maiden estate, although she was still comparatively young. She had her little ancestral house, her small vegetable garden, a tiny wood-lot from which she hired enough wood cut to supply her needs, and a very small sum of money in the bank, enough to pay her taxes and insurance, and not much besides. She had a few hens, and lived mostly on eggs and vegetables; as for her clothes, she never wore them out; she moved about softly and carefully, and never frayed the hems of her gowns, nor rubbed her elbows; and as for soil, no mortal had ever seen a speck of grime upon Martha Elder or her raiment. She seemed to pick her spotless way through life like a white dove. There was a story that Martha once wore a white dress all one summer, keeping it immaculate without washing, and it seemed quite possible. When she walked abroad she held her dress skirt at an unvarying height of modest neatness revealing snowy starched petticoats and delicate ankles in white stockings. She might have been painted as a type of elderly maiden peace and pure serenity by an artist who could see only externals. But it was very different with her from what people thought. Nobody dreamed of the fierce tension of her nerves as she sat at her window sewing through the long summer afternoons, drawing her monotonous thread in and out of dainty seams; nobody dreamed what revolt that little cottage roof, when it was covered with wintry storms, sometimes sheltered. When Martha's sister came home with her husband and beautiful first baby to visit her, her smiling calm of welcome was inimitable.

"Martha never did say much," Adeline told her husband, when they were in their room at night. "She didn't exclaim even over the baby." As she spoke she looked gloatingly at his rosy curves as he lay asleep. "Martha's an old maid if there ever was one," she added.

"It's queer, for she's pretty," said her husband.

"I don't call her pretty," said Adeline; "not a mite of color." She glanced at her high bloom and tossing black mane of hair in the mirror.

"Yes, that's so," agreed Adeline's husband. Still, sometimes he used to look at Martha with the old expression, unconsciously, even before his wife, but Martha never recognized it for the same. When he had married her sister he had established between himself and her such a veil of principle that her eyes never after could catch the true meaning of him. Yet nobody knew how glad she was when this little family outside her pale of life had gone, and she could settle back unmolested into her own tracks, which were apparently those of peace, but in reality those of a caged panther. There was a strip of carpet worn threadbare in the sitting-room by Martha's pacing up and down. At last she had to take out that breadth and place it next the wall, and replace it.

People wondered why, with all Martha's sweetness and serenity, she had not professed religion and united with the church. When the minister came to talk with her about it he was nonplussed. She said, with an innocent readiness which abashed him, that she believed in the Christian religion, and trusted that she loved God; then it was as if she folded wings of concealment over her maiden character, and he could see no more.

It was at last another woman to whom she unbosomed herself, and she was a safe confidante; no safer could have been chosen. She was a far-removed cousin, and stone-deaf from scarlet fever when she was a baby. She was a woman older than Martha, and had come to make her a visit. She lived with a married sister, to whom she was a burden, and who was glad to be rid of her for a few weeks. She could not hear one word that was spoken to her; she could only distinguish language uncertainly from the motion of the lips. She was absolutely penniless, except for a little which she earned by knitting cotton lace. To this woman Martha laid bare her soul the day before Christmas, as the two sat by the western windows, one knitting, the other darning a pair of white stockings.

"To-morrow's Christmas," said the deaf woman, suddenly, in her strange, unmodulated voice. She had a flat, pale face, with smooth loops of blond hair around the temples.

Martha said, "It ain't much Christmas to me."

"What?" returned the deaf woman.

"It ain't much Christmas to me," repeated Martha. She did not raise her voice in the least, and she moved her lips very little. Speech never disturbed the sweet serenity of her mouth. The deaf woman did not catch a word, but she was always sensitive about asking over for the second time. She knitted and acted as if she understood.

"No, it ain't much Christmas to me, and it never has been," said Martha. "I 'ain't never felt as if I had had any Christmas, for my part. I don't know where it has come in if I have. I never had a Christmas present in my whole life, unless I count in that purple crocheted shawl that Adeline gave me, that somebody gave her, and she couldn't wear, because it wasn't becomin'. I never thought much of it myself. Purple never suited me, either. That was the only Christmas present I ever had. That came a week after Christmas, ten year ago, and I suppose I might count that in. I kept it laid away, and the moths got into it."

"What?" said the deaf woman.

"The moths got into it," said Martha.

The deaf woman nodded wisely and knitted.

"Christmas!" said Martha, with a scorn at once pathetic and bitter — "talk about Christmas! What is Christmas to a woman all alone in the world as I am? If you want to see the loneliest thing in all creation, look at a woman all alone in the world. Adeline is twenty-five miles away, and she's got her family. I'm all alone. I might as well be at the north pole. What's Christmas to a woman without children, or any other women to think about, livin' with her? If I had any money to give it might be different. I might find folks to give to — other folks's children; but I 'ain't got any money. I've got nothing. I can't give any Christmas presents myself, and I can't have any. Lord! Talk about Christmas to me! I can't help if I am wicked. I'm sick and tired of livin'. I have been for some time." Just then a farmer's team loaded with evergreens surmounted with merry boys went by, and she pointed tragically; and the deaf woman's eyes followed her pointing finger, and suddenly her great, smiling face changed. "There they go with Christmas-trees for other women," said Martha; "for women who have got what I haven't. I never had a Christmas-tree. I never had a Christmas. The Lord never gave me one. I want one Christmas before I die. I've got a right to it. I want one Christmas-tree and one Christmas." Her voice rose to daring impetus; the deaf woman looked at her curiously.

"What?" said she.

"I want one Christmas," said Martha. Still the deaf woman did not hear, but suddenly the calm of her face broke up; she began to weep. It was as if she understood the other's mood by some subtler faculty than that of hearing. "Christmas is a pretty sad day to me," said she, "ever since poor mother died. I always realize more than any other time how alone I be, and how my room would be better than my company, and I don't ever have any presents. And I can't give any. I give all my knittin' money to Jane for my board, and that ain't near enough. Oh, Lord! it's a hard world!"

"I want one Christmas, and one Christmas-tree," said Martha, in a singular tone, almost as if she were demanding it of some unseen power.

"What?" said the deaf woman.

"I want one Christmas, and one Christmas-tree," repeated Martha.

The deaf woman nodded and knitted, after wiping her eyes. Her face was still quivering with repressed emotion.

Martha rose. "Well, there's no use talkin'," said she, in a hard voice; "folks can take what they get in this world, not what they want, I s'pose." Her face softened a little as she looked at the deaf woman. "I guess I'll make some toast for supper; there's enough milk," said she.

"What?" said the deaf woman.

Martha put her lips close to her ear, and shouted, "I guess I'll make some toast for supper." The deaf woman caught the word toast, and smiled happily, with a sniff of retreating grief; she was very fond of toast. "Jane 'most never has it," said she. As she sat there beside the window, she presently smelled the odor of toast coming in from the kitchen; then it began to snow. The snow fell in great, damp blobs, coating all the trees thickly. When Martha entered the sitting-room to get a dish from the china-closet the deaf woman pointed, and said it was snowing.

"Yes, I see it is," replied Martha. "Well, it can snow, for all me. I 'ain't got any Christmas-tree to go to to-night."

As she spoke, both she and the deaf woman, looking out of the window, noted the splendid fir-balsam opposite, and at the same time a man with an axe, preparing to cut it down.

"Why, that man's goin' to cut down that tree! Ain't it on your land?" cried the deaf woman.

Martha shrieked and ran out of the house, bareheaded in the dense fall of snow. She caught hold of the man's arm, and he turned and looked at her with a sort of stolid surprise fast strengthening into obstinacy. "What you cuttin' down this tree for?" asked Martha.

The man muttered that he had been sent for one for Lawyer Ede.

"Well, you can't have mine," said Martha. "This ain't Lawyer Ede's land. His is on the other side of the fence. There are trees plenty good enough over there. You let mine be."

The man's arm which held the axe twitched. Suddenly Martha snatched it away by such an unexpected motion that he yielded. Then she was mistress of the situation. She stood before the tree, brandishing the axe. "If you dare to come one step nearer my tree, I'll kill you," said she. The man paled. He was a stolid farmer, unused to women like her, or, rather, unused to such developments in women like her. "Give me that axe," he said.

"I'll give you that axe if you promise to cut down one of Lawyer Ede's trees, and let mine be!"

"All right," assented the man, sulkily.

"You go over the wall, then, and I'll hand you the axe."

The man, with a shuffling of reluctant yielding, approached the wall and climbed over. Then Martha yielded up the axe. Then she stationed herself in front of her tree, to make sure that it was not harmed. The snow fell thick and fast on her uncovered head, but she did not mind. She remembered how once the man who had married her sister had said something to her beside this tree, when it was young like herself. She remembered long summer afternoons of her youth looking out upon it. Her old dreams and hopes of youth seemed still abiding beneath it, greeting her like old friends. She felt that she would have been killed herself rather than have the tree harmed. The soothing fragrance of it came in her face. She felt suddenly as if the tree were alive. A great, protecting tenderness for it came over her. She began to hear axe strokes on the other side of the wall. Then the deaf woman came to the door of the house, and stood there staring at her through the damp veil of snow. "You'll get your death out there, Marthy," she called out.

"No, I won't," replied Martha, knowing as she spoke that she was not heard.

"What be you stayin' out there for?" called the deaf woman, in an alarmed voice. Martha made no reply.

Presently the woman came out through the snow; she paused before she reached her; it was quite evident what she feared even before she spoke. "Be you crazy?" asked she.

"I'm going to see to it that John Page don't cut down this tree," replied Martha. "I know how set the Pages are." The deaf woman stared helplessly at her, not hearing a word.

Then John Page came to the wall. "Look at here," he called out. "I ain't goin' to tech your tree. I thought it was on Ede's land. I'm cuttin' down another."

"You mind you don't," responded Martha, and she hardly knew her voice. When John Page went home that night he told his wife that he'd "never known that Martha Elder was such an up and comin' woman. Deliver me from dealin' with old maids," said he; "they're worse than barbed wire."

The snow continued until midnight, then the rain set in, then it cleared and froze. When the sun rose next morning everything was coated with ice. The fir-balsam was transfigured, wonderful. Every little twig glittered as with the glitter of precious stones, the branches spread low in rainbow radiances. Martha and the deaf woman stood at the sitting-room window looking out at it. Martha's face changed as she looked. She put her face close to the other woman's ear and shouted: "Look here, Abby, you ain't any too happy with Jane; you stay here with me this winter. I'm lonesome, and we'll get along somehow." The deaf woman heard her, and a great light came into her flat countenance.

"Stay with you?"

Martha nodded.

"I earn enough to pay for the flour and sugar," said she, eagerly, "and you've got vegetables in the cellar, and I don't want another thing to eat, and I'll do all the work if you'll let me, Marthy."

"I'll be glad to have you stay," said Martha, with the eagerness of one who grasps at a treasure.

"Do you mean you want me to stay?" asked the deaf woman, wistfully, still fearing that she had not heard aright. Martha nodded.

"I'll go out in the kitchen and make some of them biscuit I used to make for breakfast," said the deaf woman. "God bless you, Marthy!"

Martha stood staring at the glorified fir-balsam. All at once it seemed to her that she saw herself, as she was in her youth, under it. Old possessions filled her soul with rapture, and the conviction of her inalienable birthright of the happiness of life was upon her. She also seemed to see all the joys which she had possessed or longed for in the radius of its radiance; its boughs seemed overladen with fulfilment and promise, and a truth came to her for the great Christmas present of her life. She became sure that whatever happiness God gives He never retakes, and, moreover, that He holds ready the food for all longing, that one cannot exist without the other.

"Whatever I've ever had that I loved I've got," said Martha Elder, "and whatever I've wanted I'm goin' to have." Then she turned around and went out in the kitchen to help about breakfast, and the dazzle of the Christmas-tree was so great in her eyes that she was almost blinded to all the sordid conditions of her daily life.

The Great Pine

1902

It was in the summer-time that the great pine sang his loudest song of winter, for always the voice of the tree seemed to arouse in the listener a realization of that which was past and to come, rather than of the present. In the winter the tree seemed to sing of the slumberous peace under his gently fanning boughs, and the deep swell of his aromatic breath in burning noons, and when the summer traveller up the mountain-side threw himself, spent and heated, beneath his shade, then the winter song was at its best. When the wind swelled high came the song of the ice-fields, of the frozen mountain-torrents, of the trees wearing hoary beards and bent double like old men, of the little wild things trembling in their covers when the sharp reports of the frost sounded through the rigid hush of the arctic night and death was abroad. The man who lay beneath the tree had much uncultivated imagination, and, though hampered by exceeding ignorance, he yet saw and heard that which was beyond mere observation. When exhausted by the summer heat, he reflected upon the winter with that keen pleasure which comes from the mental grasp of contrast to discomfort. He did not know that he heard the voice of the tree and not his own thought, so did the personality of the great pine mingle with his own. He was a sailor, and had climbed different heights from mountains, even masts made from the kindred of the tree.

Presently he threw his head back, and stared up and up, and reflected what a fine mast the tree would make, if only it were not soft pine. There was a stir in a branch, and a bird which lived in the tree in summer cast a small, wary glance at him from an eye like a point of bright intelligence, but the man did not see it. He drew a long breath, and looked irresolutely at the upward slope beyond the tree. It was time for him to be up and on if he would cross the mountain before nightfall. He was a wayfarer without resources. He was as poor as the tree, or any of the wild creatures which were in hiding around him on the mountain. He was even poorer, for he had not their feudal tenure of an abiding-place for root and foot on the mountain by the inalienable right of past generations of his race. Even the little, wary-eyed, feathered thing had its small freehold in the branches of the great pine, but the man had nothing. He had returned to primitive conditions; he was portionless save for that with which he came into the world, except for two garments which were nearly past their use as such. His skin showed through the rents; the pockets were empty. Adam expelled from Eden was not in much worse case, and this man also had at his back the flaming sword of punishment for wrong-doing. The man arose. He stood for a moment, letting the cool wind fan his forehead a little longer; then he bent his shoulders doggedly and resumed his climb up the dry bed of a brook which was in winter a fierce conduit for the melting ice and snow. Presently he came to such a choke of fallen trees across the bed that he had to leave it; then there was a sheer rock ascent which he had to skirt and go lower down the mountain to avoid.

The tree was left alone. He stood quiescent with the wind in his green plumes. He belonged to that simplest form of life which cannot project itself beyond its own existence to judge of it. He did not know when presently the man returned and threw himself down with a violent thud against his trunk, though there was a slight shock to his majesty. But the man looked up at the tree and cursed it. He had lost his way through avoiding the rocky precipice, and had circled back to the tree. He remained there a few minutes to gain breath; then he rose, for the western sunlight was filtering in gold drops through the foliage below the pine, and plodded heavily on again.

It might have been twenty minutes before he returned. When he saw the pine he cursed more loudly than before. The sun was quite low. The mountain seemed to be growing in size, the valleys were fast becoming gulfs of black mystery. The man looked at the tree malignantly. He felt in his pocket for a knife which he used to own, then for a match, the accompaniment of the tobacco and pipe which formerly comforted him, but there was none there. The thought of the lost pipe and tobacco filled him with a childish savagery. He felt that he must vent his spite upon something outside himself. He picked up two dry sticks, and began rubbing them together. He had some skill in woodcraft. Presently a spark gleamed; then another. He scraped up a handful of dry leaves. Presently smoke arose pungently in his face, then a flame leaped to life. The man kept on his way, leaving a fire behind him, and swore with an oath that he would not be trapped by the tree again.

He struggled up the old waterway, turning aside for the prostrate skeletons of giant trees, clambering over heaps of stones which might have been the cairns of others, and clawing up precipices like a panther. After one fierce scramble he paused for breath, and, standing on a sheer rock ledge, gazed downward. Below him was a swaying, folding gloom full of vague whispers and rustlings. It seemed to wave and eddy before him like the sea from the deck of a ship, and, indeed, it was another deep, only of air instead of water. Suddenly he realized that there was no light, that the fire which he had kindled must have gone out. He stared into the waving darkness below, and sniffed hard. He could smell smoke faintly, although he could see no fire. Then all at once came a gleam of red, then a leap of orange flame. Then—no human being could have told how it happened, he himself least of all, what swift motive born of deeds and experiences in his own life, born perhaps of deeds and experiences of long-dead ancestors, actuated him. He leaped back down the mountain, stumbling headlong, falling at times, and scrambled to his feet again, sending loose stones down in avalanches, running risks of life and limb, but never faltering until he was beside the pine, standing, singing in the growing glare of the fire. Then he began beating the fire fiercely with sticks, trampling it until he blistered his feet. At last the fire was out. People on a hotel piazza down in the valley, who had been watching it, turned away. "The fire is out," they said, with the regret of those who miss a spectacular delight, although admitting the pity and shame of it, yet coddling with fierce and defiant joy the secret lust of destruction of the whole race. "The fire is out," they said; but more than the fire had burned low, and was out, on the mountain. The man who had evoked destruction to satisfy his own wrath and bitterness of spirit, and then repented, sat for a few minutes outside the blackened circle around the great pine, breathing hard. He drew his rough coat-sleeve across his wet forehead, and stared up at the tree, which loomed above him like a prophet with solemnly waving arms of benediction, prophesying in a great unknown language of his own. He gaped as he stared; his face looked vacant. He felt in his pocket for his departed pipe, then withdrew his hand forcibly, dashing it against the ground. Then he sighed, swore mildly under his breath an oath of weariness and misery rather than of wrath. Then he pulled himself up by successive stages of his stiff muscles, like an old camel, and resumed his journey.

After a while he again paused and looked back. The moon had arisen, and he could see quite plainly the great pine standing crowned with white light, tossing his boughs like spears and lances of silver. "Thunderin' big tree," he muttered, with a certain pride and self-approbation. He felt that that majestic thing owed its being to him, to his forbearance with his own hard fate. Had it not been for that it would have been a mere blackened trunk. At that moment, for the first time in his history, he rose superior to his own life. In some unknown fashion this seemingly trivial happening had, as it were, tuned him to a higher place in the scale of things than he had ever held. He, through saving the tree from himself, gained a greater spiritual growth than the tree had gained in height since it first quickened with life. Who shall determine the limit at which the intimate connection and reciprocal influence of all forms of visible creation upon one another may stop? A man may cut down a tree and plant one. Who knows what effect the tree may have upon the man, to his raising or undoing?

Presently the man frowned and shook his head in a curious fashion, as if he questioned his own identity; then he resumed his climb. After the summit was gained he went down the other side of the mountain, then northward through a narrow gorge of valley to which the moonbeams did not yet penetrate. This valley, between mighty walls of silver-crested darkness, was terrifying. The man felt his own smallness and the largeness of nature which seemed about to fall upon him. Spirit was intimidated by matter. The man, rude and unlettered, brutalized and dulled by his life, yet realized it. He rolled his eyes aloft from side to side, and ran as if pursued.

When he had reached the brow of a little decline in the valley road he paused and searched eagerly with straining eyes the side of the mountain on the right. Then he drew a long breath of relief. He had seen what he wished to see—a feeble glimmer of lamplight from a window of a house, the only one on that lonely road for five miles in either direction. It was the dwelling-house on a small farm which had been owned by the father of the woman whom the man had married fifteen years before. Ten years ago, when he had run away, there had been his wife, his little girl, and his wife's mother living on the farm. The old farmer father had died two years before that, and the man, who had wild blood in his veins, had rebelled at the hard grind necessary to wrest a livelihood by himself from the mountain soil. So one morning he was gone, leaving a note saying that he had gone to sea, and would write and send money, that he could earn more than on a farm. But he never wrote, and he never sent the money. He had met with sin and disaster, and at last he started homeward, shorn, and, if not repentant, weary of wrong-doing and its hard wages. He had retreated from the broad way with an ignoble impulse, desiring the safety of the narrow, and the loaves and fishes, which, after all, can be found in it with greater certainty; but now, as he hastened along, he became conscious of something better than that. One good impulse begat others by some law of spiritual reproduction. He began to think how he would perhaps do more work than he had formerly, and please his wife and her mother.

He looked at the light in the window ahead with something akin to thankfulness. He remembered how very gentle his wife had been, and how fond of him. His wife's mother also had been a mild woman, with reproving eyes only, never with a tongue of reproach. He remembered his little girl with a thrill of tenderness and curiosity. She would be a big girl now; she would be like her mother. He began picturing to himself what they would do and say, what they would give him for supper. He thought he would like a slice of ham cut from one of those cured on the farm, that and some new-laid eggs. He would have some of those biscuits that his wife's mother used to make, and some fresh butter, and honey from the home bees. He would have tea and cream. He seemed to smell the tea and the ham. A hunger which was sorer than any hunger of the flesh came over him. All at once the wanderer starved for home. He had been shipwrecked and at the point of death from hunger, but never was hunger like this. He had planned speeches of contrition; now he planned nothing. He feared no blame from those whom he had wronged; he feared nothing except his own need of them. Faster and faster he went. He seemed to be running a race. At last he was quite close to the house. The light was in a window facing the road, and the curtain was up. He could see a figure steadily passing and repassing it. He went closer, and saw that it was a little girl with a baby in her arms, and she was walking up and down hushing it. A feeble cry smote his ears, though the doors and windows were closed. It was chilly even in midsummer in the mountains. He went around the house to the side door. He noticed that the field on the left was waving with tall, dry grass, which should have been cut long ago; he noticed that there were no beanpoles in the garden. He noticed that the house looked gray and shabby even in the moonlight, that some blinds were gone and a window broken.

He leaned a second against the door. Then he opened it and entered. He came into a little, square entry; on one side was the kitchen door, on the other the room where the light was. He opened the door leading to this room. He stood staring, for nothing which he had anticipated met his eyes, except the little girl. She stood gazing at him, half in alarm, half in surprise, clutching close the baby, which was puny, but evidently about a year old. Two little boys stood near the table on which the lamp was burning, and they stared at him with wide-open mouths and round eyes. But the sight which filled the intruder with the most amazement and dismay was that of a man in the bed in the corner. He recognized him at once as a farmer who had lived, at the time of his departure, five miles away in the village. He remembered that his wife was recently dead when he left. The man, whose blue, ghastly face was sunken in the pillows, looked up at him. He thrust out a cadaverous hand as if to threaten. The little girl with the baby and the two little boys edged nearer the bed, as if for protection.

"Who be you?" inquired the sick man, with feeble menace. "What d' ye want comin' in here this way?" It was like the growl of a sick dog.

The other man went close to the bed.

"Where is my wife?" he asked, in a strange voice. It was expressive of horror and anger and a rage of disappointment.

"You ain't—Dick?" gasped the man in bed.

"Yes, I be; and I know you, Johnny Willet. Where is my wife? What are you here for?"

"Your wife is dead," answered the man, in a choking voice. He began to cough; he half raised himself on one elbow. His eyes bulged. He crowed like a child with the croup. The little girl promptly laid the baby on the bed and ran to a chimney cupboard for a bottle of medicine, which she administered with a spoon. The sick man lay back, gasping for breath. He looked as if already dead; his jaw dropped; there were awful blue hollows in his face.

"Dead!" repeated the visitor, thinking of his wife, and not of the other image of death before him.

"Yes, she's dead."

"Where's my little girl?"

The sick man raised one shaking hand and pointed to the little girl who had taken up the whimpering baby.

"That?"

The sick man nodded.

The other eyed the little girl, rather tall for her age, but very slim, her narrow shoulders already bent with toil. She regarded him, with serious blue eyes in a little face, with an expression of gentleness so pronounced that it gave the impression of a smile. The man's eyes wandered from the girl to the baby in her arms and the two little boys.

"What be you all a-doin' here?" he demanded, gruffly, and made a movement towards the bed. The little girl turned pale, and clutched the baby more closely. The sick man made a feeble sound of protest and deprecation. "What be you all a-doin' here?" demanded the other again.

"I married your wife after we heard your ship was lost. We knew you was aboard her from Abel Dennison. He come home, and said you was dead for sure, some eight year ago, and then she said she'd marry me. I'd been after her some time. My wife died, and my house burned down, and I was left alone without any home, and I'd always liked her. She wasn't any too willin', but finally she give in."

The man whom he had called Dick glared at him speechlessly.

"We both thought you was dead, sure," said the sick man, in a voice of mild deprecation, which was ludicrously out of proportion to the subject.

Dick looked at the children.

"We had 'em," said the sick man. "She died when the baby was two months old, and your girl Lottie has been taking care of it. It has been pretty hard for her, but I was too sick, and 'ain't been able to do anything. I can jest crawl around a little, and that's all. Lottie can milk—we've got one cow left—and she feeds the hens, and my first wife's brother has given us some flour and meal, and cuts up some wood to burn, and we've worried along, but we can't stand it when winter comes, anyhow. Somethin' has got to be done." Suddenly an expression of blank surprise before an acquisition of knowledge came over his face. "Good Lord! Dick," he gasped out, "it's all yours. It's all yours, anyway, now."

"Where's the old woman?" asked Dick, abruptly, ignoring what the other said.

"Your wife's mother? She died of pneumonia about two year ago. Your wife she took it to heart pretty bad. She was a heap of help about the children."

Dick nodded. "The old woman always was smart to work," he assented.

"Yes, and your wife she wa'n't over-strong."

"Never was."

"No."

"S'pose there was enough to put her away decent?"

"I sold the wood-lot on the back road. There's a gravestone. Luckily I had it done before I was took sick."

"S'pose you're pretty hard pinched now?"

"Awful hard. We can't get along so much longer. There's enough wood to cut, if I could do it, that would bring in somethin'; and there's the hay, that's spoilin'. I can't do nothin'. There's nothin' but this house over our heads." Suddenly that look of surprised knowledge came over his face again. "Lord! it's all yours, and the girl's, anyhow," he muttered.

"She's been doin' the work?" asked Dick, pointing to the girl.

"Yes; she does the best she can, but she ain't very big, and the children 'ain't got enough to be decent, and we can't get much cooked."

Dick made a resolute step towards the door.

"Where be you a-goin', Dick?" asked the sick man, with a curious wistfulness. "You ain't goin' to-night?"

"What is there in the house to eat?"

"What's in the house, Lottie?"

"There's some meal and milk and eggs," answered the child, in a high, sweet voice.

"Come here and give us a kiss, Lottie," said Dick, suddenly.

The little girl approached him timidly, staggering under the weight of the baby. She lifted her face, and the man kissed her with a sort of solemnity. "I'm your father, Lottie," said he.

The two looked at each other, the child shrinking, yet smiling.

"Glad I got home?" asked the man.

"Yes, sir."

Dick went out into the kitchen, and the children followed and stood in the doorway, watching. He gravely set to work with such utensils and materials as he found, which were scanty enough. He kindled a fire and made a corn-cake. He made porridge for the sick man and carried him a bowl of it smoking hot. "'Ain't had nothin' like this sence she died," said the sick man.

After supper Dick cleaned the kitchen. He also tidied up the other room and made the bed, and milked, and split some wood wherewith to cook breakfast.

"You ain't goin' to-night, Dick?" the sick man said, anxiously, when he came in after the work was done.

"No, I ain't."

"Lord! I forgot; it's your house," said the sick man.

"I wa'n't goin' anyhow," said Dick.

"Well, there's a bed up-stairs. You 'ain't got any more clothes than what you've got on, have you?"

"No, I 'ain't," replied Dick, shortly.

"Well, there's mine in the closet out of this room, and you might jest as well wear 'em till I get up. There's some shirts and some pants."

"All right," said Dick.

The next morning Dick got the breakfast, cooking eggs with wonderful skill and frying corn-cakes. Then, dressed in the sick man's shirt and trousers, he set forth, axe in hand. He toiled all day in the woods; he toiled every day until he had sufficient wood cut, then he hired a horse, to be paid for when the wood was sold. He carted loads to the hotels and farm-houses where summer-boarders were taken. He arose before dawn and worked in the field and garden. He cut the hay. He was up half the night setting the house to rights. He washed and ironed like a woman. The whole establishment was transformed. He got a doctor for the sick man, but he gave small encouragement. He had consumption, although he might linger long. "Who's going to take care of the poor fellow, I don't know," said the doctor.

"I be," said Dick.

"Then there are the children," said the doctor.

"One of 'em is mine, and I'll take care of his," said Dick.

The doctor stared, as one stares who sees a good deed in a naughty world, with a mixture of awe, of contempt, and of incredulity.

"Well," he said, "it's lucky you came along."

After that Dick simply continued in his new path of life. He worked and nursed. It was inconceivable how much the man accomplished. He developed an enormous capacity for work. In the autumn he painted the house; the cellar was full of winter vegetables, the wood-pile was compact. The children were warmly clad, and Lottie went to school. Her father had bought an old horse for a song, and he carried her to school every day. Once in January he had occasion to drive around the other side of the mountain which he had climbed the night of his return. He started early in the afternoon, that he might be in season to go for Lottie.

It was a clear, cold day. Snow was on the ground, a deep, glittering level, with a hard crust of ice. The sleigh slid over the frozen surface with long hisses. The trees were all bare and had suffered frightfully in the last storm. The rain had frozen as it fell, and there had been a high gale. The ice-mailed branches had snapped, and sometimes whole trees. Dick, slipping along on the white line of road below, gazed up at the side of the mountain. He looked and looked again. Then he desisted. He reached over and cut the horse's back with the reins. "Get up!" he cried, harshly.

The great pine had fallen from his high estate. He was no more to be seen dominating the other trees, standing out in solitary majesty among his kind. The storm had killed him. He lay prostrate on the mountain.

And the man on the road below passed like the wind, and left the mountain and the dead tree behind.

Luella Miller

1902

Close to the village street stood the one-story house in which Luella Miller, who had an evil name in the village, had dwelt. She had been dead for years, yet there were those in the village who, in spite of the clearer light which comes on a vantage-point from a long-past danger, half believed in the tale which they had heard from their childhood. In their hearts, although they scarcely would have owned it, it was a survival of the wild horror and frenzied fear of their ancestors who had dwelt in the same age with Luella Miller. Young people even would stare with a shudder at the old house as they passed, and children never played around it as was their wont around an untenanted building. Not a window in the old Miller house was broken: the panes reflected the morning sunlight in patches of emerald and blue, and the latch of the sagging front door was never lifted, although no bolt secured it. Since Luella Miller had been carried out of it, the house had had no tenant except one friendless old soul who had no choice between that and the far-off shelter of the open sky. This old woman, who had survived her kindred and friends, lived in the house one week, then one morning no smoke came out of the chimney, and a body of neighbours, a score strong, entered and found her dead in her bed. There were dark whispers as to the cause of her death, and there were those who testified to an expression of fear so exalted that it showed forth the state of the departing soul upon the dead face. The old woman had been hale and hearty when she entered the house, and in seven days she was dead; it seemed that she had fallen a victim to some uncanny power. The minister talked in the pulpit with covert severity against the sin of superstition; still the belief prevailed. Not a soul in the village but would have chosen the almshouse rather than that dwelling. No vagrant, if he heard the tale, would seek shelter beneath that old roof, unhallowed by nearly half a century of superstitious fear.

There was only one person in the village who had actually known Luella Miller. That person was a woman well over eighty, but a marvel of vitality and unextinct youth. Straight as an arrow, with the spring of one recently let loose from the bow of life, she moved about the streets, and she always went to church, rain or shine. She had never married, and had lived alone for years in a house across the road from Luella Miller's.

This woman had none of the garrulousness of age, but never in all her life had she ever held her tongue for any will save her own, and she never spared the truth when she essayed to present it. She it was who bore testimony to the life, evil, though possibly wittingly or designedly so, of Luella Miller, and to her personal appearance. When this old woman spoke— and she had the gift of description, although her thoughts were clothed in the rude vernacular of her native village—one could seem to see Luella Miller as she had really looked. According to this woman, Lydia Anderson by name, Luella Miller had been a beauty of a type rather unusual in New England. She had been a slight, pliant sort of creature, as ready with a strong yielding to fate and as unbreakable as a willow. She had glimmering lengths of straight, fair hair, which she wore softly looped round a long, lovely face. She had blue eyes full of soft pleading, little slender, clinging hands, and a wonderful grace of motion and attitude.

"Luella Miller used to sit in a way nobody else could if they sat up and studied a week of Sundays," said Lydia Anderson, "and it was a sight to see her walk. If one of them willows over there on the edge of the brook could start up and get its roots free of the ground, and move off, it would go just the way Luella Miller used to. She had a green shot silk she used to wear, too, and a hat with green ribbon streamers, and a lace veil blowing across her face and out sideways, and a green ribbon flyin' from her waist. That was what she came out bride in when she married Erastus Miller. Her name before she was married was Hill. There was always a sight of "l's" in her name, married or single. Erastus Miller was good lookin', too, better lookin' than Luella. Sometimes I used to think that Luella wa'n't so handsome after all. Erastus just about worshiped her. I used to know him pretty well. He lived next door to me, and we went to school together. Folks used to say he was waitin' on me, but he wa'n't. I never thought he was except once or twice when he said things that some girls might have suspected meant somethin'. That was before Luella came here to teach the district school. It was funny how she came to get it, for folks said she hadn't any education, and that one of the big girls, Lottie Henderson, used to do all the teachin' for her, while she sat back and did embroidery work on a cambric pocket-handkerchief. Lottie Henderson was a real smart girl, a splendid scholar, and she just set her eyes by Luella, as all the girls did. Lottie would have made a real smart woman, but she died when Luella had been here about a year—just faded away and died: nobody knew what ailed her. She dragged herself to that schoolhouse and helped Luella teach till the very last minute. The committee all knew how Luella didn't do much of the work herself, but they winked at it. It wa'n't long after Lottie died that Erastus married her. I always thought he hurried it up because she wa'n't fit to teach. One of the big boys used to help her after Lottie died, but he hadn't much government, and the school didn't do very well, and Luella might have had to give it up, for the committee couldn't have shut their eyes to things much longer. The boy that helped her was a real honest, innocent sort of fellow, and he was a good scholar, too. Folks said he overstudied, and that was the reason he was took crazy the year after Luella married, but I don't know. And I don't know what made Erastus Miller go into consumption of the blood the year after he was married: consumption wa'n't in his family. He just grew weaker and weaker, and went almost bent double when he tried to wait on Luella, and he spoke feeble, like an old man. He worked terrible hard till the last trying to save up a little to leave Luella. I've seen him out in the worst storms on a wood-sled—he used to cut and sell wood—and he was hunched up on top lookin' more dead than alive. Once I couldn't stand it: I went over and helped him pitch some wood on the cart—I was always strong in my arms. I wouldn't stop for all he told me to, and I guess he was glad enough for the help. That was only a week before he died. He fell on the kitchen floor while he was gettin' breakfast. He always got the breakfast and let Luella lay abed. He did all the sweepin' and the washin' and the ironin' and most of the cookin'. He couldn't bear to have Luella lift her finger, and she let him do for her. She lived like a queen for all the work she did. She didn't even do her sewin'. She said it made her shoulder ache to sew, and poor Erastus's sister Lily used to do all her sewin'. She wa'n't able to, either; she was never strong in her back, but she did it beautifully. She had to, to suit Luella, she was so dreadful particular. I never saw anythin' like the fagottin' and hemstitchin' that Lily Miller did for Luella. She made all Luella's weddin' outfit, and that green silk dress, after Maria Babbit cut it. Maria she cut it for nothin', and she did a lot more cuttin' and fittin' for nothin' for Luella, too. Lily Miller went to live with Luella after Erastus died. She gave up her home, although she was real attached to it and wa'n't a mite afraid to stay alone. She rented it and she went to live with Luella right away after the funeral."

Then this old woman, Lydia Anderson, who remembered Luella Miller, would go on to relate the story of Lily Miller. It seemed that on the removal of Lily Miller to the house of her dead brother, to live with his widow, the village people first began to talk. This Lily Miller had been hardly past her first youth, and a most robust and blooming woman, rosy-cheeked, with curls of strong, black hair overshadowing round, candid temples and bright dark eyes. It was not six months after she had taken up her residence with her sister-in-law that her rosy colour faded and her pretty curves became wan hollows. White shadows began to show in the black rings of her hair, and the light died out of her eyes, her features sharpened, and there were pathetic lines at her mouth, which yet wore always an expression of utter sweetness and even happiness. She was devoted to her sister; there was no doubt that she loved her with her whole heart, and was perfectly content in her service. It was her sole anxiety lest she should die and leave her alone.

"The way Lily Miller used to talk about Luella was enough to make you mad and enough to make you cry," said Lydia Anderson. "I've been in there sometimes toward the last when she was too feeble to cook and carried her some blanc-mange or custard—somethin' I thought she might relish, and she'd thank me, and when I asked her how she was, say she felt better than she did yesterday, and asked me if I didn't think she looked better, dreadful pitiful, and say poor Luella had an awful time takin' care of her and doin' the work—she wa'n't strong enough to do anythin'—when all the time Luella wa'n't liftin' her finger and poor Lily didn't get any care except what the neighbours gave her, and Luella eat up everythin' that was carried in for Lily. I had it real straight that she did. Luella used to just sit and cry and do nothin'. She did act real fond of Lily, and she pined away considerable, too. There was those that thought she'd go into a decline herself. But after Lily died, her Aunt Abby Mixter came, and then Luella picked up and grew as fat and rosy as ever. But poor Aunt Abby begun to droop just the way Lily had, and I guess somebody wrote to her married daughter, Mrs. Sam Abbot, who lived in Barre, for she wrote her mother that she must leave right away and come and make her a visit, but Aunt

Abby wouldn't go. I can see her now. She was a real good-lookin' woman, tall and large, with a big, square face and a high forehead that looked of itself kind of benevolent and good. She just tended out on Luella as if she had been a baby, and when her married daughter sent for her she wouldn't stir one inch. She'd always thought a lot of her daughter, too, but she said Luella needed her and her married daughter didn't. Her daughter kept writin' and writin', but it didn't do any good. Finally she came, and when she saw how bad her mother looked, she broke down and cried and all but went on her knees to have her come away. She spoke her mind out to Luella, too. She told her that she'd killed her husband and everybody that had anythin' to do with her, and she'd thank her to leave her mother alone. Luella went into hysterics, and Aunt Abby was so frightened that she called me after her daughter went. Mrs. Sam Abbot she went away fairly cryin' out loud in the buggy, the neighbours heard her, and well she might, for she never saw her mother again alive. I went in that night when Aunt Abby called for me, standin' in the door with her little green-checked shawl over her head. I can see her now. 'Do come over here, Miss Anderson,' she sung out, kind of gasping for breath. I didn't stop for anythin'. I put over as fast as I could, and when I got there, there was Luella laughin' and cryin' all together, and Aunt Abby trying to hush her, and all the time she herself was white as a sheet and shakin' so she could hardly stand. 'For the land sakes, Mrs. Mixter,' says I, 'you look worse than she does. You ain't fit to be up out of your bed.'

" 'Oh, there ain't anythin' the matter with me,' says she. Then she went on talkin' to Luella. 'There, there, don't, don't, poor little lamb,' says she. 'Aunt Abby is here. She ain't goin' away and leave you. Don't, poor little lamb.'

" 'Do leave her with me, Mrs. Mixter, and you get back to bed,' says I, for Aunt Abby had been layin' down considerable lately, though somehow she contrived to do the work.

" 'I'm well enough,' says she. 'Don't you think she had better have the doctor, Miss Anderson?'

" 'The doctor,' says I, 'I think you had better have the doctor. I think you need him much worse than some folks I could mention.' And I looked right straight at Luella Miller laughin' and cryin' and goin' on as if she was the centre of all creation. All the time she was actin' so—seemed as if she was too sick to sense anythin'—she was keepin' a sharp lookout as to how we took it out of the corner of one eye. I see her. You could never cheat me about Luella Miller. Finally I got real mad and I run home and I got a bottle of valerian I had, and I poured some boilin' hot water on a handful of catnip, and I mixed up that catnip tea with most half a wineglass of valerian, and I went with it over to Luella's. I marched right up to Luella, a-holdin' out of that cup, all smokin'. 'Now,' says I, 'Luella Miller, *you swaller this!*'

" 'What is—what is it, oh, what is it?' she sort of screeches out. Then she goes off a-laughin' enough to kill.

" 'Poor lamb, poor little lamb,' says Aunt Abby, standin' over her, all kind of tottery, and tryin' to bathe her head with camphor.

" '*You swaller this right down,*' says I. And I didn't waste any ceremony. I just took hold of Luella Miller's chin and I tipped her head back, and I caught her mouth open with laughin', and I clapped that cup to her lips, and I fairly hollered at her: 'Swaller, swaller, swaller!' and she gulped it right down. She had to, and I guess it did her good. Anyhow, she stopped cryin' and laughin' and let me put her to bed, and she went to sleep like a baby inside of half an hour. That was more than poor Aunt Abby did. She lay awake all that night and I stayed with her, though she tried not to have me; said she wa'n't sick enough for watchers. But I stayed, and I made some good corn-meal gruel and I fed her a teaspoon every little while all night long. It seemed to me as if she was jest dyin' from bein' all wore out. In the mornin' as soon as it was light I run over to the Bisbees and sent Johnny Bisbee for the doctor. I told him to tell the doctor to hurry, and he come pretty quick. Poor Aunt Abby didn't seem to know much of anythin' when he got there. You couldn't hardly tell she breathed, she was so used up. When the doctor had gone, Luella came into the room lookin' like a baby in her ruffled nightgown. I can see her now. Her eyes were as blue and her face all pink and white like a blossom, and she looked at Aunt Abby in the bed sort of innocent and surprised. 'Why,' says she, 'Aunt Abby ain't got up yet?'

" 'No, she ain't,' says I, pretty short.

" 'I thought I didn't smell the coffee,' says Luella.

" 'Coffee,' says I. 'I guess if you have coffee this mornin' you'll make it yourself.'

" 'I never made the coffee in all my life,' says she, dreadful astonished. 'Erastus always made the coffee as long as he lived, and then Lily she made. it, and then Aunt Abby made it. I don't believe I *can* make the coffee, Miss Anderson.'

" 'You can make it or go without, jest as you please,' says I.

"'Ain't Aunt Abby goin' to get up?' says she.

"'I guess she won't get up,' says I, 'sick as she is.' I was gettin' madder and madder. There was somethin' about that little pink-and-white thing standin' there and talkin' about coffee, when she had killed so many better folks than she was, and had jest killed another, that made me feel 'most as if I wished somebody would up and kill her before she had a chance to do any more harm.

"'Is Aunt Abby sick?' says Luella, as if she was sort of aggrieved and injured.

"'Yes,' says I, 'she's sick, and she's goin' to die, and then you'll be left alone, and you'll have to do for yourself and wait on yourself, or do without things.' I don't know but I was sort of hard, but it was the truth, and if I was any harder than Luella Miller had been I'll give up. I ain't never been sorry that I said it. Well, Luella, she up and had hysterics again at that, and I jest let her have 'em. All I did was to bundle her into the room on the other side of the entry where Aunt Abby couldn't hear her, if she wa'n't past it—I don't know but she was—and set her down hard in a chair and told her not to come back into the other room, and she minded. She had her hysterics in there till she got tired. When she found out that nobody was comin' to coddle her and do for her she stopped. At least I suppose she did. I had all I could do with poor Aunt Abby tryin' to keep the breath of life in her. The doctor had told me that she was dreadful low, and give me some very strong medicine to give to her in drops real often, and told me real particular about the nourishment. Well, I did as he told me real faithful till she wa'n't able to swaller any longer. Then I had her daughter sent for. I had begun to realize that she wouldn't last any time at all. I hadn't realized it before, though I spoke to Luella the way I did. The doctor he came, and Mrs. Sam Abbot, but when she got there it was too late; her mother was dead. Aunt Abby's daughter just give one look at her mother layin' there, then she turned sort of sharp and sudden and looked at me.

"'Where is she?' says she, and I knew she meant Luella.

"'She's out in the kitchen,' says I. 'She's too nervous to see folks die. She's afraid it will make her sick.'

"The Doctor he speaks up then. He was a young man. Old Doctor Park had died the year before, and this was a young fellow just out of college. 'Mrs. Miller is not strong,' says he, kind of severe, 'and she is quite right in not agitating herself.'

"'You are another, young man; she's got her pretty claw on you,' thinks

I, but I didn't say anythin' to him. I just said over to Mrs. Sam Abbot that
Luella was in the kitchen, and Mrs. Sam Abbot she went out there, and I
went, too, and I never heard anythin' like the way she talked to Luella Miller. I felt pretty hard to Luella myself, but this was more than I ever would
have dared to say. Luella she was too scared to go into hysterics. She jest
flopped. She seemed to jest shrink away to nothin' in that kitchen chair,
with Mrs. Sam Abbot standin' over her and talkin' and tellin' her the truth.
I guess the truth was most too much for her and no mistake, because Luella
presently actually did faint away, and there wa'n't any sham about it, the
way I always suspected there was about them hysterics. She fainted dead
away and we had to lay her flat on the floor, and the Doctor he came runnin' out and he said somethin' about a weak heart dreadful fierce to Mrs.
Sam Abbot, but she wa'n't a mite scared. She faced him jest as white as
even Luella was layin' there lookin' like death and the Doctor feelin' of her
pulse.

"'Weak heart,' says she, 'weak heart; weak fiddlesticks! There ain't
nothin' weak about that woman. She's got strength enough to hang onto
other folks till she kills 'em. Weak? It was my poor mother that was weak:
this woman killed her as sure as if she had taken a knife to her.'

"But the Doctor he didn't pay much attention. He was bendin' over
Luella layin' there with her yellow hair all streamin' and her pretty pink-
and-white face all pale, and her blue eyes like stars gone out, and he was
holdin' onto her hand and smoothin' her forehead, and tellin' me to get the
brandy in Aunt Abby's room, and I was sure as I wanted to be that Luella
had got somebody else to hang onto, now Aunt Abby was gone, and I
thought of poor Erastus Miller, and I sort of pitied the poor young Doctor,
led away by a pretty face, and I made up my mind I'd see what I could do.

"I waited till Aunt Abby had been dead and buried about a month, and
the Doctor was goin' to see Luella steady and folks were beginnin' to talk;
then one evenin', when I knew the Doctor had been called out of town and
wouldn't be around, I went over to Luella's. I found her all dressed up in a
blue muslin with white polka dots on it, and her hair curled jest as pretty,
and there wa'n't a young girl in the place could compare with her. There
was somethin' about Luella Miller seemed to draw the heart right out of
you, but she didn't draw it out of *me*. She was settin' rocking in the chair by
her sittin'-room window, and Maria Brown had gone home. Maria Brown
had been in to help her, or rather to do the work, for Luella wa'n't helped
when she didn't do anythin'. Maria Brown was real capable and she didn't

have any ties; she wa'n't married, and lived alone, so she'd offered. I couldn't see why she should do the work any more than Luella; she wa'n't any too strong; but she seemed to think she could and Luella seemed to think so, too, so she went over and did all the work—washed, and ironed, and baked, while Luella sat and rocked. Maria didn't live long afterward. She began to fade away just the same fashion the others had. Well, she was warned, but she acted real mad when folks said anythin': said Luella was a poor, abused woman, too delicate to help herself, and they'd ought to be ashamed, and if she died helpin' them that couldn't help themselves she would—and she did.

"'I s'pose Maria has gone home,' says I to Luella, when I had gone in and sat down opposite her.

"'Yes, Maria went half an hour ago, after she had got supper and washed the dishes,' says Luella, in her pretty way.

"'I suppose she has got a lot of work to do in her own house to-night,' says I, kind of bitter, but that was all thrown away on Luella Miller. It seemed to her right that other folks that wa'n't any better able than she was herself should wait on her, and she couldn't get it through her head that anybody should think it *wa'n't* right.

"'Yes,' says Luella, real sweet and pretty, 'yes, she said she had to do her washin' to-night. She has let it go for a fortnight along of comin' over here.'

"'Why don't she stay home and do her washin' instead of comin' over here and doin' *your* work, when you are just as well able, and enough sight more so, than she is to do it?' says I.

"Then Luella she looked at me like a baby who has a rattle shook at it. She sort of laughed as innocent as you please. 'Oh, I can't do the work myself, Miss Anderson,' says she. 'I never did. Maria *has* to do it.'

"Then I spoke out: 'Has to do it!' says I. 'Has to do it! She don't have to do it, either. Maria Brown has her own home and enough to live on. She ain't beholden to you to come over here and slave for you and kill herself.'

"Luella she jest set and stared at me for all the world like a doll-baby that was so abused that it was comin' to life.

"'Yes,' says I, 'she's killin' herself. She's goin' to die just the way Erastus did, and Lily, and your Aunt Abby. You're killin' her jest as you did them. I don't know what there is about you, but you seem to bring a curse,' says I. 'You kill everybody that is fool enough to care anythin' about you and do for you.'

"She stared at me and she was pretty pale.

"'And Maria ain't the only one you're goin' to kill,' says I. 'You're goin' to kill Doctor Malcom before you're done with him.'

"Then a red colour came flamin' all over her face. 'I ain't goin' to kill him, either,' says she, and she begun to cry.

"'Yes, you *be!*' says I. Then I spoke as I had never spoke before. You see, I felt it on account of Erastus. I told her that she hadn't any business to think of another man after she'd been married to one that had died for her: that she was a dreadful woman; and she was, that's true enough, but sometimes I have wondered lately if she knew it—if she wa'n't like a baby with scissors in its hand cuttin' everybody without knowin' what it was doin'.

"Luella she kept gettin' paler and paler, and she never took her eyes off my face. There was somethin' awful about the way she looked at me and never spoke one word. After awhile I quit talkin' and I went home. I watched that night, but her lamp went out before nine o'clock, and when Doctor Malcom came drivin' past and sort of slowed up he see there wa'n't any light and he drove along. I saw her sort of shy out of meetin' the next Sunday, too, so he shouldn't go home with her, and I begun to think mebbe she did have some conscience after all. It was only a week after that that Maria Brown died—sort of sudden at the last, though everybody had seen it was comin'. Well, then there was a good deal of feelin' and pretty dark whispers. Folks said the days of witchcraft had come again, and they were pretty shy of Luella. She acted sort of offish to the Doctor and he didn't go there, and there wa'n't anybody to do anythin' for her. I don't know how she *did* get along. I wouldn't go in there and offer to help her—not because I was afraid of dyin' like the rest, but I thought she was just as well able to do her own work as I was to do it for her, and I thought it was about time that she did it and stopped killin' other folks. But it wa'n't very long before folks began to say that Luella herself was goin' into a decline jest the way her husband, and Lily, and Aunt Abby and the others had, and I saw myself that she looked pretty bad. I used to see her goin' past from the store with a bundle as if she could hardly crawl, but I remembered how Erastus used to wait and 'tend when he couldn't hardly put one foot before the other, and I didn't go out to help her.

"But at last one afternoon I saw the Doctor come drivin' up like mad with his medicine chest, and Mrs. Babbit came in after supper and said that Luella was real sick.

"'I'd offer to go in and nurse her,' says she, 'but I've got my children to consider, and mebbe it ain't true what they say, but it's queer how many folks that have done for her have died.'

"I didn't say anythin', but I considered how she had been Erastus's wife and how he had set his eyes by her, and I made up my mind to go in the next mornin', unless she was better, and see what I could do; but the next mornin' I see her at the window, and pretty soon she came steppin' out as spry as you please, and a little while afterward Mrs. Babbit came in and told me that the Doctor had got a girl from out of town, a Sarah Jones, to come there, and she said she was pretty sure that the Doctor was goin' to marry Luella.

"I saw him kiss her in the door that night myself, and I knew it was true. The woman came that afternoon, and the way she flew around was a caution. I don't believe Luella had swept since Maria died. She swept and dusted, and washed and ironed; wet clothes and dusters and carpets were flyin' over there all day, and every time Luella set her foot out when the Doctor wa'n't there there was that Sarah Jones helpin' of her up and down the steps, as if she hadn't learned to walk.

"Well, everybody knew that Luella and the Doctor were goin' to be married, but it wa'n't long before they began to talk about his lookin' so poorly, jest as they had about the others; and they talked about Sarah Jones, too.

"Well, the Doctor did die, and he wanted to be married first, so as to leave what little he had to Luella, but he died before the minister could get there, and Sarah Jones died a week afterward.

"Well, that wound up everything for Luella Miller. Not another soul in the whole town would lift a finger for her. There got to be a sort of panic. Then she began to droop in good earnest. She used to have to go to the store herself, for Mrs. Babbit was afraid to let Tommy go for her, and I've seen her goin' past and stoppin' every two or three steps to rest. Well, I stood it as long as I could, but one day I see her comin' with her arms full and stoppin' to lean against the Babbit fence, and I run out and took her bundles and carried them to her house. Then I went home and never spoke one word to her though she called after me dreadful kind of pitiful. Well, that night I was taken sick with a chill, and I was sick as I wanted to be for two weeks. Mrs. Babbit had seen me run out to help Luella and she came in and told me I was goin' to die on account of it. I didn't know whether I was or not, but I considered I had done right by Erastus's wife.

"That last two weeks Luella she had a dreadful hard time, I guess. She was pretty sick, and as near as I could make out nobody dared go near her. I don't know as she was really needin' anythin' very much, for there was enough to eat in her house and it was warm weather, and she made out to cook a little flour gruel every day, I know, but I guess she had a hard time, she that had been so petted and done for all her life.

"When I got so I could go out, I went over there one morning. Mrs. Babbit had just come in to say she hadn't seen any smoke and she didn't know but it was somebody's duty to go in, but she couldn't help thinkin' of her children, and I got right up, though I hadn't been out of the house for two weeks, and I went in there, and Luella she was layin' on the bed, and she was dyin'.

"She lasted all that day and into the night. But I sat there after the new doctor had gone away. Nobody else dared to go there. It was about midnight that I left her for a minute to run home and get some medicine I had been takin', for I begun to feel rather bad.

"It was a full moon that night, and just as I started out of my door to cross the street back to Luella's, I stopped short, for I saw something."

Lydia Anderson at this juncture always said with a certain defiance that she did not expect to be believed, and then proceeded in a hushed voice:

"I saw what I saw, and I know I saw it, and I will swear on my death bed that I saw it. I saw Luella Miller and Erastus Miller, and Lily, and Aunt Abby, and Maria, and the Doctor, and Sarah, all goin' out of her door, and all but Luella shone white in the moonlight, and they were all helpin' her along till she seemed to fairly fly in the midst of them. Then it all disappeared. I stood a minute with my heart poundin', then I went over there. I thought of goin' for Mrs. Babbit, but I thought she'd be afraid. So I went alone, though I knew what had happened. Luella was layin' real peaceful, dead on her bed."

This was the story that the old woman, Lydia Anderson, told, but the sequel was told by the people who survived her, and this is the tale which has become folklore in the village.

Lydia Anderson died when she was eighty-seven. She had continued wonderfully hale and hearty for one of her years until about two weeks before her death.

One bright moonlight evening she was sitting beside a window in her parlour when she made a sudden exclamation, and was out of the house and across the street before the neighbour who was taking care of her could stop her. She followed as fast as possible and found Lydia Anderson stretched on the ground before the door of Luella Miller's deserted house, and she was quite dead.

The next night there was a red gleam of fire athwart the moonlight and the old house of Luella Miller was burned to the ground. Nothing is now left of it except a few old cellar stones and a lilac bush, and in summer a helpless trail of morning glories among the weeds, which might be considered emblematic of Luella herself.

The Lost Ghost

1903

Mrs. John Emerson, sitting with her needlework beside the window, looked out and saw Mrs. Rhoda Meserve coming down the street, and knew at once by the trend of her steps and the cant of her head that she meditated turning in at her gate. She also knew by a certain something about her general carriage—a thrusting forward of the neck, a bustling hitch of the shoulders—that she had important news. Rhoda Meserve always had the news as soon as the news was in being, and generally Mrs. John Emerson was the first to whom she imparted it. The two women had been friends ever since Mrs. Meserve had married Simon Meserve and come to the village to live.

Mrs. Meserve was a pretty woman, moving with graceful flirts of ruffling skirts; her clear-cut, nervous face, as delicately tinted as a shell, looked brightly from the plumy brim of a black hat at Mrs. Emerson in the window. Mrs. Emerson was glad to see her coming. She returned the greeting with enthusiasm, then rose hurriedly, ran into the cold parlour and brought out one of the best rocking-chairs. She was just in time, after drawing it up beside the opposite window, to greet her friend at the door.

"Good-afternoon," said she. "I declare, I'm real glad to see you. I've been alone all day. John went to the city this morning. I thought of coming over to your house this afternoon, but I couldn't bring my sewing very well. I am putting the ruffles on my new black dress skirt."

"Well, I didn't have a thing on hand except my crochet work," responded Mrs. Meserve, "and I thought I'd just run over a few minutes."

"I'm real glad you did," repeated Mrs. Emerson. "Take your things right off. Here, I'll put them on my bed in the bedroom. Take the rocking-chair."

Mrs. Meserve settled herself in the parlour rocking-chair, while Mrs. Emerson carried her shawl and hat into the little adjoining bedroom. When she returned Mrs. Meserve was rocking peacefully and was already at work hooking blue wool in and out.

"That's real pretty," said Mrs. Emerson.

"Yes, I think it's pretty," replied Mrs. Meserve.

"I suppose it's for the church fair?"

"Yes. I don't suppose it'll bring enough to pay for the worsted, let alone the work, but I suppose I've got to make something."

"How much did that one you made for the fair last year bring?"

"Twenty-five cents."

"It's wicked, ain't it?"

"I rather guess it is. It takes me a week every minute I can get to make one. I wish those that bought such things for twenty-five cents had to make them. Guess they'd sing another song. Well, I suppose I oughtn't to complain as long as it is for the Lord, but sometimes it does seem as if the Lord didn't get much out of it."

"Well, it's pretty work," said Mrs. Emerson, sitting down at the opposite window and taking up her dress skirt.

"Yes, it is real pretty work. I just *love* to crochet."

The two women rocked and sewed and crocheted in silence for two or three minutes. They were both waiting. Mrs. Meserve waited for the other's curiosity to develop in order that her news might have, as it were, a befitting stage entrance. Mrs. Emerson waited for the news. Finally she could wait no longer.

"Well, what's the news?" said she.

"Well, I don't know as there's anything very particular," hedged the other woman, prolonging the situation.

"Yes, there is; you can't cheat me," replied Mrs. Emerson.

"Now, how do you know?"

"By the way you look."

Mrs. Meserve laughed consciously and rather vainly.

"Well, Simon says my face is so expressive I can't hide anything more than five minutes no matter how hard I try," said she. "Well, there is some news. Simon came home with it this noon. He heard it in South Dayton. He had some business over there this morning. The old Sargent place is let."

Mrs. Emerson dropped her sewing and stared.

"You don't say so!"

"Yes, it is."

"Who to?"

"Why, some folks from Boston that moved to South Dayton last year. They haven't been satisfied with the house they had there—it wasn't large enough. The man has got considerable property and can afford to live pretty well. He's got a wife and his unmarried sister in the family. The sister's got money, too. He does business in Boston and it's just as easy to get to Boston from here as from South Dayton, and so they're coming here. You know the old Sargent house is a splendid place."

"Yes, it's the handsomest house in town, but———"

"Oh, Simon said they told him about that and he just laughed. Said he wasn't afraid and neither was his wife and sister. Said he'd risk ghosts rather than little tucked-up sleeping-rooms without any sun, like they've had in the Dayton house. Said he'd rather risk *seeing* ghosts, than risk being ghosts themselves. Simon said they said he was a great hand to joke."

"Oh, well" said Mrs. Emerson, "it is a beautiful house, and maybe there isn't anything in those stories. It never seemed to me they came very straight anyway. I never took much stock in them. All I thought was—if his wife was nervous."

"Nothing in creation would hire me to go into a house that I'd ever heard a word against of that kind," declared Mrs. Meserve with emphasis. "I wouldn't go into that house if they would give me the rent. I've seen enough of haunted houses to last me as long as I live."

Mrs. Emerson's face acquired the expression of a hunting hound.

"Have you?" she asked in an intense whisper.

"Yes, I have. I don't want any more of it."

"Before you came here?"

"Yes; before I was married—when I was quite a girl."

Mrs. Meserve had not married young. Mrs. Emerson had mental calculations when she heard that.

"Did you really live in a house that was———" she whispered fearfully.

Mrs. Meserve nodded solemnly.

"Did you really ever—see—anything———"

Mrs. Meserve nodded.

"You didn't see anything that did you any harm?"

"No, I didn't see anything that did me harm looking at it in one way, but it don't do anybody in this world any good to see things that haven't any business to be seen in it. You never get over it."

There was a moment's silence. Mrs. Emerson's features seemed to sharpen.

"Well, of course I don't want to urge you," said she, "if you don't feel like talking about it; but maybe it might do you good to tell it out, if it's on your mind, worrying you."

"I try to put it out of my mind," said Mrs. Meserve.

"Well, it's just as you feel."

"I never told anybody but Simon," said Mrs. Meserve. "I never felt as if it was wise perhaps. I didn't know what folks might think. So many don't believe in anything they can't understand, that they might think my mind wasn't right. Simon advised me not to talk about it. He said he didn't believe it was anything supernatural, but he had to own up that he couldn't give any explanation for it to save his life. He had to own up that he didn't believe anybody could. Then he said he wouldn't talk about it. He said lots of folks would sooner tell folks my head wasn't right than to own up they couldn't see through it."

"I'm sure I wouldn't say so," returned Mrs. Emerson reproachfully. "You know better than that, I hope."

"Yes, I do," replied Mrs. Meserve. "I know you wouldn't say so."

"And I wouldn't tell it to a soul if you didn't want me to."

"Well, I'd rather you wouldn't."

"I won't speak of it even to Mr. Emerson."

"I'd rather you wouldn't even to him."

"I won't."

Mrs. Emerson took up her dress skirt again; Mrs. Meserve hooked up another loop of blue wool. Then she began:

"Of course," said she, "I ain't going to say positively that I believe or disbelieve in ghosts, but all I tell you is what I saw. I can't explain it. I don't pretend I can, for I can't. If you can, well and good; I shall be glad, for it will stop tormenting me as it has done and always will otherwise. There hasn't been a day nor a night since it happened that I haven't thought of it, and always I have felt the shivers go down my back when I did."

"That's an awful feeling," Mrs. Emerson said.

"Ain't it? Well, it happened before I was married, when I was a girl and lived in East Wilmington. It was the first year I lived there. You know my family all died five years before that. I told you."

Mrs. Emerson nodded.

"Well, I went there to teach school, and I went to board with a Mrs.

Amelia Dennison and her sister, Mrs. Bird. Abby, her name was—Abby Bird. She was a widow; she had never had any children. She had a little money—Mrs. Dennison didn't have any—and she had come to East Wilmington and bought the house they lived in. It was a real pretty house, though it was very old and run down. It had cost Mrs. Bird a good deal to put it in order. I guess that was the reason they took me to board. I guess they thought it would help along a little. I guess what I paid for my board about kept us all in victuals. Mrs. Bird had enough to live on if they were careful, but she had spent so much fixing up the old house that they must have been a little pinched for awhile.

"Anyhow, they took me to board, and I thought I was pretty lucky to get in there. I had a nice room, big and sunny and furnished pretty, the paper and paint all new, and everything as neat as wax. Mrs. Dennison was one of the best cooks I ever saw, and I had a little stove in my room, and there was always a nice fire there when I got home from school. I thought I hadn't been in such a nice place since I lost my own home, until I had been there about three weeks.

"I had been there about three weeks before I found it out, though I guess it had been going on ever since they had been in the house, and that was most four months. They hadn't said anything about it, and I didn't wonder, for there they had just bought the house and been to so much expense and trouble fixing it up.

"Well, I went there in September. I begun my school the first Monday. I remember it was a real cold fall, there was a frost the middle of September, and I had to put on my winter coat. I remember when I came home that night (let me see, I began school on a Monday, and that was two weeks from the next Thursday), I took off my coat downstairs and laid it on the table in the front entry. It was a real nice coat—heavy black broadcloth trimmed with fur; I had had it the winter before. Mrs. Bird called after me as I went upstairs that I ought not to leave it in the front entry for fear somebody might come in and take it, but I only laughed and called back to her that I wasn't afraid. I never was much afraid of burglars.

"Well, though it was hardly the middle of September, it was a real cold night. I remember my room faced west, and the sun was getting low, and sky was a pale yellow and purple, just as you see it sometimes in the winter when there is going to be a cold snap. I rather think that was the night the frost came the first time. I know Mrs. Dennison covered up some flowers she had in the front yard, anyhow. I remember looking out and seeing an old green plaid shawl of hers over the verbena bed. There was a fire in my little wood-stove. Mrs. Bird made it, I know. She was a real motherly sort of woman; she always seemed to be the happiest when she was doing something to make other folks happy and comfortable. Mrs. Dennison told me she had always been so. She said she had coddled her husband within an inch of his life. 'It's lucky Abby never had any children,' she said, 'for she would have spoilt them.'

"Well, that night I sat down beside my nice little fire and ate an apple. There was a plate of nice apples on my table. Mrs. Bird put them there. I was always very fond of apples. Well, I sat down and ate an apple, and was having a beautiful time, and thinking how lucky I was to have got board in such a place with such nice folks, when I heard a queer little sound at my door. It was such a little hesitating sort of sound that it sounded more like a fumble than a knock, as if some one very timid, with very little hands, was feeling along the door, not quite daring to knock. For a minute I thought it was a mouse. But I waited and it came again, and then I made up my mind it was a knock, but a very little scared one, so I said, 'Come in.'

"But nobody came in, and then presently I heard the knock again. Then I got up and opened the door, thinking it was very queer, and I had a frightened feeling without knowing why.

"Well, I opened the door, and the first thing I noticed was a draught of cold air, as if the front door downstairs was open, but there was a strange close smell about the cold draught. It smelled more like a cellar that had been shut up for years, than out-of-doors. Then I saw something. I saw my coat first. The thing that held it was so small that I couldn't see much of anything else. Then I saw a little white face with eyes so scared and wishful that they seemed as if they might eat a hole in anybody's heart. It was a dreadful little face, with something about it which made it different from any other face on earth, but it was so pitiful that somehow it did away a good deal with the dreadfulness. And there were two little hands spotted purple with the cold, holding up my winter coat, and a strange little faraway voice said: 'I can't find my mother.'

"'For Heaven's sake,' I said, 'who are you?'

"Then the little voice said again: 'I can't find my mother.'

"All the time I could smell the cold and I saw that it was about the child; that cold was clinging to her as if she had come out of some deadly cold place. Well, I took my coat, I did not know what else to do, and the cold was clinging to that. It was as cold as if it had come off ice. When I had the coat I could see the child more plainly. She was dressed in one little white garment made very simply. It was a nightgown, only very long, quite covering her feet, and I could see dimly through it her little thin body mottled purple with the cold. Her face did not look so cold; that was a clear waxen white. Her hair was dark, but it looked as if it might be dark only because it was so damp, almost wet, and might really be light hair. It clung very close to her forehead, which was round and white. She would have been very beautiful if she had not been so dreadful.

"'Who are you?' says I again, looking at her.

"She looked at me with her terrible pleading eyes and did not say anything.

"'What are you?' says I. Then she went away. She did not seem to run or walk like other children. She flitted, like one of those little filmy white butterflies, that don't seem like real ones they are so light, and move as if they had no weight. But she looked back from the head of the stairs. 'I can't find my mother,' said she, and I never heard such a voice.

"'Who is your mother?' says I, but she was gone.

"Well, I thought for a moment I should faint away. The room got dark and I heard a singing in my ears. Then I flung my coat onto the bed. My hands were as cold as ice from holding it, and I stood in my door, and called first Mrs. Bird and then Mrs. Dennison. I didn't dare go down over the stairs where that had gone. It seemed to me I should go mad if I didn't see somebody or something like other folks on the face of the earth. I thought I should never make anybody hear, but I could hear them stepping about downstairs, and I could smell biscuits baking for supper. Somehow the smell of those biscuits seemed the only natural thing left to keep me in my right mind. I didn't dare go over those stairs. I just stood there and called, and finally I heard the entry door open and Mrs. Bird called back:

"'What is it? Did you call, Miss Arms?'

"'Come up here; come up here as quick as you can, both of you,' I screamed out; 'quick, quick, quick!'

"I heard Mrs. Bird tell Mrs. Dennison: 'Come quick, Amelia, something is the matter in Miss Arms' room.' It struck me even then that she expressed herself rather queerly, and it struck me as very queer, indeed, when they both got upstairs and I saw that they knew what had happened, or that they knew of what nature the happening was.

"'What is it, dear?' asked Mrs. Bird, and her pretty, loving voice had a strained sound. I saw her look at Mrs. Dennison and I saw Mrs. Dennison look back at her.

"'For God's sake,' says I, and I never spoke so before—'for God's sake, what was it brought my coat upstairs?'

"'What was it like?' asked Mrs. Dennison in a sort of failing voice, and she looked at her sister again and her sister looked back at her.

"'It was a child I have never seen here before. It looked like a child,' says I, 'but I never saw a child so dreadful, and it had on a nightgown, and said she couldn't find her mother. Who was it? What was it?'

"I thought for a minute Mrs. Dennison was going to faint, but Mrs. Bird hung onto her and rubbed her hands, and whispered in her ear (she had the cooingest kind of voice), and I ran and got her a glass of cold water. I tell you it took considerable courage to go downstairs alone, but they had set a lamp on the entry table so I could see. I don't believe I could have spunked up enough to have gone downstairs in the dark, thinking every second that child might be close to me. The lamp and the smell of the biscuits baking seemed to sort of keep my courage up, but I tell you I didn't waste much time going down those stairs and out into the kitchen for a glass of water. I pumped as if the house was afire, and I grabbed the first thing I came across in the shape of a tumbler: it was a painted one that Mrs. Dennison's Sunday school class gave her, and it was meant for a flower vase.

"Well, I filled it and then ran upstairs. I felt every minute as if something would catch my feet, and I held the glass to Mrs. Dennison's lips, while Mrs. Bird held her head up, and she took a good long swallow, then she looked hard at the tumbler.

"'Yes,' says I, 'I know I got this one, but I took the first I came across, and it isn't hurt a mite.'

"'Don't get the painted flowers wet,' says Mrs. Dennison very feebly, 'they'll wash off if you do.'

"'I'll be real careful,' says I. I knew she set a sight by that painted tumbler.

"The water seemed to do Mrs. Dennison good, for presently she pushed Mrs. Bird away and sat up. She had been laying down on my bed.

"'I'm all over it now,' says she, but she was terribly white, and her eyes looked as if they saw something outside things. Mrs. Bird wasn't much better, but she always had a sort of settled sweet, good look that nothing could disturb to any great extent. I knew I looked dreadful, for I caught a glimpse of myself in the glass, and I would hardly have known who it was.

"Mrs. Dennison, she slid off the bed and walked sort of tottery to a chair. 'I was silly to give way so,' says she.

"'No, you wasn't silly, sister,' says Mrs. Bird. 'I don't know what this means any more than you do, but whatever it is, no one ought to be called silly for being overcome by anything so different from other things which we have known all our lives.'

"Mrs. Dennison looked at her sister, then she looked at me, then back at her sister again, and Mrs. Bird spoke as if she had been asked a question.

"'Yes,' says she, 'I do think Miss Arms ought to be told—that is, I think she ought to be told all we know ourselves.'

"'That isn't much,' said Mrs. Dennison with a dying-away sort of sigh. She looked as if she might faint away again any minute. She was a real delicate-looking woman, but it turned out she was a good deal stronger than poor Mrs. Bird.

"'No, there isn't much we do know,' says Mrs. Bird, 'but what little there is she ought to know. I felt as if she ought to when she first came here.'

"'Well, I didn't feel quite right about it,' said Mrs. Dennison, 'but I kept hoping it might stop, and any way, that it might never trouble her, and you had put so much in the house, and we needed the money, and I didn't know but she might be nervous and think she couldn't come, and I didn't want to take a man boarder.'

"'And aside from the money, we were very anxious to have you come, my dear,' says Mrs. Bird.

"'Yes,' says Mrs. Dennison, 'we wanted the young company in the house; we were lonesome, and we both of us took a great liking to you the minute we set eyes on you.'

"And I guess they meant what they said, both of them. They were beautiful women, and nobody could be any kinder to me than they were, and I never blamed them for not telling me before, and, as they said, there wasn't really much to tell.

"They hadn't any sooner fairly bought the house, and moved into it, than they began to see and hear things. Mrs. Bird said they were sitting together in the sitting-room one evening when they heard it the first time. She said her sister was knitting lace (Mrs. Dennison made beautiful knitted lace) and she was reading the *Missionary Herald* (Mrs. Bird was very much interested in mission work), when all of a sudden they heard something. She heard it first and she laid down her *Missionary Herald* and listened, and then Mrs. Dennison she saw her listening and she drops her lace.

'What is it you are listening to, Abby?' says she. Then it came again and they both heard, and the cold shivers went down their backs to hear it, though they didn't know why. 'It's the cat, isn't it?' says Mrs. Bird.

"'It isn't any cat,' says Mrs. Dennison.

"'Oh, I guess it *must* be the cat; maybe she's got a mouse,' says Mrs. Bird, real cheerful, to calm down Mrs. Dennison, for she saw she was 'most scared to death, and she was always afraid of her fainting away. Then she opens the door and calls, 'Kitty, kitty, kitty!" They had brought their cat with them in a basket when they came to East Wilmington to live. It was a real handsome tiger cat, a tommy, and he knew a lot.

"Well, she called 'Kitty, kitty, kitty!' and sure enough the kitty came, and when he came in the door he gave a big yawl that didn't sound unlike what they had heard.

"'There, sister, here he is; you see it was the cat,' says Mrs. Bird. 'Poor kitty!'

"But Mrs. Dennison she eyed the cat, and she give a great screech.

"'What's that? What's that?' says she.

"'What's what?' says Mrs. Bird, pretending to herself that she didn't see what her sister meant.

"'Somethin's got hold of that cat's tail,' says Mrs. Dennison. 'Somethin's got hold of his tail. It's pulled straight out, an' he can't get away. Just hear him yawl!'

"'It isn't anything,' says Mrs. Bird, but even as she said that she could see a little hand holding fast to that cat's tail, and then the child seemed to sort of clear out of the dimness behind the hand, and the child was sort of laughing then, instead of looking sad, and she said that was a great deal worse. She said that laugh was the most awful and the saddest thing she ever heard.

"Well, she was so dumfounded that she didn't know what to do, and she couldn't sense at first that it was anything supernatural. She thought it must be one of the neighbour's children who had run away and was making free of their house, and was teasing their cat, and that they must be just nervous to feel so upset by it. So she speaks up sort of sharp.

"'Don't you know that you mustn't pull the kitty's tail?' says she. 'Don't you know you hurt the poor kitty, and she'll scratch you if you don't take care. Poor kitty, you mustn't hurt her.'

"And with that she said the child stopped pulling that cat's tail and went to stroking her just as soft and pitiful, and the cat put his back up and rubbed and purred as if he liked it. The cat never seemed a mite afraid, and that seemed queer, for I had always heard that animals were dreadfully afraid of ghosts; but then, that was a pretty harmless little sort of ghost.

"Well, Mrs. Bird said the child stroked that cat, while she and Mrs. Dennison stood watching it, and holding onto each other, for, no matter how hard they tried to think it was all right, it didn't look right. Finally Mrs. Dennison she spoke.

"'What's your name, little girl?' says she.

"Then the child looks up and stops stroking the cat, and says she can't find her mother, just the way she said it to me. Then Mrs. Dennison she gave such a gasp that Mrs. Bird thought she was going to faint away, but she didn't. 'Well, who is your mother?' says she. But the child just says again 'I can't find my mother—I can't find my mother.'

"'Where do you live, dear?' says Mrs. Bird.

"'I can't find my mother,' says the child.

"Well, that was the way it was. Nothing happened. Those two women stood there hanging onto each other, and the child stood in front of them, and they asked her questions, and everything she would say was: 'I can't find my mother.'

"Then Mrs. Bird tried to catch hold of the child, for she thought in spite of what she saw that perhaps she was nervous and it was a real child, only perhaps not quite right in its head, that had run away in her little nightgown after she had been put to bed.

"She tried to catch the child. She had an idea of putting a shawl around it and going out—she was such a little thing she could have carried her easy enough—and trying to find out to which of the neighbours she belonged. But the minute she moved toward the child there wasn't any child there; there was only that little voice seeming to come from nothing, saying 'I can't find my mother,' and presently that died away.

"Well, that same thing kept happening, or something very much the same. Once in awhile Mrs. Bird would be washing dishes, and all at once the child would be standing beside her with the dish-towel, wiping them. Of course, that was terrible. Mrs. Bird would wash the dishes all over. Sometimes she didn't tell Mrs. Dennison, it made her so nervous. Sometimes when they were making cake they would find the raisins all picked over, and sometimes little sticks of kindling-wood would be found laying beside the kitchen stove. They never knew when they would come across that child, and always she kept saying over and over that she couldn't find her mother. They never tried talking to her, except once in awhile Mrs. Bird would get desperate and ask her something, but the child never seemed to hear it; she always kept right on saying that she couldn't find her mother.

"After they had told me all they had to tell about their experience with the child, they told me about the house and the people that had lived there before they did. It seemed something dreadful had happened in that house. And the land agent had never let on to them. I don't think they would have bought it if he had, no matter how cheap it was, for even if folks aren't really afraid of anything, they don't want to live in houses where such dreadful things have happened that you keep thinking about them. I know after they told me I should never have stayed there another night, if I hadn't thought so much of them, no matter how comfortable I was made; and I never was nervous, either. But I stayed. Of course, it didn't happen in my room. If it had I could not have stayed."

"What was it?" asked Mrs. Emerson in an awed voice.

"It was an awful thing. That child had lived in the house with her father and mother two years before. They had come—or the father had—from a real good family. He had a good situation: he was a drummer for a big leather house in the city, and they lived real pretty, with plenty to do with. But the mother was a real wicked woman. She was as handsome as a picture, and they said she came from good sort of people enough in Boston, but she was bad clean through, though she was real pretty spoken and most everybody liked her. She used to dress out and make a great show, and she never seemed to take much interest in the child, and folks began to say she wasn't treated right.

"The woman had a hard time keeping a girl. For some reason one wouldn't stay. They would leave and then talk about her awfully, telling all kinds of things. People didn't believe it at first; then they began to. They said that the woman made that little thing, though she wasn't much over five years old, and small and babyish for her age, do most of the work, what there was done; they said the house used to look like a pigsty when she didn't have help. They said the little thing used to stand on a chair and wash dishes, and they'd seen her carrying in sticks of wood most as big as she was many a time, and they'd heard her mother scolding her. The woman was a fine singer, and had a voice like a screech-owl when she scolded.

"The father was away most of the time, and when that happened he had been away out West for some weeks. There had been a married man hanging about the mother for some time, and folks had talked some; but they weren't sure there was anything wrong, and he was a man very high up, with money, so they kept pretty still for fear he would hear of it and make trouble for them, and of course nobody was sure, though folks did say afterward that the father of the child had ought to have been told.

"But that was very easy to say; it wouldn't have been so easy to find anybody who would have been willing to tell him such a thing as that, especially when they weren't any too sure. He set his eyes by his wife, too. They said all he seemed to think of was to earn money to buy things to deck her out in. And he about worshiped the child, too. They said he was a real nice man. The men that are treated so bad mostly are real nice men. I've always noticed that.

"Well, one morning that man that there had been whispers about was missing. He had been gone quite a while, though, before they really knew that he was missing, because he had gone away and told his wife that he had to go to New York on business and might be gone a week, and not to worry if he didn't get home, and not to worry if he didn't write, because he should be thinking from day to day that he might take the next train home and there would be no use in writing. So the wife waited, and she tried not to worry until it was two days over the week, then she run into a neighbour's and fainted dead away on the floor; and then they made inquiries and found out that he had skipped—with some money that didn't belong to him, too.

"Then folks began to ask where was that woman, and they found out by comparing notes that nobody had seen her since the man went away; but three or four women remembered that she had told them that she thought of taking the child and going to Boston to visit her folks, so when they hadn't seen her around, and the house shut, they jumped to the conclusion that was where she was. They were the neighbours that lived right around her, but they didn't have much to do with her, and she'd gone out of her way to tell them about her Boston plan, and they didn't make much reply when she did.

"Well, there was this house shut up, and the man and woman missing and the child. Then all of a sudden one of the women that lived the nearest remembered something. She remembered that she had waked up three nights running, thinking she heard a child crying somewhere, and once she waked up her husband, but he said it must be the Bisbees' little girl, and she thought it must be. The child wasn't well and was always crying. It used to have colic spells, especially at night. So she didn't think any more about it until this came up, then all of a sudden she did think of it. She told what she had heard, and finally folks began to think they had better enter that house and see if there was anything wrong.

"Well, they did enter it, and they found that child dead, locked in one of the rooms. (Mrs. Dennison and Mrs. Bird never used that room; it was a back bedroom on the second floor.)

"Yes, they found that poor child there, starved to death, and frozen, though they weren't sure she had frozen to death, for she was in bed with clothes enough to keep her pretty warm when she was alive. But she had been there a week, and she was nothing but skin and bone. It looked as if the mother had locked her into the house when she went away, and told her not to make any noise for fear the neighbours would hear her and find out that she herself had gone.

"Mrs. Dennison said she couldn't really believe that the woman had meant to have her own child starved to death. Probably she thought the little thing would raise somebody, or folks would try to get in the house and find her. Well, whatever she thought, there the child was, dead.

"But that wasn't all. The father came home, right in the midst of it; the child was just buried, and he was beside himself. And—he went on the track of his wife, and he found her, and he shot her dead; it was in all the papers at the time; then he disappeared. Nothing had been seen of him since. Mrs. Dennison said that she thought he had either made way with himself or got out of the country, nobody knew, but they did know there was something wrong with the house.

"'I knew folks acted queer when they asked me how I liked it when we first came here,' says Mrs. Dennison, 'but I never dreamed why till we saw the child that night.'"

"I never heard anything like it in my life," said Mrs. Emerson, staring at the other woman with awestruck eyes.

"I thought you'd say so," said Mrs. Meserve. "You don't wonder that I ain't disposed to speak light when I hear there is anything queer about a house, do you?"

"No, I don't, after that," Mrs. Emerson said.

"But that ain't all," said Mrs. Meserve.

"Did you see it again?" Mrs. Emerson asked.

"Yes, I saw it a number of times before the last time. It was lucky I wasn't nervous, or I never could have stayed there, much as I liked the place and much as I thought of those two women; they were beautiful women, and no mistake. I loved those women. I hope Mrs. Dennison will come and see me sometime.

"Well, I stayed, and I never knew when I'd see that child. I got so I was very careful to bring everything of mine upstairs, and not leave any little thing in my room that needed doing, for fear she would come lugging up my coat or hat or gloves or I'd find things done when there'd been no live being in the room to do them. I can't tell you how I dreaded seeing her; and worse than the seeing her was the hearing her say, 'I can't find my mother.' It was enough to make your blood run cold. I never heard a living child cry for its mother that was anything so pitiful as that dead one. It was enough to break your heart.

"She used to come and say that to Mrs. Bird oftener than to any one else. Once I heard Mrs. Bird say she wondered if it was possible that the poor little thing couldn't really find her mother in the other world, she had been such a wicked woman.

"But Mrs. Dennison told her she didn't think she ought to speak so nor even think so, and Mrs. Bird said she shouldn't wonder if she was right. Mrs. Bird was always very easy to put in the wrong. She was a good woman, and one that couldn't do things enough for other folks. It seemed as if that was what she lived on. I don't think she was ever so scared by that poor little ghost, as much as she pitied it, and she was 'most heartbroken because she couldn't do anything for it, as she could have done for a live child.

"'It seems to me sometimes as if I should die if I can't get that awful little white robe off that child and get her in some clothes and feed her and stop her looking for her mother,' I heard her say once, and she was in earnest. She cried when she said it. That wasn't long before she died.

"Now I am coming to the strangest part of it all. Mrs. Bird died very sudden. One morning—it was Saturday, and there wasn't any school—I went downstairs to breakfast, and Mrs. Bird wasn't there; there was nobody but Mrs. Dennison. She was pouring out the coffee when I came in. 'Why, where's Mrs. Bird?' says I.

"'Abby ain't feeling very well this morning,' says she; 'there isn't much the matter, I guess, but she didn't sleep very well, and her head aches, and she's sort of chilly, and I told her I thought she'd better stay in bed till the house gets warm.' It was a very cold morning.

"'Maybe she's got cold,' says I.

"'Yes, I guess she has,' says Mrs. Dennison. 'I guess she's got cold. She'll be up before long. Abby ain't one to stay in bed a minute longer than she can help.'

"Well, we went on eating our breakfast, and all at once a shadow flickered across one wall of the room and over the ceiling the way a shadow will sometimes when somebody passes the window outside. Mrs. Dennison and I both looked up, then out of the window; then Mrs. Dennison she gives a scream.

"'Why, Abby's crazy!' says she. 'There she is out this bitter cold morning, and—and———' She didn't finish, but she meant the child. For we were both looking out, and we saw, as plain as we ever saw anything in our lives, Mrs. Abby Bird walking off over the white snow-path with that child holding fast to her hand, nestling close to her as if she had found her own mother.

"'She's dead,' says Mrs. Dennison, clutching hold of me hard. 'She's dead; my sister is dead!'

"She was. We hurried upstairs as fast as we could go, and she was dead in her bed, and smiling as if she was dreaming, and one arm and hand was stretched out as if something had hold of it; and it couldn't be straightened even at the last—it lay out over her casket at the funeral."

"Was the child ever seen again?" asked Mrs. Emerson in a shaking voice.

"No," replied Mrs. Meserve; "that child was never seen again after she went out of the yard with Mrs. Bird."

Part Three

Stories from

Eglantina

1902

"Eglantina, tall and fair,
   Queen of Beauty and of Grace,
All my darkened house of life
   Is illumined by thy face.

"Shinest thou unto my heart
   As the dew in morning field,
When beneath the eastern sun
   Gems of Zion blaze revealed.

"Sweet'nest thou my every thought
   Like the bud when night hath passed,
And she breaks her seal of bloom
   To become a rose at last.

"Though in gloom thy lover sighs,
   Eglantina, tall and fair,
Love the Blind hath touched his eyes,
   And he sees thee past compare."

These verses abounding in conceits, and appealing to the purely personal rather than to the broadly human side of love and tender sentiment, were cut and skilfully colored, illuminated after a simple fashion, on a window-shutter in the east parlor of the old Litchfield house, in Litchfield village. The furniture of the east parlor was after the fashion of Queen Anne.

There were bulky-drawered pieces rearing themselves with precarious grace on tall, slim, and fragile legs; there were tables which seemed to have a perpetual swaying motion of their own, the ornaments whereon—the shells and china vases and card-baskets—faintly jingled when one crossed the room; there were sofas and chairs which creaked with faint remonstrance but never succumbed under weight. The sofas and chairs had been upholstered with sea-green, then it faded to a green like a dim reminiscence of the color which might have served as a background for memories of old bloom—the long-past roses and pinks and heartsease of old gardens, of the old garden behind the Litchfield house, and, if one chose to think further, of the youthful joys of the dwellers in the house.

That was Eglantina's favorite room, and there she used to sit with Roger Proctor. Eglantina's father had married for the second time when her mother had been dead ten years and she was eleven. The new wife had been a widow with one child, Roger Proctor, a year younger than Eglantina. Dr. Eliphalet Litchfield had been jealous of this son by a former husband, and had insisted upon the mother's practically separating from him upon her marriage with himself.

So the boy, who had been blind from scarlet-fever ever since his infancy, was put to board with a distant relative of his mother's, and was seldom seen by her.

Dr. Eliphalet Litchfield was a man of such concentrated tenderness towards a few that it gave rise to cruelty towards others. All his life he had also been suspicious of that which he loved, lest it not belong wholly and unreservedly to him, and he fought for his own against the phantoms of his brain and not against real foes. Although he always feared that she did not, the new wife easily loved him better than she loved her blind son, for Dr. Litchfield was a personable and masterful man, who could compel, although long past youth, almost any woman to his will. The new wife was scarcely more than a girl, although a widow with a son of ten. She was a mild and delicate creature, whose only force of character lay in loving devotion, and that proved too strenuous for her fragile constitution. She died a year after her marriage, and her little daughter died with her.

Then Dr. Litchfield sent for the blind son of the dead woman, and lavished upon him a curious affection, which was at first not so much affection as a sentiment of duty and remorse. This man, given to fierce strains of mood, chose to fancy that his young wife's untimely death was to be held in the light of a judgment of God for their desertion of her blind son. He never looked in the boy's sightless face without seeing that of a long-since-dead but nevertheless triumphant rival, and he saw also, in the boy himself, another aspirant, and a rightful one, to his lost wife's love; but he was devoted to his welfare. From the time that Roger Proctor came to live in the Litchfield house his lines were cast in pleasant places. Dr. Litchfield enjoined upon his daughter Eglantina that she was to treat the strange little boy as her own brother, and he himself showed more indulgence towards him than towards her. Roger, although a boy, and blind, went clad in finer raiment than Eglantina; he had a pony and rode when she walked. He was taught by expensive teachers, while Eglantina had to be satisfied with simpler and less expensive instruction, for Dr. Litchfield was not a rich man. Roger had the best bedroom in the house, and Eglantina a small one, hot in summer and cold in winter. Had the girl anything she loved for which the boy expressed a preference, she was straightway reminded that she must give it up cheerfully to her blind brother. However, Eglantina needed no such reminding. From the minute that the blind child entered the house the other child was his willing slave. Nothing was ever seen more appealing to old and young than that little blind boy, Roger Proctor. His hair, which hung in straight, smooth lengths, had a wonderful high light around his head which suggested an aureole. His young face, between these lines of gold, was an oval so pure that it had an effect of majesty and peace even in the child. His blind eyes, large and blue, seeming to give instead of receive light, gazed with unswerving directness from under a high forehead of innocent seriousness. Although his forehead seemed almost frowning with gravity, Roger's mouth was always smiling with a wonderful smile, before which people shrank a little. "He looks like an angel," they said. It was a smile of inward cognizance rather than observation, and revealed, as nothing else could have done, the nature of the boy. It gave evidence of the estimation in which a perfectly simple and guileless soul held those around him who appealed to his crippled senses. There was that about the boy which excited a certain fear and awe. His was a most perfect limpidity of nature. One looking therein saw everything—reflections and depths of innocence. His motives shone through all his actions with unmistakable radiance. The blind boy gave, as no seeing child could have done, an impression of light and clearness. Soon his step-father adored him, and as for Eglantina, she worshipped him from the first. No greater contrast could

have been imagined than there was between the girl and the boy. They
were of about the same age, but Eglantina was head and shoulders above
Roger, though he was not below the usual height. But Eglantina was abnormally tall; her stature was almost a deformity, especially since she was
exceedingly slender. And that was not all. Crowning that slim height was a
head and face unfortunate not so much from lack of beauty as from a mark
on one cheek which had been there from birth. A story was told in the village of how Dr. Litchfield's wife had longed for roses in winter when there
were none, and talked of the rose which climbed over the front porch in the
summer-time, and declared that she could smell them when none were
there, and how at last when Eglantina was born, there on one little cheek
was that hideous travesty of a red rose which she must bear until the day of
her death. The mother, who had a strong vein of romance, had called the
child Eglantina, and mourned until she died, not long after, because of her
disfigurement, and often kissed with tears of self-reproach and the most
passionate tenderness and pity the mark on the little cheek, as if she would
kiss it away.

Dr. Litchfield ever after hated roses; he would have none in his garden,
and the eglantine over the front porch was rooted up. Eglantina herself had
an antipathy to roses, and never could she have a whiff of rose scent unless
she turned faint and ill. Nothing could exceed the child's sensitiveness with
regard to the mark on her cheek. She never looked in her glass without seeing that, and that only. That dreadful blur of youth and beauty seemed all
her face; she was blind to all else. She shrank from strangers with a shyness
that was almost panic. Eyes upon her face seemed to scorch her very heart.
But as she grew older, although the inward suffering was much the same,
she learned to give less outward evidence of it. She no longer shrank so involuntarily from strangers; she even endured pitying glances, or repulsion,
with a certain gentleness which gave evidence of enormous patience rather
than bravery. When Roger had been in her father's house some years, she
became conscious of a feeling which filled her with horror. She strove
against it, she tried to imagine that it was not so, that she could not be such
a monster, but she knew all of a sudden that she was glad that Roger was
blind. Whenever she looked at him came the wild, selfish triumph and joy
that he could not see her. Her consciousness of this came upon her in full
force for the first time one afternoon in August, when she was eighteen and
Roger a few months younger. They were crossing a field behind the house,
hand-in-hand as usual, for, although Roger could walk very well alone, he

moved with more certainty—and that not alone from his lack of sight, but from the lack of something in his nature—if he were in leading of some one. Eglantina was still much taller. They strolled together across the wide field sloping to the south. The field was rosy with sorrel, out of which flew butterflies of much the same color with a curious effect as if the flowers themselves had taken wings. Eglantina told Roger. "The butterflies fly up in clouds, and it looks as if the flowers themselves had broken loose from the ground; they are of the same color," said she.

Roger turned his sightless eyes towards the sorrel, and nodded and smiled as if he saw. "I have made a poem to you, Eglantina," said he.

Eglantina colored until the rest of her face was as red as the rose-mark on her left cheek, then she turned pale, and that brought it into stronger relief. "You must not," she said, faintly.

"Why not? There is no one in the whole world as beautiful as you are, Eglantina."

"No, I am not," she returned, in a pitiful, hesitating voice, as if the truth were stifling her.

"Yes."

"You do not know; you never saw me."

"I have seen you with my whole soul. You are the most beautiful girl in the whole world, Eglantina."

Eglantina shut her mouth hard. She pulled her broad-brimmed hat over her face by the green bridle-ribbon, and cast her disfigured cheek into a deep shadow.

It was a burning day, the ground was hot to their feet, perfumed waves of steaming air came in their faces. There was a loud din of locusts. Over in another field some men were mowing, swinging their scythes in glittering circles, and now and then calling to one another with hoarse laughter. Then came the liquid call of a quail, then shouts of children over in the road. It seemed to Eglantina as if the whole world was in a merry dance of love and progress, and that she alone was caught motionless in the current of fate.

Roger looked at her anxiously. "What is the matter, Eglantina?" he asked, softly.

"Nothing," said she.

When they reached home, she ran up to her own chamber. She went to her little mirror over her white-draped dressing-table and gazed long in it. Then she sank down before it on the floor in an agony of self-abasement.

After a while she rose and pulled the muslin drapery over the glass, and did not look in it again. When she went down-stairs there was Roger's poem cut skilfully on the shutter in the east parlor. Roger could not use pen or pencil to much advantage, but he could cut the letters plainly, feeling them with his long, sensitive fingers. Eglantina held her cambric pocket-handkerchief over her marred cheek and read every word, smiling tenderly. Then she put the handkerchief to her eyes and leaned against the shutter and sobbed softly. Then Roger came into the room, feeling his way towards her, and she choked her sobs back and dried her eyes. Roger wished to color the letters of his poem, and Eglantina sorted out the colors from her paint-box, and he painted them.

Then every time that she saw that poem to Eglantina, tall and fair, she tried to picture herself as Roger saw her, and not as she really was. She tried to forget the birthmark, she tried not to think of it when she spoke to Roger, lest the consciousness of it be evident in her voice, but that she could not compass. She thought of it always, and the more she strove against it the more she was conscious of it, until she grew to feel as if the mark were on her very soul.

But her patience grew and grew to keep pace with it. Eglantina had been an impatient child, nervous and irritable, but all that had gone. There were in her heart ceaseless torture and suffering, but never rebellion. She thought of the mark as her shame and her fault; she unreasoningly reproached herself because of it, but she never complained of her hard fate.

Everybody who knew Eglantina spoke well of her. They said what a pity that such a good girl should be under such an affliction, and they also said when they saw the piteous couple together—the man who could not see and the woman who should not be seen—that there was an ideal match. Eglantina's father began also to have that fancy. He had grown old of late years, and had the troubled persistency of a child for his way, when once he had begun to dwell upon it. It was not long after Roger had cut his verses to Eglantina, tall and fair, on the shutter. The old man spied them one afternoon when he had returned from a call in the village, for his professional services were still in demand. The shutter had swung into the room in a sudden gust of east wind, and he had caught sight of something unwonted upon it. He put on his glasses and stood close to the shutter, reading laboriously. That evening he called Eglantina back after she had started upstairs with her candle. "Eglantina, come here a moment," he said. "I want to speak to you."

Eglantina returned and stood before him, the candle-light illuminating her poor face, which her father had never seen without a qualm of pain and rebellion. That mark was for him like a blot on the fair face of love itself, and his will rose up against it in futile revolt.

Her father looked at her, his forehead contracted, then he turned towards the shutter, and again towards her with a half-smile, while one long finger pointed to the verses. "Have you seen these, Eglantina?" he said.

"Yes, sir," replied Eglantina, gravely. She looked full at her father with a look which was fairly eloquent. "See what I am," it said. "What have I to do with love-verses? Why do you mock me by speaking of this?"

But her father shook his head stubbornly as if in direct answer to such unspoken speech of hers. "If," he said, with a sort of stern abashedness, for he had never spoken of such things to his daughter—"if your own heart leads you in that direction, Eglantina, there is no possible objection, and I should like to see you settled. I am growing old."

Eglantina, still speechless, raised one arm, her lace sleeve falling back from her wrist, and pointed to her marred left cheek. There was in the gesture utmost resignation and pride, and her eyes reproved her father mutely.

Her father frowned and continued shaking his head in denial. "I still say that under the circumstances there can be no possible objection," he said. "What difference can that make to a blind man, who has learned to esteem you for your own true worth, and has invested you in his own mind with the graces of person to correspond with those of your character?"

Eglantina looked at him. After all, she was eager to be persuaded. "I cannot keep it secret from him," she faltered.

"How can you do aught else? How can you describe your face to a blind man?"

Eglantina continued to regard her father with eyes of painful searching, as one who would discover hope against conviction and find refutation for her own argument.

"Roger has been told repeatedly," said her father.

Eglantina nodded. She herself had told him, and he had laughed at her.

"And the telling conveys no meaning to him," said her father. "What does beauty or deformity of the flesh signify to a blind man."

"I can see, and I can see that which he loves mistakenly," replied Eglantina, in a pitiful voice.

The two stood facing each other, both the father and daughter above middle height, for Eglantina got her height from her father. The two faces were on a level—Dr. Litchfield's, thin to asceticism, domed by a high, bald forehead, confronted the other face illuminated by the upward gleam of the candle, and his lightened unexpectedly with surprise and approbation. The east wind, salt with the sea, came in at the open window. The girl's white gown wound around her in ruffling folds, for the window was at her back; her brown hair, which was long and fine and curling, blew over her disfigured cheek, partly concealing it. That of her face which was visible was not unpleasing, though irregular, being too full of curves, even her profile having no clearly cut lines. Eglantina's face gave the impression of a sweet dissonance of overlapping curves, and suggested a rose. Moreover, under the upward light of the candle, it took on, as to lips and eyes, a radiant sparkle of dewy youth. She looked fairly beautiful to her father. For the first time the girl saw a look of admiration fixed upon her poor face. "You are not so bad-looking, after all, my child," her father said, in a new voice, and Eglantina's heart leaped, and for the minute she was actually beautiful. She was triumphant over her deformity.

"Do as your heart dictates, my daughter," said her father, "and have no fear."

Eglantina pulled her hair farther over the disfigured cheek; she looked at her father with a smile at once foolish, doubtful, and beatific, then she turned without a word and went out with white robes and brown hair streaming back, and her candle was extinguished in the draught as she passed the door.

The next day, in the afternoon, she was seated in the arbor in the garden with her embroidery work. She worked cunning eyelet holes in a strip of linen, and the shadow of the vines made a soft, green gloom in the place, and near by was a hive of bees, and she could hear their drowsy hum and see their winged flights to a great bed of pinks, wilting in the full blaze of the sunlight, and giving out a great, panting fragrance of spice and honey. There were no roses in the garden, and there were virgin's-bower and a hop-vine over the arbor, instead of the eglantine which had formerly shaded it.

Presently Eglantina saw Roger coming, walking almost as if he saw, with no outstretching of feeling hands. In fact, he knew his way well enough between the flower-beds, being guided by their various odors. His direct path to Eglantina in the arbor lay between mignonette and pinks on one side and sweet alyssum and thyme on the other.

Eglantina, watching him approach, swept a great bunch of brown curls completely over her disfigured cheek, and sat so when he entered.

"Pass all the other lesser flowers by until you find the rose," he said, laughing tenderly.

"I am no rose," said Eglantina.

"The rose does not know she is herself, else she would be no rose," said Roger.

"I am a poor mockery of a rose, from this dreadful mark on my cheek," said Eglantina, and she felt as if she were about to die, for it seemed to her that such brutal frankness must convince.

But Roger only laughed. "The rose has a scratch from a thorn on one of her petals," he returned, "or a bee has sucked too greedily for honey. What of it? Is there not enough beauty left? There is no one in the whole world so beautiful as you, Eglantina. A mark on your cheek! What is a mark on your cheek but a beauty, since it is a part of you? Fret no more about it, sweetheart."

Eglantina looked at him, at the beautiful face in a cloud of golden beard, at the sightless blue eyes, and she pulled the curls closer over her cheek and resisted no longer.

It was then the 1st of September, and it was decided to have the marriage the next month—there was no reason why they should wait, and Dr. Litchfield was disposed to hasten the wedding. Soon the simple preparations were nearly finished. Roger's chamber had been newly papered with a pale-green satin paper, sprinkled with bouquets of flowers. Roger's wedding-suit was ready and Eglantina's gown. The gown was a peach-blow silk, and it lay in shimmering folds on the high bed in the spare chamber, and from the tester floated the veil, and a pair of little rose-colored slippers toed out daintily beside the dimity dressing-table, and in a little box thereon was a brooch which Roger had given her—a knot of his fair hair set in a circle of pearls.

The summer was still fervid. One evening, after a very warm day, Roger and Eglantina had been walking a long way down the country road towards the village, and it was late when they returned and went into the house. The moon was long risen and the dew was heavy, like a hoar-frost over the meadows and gardens, and all things sweetened in it. There was a great breath of rowen hay over the land, and of wild grapes and apples and pears. Now and then came a dark flap of a wing of mystery, and a whippoorwill called out of the willows on the border of a brook.

Roger and Eglantina kissed each other in the front entry, then Roger went up-stairs in the dark and Eglantina lighted her chamber candle.

But her father called her again, and she went into the east parlor as before, with the candle throwing an upward light upon her face. This time Dr. Litchfield hesitated long before speaking, so long that she looked at him in surprise, thinking that she had, perhaps, not understood and he had not called her. "Did you want to see me, father?" she asked.

"Yes, Eglantina," he replied, but still he hesitated, and she waited in growing wonder and alarm.

"Eglantina," Dr. Litchfield said, presently.

"Yes, father."

"Dr. David Lyman is in the south village. He has been attending the daughter of Squire Eggleston, who lost her sight from scarlet-fever," her father said, abruptly.

Eglantina turned white and gave a quick gasp.

"He will restore her sight," said her father, "and—" he paused. Eglantina was silent and motionless. She stood with her mouth set hard and her eyes averted.

"It might be well to have him see Roger," said her father. He did not look at her.

Eglantina turned and went out of the room without a word.

That night she did not sleep. She was awake all night, pleading pitilessly for and against herself, as if she had been a stranger. Monstrous as it might seem, there was something to be said in favor of letting the physician who might restore Roger's sight pass by and keeping her lover blind until the day of his death. Eglantina, reflecting impartially, knew quite well that if it were her own case, and she had to choose between love and sight, what she should do. "If Roger gains his sight he loses love," she said. "And he is one who, if love go amiss, will come to harm in himself." And that was quite true, for Roger Proctor was a man to be made or marred by love, for he lacked that in his character which would make him stand or fall unto himself alone.

"Will he not lose more than he gains?" Eglantina asked herself, and though her judgment told her yes, yet she dared not trust to her judgment when her inclination so swayed her. Then, moreover, to such strength her love had grown that all the old, guilty, secret gladness over his blindness was gone, and instead was a great tenderness and pity for her lover that he must go blind and miss so much. "He can see a plenty that is beautiful if he miss the beauty in me," thought Eglantina; "and who am I to say that no other woman besides me can make him happy?"

But always she went back to the fear as to how he would endure the awful shock when, after his eyesight was restored, he should look for the first time on her face and see what he had loved and kissed. She thought truly not then of her own distress and humiliation, but of him, and what he would suffer, and she could not argue that away. Then all at once her mind was at rest, for a great and unselfish, though fantastic, plan had occurred to her, and she knew what she could do to spare him.

The next morning her father looked at her, and looked again as if to be sure he saw aright, for he did not seem to see the birthmark at all. There was a strange expression in her face which dominated all disfigurement, and would have dominated beauty as well.

"When will he come?" she asked her father, when Roger was not within hearing.

"This afternoon if I go for him," replied her father, with his eyes still on her face; "but you had best not tell Roger until the doctor has pronounced on the case. You had best not hold up hope that may come to naught."

"It will not come to naught," she replied, and after breakfast she told Roger that a doctor was coming who would cure his eyes and he would see.

Roger received the news with a curious calmness at first, but as he reflected a great joy grew and strengthened in his face. Then he cried out, suddenly, "Then I shall see you; I shall see you!"

"Yes," said Eglantina.

"Why do you speak so, Eglantina? Your voice sounds strange." There was a peculiar quality in Eglantina's voice, a peculiarity of intonation which made it unmistakable among others, and just then it had disappeared.

"Why strange?" said she.

"It is strange now. Are you not glad that I am to see—to see you, sweetheart?"

"I am more than glad," replied Eglantina. Then she went away hurriedly, though Roger called wonderingly and in a hurt fashion after her.

That afternoon before the doctor came Eglantina sent a letter to her cousin Charlotte Wyatt, who lived in Boston, and who was to be present at the wedding, to hasten her coming. The two were great friends, though Charlotte had visited Eglantina but once, when Roger was away, and so had never seen him; but Eglantina had often visited Boston, and the two wrote frequent letters.

"Come if you can in a fortnight's time, dear Charlotte," wrote Eglantina, "though that be a fortnight before the day set for the wedding, for I am in sore trouble and distress of mind, and only you can comfort and help me." And she wrote not a word with regard to Roger's eyes. And she did not mention Charlotte's coming to Roger.

That afternoon Dr. David Lyman came at Dr. Litchfield's bidding, and the operation on Roger's eyes was performed with great hope of success, though the result could not be certainly known for the space of two weeks, when the bandages should be removed and Dr. Lyman would return. During those two weeks Eglantina nursed Roger tenderly and let no trace of her own sadness appear. Indeed, she began to feel that she should have joy enough if Roger regained his sight, even if she lost him thereby, for the blind man was full of delight, and for the first time revealed how he had suffered in his mind because of his loss of sight.

Then the day before the one appointed for the removing of the bandages came Charlotte Wyatt, stepping out of the stage-coach at the door, a tall and most beautiful and stately maiden, who was held in great renown for her beauty, being called the beautiful Charlotte Wyatt, and being the toast of all the young men and sought in marriage by many. Charlotte Wyatt, with all her beauty, bore a certain family resemblance to her cousin. She was of the same height, she was shaped like her, she moved and spoke like her, having the same trick of intonation in her grave, sweet voice. But this resemblance only served to make Eglantina's defects a more lamentable contrast to the other's beauty. It was like a perfect and a deformed rose on the same bush. The deformed flower was the worse deformed for being a rose beside the other.

That night the two girls lay awake all night in bed and talked, and Eglantina told the other her trouble, and yet not all, for she did not discover to her the plan which she had made. Charlotte held her cousin in her arms and wept over her, and pitied her with a pity which bore a cruel sting in it. "I do not wonder that your heart aches, sweetheart, for surely never was a man like Roger, and you might well love him better blind than any other man with his sight," said Charlotte Wyatt, fervently. She had not spoken to Roger, but she had peeped into the room where he sat with his eyes bandaged, with Eglantina reading to him. Eglantina shrank from her suddenly when she said that. "What is the matter? What have I said to hurt you, sweet?" cried Charlotte.

"Nothing, dear," replied Eglantina, and held the other girl close in her arms as they lay in bed.

"I never loved any man overmuch, though so many have said that they loved me, but I can see how you love Roger," Charlotte said, innocently.

"There is no one like him," Eglantina agreed, and she began sobbing in a despairing fashion, and Charlotte strove to comfort her. "He will love you just the same when he can see," she said. "Beauty is but skin deep, sweetheart."

"I care not—oh, I care not, so he is not hurt," sobbed Eglantina.

"How you love him!" whispered the other girl. "If he is not true to love like yours, he is more blind when he sees than when he saw not."

"No, he will not be one whit to blame," cried Eglantina, angrily. She sprang out of bed and ran to her looking-glass, and she looked in it, and the candle was burning at the side, and she saw her face plainly, and Charlotte also saw it in the glass. Then Eglantina turned and looked at her cousin, and Charlotte's eyes fell. "Oh, Eglantina, I—I wish—" she began, brokenly. Then she wept aloud for pity and confusion. "I will always love you. Your face is beautiful to me. I will always love you," she sobbed, and it was the same as if she had owned that Roger would not.

It was the next afternoon that the bandages were to be removed from Roger Proctor's eyes, and it would then be known if the operation were a success. The great doctor and Eglantina's father and the nurse were in the room with Roger. Eglantina and Charlotte waited outside. Charlotte was dressed in a lilac satin gown falling in soft folds around her lovely height, and her fair hair was twisted into a great knot from which fell a shower of loose curls around her rosy face, and since she had come away without a certain tucker of wrought lace which she much affected, Eglantina had dressed her in one of her own, taking it from a drawer where it had lain with a sachet of lavender, and she had fastened it with her brooch of Roger's hair set in pearls.

The two moved up and down; neither could rest, for an uneasiness as great as Eglantina's was apparently over the other girl. The girls of the same height, with the same fashion of wearing their hair, with the same tricks of motion, with the lamentable difference of likeness in their faces, seemed to fill all the east parlor with the same fluttering wind of agitation. Charlotte espied the verses to "Eglantina, tall and fair" on the shutter, and began to read them aloud, then paused for shame and confusion before she said 'fair,' and Eglantina listened unmoved. Then Charlotte ran to her and laid her beautiful, rosy cheek against her cousin's disfigured one and kissed her, and the kiss seemed to burn Eglantina, but she did not shrink.

They listened to every sound from the next room, the doctor's study, where Roger and the two physicians were, and presently out came Dr. Eliphalet Litchfield, not with the gladness of his profession after a successful operation, but falteringly, with pitiful eyes upon his daughter.

"Well?" said Eglantina to him.

"He sees," replied Dr. Litchfield, in a husky voice. He looked hesitatingly at Eglantina. The door of the next room was opened again, and Dr. David Lyman looked out. "He is asking for your daughter," he said to Eliphalet Litchfield, and after a swift glance at Eglantina he fastened his gaze upon Charlotte. He had seen neither before, Eglantina having kept herself out of his sight, and he thought Charlotte was she.

"Eglantina, Eglantina," called Roger's voice, high with nervousness, from the next room. He was too weak to stir; the strain had been severe, and he was of a delicate physique. "You had best come at once," whispered Dr. David Lyman, who was a small, fair man with a manner of imperious incisiveness, to Charlotte. "He has been under a great stress, and it is not advisable to cross him; even his sight may depend upon it." Then he turned impatiently to Dr. Litchfield. "Your daughter had better come," he said.

Before Charlotte could speak, Eglantina laid a hand with a weight of steel on her arm. "Go," she said.

Charlotte stared at her, pale and scared.

"Go," said Eglantina.

Dr. Litchfield made a motion forward, but Eglantina stopped him with a look. She pushed Charlotte towards the study door, and whispered sharply in her ear. "You heard what the doctor said," she whispered. "Don't let him know. Go."

Charlotte went into the room, half by force, half with bewildered quiescence. Then the three outside heard a great cry of rapture from Roger.

Eglantina went away hurriedly. The two men stood looking at each other. "She is my daughter," said Dr. Eliphalet Litchfield.

"My God," said the other.

It was nearly time for the stage-coach to pass the house. Eglantina was waiting for it at the turn of the road beyond. She wore her long green cloak and carried a bandbox. No one had seen her leave the house. An hour later Dr. Litchfield found a letter pinned to his cloak, which hung in the entry. It was very brief:

"Dear Father,—This is to inform you that I have gone to Aunt Pamela's. Do not undeceive Roger at present, and do not let Charlotte. Your respectful and obedient daughter to command,

"Eglantina."

Eglantina's aunt Pamela Litchfield lived in the next village of Stonybrook. She was a maiden woman with a large estate, and she lived alone, with the exception of one old servant. When her niece arrived and told her story, or a great part of her story, she listened with amazement and a large mixture of admiration and sympathy. A considerable vein of romance had this old maiden lady, although she held it for the most part well in check, and was considered to have disdained many good opportunities for matrimony.

"And do you propose that your father and cousin should continue this deception long, my dear?" she said.

"As long as may be needful," replied Eglantina.

"Until Roger falls in love with Charlotte?" asked the old lady, shrewdly.

"He is in love with her now."

"Because he thinks Charlotte Eglantina."

"She is the Eglantina whom he loved."

"Nonsense, dear child; she is not the Eglantina whom he loved, unless 'twas a surface affection not worthy the name of love."

"He could not love a face like mine," said Eglantina, gently and proudly.

"Think you that your father and cousin will consent to such deceit?"

"They must until he is recovered."

"And when they tell him, what then?"

"Then he will love Charlotte, and she will love him, and all will be well."

"All will not be well," said Pamela Litchfield, firmly. But she said no more; she coaxed her niece to eat, and by-and-by to sleep, after a composing draught of orange-flower water. Next morning she sent a letter to her brother, but she kept Eglantina, and let no one see her, and tended her, and made much of her, secretly adoring her as a heroine who had done a noble and unheard-of deed for love. Eglantina had been with her aunt Pamela a week, when one afternoon came Charlotte, riding in the doctor's chaise, herself driving with a pretty skill, holding the reins high, slapping the white horse's back with them, and clucking to him like a bird to hasten his pace. And she, running into Miss Pamela Litchfield's house, and finding Eglantina by herself embroidering in the parlor, in the deep window-seat, caught her round the waist, and talked fast, half laughing and half crying. "He will not have me," she said. "He yet believes me to be you, though my conscience chides me sore for the deceit. Your father has been silent, too, though 'twas against his will; yet what could we do, since you left us in such a plaguy lurch, and Dr. Lyman saying he must not be crossed. But he will have none of me, and this morning he told me, with as near tears as a man may, that he accounted himself as worthy of great blame, but held that he might be worthy of more did he dissemble. Then did my pretty gentleman inform me—me, Charlotte Wyatt, that his feelings had changed, that he held himself in great despite for the change, and considered that in gaining his sight he had lost that which was infinitely more precious, and also his good esteem for himself, but he saw nothing for it but the truth, though sorely troubled to speak it. This to me, and to my uncle, your father, he said more. This he said of me, of me who has had some praise, whether deserved or not, for her looks, and hath been sought of many men with eyesight of the best—that he was disappointed in my poor face, that it was not what he had deemed it to be, that it was less fair. Nay, he even went further, this blind man who now sees, and called it, not hideous, for he is too gentle a man for that, but he admitted that it hath a repulsion for his fastidiousness. And then I, having heard what he said to my uncle, and being, I will admit, something taken aback by such slighting, must needs march in and tell this particular gentleman, Roger Proctor, the truth, or at least a part of the truth, for your magnanimity I kept from him, for I began to have an inkling that he would be sorely hurt instead of pleased by it. I told him that it was all a deception, that I was my poor self instead of his beloved Eglantina, that she had been unexpectedly called away, and that we had deceived him for his health's sake, and, Lord! had you but seen how he brightened! And now you must go to him, sweetheart."

But Eglantina at that lost all the firmness which had sustained her, and wept and implored, and declared that she could not, but Charlotte and Pamela Litchfield pleaded with her, and comforted and encouraged her, Charlotte saying that it was considered highly dangerous even yet for Roger to be thwarted in any way, since he was exceeding nervous, and a mental strain might bring about inflammation to the eyes, and finally she yielded.

It was evening when Eglantina and Charlotte, in the doctor's chaise, rode into the yard of the Litchfield house, and Eglantina did not see Roger until the next morning. In the morning she went into the east parlor where he sat. She opened the door abruptly, for she had no courage for delay, and entered, and stood before Roger Proctor, and a sunbeam from the east window, the lettered shutter of which had been thrown open, fell upon her poor face with the monstrous travesty of a rose disfiguring her cheek, and Roger gave one great, glad cry of recognition, and she was in his arms, and he was covering her face with kisses, and looking at it with ecstasy, as if it were the face of an angel. "Oh, Eglantina," he said. "It is you, sweetheart, you and no other; no other could have such beauty as thine, the beauty I have seen with my soul and now see with my twice-blessed eyes."

For, strange as it may seem, this poor Eglantina seemed to Roger Proctor more beautiful than one of the greatest beauties of her day. It may have been from a false standard of taste, or he may have been always blinded by love, even after he had gained his sight, or, as some held, it may have been that the mark on Eglantina's face had in some way so chastened and influenced her character of humility and patience and unselfishness that a harmony deeper and truer than any ordinary loveliness had been established between her affliction and her soul, and she had become in a high and spiritual sense a beauty, indeed, to those who might be able to see.

Eglantina lived and died, and her long grave is in the graveyard of Litchfield village, and at the head is a marble stone on which are cut the verses beginning, "Eglantina, tall and fair."

They who read may well imagine that she who was buried there was fair beyond her compeers. And it is true that she who lies under the green sod whence has sprung a wild rose-bush, self-sown, was to one loving heart one of the greatest and most marvellous beauties who ever lived; and who shall deny that she was, indeed, "Queen of Beauty and of Grace"?

The Revolt of Sophia Lane
(The Givers)

1903

The level of new snow in Sophia Lane's north yard was broken by horse's tracks and the marks of sleigh-runners. Sophia's second cousin, Mrs. Adoniram Cutting, her married daughter Abby Dodd, and unmarried daughter Eunice had driven over from Addison, and put up their horse and sleigh in Sophia's clean, unused barn.

When Sophia had heard the sleigh-bells she had peered eagerly out of the window of the sitting-room and dropped her sewing. "Here's Ellen and Abby and Eunice," she cried, "and they've brought you some wedding-presents. Flora Bell, you put the shawl over your head, and go out through the shed and open the barn. I'll tell them to drive right in."

With that the girl and the woman scuttled—Flora Bell through the house and shed to the barn which joined it; Sophia, to the front door of the house, which she pushed open with some difficulty on account of the banked snow. Then she called to the women in the sleigh, which had stopped at the entrance to the north yard: "Drive right in—drive right in. Flora has gone to open the barn doors. She'll be there by the time you get there."

Then Sophia ran through the house to the kitchen, set the teakettle forward, and measured some tea into the teapot. She moved with the greatest swiftness, as if the tea in so many seconds were a vital necessity. When the guests came in from the barn she greeted them breathlessly. "Go right into the sittin'-room," said she. "Flora, you take their things and put them on the bedroom bed. Set right down by the stove and get warm, and the tea 'll be ready in a minute. The water's 'most boilin'. You must be 'most froze." The three women, who were shapeless bundles from their wraps, moved clumsily into the sitting-room as before a spanking breeze of will. Flora followed them; she moved more slowly than her aunt, who was a miracle of nervous speed. Sophia Lane never walked; she ran to all her duties and pleasures as if she were racing against time. She hastened the boiling of the teakettle—she poked the fire; she thrust light slivers of wood into the stove. When the water boiled she made the tea with a rush, and carried the tray with cups and saucers into the sitting-room with a perilous side-wise tilt and flirt. But nothing was spilled. It was very seldom that Sophia came to grief through her haste.

The three women had their wraps removed, and were sitting around the stove. The eldest, Mrs. Ellen Cutting—a stout woman with a handsome face reddened with cold—spoke when Sophia entered.

"Land! if you haven't gone and made hot tea!" said she.

Sophia set the tray down with a jerk, and the cups hopped in their saucers. "Well, I guess you need some," said she, speaking as fast as she moved. "It's a bitter day; you must be froze."

"Yes, it is awful cold," assented Abby Dodd, the married daughter, "but I told mother and Eunice we'd got to come to-day, whether or no. I was bound we should get over here before the wedding."

"Look at Flora blush!" giggled Eunice, the youngest and the unmarried daughter.

Indeed, Flora Bell, who was not pretty, but tall and slender and graceful, was a deep pink all over her delicate face to the roots of her fair hair.

"You wait till your turn comes, Sis, and see what you'll do," said Abby Dodd, who resembled her mother, being fat and pink and white, with a dumpy, slightly round-shouldered figure in a pink flannel shirt-waist frilled with lace. All the new-comers were well dressed, the youngest daughter especially. They had a prosperous air, and they made Sophia's small and frugal sitting-room seem more contracted than usual. Both Sophia and her niece were dressed in garments which the visitors would characterize later among themselves, with a certain scorn tinctured with pity, as "fadged up." They were not shabby, they were not exactly poor, but they were painfully and futilely aspiring. "If only they would not trim quite so much," Eunice Cutting said later. But Sophia dearly loved trimming; and as for Flora, she loved whatever her aunt Sophia did. Sophia had adopted her when her parents died, when she was a baby, and had brought her up on a pittance a year. Flora was to be married to Herbert Bennet on the next day but one. She was hurrying her bridal preparations, and she was in a sort of delirium of triumph, of pride, of happiness and timidity.

She was the centre of attention to-day. The visitors' eyes were all upon her with a half-kindly, half-humorous curiosity.

On the lounge at the side of the room opposite the stove were three packages, beautifully done up in white paper and tied with red and green ribbons. Sophia had spied them the moment she entered the room.

The guests comfortably sipped their tea.

"Is it sweet enough?" asked Sophia of Mrs. Cutting, thrusting the white sugar-bowl at her.

"Plenty," replied Mrs. Cutting. "This tea does go right to the spot. I did get chilled."

"I thought you would."

"Yes, and I don't like to, especially since it is just a year ago since I had pneumonia, but Abby thought we must come to-day, and I thought so myself. I thought we wanted to have one more look at Flora before she was a bride."

"Flora's got to go out now to try on her weddin'-dress the last time," said Sophia. "Miss Beals has been awful hurried at the last minute; she don't turn off work very fast, and the dress won't be done till to-night; but everything else is finished."

"I suppose you've had a lot of presents, Flora?" said Abby Dodd.

"Quite a lot," replied Flora, blushing.

"Yes, she's had some real nice presents, and two or three that ain't quite so nice," said Sophia, "but I guess those can be changed."

Mrs. Cutting glanced at the packages on the sofa with an air of confidence and pride. "We have brought over some little things," said she. "Adoniram and I give one, and Abby and Eunice each one. I hope you'll like them, Flora."

Flora was very rosy; she smiled with a charming effect, as if she were timid before her own delight. "Thank you," she murmured. "I know they are lovely."

"Do go and open them, Flora," said Eunice. "See if you have any other presents like them."

"Yes, open them, Flora," said Mrs. Cutting, with pleasant patronage.

Flora made an eager little movement toward the presents, then she looked wistfully at her aunt Sophia.

Sophia was smiling with a little reserve. "Yes, go and open them, Flora," said she; "then bring out your other presents and show them."

Flora's drab skirt and purple ruffles swayed gracefully across the room; she gathered up the packages in her slender arms, and brought them over to the table between the windows, where her aunt sat. Flora began untying the red and green ribbons, while the visitors looked on with joyful and smiling importance. On one package was marked, "Flora, with all best wishes for her future happiness, from Mr. and Mrs. Adoniram Cutting."

"That is ours," said Mrs. Cutting.

Flora took off the white paper, and a nice white box was revealed. She removed the lid and took out a mass of crumpled tissue-paper. At last she drew forth the present. It was in three pieces. When she had set them on the table, she viewed them with admiration but bewilderment. She looked from one to the other, smiling vaguely.

Abby Dodd laughed. "Why, she doesn't know how to put them to-gether!" said she. She went to the table and quickly adjusted the different parts of the present. "There!" said she, triumphantly.

"What a beautiful—teakettle!" said Flora, but still in a bewildered fashion.

Sophia was regarding it with an odd expression. "What is it?" she asked, shortly.

"Why, Sophia," cried Mrs. Cutting, "don't you know? It is an after-noon-tea kettle."

"What's that thing under it?" asked Sophia.

"Why, that's the alcohol-lamp. It swings on that little frame over the lamp and heats the water. I thought it would be so nice for her."

"It's beautiful," said Flora.

Sophia said nothing.

"It is real silver; it isn't plated," said Mrs. Cutting, in a slightly grieved tone.

"It is beautiful," Flora murmured again, but Sophia said nothing.

Flora began opening another package. It was quite bulky. It was marked, "Flora, with best wishes for a life of love and happiness, from Abby Dodd."

"Be careful," charged Abby Dodd. "It's glass."

Flora removed the paper gingerly. The present was rolled in tissue-paper.

"What beautiful dishes!" said she, but her voice was again slightly be-wildered.

Sophia looked at the present with considerable interest. "What be the bowls for?" said she. "Oatmeal?"

The visitors all laughed.

"Oatmeal!" cried Abby. "Why, they are finger-bowls!"

"Finger-bowls?" repeated Sophia, with a plainly hostile air.

"Yes—bowls to dip your fingers in after dinner," said Abby.

"What for?" asked Sophia.

"Why, to—to wash them."

"We wash our hands in the wash-basin in the kitchen with good hot water and soap," said Sophia.

"Oh, but these are not really to wash the hands in—just to dabble the fingers in," said Eunice, still giggling. "It's the style. You have them in little plates with doilies and pass them around after dinner."

"They are real pretty," said Flora.

Sophia said nothing.

"They are real cut glass," said Mrs. Cutting.

Flora turned to the third package, that was small and flat and exceedingly dainty. The red-and-green ribbon was tied in a charming bow, with Eunice's visiting-card. On the back of the card was written, "Flora, with dearest love, and wishes for a life of happiness, from Eunice." Flora removed the ribbons and the white paper, and opened a flat, white box, disclosing six dainty squares of linen embroidered with violets.

"What lovely mats!" said she.

"They are finger-bowl doilies," said Eunice, radiantly.

"To set the bowls on?" said Flora.

"Yes; you use pretty plates, put a doily in each plate, and then the finger-bowl on the doily."

"They are lovely," said Flora.

Sophia said nothing.

Abby looked rather aggrievedly at Sophia. "Eunice and I thought Flora would like them as well as anything we could give her," said she.

"They are lovely," Flora said again.

"You haven't any like them, have you?" Abby asked, rather uneasily.

"No, she hasn't," answered Sophia, for her niece.

"We tried to think of some things that everybody else wouldn't give her," said Mrs. Cutting.

"Yes, you have," Sophia answered, dryly.

"They are all beautiful," said Flora, in a soft, anxiously deprecating voice, as she gathered up the presents. "I keep my presents in the parlor," she remarked further. "I guess I'll put these in there with the rest."

Presently she returned, bringing a large box; she set it down and returned for another. They were large suit-boxes. She placed them on the table, and the visitors gathered round.

"I've had beautiful presents," said Flora.

"Yes, she has had *some* pretty nice presents," assented Sophia. "Most of them are real nice."

Flora stood beside the table and lifted tenderly from the box one wedding-gift after another. She was full of shy pride. The visitors admired everything. When Flora had displayed the contents of the two boxes, she brought out a large picture in an ornate gilt frame, and finally wheeled through the door with difficulty a patent rocker upholstered with red, crushed plush.

"That's from some of his folks," said Sophia. "I call it a handsome present."

"I'm going to have a table from his aunt Jane," remarked Flora.

"Sit down in that chair and see how easy it is," said Sophia, imperatively, to Mrs. Cutting, who obeyed meekly, although the crushed plush was so icy cold from its sojourn in the parlor that it seemed to embrace her with deadly arms and made her have visions of pneumonia.

"It's as easy a chair as I ever sat in," she said, rising hastily.

"Leave it out here and let her set in it while she is here," said Sophia and Mrs. Cutting sank back into the chair, although she did ask for a little shawl for her shoulders.

Mrs. Cutting had always had a wholesome respect for her cousin Sophia Lane, although she had a certain feeling of superiority by reason of her wealth. Even while she looked about Sophia's poor little sitting-room and recalled her own fine parlors, she had a sense that Sophia was throned on such mental heights above mahogany and plush and tapestry that she could not touch her with a finger of petty scorn even if she wished.

After Flora had displayed her presents and carried them back to the parlor, she excused herself and went to the dressmaker's to try on her wedding-dress.

After Flora had gone out of the yard, looking abnormally stout with a gay plaid shawl over the coat and her head rolled in a thick, old, worsted hood of Sophia's, Mrs. Cutting opened on a subject about which she was exceedingly curious.

"I'm real sorry we can't have a glimpse of the wedding-dress," said she, ingratiatingly.

Sophia gave an odd sort of grunt in response. Sophia always gave utterance to that nondescript sound, which was neither assent nor dissent, but open to almost any interpretation, when she wished to evade a lie. She was in reality very glad that the wedding-dress was not on exhibition. She thought it much better that it should not be seen in its full glory until the wedding-day.

"Flora has got many good presents," said Sophia, "and a few tomfool ones, thanks to me and what I did last Christmas."

"What do you mean, Sophia?" asked Mrs. Cutting.

"Didn't you hear what I did, Ellen Cutting?"

"No, I didn't hear a word about it."

"Well, I didn't know but somebody might have told. I wasn't a mite ashamed of it, and I ain't now. I'd do the same thing over again if it was necessary, but I guess it won't be; I guess they got a good lesson. I dare say they were kind of huffy at the time. I guess they got over it. They've all give Flora presents now, anyhow, except Angeline White, and I guess she will."

"Why, what did you do?" asked Abby Dodd, with round eyes of interest on Sophia.

"Why, I'd jest as soon tell you as not," replied Sophia. "I've got some cake in the oven. Jest let me take a peek at that first."

"Wedding-cake?" asked Eunice, as Sophia ran out of the room.

"Land, no!" she called back. "That was made six weeks ago. Weddin'-cake wouldn't be worth anything baked now."

"Eunice, didn't you know better than that?" cried her mother.

"It's white cake," Sophia's explanatory voice came from the kitchen, whence sweet odors floated into the room. The oven door opened and shut with an exceedingly swift click like a pistol-shot.

"I should think she'd make the cake fall, slamming the oven door like that," murmured Abby Dodd.

"So should I; but it won't," assented her mother. "I never knew Sophia to fail with her cake."

Sophia flew back into the sitting-room and plumped into her chair; she had, indeed, risen with such impetus and been so quick that the chair had not ceased rocking since she left it. "It's done," said she; "I took it out. I'll let it stand in the pan and steam awhile before I do anything more with it. Now I'll tell you what I did about Flora's Christmas presents last year if you want me to. I'd jest as soon as not. If I hadn't done what I did, there wouldn't have been any weddin' this winter, I can tell you that."

"You don't say so!" cried Mrs. Cutting, and the others stared.

"No, there wouldn't. You know, Herbert and Flora have been goin' together three years this December. Well, they'd have been goin' together three years more, and I don't know but they'd been goin' together till doomsday, if I hadn't taken matters into my own hand. I ain't never been married myself, and maybe folks think I ain't any right to my opinion, but I've always said I didn't approve of young folks goin' together so long unless they get married. When they're married, and any little thing comes up that one or the other don't think quite so nice, why, they put up with it, and make the best of it, and kind of belittle that and make more of the things that they do like. But when they ain't married it's different. I don't care how much they think of each other, something may come up to make him or her kind of wonder if t'other is good enough to marry, after all. Well, nothin' of that kind has happened with Flora and Herbert Bennet, and I ain't sayin' there has. They went together them three years, and, far as I can see, they think each other is better than in the beginnin'. Well, as I was sayin', it seemed to me that those two had ought to get married before long if they were ever goin' to, but I must confess I didn't see how they were any nearer it than when they started keepin' company."

"Herbert has been pretty handicapped," remarked Mrs. Cutting.

"Handicapped? Well, I rather guess he has! He was young when his father died, and when his mother had that dreadful sickness and had to go to the hospital, he couldn't keep up the taxes, and the interest on the mortgage got behindhand; the house was mortgaged when his father died, and it had to go; he's had to hire ever since. They're comin' here to live; you knew that, I s'pose?"

"Sophia, you don't mean his mother is coming here to live?"

"Why not? I'm mighty glad the poor woman's goin' to have a good home in her old age. She's a good woman as ever was, just as mild-spoken, and smart too. I'm tickled to death to think she's comin', and so's Flora. Flora sets her eyes by his mother."

"Well, you know your own business, but I must say I think it's a considerable undertaking."

"Well, I don't. I'd like to know what you'd have her do. Herbert can't afford to support two establishments, no more than he earns, and he ain't goin' to turn his mother out to earn her bread an' butter at her time of life, I rather guess. No; she's comin' here, and she's goin' to have the south chamber; she's goin' to furnish it. I never see a happier woman; and as for Herbert—well, he has had a hard time, and now things begin to look brighter; but I declare, about a year ago, as far as I could see, it didn't look as if he and Flora ever could get married. One evenin' the poor fellow came here, and he talked real plain; he said he felt as if he'd ought to. He said he'd been comin' here a long time, and he'd begun to think that he and Flora might keep on that way until they were gray, so far as he could help it. There he was, he said, workin' in Edgcomb's store at seven dollars a week, and had his mother to keep, and he couldn't see any prospect of anything better. He said maybe if he wasn't goin' with Flora she might get somebody else. 'It ain't fair to Flora,' said he. And with that he heaves a great sigh, and the first thing I knew, right before me, Flora she was in his lap, huggin' him, and cryin', and sayin' she'd never leave him for any man on the face of the earth, and she didn't ask anything any better than to wait. They'd both wait and be patient and trust in God, and she was jest as happy as she could be, and she wouldn't change places with the Queen. First thing I knew I was cryin' too; I couldn't help it; and Herbert, poor fellow, he fetched a big sob himself, and I didn't think none the worse of him for it. 'Seems as if I must be sort of lackin' somehow, to make such a failure of things,' says he, kind of broken like.

"'You ain't lackin',' says Flora, real fierce like. 'It ain't you that's to blame. Fate's against you and always has been.'

"'Now you look round before you blame the Lord,' says I at that—for when folks say fate they always mean the Lord. 'Mebbe it ain't the Lord,' says I; 'mebbe it's folks. Wouldn't your uncle Hiram give you a lift, Herbert?'

"'Uncle Hiram!' says he; but not a bit scornful—real good-natured.

"'Why? I don't see why not,' says I. 'He always gives nice Christmas presents to you and your mother, don't he?'

"'Yes,' says he. 'He gives Christmas presents.'

"'Real nice ones?'

"'Yes,' said poor Herbert, kind of chucklin', but real good-natured. 'Last Christmas Uncle Hiram gave mother a silver card-case, and me a silver ash-receiver.'

"'But you don't smoke?' says I.

"'No,' says he, 'and mother hasn't got any visitin'-cards.'

"'I suppose he didn't know, along of not livin' in the same place,' says I.

"'No,' says he. 'They were real handsome things—solid; must have cost a lot of money.'

"'What would you do it you could get a little money, Herbert?' says I.

"Bless you! he knew quick enough. Didn't have to study over it a minute.

"'I'd buy that piece of land next your house here,' says he, 'and I'd keep cows and start a milk route. There's need of one here,' says he, 'and it's just what I've always thought I'd like to do; but it takes money,' he finishes up, with another of them heart-breakin' sighs of his, 'an' I ain't got a cent.'

"'Something will happen so you can have the milk route,' says Flora, and she kisses him right before me, and I was glad she did. I never approved of young folks bein' silly, but this was different. When a man feels as bad as Herbert Bennet did that day, if the woman that's goin' to marry him can comfort him any, she'd ought to.

"'Yes,' says I, 'something will surely happen. You jest keep your grit up, Herbert.'

"'How you women do stand by me!' says Herbert, and his voice broke again, and I was pretty near cryin'.

"'Well, we're goin' to stand by you jest as long as you are as good as you be now,' says I. 'The tide 'll turn before long.'

"I hadn't any more than got the words out of my mouth before the express drove up to the door, and there were three Christmas presents for Flora, early as it was, three days before Christmas. Christmas presents so long beforehand always make me a little suspicious, as if mebbe folks wanted other folks to be sure they were goin' to have something. Flora she'd always made real handsome presents to every one of them three that sent those that day. One was Herbert's aunt Harriet Morse, one was Cousin Jane Adkins over to Gorham, and the other was Mis' Crocker, she that was Emma Ladd; she's a second cousin of Flora's father's. Well, them three presents came, and we undid them. Then we looked at 'em. 'Great Jehosophat!' says I. Herbert he grinned, then he said something I didn't hear, and Flora she looked as if she didn't know whether to laugh or cry. There Flora she didn't have any money to put into presents, of course, but you know what beautiful fancy-work she does, and there she'd been workin' ever since the Christmas before, and she made a beautiful centre-piece and a bureau-scarf and a lace handkerchief for those three women, and there they had sent her a sort of a dewdab to wear in her hair! Pretty enough, looked as if it cost considerable—a pink rose with spangles, and a feather shootin' out of it; but Lord! if Flora had come out in that thing anywhere she'd go in Brookville she'd scared the natives. It was all right where Herbert's aunt Harriet lived. Ayres is a city, but in this town, 'way from a railroad—goodness!

"Well, there was that; and Cousin Jane Adkins had sent her a Japanese silk shawl, all over embroidery, as handsome as a picture; but there was poor Flora wantin' some cotton cloth for her weddin' fix, and not a cent to buy a thing with. My sheets and pillowcases and table-linen that I had from poor mother was about worn out, and Flora was wonderin' how she'd ever get any. But there Jane had sent that shawl, that cost nobody knew how much, when she knew Flora wanted the other things—because I'd told her. But Mis' Crocker's was the worst of all. She's a widow with a lot of money, and she's put on a good many airs. I dun'no' as you know her. No, I thought you didn't. Well, she does feel terrible airy. She sent poor Flora a set of chessmen, all red and white ivory, beautifully carved, and a table to keep 'em on. I must say I was so green I didn't know what they were when I first saw 'em. Flora knew; she'd seen some somewheres she'd been.

" 'For the land sake! what's them little dolls and horses for?' says I. 'It looks like Noah's ark without the ark.'

" 'It's a set of chess and a table,' said Flora, and she looked ready to cry, poor child. She thought, when she got that great package, that she really had got something she wanted that time, sure.

" 'Chess?' says I.

" 'A game,' says Flora.

" 'A game?' says I.

" 'To play,' says she.

" 'Do you know how to play it, Flora?' says I.

" 'No,' says she.

" 'Does Herbert?'

" 'No.'

" 'Well,' says I, and I spoke right out, 'of all the things to give anybody that needs things!'

"Flora was readin' the note that came with it. Jane Crocker said in the note that in givin' her Christmas present this year she was havin' a little eye on the future—and she underlined the future. She was twittin' Flora a little about her waitin' so long, and I knew it. Jane Crocker is a good woman enough, but she's got claws. She said she had an eye on the *underlined* future, and she said a chess set and a table were so stylish in a parlor. She didn't say a word about playin'.

"'Does she play that game?' says I to Flora.

"'I don't know,' says Flora. She didn't; I found out afterwards. She didn't know a single blessed thing about the game.

"Well, I looked at that present of poor Flora's, and I felt as if I should give up. 'How much do you s'pose that thing cost?' says I. Then I saw she had left the tag on. I looked. I didn't care a mite. I don't know where she got it. Wherever it was, she got cheated, if I know anything about it. There Jane Crocker had paid forty dollars for that thing.

"'Why didn't she give forty dollars for a Noah's ark and done with it?' says I. 'I'd jest as soon have one. Go and put it in the parlor,' says I.

"And poor Flora and Herbert lugged it into the parlor. She was almost cryin'.

"Well, the things kept comin' that Christmas. We both had a good many presents, and it did seem as if they were worse than they had ever been before. They had always been pretty bad. I don't care if I do say it."

There was a faint defiance in Sophia's voice. Mrs. Cutting and her daughters glanced imperceptibly at one another. A faint red showed on Mrs. Cutting's cheeks.

"Yes," repeated Sophia, firmly, "they always had been pretty bad. We had tried to be grateful, but it was the truth. There were so many things Flora and I wanted, and it did seem sometimes as if everybody that gave us Christmas presents sat up a week of Sundays tryin' to think of something to give us that we didn't want. There was Lizzie Starkwether; she gave us bed-shoes. She gave us bed-shoes the winter before, and the winter before that, but that didn't make a mite of difference. She kept right on givin' 'em, red-and-black bed-shoes. There she knits beautiful mittens and wristers, and we both wanted mittens or wristers; but no, we got bed-shoes. Flora and me never wear bed-shoes, and, what's more, I'd told Lizzie Starkwether so. I had a chance to do it when I thought I wouldn't hurt her feelin's. But that didn't make any difference; the bed-shoes come right along. I must say I was mad when I saw them that last time. 'I must say I don't call this a present; I call it a kick,' says I, and I'm ashamed to say I gave them bed-shoes a fling. There poor Flora had been sittin' up nights makin' a white apron trimmed with knit lace for Lizzie, because she knew she wanted one.

"Well, so it went; everything that come was a little more something we didn't want, especially Flora's; and she didn't say anything, but tried to look as if she was tickled to death; and she sent off the nice, pretty things she'd worked so hard to make, and every single one of them things, if I do say it, had been studied over an hour to every minute the ones she got had. Flora always tried not to give so much what she likes as what the one she's givin' to likes; and when I saw what she was gettin' back I got madder an' madder. I s'pose I wasn't showin' a Christian spirit, and Flora said so. She said she didn't give presents to get their worth back, and if they liked what she gave, that was worth more than anything. I could have felt that way if they'd been mine, but I couldn't when they were Flora's, and when the poor child had so little, and couldn't get married on account of it, too. Christmas mornin' came Herbert's rich uncle Hiram's present. It came while we were eatin' breakfast, about eight o'clock. We were rather late that mornin'. Well, the expressman drove into the yard, and he left a nice little package, and I saw the Leviston express mark on it, and I says to Flora, 'This must come from Herbert's uncle Hiram, and I shouldn't wonder if you had got something real nice.'

"Well, we undid it, and if there wasn't another silver card-case, the same style as Herbert's mother had given her the Christmas before. Well, Flora has got some visitin'-cards, but the idea of her carryin' a silver card-case like that when she went callin'! Why, she wouldn't have had anything else that come up to that card-case! Flora didn't say much, but I could see her lips quiver. She jest put it away, and pretty soon Herbert run in—he was out with the delivery-wagon from the store, and he stopped a second. He didn't stay long—he was too conscientious about his employer's time—but he stayed long enough to tell about his and his mother's Christmas presents from his uncle Hiram, and what do you think they had that time? Why, Herbert had a silver cigarette-case, and he never smokin' at all, and his mother had a cut-glass wine-set.

"Well, I didn't say much, but I was makin' up my mind. I was makin' it up slow, but I was makin' it up firm. Some more presents came that afternoon, and not a thing Flora wanted, except some ironin' holders from Cousin Ann Drake, and me a gingham apron from her. Yes, Flora did have another present she wanted, and that was a handkerchief come through the mail from the school-teacher that used to board here—a real nice, fine one. But the rest—well, there was a sofa-pillow painted with wild roses on boltin'-cloth, and there every sofa we'd got to lay down on in the house was this lounge here. We'd never had a sofa in the parlor, and Minerva Saunders—she sent it—knew it; and I'd like to know how much we could use a painted white boltin'-cloth pillow here? Minerva was rich, too, and I knew the pillow cost enough. And Mis' George Harris, she that was Minnie Beals—she was Flora's own cousin, you know—what did she send but a brass fire-set—poker and tongs and things—and here we ain't got an open fireplace in the house, and she knew it. But Minnie never did have much sense; I never laid it up against her. She meant well, and she's sent Flora some beautiful napkins and table-cloths; I told her that was what she wanted for a weddin'-present. Well, as I was sayin', I was makin' up my mind slow but firm, and by afternoon it was made up. Says I to Flora: 'I wish you'd go over to Mr. Martin's and ask him if I can have his horse and sleigh this afternoon. Tell him I'll pay him.' He never takes any pay, but I always offer. Flora said: 'Why, Aunt Sophia, you ain't goin' out this afternoon! It looks as if it would snow every minute.'

"'Yes, I be,' says I.

"Well, Flora went over and asked, and Mr. Martin said I was welcome to the horse and sleigh—he's always real accommodatin'—and he hitched up himself and brought it over about one o'clock. I thought I'd start early, because it did threaten snow. I got Flora out of the way—sent her down to the store to get some sugar; we were goin' to make cake when I got home, and we were all out of powdered sugar. When that sleigh come I jest bundled all them presents—except the apron and holders and the two or three other things that was presents, because the folks that give 'em had studied up what Flora wanted, and give to her instead of themselves—an' I stowed them all in that sleigh, under the seat and on it, and covered them up with the robe.

"Then I wrapped up real warm, because it was bitter cold—seemed almost too cold to snow—and I put a hot soapstone in the sleigh, and I gathered up the reins, an' I slapped 'em over the old horse's back, and I set out.

"I thought I'd go to Jane Crocker's first—I wanted to get rid of that chess-table; it took up so much room in the sleigh I hadn't any place to put my feet, and the robe kept slippin' off it. So I drove right there. Jane was to home; the girl came to the door, and I went into the parlor. I hadn't been to call on Jane for some time, and she'd got a number of new things I hadn't seen, and the first thing I saw was a chess-table and all them little red and white Noah's-ark things, jest like the one she sent us. When Jane come in, dressed in black silk stiff enough to stand alone—though she wa'n't goin' anywheres and it looked like snow—I jest stood right up. I'd brought in the table and the box of little jiggers, and I goes right to the point. I had to. I had to drive six miles to Ayres before I got through, and there it was spittin' snow already.

"'Good-afternoon, Jane,' says I. 'I've brought back your presents.'

"Jane she kind of gasped, and she turned pale. She has a good deal of color; she's a pretty woman; well, it jest slumped right out of her cheeks. 'Mercy! Sophia,' says she, 'what do you mean?'

"'Jest what I say, Jane,' says I. 'You've sent Flora some playthings that cost forty dollars—you left the tags on, so we know—and they ain't anything she has any use for. She don't know how to play chess, and neither does Herbert; and if they did know, they wouldn't neither of 'em have any time, unless it was Sundays, and then it would be wicked.'

"'Oh, Lord! Sophia,' says she, kind of chokin', 'I don't know how to play myself, but I've got one for an ornament, and I thought Flora—'

"'Flora will have to do without forty-dollar ornaments, if ever she gets money enough to get married at all,' says I, 'and I don't think a Noah's ark set on a table marked up in squares is much of an ornament, anyhow.'

"I didn't say any more. I jest marched out and left the presents. But Jane she came runnin' after me. 'Sophia,' says she—and she spoke as if she was sort of scared. She never had much spunk, for all she looks so up an' comin'—'Sophia,' says she, 'I thought she'd like it. I thought—'

"'No, you didn't, Jane Crocker,' says I. 'You jest thought what you'd like to give, and not what she'd like to have.'

"'What would she like to have?' says she, and she was 'most cryin'. 'I'll get her anything she wants, if you'll jest tell me, Sophia.'

"'I ain't goin' to tell you, Jane,' says I, but I spoke softer, for I saw that she meant well, after all—'I ain't goin' to tell you. You jest put yourself in her place; you make believe you was a poor young girl goin' to get married, and you think over what little the poor child has got now and what she has to set alongside *new* things, and you kind of study it out for yourself,' says I. And then I jest said good-bye, though she kept callin' after me, and I run out and climbed in the sleigh and tucked myself in and drove off.

"The very next day Jane Crocker sent Flora a beautiful new carpet for the front chamber, and a rug to go with it. She knew Flora was goin' to have the front chamber fixed up when she got married; she'd heard me say so; and the carpet was all worn out.

"Well, I kept right on. I carried back Cousin Abby Adkins's white silk shawl, and she acted awful mad; but she thought better of it as I was goin' out to the sleigh, and she called after me to know what Flora wanted, and I told her jest what I had Jane Crocker. And I carried back Minerva Saunders's boltin'-cloth sofa-pillow, and she was more astonished than anything else—she was real good-natured. You know how easy she is. She jest laughed after she'd got over bein' astonished. 'Why,' says she, 'I don't know but it *is* kind of silly, now I come to think of it. I declare I clean forgot you didn't have a sofa in the parlor. When I've been in there I've been so took up seein' you and Flora, Sophia, that I never took any account at all of the furniture.'

"So I went away from there feelin' real good, and the next day but one there come a nice hair-cloth sofa for Flora to put in the parlor.

"Then I took back Minnie Harris's fire-set, and she acted kind of dazed. 'Why, don't you think it's handsome?' says she. You know she's a young thing, younger than Flora. She's always called me Aunt Sophia, too. 'Why, Aunt Sophia,' says she, 'didn't Flora think it was handsome?'

"'Handsome enough, child,' says I, and I couldn't help laughin' myself, she looked like sech a baby—'handsome enough, but what did you think Flora was goin' to do with a poker and tongs to poke a fire, when there ain't any fire to poke?'

"Then Minnie she sort of giggled. 'Why, sure enough, Aunt Sophia,' says she. 'I never thought of that.'

"'Where did you think she would put them?' says I. 'On the parlor mantel-shelf for ornaments?'

"Then Minnie she laughed sort of hysterical. 'Give 'em right here, Aunt Sophia,' says she.

"The next day she sent a clock—that wasn't much account, though it was real pretty; it won't go long at a time—but it looks nice on the parlor shelf, and it was so much better than the poker and tongs that I didn't say anything. It takes sense to give a present, and Minnie Harris never had a mite, though she's a pretty little thing.

"Then I took home Lizzie Starkwether's bed-shoes, and she took it the worst of all.

"'Don't they fit?' says she.

"'Fit well 'nough,' says I. 'We don't want 'em.'

"'I'd like to know why not,' says she.

"'Because you've given us a pair every Christmas for three years,' says I, 'and I've told you we never wear bed-shoes; and even if we did wear 'em,' says I, 'we couldn't have worn out the others to save our lives. When we go to bed, we go to sleep,' says I. 'We don't travel round to wear out shoes. We've got two pairs apiece laid away,' says I, 'and I think you'd better give these to somebody that wants 'em—mebbe somebody that you've been givin' mittens to for three years, that don't wear mittens.'

"Well, she was hoppin', but she got over it, too; and I guess she did some thinkin', for in a week came the prettiest mittens for each of us I ever laid eyes on, and Minerva herself came over and called, and thanked Flora for her apron as sweet as pie.

"Well, I went to all the others in town, and then I started for Ayres, and carried back the dewdab to Herbert's aunt Harriet Morse. I hated to do that, for I didn't know her very well; but I went, and she was real nice. She made me drink a cup of tea and eat a slice of her cake, and she thanked me for comin'. She said she didn't know what young girls liked, and she had an idea that they cared more about something to dress up in than anything else, even if they didn't have a great deal to do with, and she had ought to have known better than to send such a silly thing. She spoke real kind about Herbert, and hoped he could get married before long; and the next day she sent Flora a pair of beautiful blankets, and now she's given Flora all her bed linen and towels for a weddin'-present. I heated up my soapstone in her kitchen oven and started for home. It was almost dark, and snowin' quite hard, and she said she hated to have me go, but I said I didn't mind. I was goin' to stop at Herbert's uncle Hiram's on my way home. You know he lives in Leviston, half-way from Ayres.

"When I got there it was snowin' hard, comin' real thick.

"I drew up at the front gate and hitched the horse, and waded through the snow to the front door and rung the bell; and Uncle Hiram's housekeeper came to the door. She is a sort of cousin of his—a widow woman from Ayres. I don't know as you know who she is. She's a dreadful lackada'sical woman, kind of pretty, long-faced and slopin'-shouldered, and she speaks kind of slow and sweet. I asked if Mr. Hiram Snell was in, and she said she guessed so, and asked me in, and showed me into the sittin'-room, which was furnished rich; but it was awful dirty and needed dustin'. I guess she ain't much of a housekeeper. Uncle Hiram was in the sittin'-room, smokin' a pipe and readin'. You know Hiram Snell. He's kind of gruff-spoken, but he ain't bad-meanin'. It's more because he's kind of blunderin' about little things, like most men; ain't got a small enough grip to fit 'em. Well, he stood up when I come in. He knew me by sight, and I said who I was—that I was aunt to Flora Bell that his nephew Herbert Bennet was goin' to marry; and he asked me to sit down, but I said I couldn't because I had to drive a matter of three miles to get home, and it was snowin' so hard. Then I out with that little fool card-case, and I said I'd brought it back.

"'What's the matter? Ain't it good enough?' says he, real short. He's got real shaggy eyebrows, an' I tell you his eyes looked fierce under 'em.

"'Too good,' says I. 'Flora she ain't got anything good enough to go with it. This card-case can't be carried by a woman unless she has a handsome silk dress, and fine white kid gloves, and a sealskin sack, and a hat with an ostrich feather,' says I.

"'Do you want me to give her all those things to go with the card-case?' says he, kind of sarcastic.

"'If you did, they'd come back quicker than you could say Jack Robinson,' says I, for I was gettin' mad myself.

"But all of a sudden he burst right out laughin'. 'Well,' says he, 'you've got horse-sense, an' that's more than I can say of most women.' Then he takes the card-case and he looks hard at it. 'Why, Mrs. Pendergrass said she'd be sure to like it!' says he. 'Said she'd got one for Herbert's mother last year. Mrs. Pendergrass buys all my Christmas presents for me. I don't make many.'

"'I shouldn't think you'd better if you can't get more sensible ones to send,' says I. I knew I was saucy, but he was kind of smilin', and I laughed when I said it, though I meant it all the same.

"'Why, weren't Herbert's all right?' says he.

"'Right?' says I. 'Do you know what he had last year?'

"'No, I don't,' says he.

"'Well, last year you sent him a silver ash-tray, and his mother a card-case, and this year he had a silver cigarette-case, and his mother a cut-glass wine-set.'

"'Well?'

"'Nothin', only Herbert never smokes, and his mother hasn't got any visitin'-cards, and she don't have much wine, I guess.'

"Hiram Snell laughed again. 'Well, I left it all to Mrs. Pendergrass,' says he. 'I never thought she had brains to spare, but then I never thought it took brains to buy Christmas presents.'

"'It does,' says I,—'brains and consider'ble love for the folks you are buyin' for.'

"'Christmas is tomfoolery, anyhow,' says he.

"'That's as you look at it,' says I.

"He stood eyin' me sort of gruff, and yet as if he were sort of tickled at the same time. 'Well,' says he, finally, 'you've brought this fool thing back. Now what shall I give your niece instead?'

"'I don't go round beggin' for presents,' says I.

"'How the devil am I going to get anything that she'll like any better if I don't know?' says he. 'And Mrs. Pendergrass can't help me out any. You've got to say something.'

"'I sha'n't,' says I, real set. 'You ain't no call to give my niece anything, anyway; you ain't no call to give her anything she wants, and you certainly ain't no call to give her anything she don't want.'

"'You don't believe in keepin' presents you don't want?'

"'No,' says I, 'I don't—and thankin' folks for 'em as if you liked 'em. It's hypocrisy.'

"He kind of grunted, and laughed again.

"'It don't make any odds about Flora,' says I; 'and as for your nephew and your sister, you know about them and what they want as well as I do, or you'd ought to. I ain't goin' to tell you.'

"'So Maria hasn't got any cards, and Herbert don't smoke,' says he, and he grinned as if it was awful funny.

"Well, I thought it was time for me to be goin', and jest then Mrs. Pendergrass came in with a lighted lamp. It had darkened all of a sudden, and I could hear the sleet on the window, and there I had three miles to drive.

"So I started, and Hiram Snell he followed me to the door. He seemed sort of anxious about my goin' out in the storm, and come out himself through all the snow, and unhitched my horse and held him till I got nicely tucked in the sleigh. Then jest as I gathered up the reins, he says, speakin' up loud against the wind,

"'When is Herbert and your niece goin' to get married?'

"'When Herbert gets enough money to buy a piece of land and some stock and start a milk route,' says I. Then off I goes."

Sophia paused for a climax. Her guests were listening, breathless.

"Well, what did he give Herbert?" asked Mrs. Cutting.

"He gave him three thousand dollars to buy that land and some cows and put up a barn," said Sophia, and her audience drew a long, simultaneous breath.

"That was great," said Eunice.

"And he's made Flora a wedding-present of five shares in the Ayres street-railroad stock, so she should have a little spendin'-money," said Sophia.

"I call him a pretty generous man," said Abby Dodd.

"Generous enough," said Sophia Lane, "only he didn't know how to steer his generosity."

The guests rose; they were looking somewhat uncomfortable and embarrassed. Sophia went into the bedroom to get their wraps, letting a breath of ice into the sitting-room. While she was gone the guests conferred hastily with one another.

When she returned, Mrs. Cutting faced her, not unamiably, but confusedly. "Now look here, Sophia Lane," said she, "I want you to speak right out. You needn't hesitate. We all want the truth. Is—anything the matter with our presents we brought to-day?"

"Use your own jedgment," replied Sophia Lane.

"Where are those presents we brought?" asked Mrs. Cutting. She and her daughters all looked sober and doubtful, but not precisely angry.

"They are in the parlor," replied Sophia.

"Suppose you get them," said Mrs. Cutting.

When Sophia returned with the alcohol-lamp and afternoon-tea kettle, the finger-bowls and the doilies, the guests had on their wraps. Abby Dodd and Eunice at once went about tying up the presents. Mrs. Cutting looked on. Sophia got her little shawl and hood. She was going out to the barn to assist her guests in getting their horse out.

"Has Flora got any dishes?" asked Mrs. Cutting, thoughtfully.

"No, she hasn't got anything but her mother's china tea-set," replied Sophia. "She hasn't got any good dishes for common use."

"No dinner-set?"

"No; mine are about used up, and I've been careful with 'em too."

Mrs. Cutting considered a minute longer. "Has she got some good tumblers?" she asked.

"No, she hasn't. We haven't any too many tumblers in the house."

"How is she off for napkins?" asked Eunice, tying up her doilies.

"She ain't any too well off. She's had a dozen give her, and that's all."

The guests, laden with the slighted wedding-gifts, followed Sophia through the house, the kitchen, and the clean, cold wood-shed to the barn. Sophia slid back the heavy doors.

"Well, good-bye, Sophia," said Mrs. Cutting. "We've had a nice time, and we've enjoyed seeing Flora's presents."

"Yes, so have I," said Eunice.

"I think she's fared real well," said Abby.

"Yes, she has," said Sophia.

"We shall be over in good season," said Eunice.

"Yes, we shall," assented Abby.

Sophia untied the horse, which had been fastened to a ring beside the door; still the guests did not move to get into the sleigh. A curious air of constraint was over them. Sophia also looked constrained and troubled. Her poor faithful face peering from the folds of her gray wool hood was defiant and firm, but still anxious. She looked at Mrs. Cutting, and the two women's eyes met; there was a certain wistfulness in Sophia's.

"I think a good deal of Flora," said she, and there was a hint of apology in her tone.

Simultaneously the three women moved upon Sophia, their faces cleared; lovely expressions of sympathy and kindly understanding appeared upon them.

"Good-bye, Sophia," said Mrs. Cutting, and kissed her.

"Good-bye, Cousin Sophia," said the daughters, and they also kissed her.

When they drove out of the snowy yard, three smiling faces turned back for a last greeting to Sophia. She slid together the heavy barn doors. She was smiling happily, though there were tears in her eyes.

"Everybody in this world means to be pretty good to other folks," she muttered to herself, "and when they ain't, it ain't always their fault; sometimes it's other folks'."

The Reign of the Doll

1904

There was a great storm. Fidelia Nutting was too frightened and excited to go to bed. It was eleven o'clock; three hours before, at eight o'clock, she had opened the door into her bedroom in order that the warmth of the sitting-room should temper the freezing atmosphere before she retired. She sat where she could see the peaceful white slope of the feather-bed; her head was heavy with sleep, but the strain of her nerves kept her awake. Fidelia was exceedingly timid, and even overawed, by any unusual stress of nature. Summer thunder-storms had always rendered her for the time a mild maniac, winds seemed to penetrate her soul, winter snows to enter and sift into the farthest crannies of her thoughts. This storm was sleet rather than snow. The wind raged. It seemed to pounce upon the house and shake it like a wild beast, then retreat, muttering, to some awful lair of storm, to return with a new gathering of fury.

Fidelia cowered and shivered, with a roll of fearful eyes. She was a large, elderly woman with the soul of a child. She was entirely alone in her little house; over across the street, in the large, old mansion-house of the Nuttings, her sister Diantha was also alone. Now and then Fidelia went to her window, that looked across the street, and saw with a thrill of half-resentful comfort her sister Diantha's light. She reflected that Diantha also had always been afraid in a storm, though not as afraid as she—or not owning to it.

"She always used to keep her lamp burning when there was a thunder-storm and when the wind was high," reflected Fidelia. Diantha's lamp was set on a table in the centre of her sitting-room, in a direct line with Fidelia's window. A great beam of yellow light shone through the window—through the shreds of snow which clung like wool to the sashes, through the icy veil of sleet, through the foliage of the geraniums in Fidelia's beautiful window garden. Fidelia was a little afraid that the cold wind might injure her flowers, but she would not lower her curtain, because she was shame-facedly desirous of the company of Diantha's light.

Suddenly she heard a gathering flurry of sleigh-bells. They increased un-til they seemed in the room; then they stopped suddenly. Fidelia's heart leaped for fear.

"Something has stopped here," she gasped. It was unprecedented for anything to stop there at that hour and in such a storm. She shaded her eyes, and peered fearfully and cautiously from the window around her ge-raniums. She could see a dark shape at the opposite window, blotting out the lamplight, and she knew that Diantha was also looking. A man's figure, gigantic in a fur coat, lumbered slantingly through the drifts of the path to the front door. Fidelia put a little worsted shawl over her head, took her lamp, and crept tremblingly through the freezing front entry in response to the knock. Her bell was out of order.

"Who's there?" she asked.

"Express!" he shouted, in an angry voice, and Fidelia turned the key and opened the door. The fur of the expressman's coat stood out, stiffly pointed with ice; his cap looked like an ice helmet. "Express, ma'am," he said, in a hoarse voice, and the package was in Fidelia's hand and he was gone. Then the wind came in a wild gust, and Fidelia fled before it with her streaming lamp. Back in the warm sitting-room she set the lamp safely on the table; then she stood gazing at her package. It was a long box, very nicely wrapped in thick paper and securely tied. Fidelia did not connect it with Christmas; Christmas presents were not within her present environments. She examined the package carefully, and saw that the address was cor-rect—Miss Fidelia Nutting, North Abbot, and it was marked paid, with a blue pencil. She laid the package on the table, and seated herself near it in her rocking-chair. Another gust of wind came, and the bombardment of the sleet upon the window was frightful; it seemed as if the panes must be shattered. She looked at the package on the table, and a curious fear of it came over her. The unwontedness of that and the unwontedness of the storm seemed one, and instinct with terror.

"I'd like to know what's in that bundle," she whispered, with fearful eyes on it. She got up and gazed across the street at her sister's lamp, which still shone to comfort her. The dark figure, however, moved before it in a second. "She's looking out," she thought, with that curious mixture of timidity and anger and affection with which she always thought of her sister. She and Diantha had quarrelled over the distribution of the property after their mother died. Diantha had taken the old homestead and less money, and gone to live there alone. Fidelia had taken more money and the small cottage, and gone to live there. They spoke sternly when they met; they never exchanged visits; there was between them a sort of dignified hostility, to which they did not own. Although all the village knew that there was enmity between the sisters, none knew which of the two originated it, which had demanded the peculiar arrangement of property and the living part. Fidelia felt a certain sympathy with Diantha because of the express package. She knew how curious Diantha was, though she would not own to it. Curiosity at its extreme is like unslaked thirst. "Poor Diantha, she's just dying to know what is in that bundle," she said to herself. She, aside from her vague alarm over it, was loath to open it in the face of this eager, unsatisfied curiosity over the way. She watched her sister's light opposite. She had a desperate hope that she would keep it burning all night; but about half-past ten it went suddenly out. "Oh, dear," groaned Fidelia. Loneliness went over her like a deep sea. New terror of the package seized her. She felt that nobody would send it to her with any good purpose. Her nervous terror had fairly for the time being unsettled her reason. Then she heard some one at the door. She waited, hoping that she might be mistaken, that it was the wind. But it came again. There was a sharp pounding on the door panels; it was impossible to think it was anything else.

Fidelia pulled her little shawl closely over her head, took up her lamp, and went forth into the cold front entry. The pounding came on the door with redoubled impetus. The caller had seen the lamp through the sidelights.

"Who is it?" cried Fidelia, in a voice which rang strange to her own ears. She was almost in convulsions of terror.

"Diantha," responded a shrill voice from outside. "Let me in quick; it's a terrible storm."

Then Fidelia set her lamp on the entry table, and fumbled in a tumult of surprise and delight with the bolt and the key and a chain. As the door opened, the lamp blazed high and went out. Diantha and Fidelia rushed upon the door, and together forced it back and locked it.

"Come into the sitting-room, Diantha," said Fidelia, in a trembling voice. "Look out you don't run into anything; it's very dark." Fidelia felt timidly for her sister's hand, and led her, feeling her way carefully, into the sitting-room.

Fidelia got a match and fumbled her way back to the entry, got the lamp and lighted it, and put it in its usual place on the sitting-room table. Then the sisters looked at each other. Each looked curiously shamefaced. Diantha was smaller than Fidelia, but more incisive. She was rather pretty, with a sharply cut, cameo-like face framed in white hair, which was now indecorously tossed about her temples. She began smoothing it impatiently.

"I never saw a worse night," said she.

"It's a terrible storm," assented Fidelia. It was pleasant to find a common grievance. "Do you want a brush and comb?" asked she.

"Yes, I guess I'd better smooth my hair a little," said Diantha; and Fidelia got her brush and comb from the bedroom. She watched her sister standing before the sitting-room mirror, which hung between the front windows, and her whole face was changed. Whatever bitterness had been in her heart towards Diantha was lost sight of in her joy over companionship in this night of storm.

"It's a dreadful storm," said she.

"Yes, it is," assented Diantha. "I could hardly get over here. The telephone-wire is down, and the branches are crashing off the trees. There's a big maple branch right 'side of your front gate. I had to step over the end of it. It's awful."

"It's worse than it was," said Fidelia.

"Yes, it's worse than it was when the expressman came." Diantha looked hard at the package on the table.

Fidelia was slow to wrath, but all at once she had an impulse of indignation. So that was all her sister had come over there for—just curiosity to see what was in that package, when she knew how frightened she was in a storm, how frightened she had always been. She sat down in the rocking-chair, and her large face took on an expression at once sulky and obstinate.

"Yes," she said, dryly, "I guess it is worse than it was when the expressman came." Then she said no more. She rocked slowly back and forth; a fierce rattle of sleet came on the window-panes. Diantha carried the brush and comb back to the bedroom; her white hair shone like silver; then she returned, and stood looking out at the black night pierced by the whiteness of the storm.

"Don't you feel afraid that your geraniums will get frozen, quite so close to the window?" she asked. "That Lady Washington lays right against the pane, and it is so cold that the window is frosting, beside the sleet."

Fidelia softened a little. "Maybe there is some danger," she said.

"Suppose we move them back a little?" said Diantha. "We can move them together, I guess."

Fidelia rose, and she and Diantha took hold of the flower-stand and moved it slightly away from the window.

"I guess that is safer," said Diantha. She looked at the package on the table again, but Fidelia was rocking back and forth with the old look of obstinacy on her face. Diantha also sat down near the stove. A great gust of wind shook the house; a tree crashed somewhere.

"It is an awful storm," remarked Diantha.

Fidelia felt such a thrill of thankfulness for companionship in the midst of that terrible attack of wind that she melted. "Yes," she said, "it is awful."

"It makes me think of stories I used to read of folks in a fort being besieged by Indians," said Diantha, looking at the package.

Fidelia's eyes followed hers. "Yes," she said, "it does."

"I suppose you don't want to go to bed yet?" said Diantha, rather formally. "I am not keeping you up?"

"No," said Fidelia.

"I thought you didn't use to go to bed in a hard storm," said Diantha, "and I felt kind of nervous alone, and I saw your light burning."

Fidelia's face lightened. So Diantha had not come over wholly for the sake of curiosity. Fidelia felt pleased to think her sister had felt the need of her, even selfishly. Her eyes and Diantha's both fell upon the package at the same time; then they met.

"I haven't opened it yet," said Fidelia, quite easily. She laughed.

Diantha laughed too. "You don't seem to be in much of a hurry to see your Christmas present," said she.

"Oh, I don't believe it can be a Christmas present."

"It must be."

"Who could have sent me one?"

"I don't know, but somebody must have."

"Perhaps I had better see what it is," said Fidelia. She rose, and Diantha hesitated a second; then she rose, and both women stood over the package on the table. Fidelia began carefully untying the string.

"Why don't you cut it?" asked Diantha.

"It's a very nice string," replied Fidelia, who was thrifty. Her thrift had made some of the difference between herself and her sister.

She strove hard with the knot, which was difficult. Diantha pushed her away, and untied it herself with firm, nervous fingers. Then she flung the string to her sister.

"Here's your string," said she, but with entire good-nature. She even laughed indulgently. Fidelia then wound the string carefully, while Diantha lifted the lid from the box. Both women gave little gasps of astonishment.

"Goodness!" cried Diantha. "Who ever could have?"

"I don't know," responded Fidelia, feebly. They both stared a second at each other, then again at the box. In the box, in a nest of tissue-paper, lay a large doll. The doll's eyes were closed, but she smiled in her doll-sleep—a smile of everlasting amiability and peace. Golden ringlets clustered around her pink-and-white countenance, her little kid arms and hands lay supine at her side, her little kid toes stuck up meekly side by side. The doll was entirely undressed, except for a very brief under-garment of coarse muslin.

"It's a doll," gasped Diantha.

"Yes, Diantha," gasped Fidelia.

"Who could have sent you a doll?" inquired Diantha, with some sternness.

"I don't know," replied Fidelia.

"There must be some mistake," said Diantha.

Fidelia's face, which had worn an expression of secret delight, fell. "I suppose so," she said.

Both women stared at the doll, as if under a species of fascination. The storm roared harder, the sleet beat against the window as if it would break the glass, another tree branch crashed, but they did not heed it. They continued to stare at the doll.

"She isn't dressed," said Fidelia, finally, with a tender cadence in her voice.

"No, she isn't," returned Diantha.

Diantha then lifted the doll very carefully and delicately by the middle of its small back. The doll's eyes immediately flew open, and seemed to survey them with intelligent and unswerving joy.

"Her eyes open and shut," remarked Diantha. She then pressed the small body a little harder, and there came a tiny, squeaking cry. "It cries," proclaimed Diantha.

Fidelia simply stared.

Diantha looked speculative. "Most probably this doll belongs to the little Merrill girl that lives next door," said she.

"Perhaps it does," replied Fidelia.

"I guess you had better take it over there to-morrow morning and ask her mother."

"I suppose I had."

Diantha and Fidelia sat down after Diantha had placed the doll carefully back in the box, but she did not replace the lid. The two women rocked, and listened to the storm, which seemed to increase.

"There's no going to bed to-night, I suppose," said Diantha, with an angry inflection. She scowled at the storm beating at the windows.

The two rocked awhile longer. It was past midnight.

"That doll makes me think of that one I had when I was a child," said Diantha, in a tone of indignant reminiscence.

"It looks a good deal like mine, too," said Fidelia, in a softer tone.

"It seems," said Diantha, still in an indignant tone, "a pity to give away a doll to any child, not dressed."

Fidelia, looking at Diantha, blushed all over her delicate old face, and Diantha also blushed.

"Yes, it does," said Fidelia, in a hesitating voice.

"It's a shame," said Diantha.

"Yes," said Fidelia—"yes, I think it is a shame."

"I suppose you have a lot of pieces in the house?" said Diantha. She did not look at Fidelia then; she gazed out of the window. "It is a dreadful storm," she murmured, before Fidelia had a chance to reply, as if her mind were really not upon the doll at all.

"Yes, I have," replied Fidelia, with subdued eagerness.

"Well, I suppose the little Merrill girl would think a lot more of the doll if it was dressed; it would be a shame to give her one that wasn't, and if we've got to sit up for the storm we may as well do something. It wasn't ever my way to sit idle."

"I know it wasn't, sister," agreed Fidelia, falling insensibly into her old manner of addressing Diantha. "I've got a great many real pretty pieces," she said.

"Handy?"

"They are up-garret."

"Well, what if they are? I ain't afraid to go up-garret for them. You'd better light the lantern, that's all. I don't think we'd better carry a lamp up there; the wind blows too hard."

"I'll get it right away," said Fidelia, fairly tremulous with excitement.

"Have you got any pieces of that blue silk dress you had when you were nineteen years old?"

"Yes, I have some nice pieces."

"My green silk would make something handsome, but the pieces of that are all over at my house."

"I've got a big piece of that," said Fidelia. "You gave me some for patchwork years ago, and I did not begin to use it up; and I've got some of that pink satin I had when Abigail Upham was married; and I've got some dotted muslin, and some of that spriggled muslin, and plenty of old linen, and some narrow lace, and some ribbon."

"You'd better get the lantern, and we'll get the pieces and go right to work," said Diantha, rising with alacrity.

The two women went forthwith to the garret, stepping cautiously over the loose flooring, and peering timorously into the recumbent shadows beneath the eaves by the flashing light of the lantern which Fidelia carried. The pieces were in two old trunks and a blue cotton bag. They collected a quantity of remnants of silk and satin and linen, and went back downstairs to the sitting-room. Fidelia was trembling with the cold.

"You'd better sit close to the stove, or you'll catch your death," said Diantha, and she looked kindly at her sister.

"Yes, I will," replied Fidelia, gratefully.

"I'll set the lamp on the stand, and then you can see," said Diantha.

The two sisters, seated close to the warm stove, with the stand between them, went to work with half-shamed delight. They cut and made the tiny garments for the smiling doll, while the storm raged outside. They paid very little attention to it. They were absorbed.

"Suppose we make the pink satin just the way yours was made," suggested Diantha.

"With a crosswise flounce," said Fidelia, happily.

"And a little lace spencer cape."

"My old doll had one," said Fidelia.

"And so did mine."

"All our dolls used to dress alike."

"Yes, I know they did."

"We used to take a sight of comfort playing with them, sister."

"Yes, we did," agreed Diantha, harshly, "but those days are over."

Fidelia felt a little rebuked. "Yes, I know they are," she replied meekly.

"We might make a dress of dotted muslin over the blue silk, like those our dolls used to have," said Diantha, in a softer voice.

"Yes, we might," Fidelia said, delighted.

As the two women worked, their faces seemed to change. They were tall and bent, with a rigorous bend of muscles not apparently so much from the feebleness and relaxing of age as from defiance to the stresses of life; both sisters' backs had the effect of stern walkers before fierce winds; their hair was sparse and faded, brushed back from thin temples, with nothing of the grace of childhood, and yet there was something of the immortal child in each as she bent over her doll-clothes. The contour of childhood was evident in their gaunt faces, which suddenly appeared like transparent masks of age; the light of childhood sparkled in their eyes; when they chattered and laughed one would have sworn there were children in the room. And, strangest of all, their rancor and difference seemed to have vanished; they were in the most perfect accord.

They worked all night, until the triumphant pallor of dawn overcame the darkness and the window-panes were outlined in blue through the white shades. It cleared just before daylight.

"I declare, it's morning," said Diantha.

"We've worked all night," said Fidelia, in an awed tone.

"Better work than sit still," said Diantha. "You'd better put the lamp out."

Fidelia put out the lamp and pulled up a window-curtain.

"The storm is over," said she, "but it it awful! Just look, sister."

Diantha and Fidelia stood at the window and surveyed the ruin outside. The yard and the road were strewn with the branches of the trees; the trees, lopped and mutilated, stood cased in a glittering white mail over their lost members. It was a sylvan battlefield, where the victors had barely come off with their lives.

"It's dreadful; you can't get home yet a while," said Fidelia.

"I guess I can manage," said Diantha, suspiciously. She wondered if Fidelia wanted to be rid of her.

But Fidelia was looking at her with the expression of a child who wants to make up. "I thought I'd make some of those light biscuits you used to like for breakfast," said she.

"I don't see as I can get home before breakfast," said Diantha. Then she added, in another voice, "Yes, I always did like those light biscuits, sister."

"I've got some honey, too," said Fidelia.

"If there is anything I do like it is light biscuit and honey," said Diantha.

"We can finish dressing the doll after breakfast," ventured Fidelia, radiantly.

"Yes, we can. It's a shame to give a child a doll that ain't dressed."

The sisters worked until late afternoon on the doll's small wardrobe. Everything was complete, from the tiny stockings and slippers to the hat of drawn pink silk, after the style of one which Diantha's doll had owned a half-century before. When at last the doll was arrayed in her pink silk frock, her lace spencer cape, her pink hat trimmed with a fall of lace, under which her rosy face with its unswerving smile looked at her benefactors, they were radiant.

"I call that a very beautiful doll, sister," said Fidelia.

"She certainly is," agreed Diantha.

Fidelia looked at Diantha, and Diantha returned the look. A sudden cloud was over both faces.

"I suppose," said Fidelia, slowly, "we had better—"

"Yes, I suppose so," said Diantha, harshly.

"Before it gets any later," said Fidelia, with a sigh.

"Yes, I suppose so."

"To-morrow is Christmas. Maybe her mother wants to hang it on the tree."

"Very likely."

"Well, will you take it over, or will I?"

"I had just as lief."

"I will if you don't feel like it."

Still neither offered to move. Both regarded the doll, then again each other.

"That Merrill child is not nearly old enough to have doll like that," said Diantha, suddenly.

"I don't think she is either," said Fidelia.

"No, she is not. It is strange people will buy such dolls for children who are no older."

"Especially since she has such handsome clothes."

"She would spoil the clothes in no time."

"Yes; she would let her wear that pink silk and her best hat every day."

"That little Merrill girl is not old enough to take care of that doll," said

Diantha, with emphasis, and with much the same tone as if she had spoken of a baby. She gathered up the doll with determination.

Fidelia sighed. "Are you going to take her over there now?" said she. It was noticeable that both sisters now spoke of the doll as she and her.

"No, I am not. I am going to take her home," declared Diantha.

"You are not going to take her over to the Merrills, sister?"

"No, I am not. That child is not old enough."

Fidelia looked scared, and also aggrieved. "But," she said, "that doll was left here; I don't think you have any right to take her away, Diantha. If either of us is going to keep her, it ought to be the one to whom it was sent."

Diantha surveyed her sister with an injured expression. "Fidelia Nutting," said she, "you don't think—you don't really think—I would do such a thing as that? Of course I wasn't going to take the doll away from you, although she does not really belong to either of us. Of course I know that you have the first claim. I was just going to take her to my house for a while, and I thought you would come over and have tea with me. I have some of that damson sauce you like, and the pound-cake and a mince-pie, and I will make some of those griddle-cakes with butter and sugar and nutmeg on them. It's lonesome for you here alone, with the roads not cleared enough so anybody can get in very easy, and it's lonesome for me. I thought maybe you'd come over, but if—you don't want to—"

"Oh, sister, I shall be very happy to come over, and I haven't had any of those griddle-cakes since mother died. I never got the knack of making them myself. I'll get my shawl and hood."

"You'd better wrap up warm," said Diantha; "it's cleared off cold by the looks. And you'd better fix your fire so you can leave it. Maybe you'll feel as if you could stay all night."

When the two sisters crossed the road together, stepping among the débris of the storm, which had not yet been fully cleared away, the neighbors within range stared. In the Merrill house, next to Fidelia's, the width of a wide yard distant, three faces were in the sitting-room window—Mrs. Merrill's, her unmarried sister's, and little Abby Merrill's, round and rosy, flattened against the glass.

"Did you ever!" cried Annie Bennett, Mrs. Merrill's sister. "There go the Nuttings across the street together. I wonder if they have made up."

"They are going into Diantha's house," said Mrs. Merrill, with wonder. "I wonder if they have made up. I don't believe one has been into the other's house since their mother's funeral."

"Maybe they have," said Annie Bennett.

"Mamma," said little Abby Merrill, "what do you spect Miss Nutting is carrying under her shawl?"

"I don't know, dear," said Mrs. Merrill.

"It looks like a dolly," said little Abby Merrill, wisely.

Mrs. Merrill and Annie Bennett laughed. "I guess Miss Diantha Nutting isn't going around carrying dollies," said Mrs. Merrill. "I guess you must be mistaken, darling."

Annie Bennett could scarcely stop laughing at the idea of Diantha Nutting carrying about a doll. But she suddenly remembered something. "Why, there's that parcel that came here for Fidelia by mistake last night," she said, chokingly. "Seeing her carry a parcel makes me remember that. I had quite forgotten it. She ought to have it, I suppose. Perhaps it is a Christmas present."

"Yes, she ought to have it," said Mrs. Merrill, turning away from the window as the door of the opposite house closed after Diantha's and Fidelia's shawled and hooded figures.

"I'll run over there and carry it," said Annie Bennett.

But little Abby interposed. She was wild to get out-of-doors after her imprisonment by the storm, and she was wild to carry a Christmas present. "Oh, mamma, let me carry it," she begged.

Her mother looked doubtful. "I don't know whether you can get over all those tree-branches without falling and hurting yourself, darling," she said.

"Oh yes, I can," pleaded little Abby.

"I don't believe it will hurt her any if she wants to go," said her aunt, Annie Bennett.

So little Abby Merrill, carefully wrapped against the cold, went across the street, picking her way among the fallen branches, with her mother watching anxiously, and carried the parcel to Diantha Nutting's door. "My mamma sent me over wif zis," said she—for Abby could not say "th"—"my mamma sent me over wif zis, zat was left at our house by a spressman by mistake last night." Little Abby Merrill never knew why Miss Diantha Nutting's face looked suddenly very strange to her, but she felt vaguely alarmed, and shrank back when Diantha spoke.

"Thank you, child," said she, in rather a deep voice, and she took the parcel.

Miss Fidelia Nutting's face was visible behind her sister's, and it wore a similar expression. "Oh, sister!" she gasped when little Abby Merrill had gone trotting, stepping high in her little red leggings, across the street. She was a stout little girl, and planted her little feet in a sturdy fashion. "Oh, sister!"

Diantha clutched her hard. "Come into the house," said she.

The two returned to the warm sitting-room, and then they looked at each other like two confederates in crime.

"Oh, sister, it is dreadful!" said Fidelia, faintly. "That doll must belong to little Abby Merrill, and this bundle she brought must be a Christmas present that somebody has sent me, and somehow the expressman made a mistake. She ought to have her, sister."

"Well," said Diantha, "go over there and carry her if you want to, then."

Fidelia hung her head. "She is a pretty small child to have such a doll, I suppose," she faltered.

"Then don't talk about it," said Diantha. "Why don't you open your parcel?"

Fidelia opened the parcel; inside the brown wrapping-paper was a nice white one tied with lavender ribbon. She untied the dainty bows, and unfolded a fleecy white shawl.

"Who gave it to you?" said Diantha.

Fidelia looked at the slip of paper pinned to a corner of the shawl. On it was written, "With Xmas greetings from Salome H. May."

"It's Salome May," she said.

"She always makes a sight of Christmas," said Diantha.

"I suppose she sent it because I gave her old-fashioned pinks out of my garden last summer," said Fidelia.

"It's a pretty shawl," said Diantha, with no enthusiasm.

"Yes, it is," said Fidelia; "but I never was in the habit of wearing a knit shawl in the house much." She laid the shawl on the table. "I suppose she sent the doll to the little Merrill girl," she added, after a pause.

"Very likely. She and Annie Bennett are intimate."

"Diantha, don't you suppose we are doing a dreadful thing?"

"No, I don't. I don't see why we are. We are not stealing that doll, are we?"

"No-o, I don't suppose we are stealing her," said Fidelia, hesitatingly.

"I am not stealing her, anyway. My conscience is clear. All I am doing is keeping her a little while, until the little Merrill girl is old enough to play with her and not destroy her."

"Oh, of course, that is all I am doing, too, sister."

Diantha Nutting prepared tea in the old dining-room, and she set the table with her mother's old blue Canton china and the best silver teapot and cream-pitcher. There were the griddle-cakes piled in a golden mound sprinkled with sugar and nutmeg; there was the damson sauce; there the pound-cake; but neither sister could eat much. The doll in her brave attire lay on the sitting-room table beside the shawl. Both felt, though they would not confess it to each other or herself, like greedy and dishonest children stealing another child's doll on Christmas-eve. But they were yet firm. Fidelia remained with Diantha that night, and Fidelia occupied her old room out of Diantha's. Neither slept much. Often one called to the other in the darkness of the night: "Fidelia, are you asleep?" "Diantha, are you asleep?" Both were thinking of the doll and the little Merrill girl, and their consciences, which were their New England birthrights, never slumbered nor slept.

The next morning at breakfast—which they did not care for, although it was as desirable as the tea of the night before, being composed of hot biscuits and honey, and ham and eggs and coffee—they looked at each other.

"Sister, I can't do it. I can't keep it up any longer," said Fidelia, suddenly and piteously.

"Well, I suppose she'll have to have her, if she does destroy her," said Diantha, grimly. Then she took another biscuit.

"I guess I'll have another biscuit too," said Fidelia.

After breakfast Fidelia crossed the road to the Merrill house. She rang the bell, trembling, and Annie Bennett came to the door.

"Here is a doll," said Fidelia, trembling. She extended the doll in her pink silk hat and her spencer cape. "Here is a doll that was left at my house by mistake. My name was on the paper, but I guess she made a mistake on account of sending so many presents. Salome H. May sent me a shawl, and I guess she must have meant the doll for little Abby."

But Annie Bennett stared wonderingly at the doll. "Why, no," said she. "Salome sent a doll for Abby two days ago. She can't have sent this to Abby. Abby has five dolls this Christmas, anyway. It can't be Abby's. I don't know of any one else who could have sent her a doll. Was your name on the wrapper?"

"Yes, it was," admitted Fidelia, a great shamefaced hope in her heart.

Annie Bennett laughed. "Well," she said, "as near as I can find out, the doll is yours, Miss Fidelia. I guess somebody thought you and your sister needed a doll to play with."

Fidelia was aware of the friendly sarcasm, but quite unmoved by it. She blushed, but she smiled happily. "It is queer who could have sent it," said she, "but I guess it can't belong to little Abby."

"No, I know it can't," said Annie Bennett.

Annie Bennett and Mrs. Merrill and little Abby Merrill, with her new doll from Salome H. May in her arms, all watched Fidelia Nutting cross the street to Diantha's.

"She skips along like a child," said Mrs. Merrill.

"She is a good deal spryer than Abby," laughed Annie Bennett. "You ought to have seen how that doll was dressed; the funniest old-fashioned things. I wonder if she and Miss Diantha dressed it. I didn't know but she would leave it for Abby anyhow."

"I suppose they will give it to some child," said Mrs. Merrill. "I suppose she thought Abby had dolls enough. I'd like to know who sent her that doll."

"I know what I think," said Annie Bennett. "I think Salome May had a doll left over, and sent it to Fidelia Nutting for a joke. It's just like her."

"Maybe she did," said Mrs. Merrill, laughing.

But Fidelia and Diantha themselves were the children who loved the doll, and they could not spare her to another child. When Fidelia ran into the sitting-room of her sister's house with the doll in her arms, Diantha stared.

"What have you brought her back for?" she asked, shortly.

"Oh, sister, the little Merrill girl has a doll from Salome H. May. This isn't her doll. It must have been sent to me."

"Fidelia Nutting, who do you suppose did such a silly thing as to send a doll to you?"

"I don't know, sister."

"Well," said Diantha, "there's one thing certain: if we don't know whom she belongs to, there's nothing to do but to keep her. If she wasn't meant for you, it's the fault of the sender."

"May be we shall find out sometime about her," said Fidelia. But they never did.

"Well, you had better stay to dinner," said Diantha. "I hailed the butcher and got a chicken, and I've got pudding on boiling."

When the two sat at dinner, casting stray glances at the doll on the sitting-room table, Diantha spoke.

"Look here, Fidelia," said she. "I've been thinking. Suppose you rent that house you live in, and come and live with me. Nobody knows how much longer we've got to live, anyhow, and we can put our means together and have a girl to wait on us; we ain't either of us fit to live alone, and I guess we can get along. We used to get along well enough when we were children."

"Yes, we did," said Fidelia, cheerfully. "I'll come if you want me to, sister."

In the afternoon the sisters sat together in the sitting-room of the Nutting house. They were making some more clothes for a doll—a lavender silk frock from an old one of Diantha's, and a little black silk mantilla. They sat close to the window to catch the waning wintry sunlight—two old sisters, come together after years of estrangement, through the mediation of the universal plaything of childhood, which had come to them out of a mystery, into a common ground of old love and memories.

"I suppose we ought to name this doll," said Diantha. "We always did name our dolls."

"Yes, I guess we had better name it," agreed Fidelia.

"We will keep her for little girls to play with if any happen in with their mothers," said Diantha. "And if a child asks what her name is, we ought to have something to say."

"Yes, I think so."

"Well?" said Diantha, interrogatively.

Fidelia blushed redly before her own sentiment; then she spoke. "I guess Peace would be a good name," said she, with a soft little shamed laugh at her sister.

"Well?" said Diantha.

The two sisters continued sewing on the doll's clothes while the light lasted, their heads bent close together with loving accord, and the doll was between them, smiling with inscrutable inanity.

The Gold

1904

The colonies had but recently declared war with the old country; and Abraham Duke, being an able-bodied man, although no longer young, was going to fight for the cause. He was fastening on his old sword, which his father before him had wielded well, and his wife Catherine was standing watching him, with an angry cant to her head. "Wherefore cannot you tell me where the gold is, Abraham Duke?" said she.

Abraham Duke regarded his wife with stern melancholy, and his glance of fixedness in his own purpose was more impregnable than any fort.

"I can tell you not, Catherine," replied he, "because no man can tell any woman anything which he wants not the whole world to know, and there are plenty of evil-disposed folk abroad in these troublous times, and 'tis for your own sake, since, in case robbers come, you can tell them without perjury that you know not where the gold is."

"For *my* sake!" returned Catherine, with a high sniff. "You tell me not for fear I shall spend the gold, and you always loved gold better than your wife. You fear lest I should buy a new gown to my back, or a new cap-ribbon. Never fear, Abraham Duke, for I have gone poorly clad so long that, faith, a new cap ribbon even would frighten me."

"I have given you all that I could, Catherine," returned Abraham, gravely.

"But now that you have all this wealth, five thousand pounds, you hide it away, and tell me not where it is—me, your wife, who has kept your house for scarce anything save a poor measure of daily bread, all these years. You wrong me, Abraham Duke."

But Abraham Duke only kept his mouth shut more tightly. He was perhaps ten years older than his wife, but he was handsome, with a stern, almost a sad, majesty of carriage. It was only some few weeks before that the money, a legacy from his father in England, five thousand pounds in gold, had come on the English ship *The Queen Mary*. It was the day afterwards that he had sent his wife away by stagecoach fifty miles inland on a visit to her sister, Mistress Abigail Endicott. He had charged her while on her visit to say nothing about the five thousand pounds, but well he knew that she had talked of nothing but the gold, and had bragged much, and now, when she had returned and her husband was about to join the army, the gold was hidden, and she was to know nothing of it and have nothing of it all to spend until her husband's return. He regarded her at the last with the sort of restrained tenderness of his kind. She was still a most charming woman to look upon, fair-skinned and fair-haired, and, in spite of her complaints, attired daintily, although she had spun and woven the blue petticoat which she wore, and worked herself the lace kerchief which veiled her bosom, and the cap which crowned her fair head. "When I come home, you shall have what you will to spend," said he, "but not now. Now is a time when a good wife needs nothing except the wherewithal to live, with her goodman away, and war in the land."

"Abraham, tell me where you have hid the gold?"

"I will not tell you, Catherine," said Abraham Duke, and now he was all equipped to start. "If, perchance, I should never come back, you may go to Parson Rawson, who holds a sealed letter for you, but in no case will he give it to you unless I fall and he has ample proof of it. He has promised me upon his honor, and no man living ever knew Parson Ebenezer Rawson to forswear his word."

"And in the mean time, while you fight I am to stay alone at home and starve."

"There is no need for a woman of industry to starve in a good home, with a bound boy to cut wood and dig the garden for her, and cows and sheep and chickens," said Abraham.

"But should the enemy come and take them all, as they may do, since we are on the seashore!" cried Catherine.

"In that case you will go to your sister, Mistress Endicott, in Rexham," replied Abraham. He was advancing towards his wife for a decorous last embrace, should she be disposed to yield it in her rancor, when little Harry Evarts, the son of Abraham's friend and neighbor, the goldsmith, came rushing in, and he was all bloody, and his pretty face was deadly white, and his fair curls, like a girl's, seemed to stand up and wave like plumes over his head, he was in such a fright. Then Catherine Duke forgot the gold, for she had no child of her own, and she loved the boy. "Harry! Harry!" she shrieked, running to him and holding him to her breast. "What is it, child? Speak! Are you hurt?"

"Father! father!" gasped the boy, and then he hung almost lifeless on Catherine's arm.

"What ails your father? Speak!" cried Catherine.

"Father is killed," replied the boy, faintly.

"Killed! What, your father killed! Abraham, do you hear? Joseph Evarts is killed. Hear what this child says! Run, quick, Abraham!"

But when Catherine turned to look at her husband there was no one there, and she for the moment thought nothing of it, inferring that at the child's first word he had hastened to see what had happened to his friend.

But Abraham Duke did not return, and it was known on good authority that he had never set foot in Joseph Evarts' house to ascertain what had happened to him, but had made his way straight out of the village to the army, the company of which he was a member being assembled in Suffield, about ten miles away.

Catherine, although she had had the difference with her husband concerning the hiding of the gold, felt hurt that he should have slipped away in such wise without a word of farewell while she was in such anxiety over the bereft child, but she had no suspicions then, or afterwards, and nobody spoke of suspicions to her. But suspicions there were, although they slumbered in the general excitement of the war and the ever-recurring rumors of a ship of the enemy in sight and about to land in the harbor of the little village of South Suffield. It was said that Abraham Duke was the last one seen entering and leaving the house of Joseph Evarts the evening before his dead body was found by his little son, who was returning from a visit to his grandmother; his mother was dead. Little Harry Evarts had, indeed, found the door of his home blocked by something, and pushed with all his childish strength, and found, when the door yielded a gap, that it was the body of his father, dead of a sword-thrust in the side, which blocked the door. Evarts had been a goldsmith by trade in the old country; since he had been in the new, finding little opportunity for the exercise of his craft, he had supported himself and his little son by working his farm. It was held that Abraham Duke had gone the night before to bid him farewell. Mistress Prudence Dexter, who lived next door, had distinctly seen him enter and leave, and she had seen no one else that evening, and it was bright moon-

light and she had been sitting beside her window with no light, to save candles. Still, in spite of the sinister report, Abraham Duke's standing—he
was tithing-man in the meeting-house, and esteemed by all—and the utter
absence of any known motive served to keep the suspicion well within
bounds, and would have done so even had not everybody's mind been distracted by the war and the rumors of strange sails on the horizon.

Meantime Catherine Duke lived on alone, save for the bound boy, who
was none too bright as to his wits, although strong and a good worker, and
night and day she searched for the gold, which she was confident her husband had hidden somewhere about the house, if he had not buried it in
the field. Her husband had not been gone twenty-four hours before all the
usual hiding-places of treasure were overhauled, such as old teapots, the
drawers of dressers, secret drawers, and the clock. She searched the clock
particularly, since she heard that her husband had been seen coming from
Joseph Evarts' with some of the works of the clock that night before he
went away. Prudence Dexter had averred that she had distinctly seen the
dangling pendulum of a clock from under Abraham's cloak as he went
down the street. Catherine, knowing that the dead man, Joseph Evarts,
had been a cunning workman in many ways, thought that he might have
rigged for his friend a secret closet in the clock, and she searched it well, but
found nothing. She thought that it might have been possible for her husband to carry the main body of the clock under his cloak, for the purpose
of the secret closet, but, although she sounded every inch and poked the inmost recesses of the clock well over, no gold did she discover. She therefore
let it be, ticking with the solemn majesty of its kind; it was an eight-day
clock, taller than a man, standing like Time itself in the corner of the living-
room, and casting a shadow like the shadow of a man across the floor every morning when the sun shone into the room. But she searched, after she
had searched the clock, every inch of the house. She even had the hearth-
stones taken up, she and the dull-witted bound boy, working by candle-
light, with the curtains drawn, that the neighbors might suspect nothing,
and she replaced them in a masterly fashion; for Catherine Duke was in reality a masterly woman. And then she had out many of the chimney bricks,
as many as she dared, and she even had up some of the flooring, but she
found nothing.

Then she and the bound boy dug up the cellar bottom, and then the
bound boy ploughed every inch of land which had hitherto remained uncultivated. She could do that openly, and people began to say that Cath-

erine would make more of the farm than her husband had done. But the land that was too stony for the plough she was more secret about, she and the boy digging it up by moonlight and replacing the sods.

Once she ventured forth with a lantern in her impatience, but the light, seen flitting along the field near the shore, occasioned a rumor in the village that a ship of the British had landed and a drum beat to arms. Then all the old men and boys left in the place sallied forth, and Catherine and the bound boy, whose name, which belied his character, was Solomon—last name he had none at all that anybody knew, for he was a foundling—had hard work to reach the house undiscovered, although she blew out the lantern and scudded for her life with her petticoats lifted, while the boy sped with her, the more afraid that he knew not what he feared.

However, all Catherine's searching came to nothing, although she worked hard—and hard work it was, with what she had to do on the farm. No woman in South Suffield was considered a better housewife than she, and she had to live up to her reputation. She and the boy sheared and washed sheep, and she spun and wove the wool. She tended the flax and made of that lengths of linen cloth; she made her soap and her candles, and kept her house as neat as wax, and all the while the search for the hidden gold was in her mind. Many a time in the dead of night would she, lying awake and pondering over it, and striving to place her own mind in the attitude of her husband's when he had hidden the treasure, think of another place where she had not looked, and be up, with her candle lit, and over the house, in her bed-gown, to find nothing at all.

Catherine grew old with the loneliness and the ever-increasing wrath with her husband, who had so mistreated her after her years of self-denial and toil for his sake. The sense of injury is like a fermenting canker in the mind when once it is allowed to work with no protest. Catherine's pretty, round face grew long and sour, her smooth forehead knitted. Her blue eyes got an expression of sharp peering which never left them. She even looked at her friends as if she suspected that the hiding-place of the gold might be in their minds. And yet all the time she had in reality no desire for the gold itself, for she had enough and to spare. Had she found the gold she would directly have hid it again and spent not one shilling until her husband's return, but the sense of injury ever spurred her on with a goading which almost produced madness. She asked herself over and over why she should not know—why her husband, for whom she had saved and toiled, could not have trusted her? Of a Sabbath-day, when she went to meeting, she regarded the parson, Ebenezer Rawson, with a covert hatred, since he held the sealed letter, and had been trusted to a greater extent than she. Sometimes, although, in spite of her wrath and sense of ill treatment, which warped her mind, she still loved her husband and prayed for his safety, the imagination would come to her how, in the case of his falling before the enemy, she should go to the parson and demand the sealed letter, and know at last what she had a right to know—the hiding-place of the gold.

After her husband had been away some six months and she had had one letter from him, with not a word about the gold, she dressed herself in her best—in her red cloak, which she had had as a bride and kept carefully, and a hat with a plume which would have become her had she not gotten the expression on her fair face of the seeker after dross, which disfigures more than aught in the world—and she made her way to the parson's house. He was a widower, and always had a kindly word for a pretty woman, although esteemed, as her husband had said, a man who kept his own counsel. Past the parson's housekeeper, an ancient aunt of his, declaring that she had need of spiritual consolation, and leaving her staring, suspicious because of the red cloak and the plume, she marched into the study, lined with books which damned all mankind by reason of the love of God, according to the tenets of the day, and she found the parson at his desk, with his forehead knitted over the tenthly of his next Sabbath-day's sermon. And then calling to her aid old blandishments of hers, she beset the parson for the letter, although the conditions of its delivery were not fulfilled, and she gave good and sufficient reasons why she should know the secret, since lately the rumors of the enemy on the coast had increased, and she argued that she should know the hiding-place of the treasure, that she might bury it safely away from the greed of the redcoats.

But Parson Ebenezer Rawson, who was a handsome man in a powdered wig, and had something of the diplomat in him, only laughed, and spoke to her with a pleasant chiding, the while he noted that she was no longer, in spite of her red cloak and her feather, as goodly to see as she had been, and had an apposite verse of Scripture concerning the frailty of the flesh and the evanescence of beauty enter his mind.

"Mistress Duke," said Parson Rawson, "it truly seemeth to me that, since you yourself cannot find the gold, no safer hiding-place can be discovered from the enemy."

Catherine blushed high with anger. "But I am in want of goods for household use," said she. In response to that, Parson Rawson surveyed her rounded form and the sumptuous folds of her red cloak, and said that he could not betray his trust, since his word, once given, was like a lock and seal upon his soul, and that did she want for the necessaries of life he would advance the money needful to her upon a loan.

At last Catherine Duke went away, still unsatisfied, and she walked—for thoroughly feminine she was—with a graceful movement, being conscious of the carriage of her head and the folds of her red cloak, until she was out of view of the parson's windows, and then she broke into an angry switch, and she even wept like a crossed child, as she went along where there were no houses.

Before she came to her own house, some quarter of a mile distant, she had to pass the house where Joseph Evarts had lived and wherein he had come to his death by foul means. Catherine Duke was not a nervous woman, nor timid, but as stanch and stout-hearted as women needed to be in those times. Still, for all that, and although she had not heard of the suspicions which were directed against her husband, she never passed this house without an involuntary quickening of her steps, especially when it was nightfall, as now, and she was alone. The house had remained deserted since poor Joseph Evarts's dead body had been carried forth from it, for the little boy had been taken to live with his grandmother in an adjoining town. Now, in this gray, weather-stained house seemed to abide the spirit of mystery and murder, and to glare forth from the desolate blanks of its windows upon all passers-by. Thus Catherine Duke, stout-hearted as she was, quickened her steps that evening, and scudded by in her red cloak, with her best plume waving in the breeze; but as she passed she gave a terrified roll of her blue eyes at the house, and she could have sworn that she saw a gleam of light in one of the rooms of the second story. She looked instinctively at the opposite side of the road for a light which could produce a reflection, but there was no house there, and no bonfire. She looked again, and it seemed certain to her that there was a candlelight in the east room on the second floor. Then she fairly ran, for a vague horror was upon her, and it seemed to her that she heard footsteps behind her, although, when she reached her own door and turned around, with the latch in her hand and Solomon gazing at her from the lighted living-room, there was not a person in sight on the road, which made a sharp turn a short distance from the Duke house. That turn swerved the road from the sea, and gave room on both sides for houses. The Evarts house was on the sea-side of the road. All that could be seen from the front door of the Duke house was the desolate, moaning waste of waters, which had lately acquired a terrible significance as a possible highway for the enemy, and the road, with no dwelling as far as the turn. Catherine called Solomon to the door. "Look," said she, sharply, "and see if you can spy out anybody on the road."

Solomon came and stood beside her, projecting his simple, gaping face, with its prominent light-blue eyes, into the gathering gloom, and whimpered—for he had some vague idea that he was being blamed, and he held his mistress in awe—that he saw no one. "Go as far as the turn in the road," said Catherine, imperiously, "and see if you see anybody; and, if you do, come back quickly and let us lock the door."

Solomon started, although he was afraid—for he was more afraid of his mistress's anger than of any unknown quantity—but she called him back. "If you see no one on the road," said she, "keep on until you reach the Evarts house, and look and see if you spy a light in the east chamber." Solomon sped away, although his legs trembled under him, for the fear in his mistress's heart infected his own.

Catherine went into the house and hung on the porridge-kettle, and very soon Solomon came back, saying that he had seen no one, and there was no light in the east chamber of the Evarts house, but there was a boat moored behind the house, on the sea-shore.

"You cannot have seen rightly," said Catherine, for now her confidence had returned. "You saw the old wreck that has lain behind the house for the last three years."

"Nay, mistress, 'twas a boat," persisted the boy; but when Catherine insisted that he had seen wrongly, he yielded and agreed with her, and said it was the wreck, for he had no mind of his own when the pressure of another was brought to bear upon it.

But the poor lad was right, and it had been well for poor Catherine Duke had she heeded him and taken the candle-gleam in the chamber of the deserted house and the boat on the sand behind it as a warning, instead of recovering her bravery of outlook and going about her evening tasks as usual. After supper she set Solomon to paring apples to dry, and she herself spun at her flax-wheel. They found her hard by it the next day, and she was murdered even as Joseph Evarts had been; but she had not come to her death so easily, for she had been tortured first, and there were the marks of fire on her feet and hands. As for the bound boy, he had leaped out of the window as the men beat down the door, and he had sped away on his long legs, with what little wit he had ever owned wellnigh gone forever. When he was found and brought back, he shook like one with palsy, and he went through his life so, and he could only speak in disjointed stammers. As for answering questions to any purpose, there was no hope of it from him, although the people gathered some confirmation of what they at first suspected, that Catherine had been first tortured to make her reveal the hiding-place of her gold, and then, when she did not reveal it, as she could not, poor soul, she was finished. Then the whole house had been ransacked for the gold, but the robbers and murderers found it no more than Catherine had done, although people were not sure of it. Indeed, it was said by many that the men, who were supposed to have come ashore in the boat which had been moored behind the Evarts house, and which had been seen by a man passing as well as by Solomon, had found the gold and taken it away. Catherine had talked much, to her own hurt, about the treasure, and there were stragglers from the army, as well as the enemy, to fear. Some said they were British soldiers who had come ashore in the boat, and some said they were men from the Colonial army, a company of which had been recently stationed for a short time at Suffield, but no one ever knew certainly.

When Abraham Duke came home, with only one arm, having lost the other by a British shot, he found a deserted home and a devastated farm, for there had been a raid by the enemy after Catherine's death. They had left the house standing, with its contents, but the livestock had been taken.

Abraham lived on alone, and worked his poor fields painfully, being so crippled with only one sound arm and hand, and he barely kept soul and body together, for, if the gold had not been stolen, he made no use of it. Sometimes the neighbors, albeit grudgingly and doubtfully, being still uncertain as to whether he was hoarding his treasure or not, came and helped the poor man with his scanty harvesting. However, they seemed to meet with but little gratitude, for Abraham Duke, always taciturn and cold of bearing, had become more so. He spoke to no man unless he were first spoken to, and then he made scant reply. And although he still attended all the services on the Sabbath-day in the meeting-house, he had given up his office of tithing-man, and would not have it; and people said he had doctrinal doubts, because of his afflictions, which were not to his credit, even if he were innocent of the crime which those who were more ready to think evil laid at his door.

As time went on, people look more and more askance at him, for his face grew more and more bitter and forbidding, even terrifying. The children became afraid of him, and gradually the old suspicion became more assured. He was held (although no one had any proof, and, there being no known motive for the crime, there was no talk of bringing him to justice) as a man accursed, and when he was helped it was more and more grudgingly and with serious doubts as to the blessings to be received for the deed.

Joseph Evarts's son had grown up, and he was living in his father's old house with his grandmother, who still lived, although very old, and never did Abraham Duke pass the house that he was not conscious of the young man's eyes upon him. Abraham had become aware of the suspicion, and it looked more keenly from Harry Evarts's eyes than any other's. Abraham rarely looked the young man in the face, for it had become to him the face of an avenging fate. He went past the house with his head bent, but always he knew there was an eye upon him—if not the young man's, his grand-mother's, for she too suspected, and voiced her suspicions openly. Her old face, set in the narrow window-frame, was as malignant as a witch's upon Abraham Duke passing by, and he felt it, although he did not look up.

Affairs grew worse and worse with him. Rheumatism beset him one winter, and he was crippled with that, as well as his maimed arm and his age, for he was now an old man. He sat all day by his fireless hearth; for it was often fireless, since he could not cut wood nor hire it cut, and often he went a day without food, for he was more and more abhorred for the shadow of suspicion of an evil deed which had fallen upon him. Old Parson Rawson had died years before. He had given up the sealed letter to Abraham when he returned from the army, and Abraham had taken it without a word, and nobody knew what had become of it.

Abraham Duke lived on, hanging to life with a feeble clutch, like an old leaf to an autumn bough, and he was near eighty, and suffering all that one could suffer and live. He was slowly freezing and starving to death, and the occasional aid from his kind only served to prolong his misery. At last, when he was eighty, there came a fierce winter, and one morning Harry Evarts, who had lately married, and whose heart, embittered with suspi-cion and the desire for vengeance, was somewhat softened by the thankful-ness for love, thought of the old man, and, walking down to the turn of the road, and seeing no smoke from the chimney, he returned home for his hand-sled, and drew a good store of fire-wood, with a basket of provisions, to the Duke house.

It was a bright, freezing morning, a day glittering as if strung with dia-monds, and the wind from the north was like a flail of death. Harry Evarts shuddered as he dragged his sled up to the door of the Duke house, and he hesitated a second for dread of what he might find when he entered. Then he heard a sweet voice from behind calling, and the girl he had married came running to join him, her fair face all glowing with the cold.

When she came alongside, Harry pounded on the door, and a horrible, dull echo, as of the vacancy of death itself, came in their ears. The young wife, Elizabeth, caught hold of her husband's arm, and she was almost weeping. "Oh, Harry! oh, Harry!" she whispered. "The poor old man must be dead."

Harry shut his mouth hard and pounded again, and again came the echo like a voice of desolate mockery from the outside of life. Then Harry shut his mouth harder, and opened the door, which was unlocked, as if the old man had left it on the latch for death, and he entered, Elizabeth shrinking behind him.

And on the hearth sat old Abraham Duke, frozen and starved, but his face had an expression of such exceeding peace and humility that even the girl was not frightened, but she began to weep bitterly. "Poor old man! oh, poor old man!" she sobbed. "And he does not look, dead, as he did alive."

The room was full of brilliant sunlight, but bitter cold, and on the hearth were only ashes, but the andirons and the tops of the fire-set caught the sunlight and glowed warmly. So also did the ornaments on the desk and the high-boy and the clock, and the pendulum of the clock, which still ticked, seemed to swing in an arc of gold. Harry was deadly white, standing looking at the old man on the hearth. Elizabeth continued to sob; then, being led by her sweet, womanly instincts, she went nearer to the old man, and placed one of her little hands with a caressing gesture like a blessing on his sunken forehead. Then she started. "Harry," she said—"Harry, there is a letter in his hand."

Harry did not stir. He was thinking of his father, and how he had come home to find him lying dead across the door.

"Harry," said the girl again, "there is a letter." Then she reached down and softly took the letter from the dead man's hand, which seemed to yield it up willingly. "Harry, the letter is for you!" cried Elizabeth, in an awed whisper.

Then she handed the letter to her husband. "Open it," said she.

"I can't," said the young man, hoarsely, for he was fighting a fight with himself.

"I will open it!" cried the girl, who was full of quick impulses, and she broke the seal. There were only a few words in the letter, which was, in fact, more a memorandum than a letter, and she read them aloud: "The andirons, the fire-set, the handles on the high-boy, the handles on the desk, the trimmings of the clock, the pendulum, the trimmings on the best bed, the handles on the dresser, the key of the desk—Gold."

"My father did the work; he made the things of gold instead of brass, and he *knew!*" exclaimed Harry.

The girl was ghastly white. She continued to look with a wild gaze of awful understanding at the old man sitting stark and dead on his fireless hearth, where he had sat so long with the great god Mammon, whom he had not dared command to his own needs lest he destroy him. She reflected how he had sat there and starved with his wealth glittering in his eyes, and she also reflected, considering the look on his dead face, that perhaps his earthly retribution had won him heavenly peace. But she shuddered convulsively, and the gold light reflected from the tops of the andirons seemed to wink at her like eyes of infernal understanding and mockery. She looked at the letter again, and called out its contents again in a voice shrill with hysteria: "The andirons, the fire-set, the handles on the high-boy, the handles on the desk, the trimmings of the clock, the pendulum, the trimmings on the best bed, the handles on the dresser, the key of the desk—Gold."

The Old-Maid Aunt

1908

I am relegated here in Eastridge to the position in which I suppose I properly belong, and I dare say it is for my best spiritual and temporal good. Here I am the old-maid aunt. Not a day, not an hour, not a minute, when I am with other people, passes that I do not see myself in their estimation playing that rôle as plainly as if I saw myself in a looking-glass. It is a moral lesson which I presume I need. I have just returned from my visit at the Pollard's country-house in Lancaster, where I most assuredly did not have it. I do not think I deceive myself. I know it is the popular opinion that old maids are exceedingly prone to deceive themselves concerning the endurance of their youth and charms, and the views of other people with regard to them. But I am willing, even anxious, to be quite frank with myself. Since—well, never mind since what time—I have not cared an iota whether I was considered an old maid or not. The situation has seemed to me rather amusing, inasmuch as it has involved a secret willingness to be what everybody has considered me as very unwilling to be. I have regarded it as a sort of joke upon other people.

But I think I am honest—I really mean to be, and I think I am—when I say that outside Eastridge the rôle of an old-maid aunt is the very last one which I can take to any advantage. Here I am estimated according to what people think I am, rather than what I actually am. In the first place, I am only fifteen years older than Peggy, who has just become engaged, but those fifteen years seem countless æons to the child herself and the other members of the family. I am ten years younger than my brother's wife, but she and my brother regard me as old enough to be her mother. As for

Grandmother Evarts, she fairly looks up to me as her superior in age, although she *does* patronize me. She would patronize the prophets of old. I don't believe she ever says her prayers without infusing a little patronage into her petitions. The other day Grandmother Evarts actually inquired of me, of *me!* concerning a knitting-stitch. I had half a mind to retort, "Would you like a lesson in bridge, dear old soul?" She never heard of bridge, and I suppose she would have thought I meant bridge-building. I sometimes wonder why it is that all my brother's family are so singularly unsophisticated, even Cyrus himself, able as he is and dear as he is.

Sometimes I speculate as to whether it can be due to the mansard-roof of their house. I have always had a theory that inanimate things exerted more of an influence over people than they dreamed, and a mansard-roof, to my mind, belongs to a period which was most unsophisticated and fatuous, not merely concerning æsthetics, but simple comfort. Those bedrooms under the mansard-roof are miracles not only of ugliness, but discomfort, and there is no attic. I think that a house without a good roomy attic is like a man without brains. Possibly living in a brainless house has affected the mental outlook of my relatives, although their brains are well enough. Peggy is not exactly remarkable for hers, but she is charmingly pretty, and has a wonderful knack at putting on her clothes, which might be esteemed a purely feminine brain, in her fingers. Charles Edward really has brains, although he is a round peg in a square hole, and as for Alice, her brains are above the normal, although she unfortunately knows it, and Billy, if he ever gets away from Alice, will show what he is made of. Maria's intellect is all right, although cast in a petty mould. She repeats Grandmother Evarts, which is a pity, because there are types not worth repeating. Maria if she had not her husband Tom to manage, would simply fall on her face. It goes hard with a purely patronizing soul when there is nobody to manage; there is apt to be an explosion. However, Maria *has* Tom. But none of my brother's family, not even my dear sister-in-law, Cyrus's wife, have the right point of view with regard to the present, possibly on account of the mansard-roof which has overshadowed them. They do not know that to-day an old-maid aunt is as much of an anomaly as a spinning-wheel, that she has ceased to exist, that she is prehistoric, that even grandmothers have almost disappeared from off the face of the earth. In short, they do not know what I am not an old-maid aunt except under this blessed mansard-roof, and some other roofs of Eastridge, many of which are also mansard, where the influence of their fixed belief prevails. For instance, they told the people next door, who have moved here recently, that the old-maid aunt was coming, and so, when I went to call with my sister-in-law, Mrs. Temple saw her quite distinctly. To think of Ned Temple being married to a woman like that, who takes things on trust and does not use her own eyes! Her two little girls are exactly like her. I wonder what Ned himself will think. I wonder if he will see that my hair is as red-gold as Peggy's, that I am quite as slim, that there is not a line on my face, that I still keep my girl color with no aid, that I wear frills of the latest fashion, and look no older than when he first saw me. I really do not know myself how I have managed to remain so intact; possibly because I have always grasped all the minor sweets of life, even if I could not have the really big worth-while ones. I honestly do not think that I have had the latter. But I have not taken the position of some people, that if I cannot have what I want most I will have nothing. I have taken whatever Providence chose to give me in the way of small sweets, and made the most of them. Then I have had much womanly pride, and that is a powerful tonic.

For instance, years ago, when my best lamp of life went out, so to speak, I lit all my candles and kept my path. I took just as much pains with my hair and my dress, and if I was unhappy I kept it out of evidence on my face. I let my heart ache and bleed, but I would have died before I wrinkled my forehead and dimmed my eyes with tears and let everybody else know. That was about the time when I met Ned Temple, and he fell so madly in love with me, and threatened to shoot himself if I would not marry him. He did not. Most men do not. I wonder if he placed me when he heard of my anticipated coming. Probably he did not. They have probably alluded to me as dear old Aunt Elizabeth, and when he met me (I was staying at Harriet Munroe's before she was married) nobody called me Elizabeth, but Lily. Miss Elizabeth Talbert, instead of Lily Talbert, might naturally set him wrong. Everybody here calls me Elizabeth. Outside Eastridge I am Lily. I dare say Ned Temple has not dreamed who I am. I hear that he is quite brilliant, although the poor fellow must be limited as to his income. However, in some respects it must be just as well. It would be a great trial to a man with a large income to have a wife like Mrs. Temple, who could make no good use of it. You might load that poor soul with crown jewels and she would make them look as if she had bought them at a department store for ninety-eight cents. And the way she keeps her house must be maddening, I should think, to a brilliant man. Fancy the books on the table being all arranged with the large ones under the small ones in perfectly even piles! I am sure that he has his meals on time, and I am equally sure that the principal dishes are preserves and hot biscuits and cake. That sort of diet simply shows forth in Mrs. Temple and her children. I am sure that his socks are always mended, but I know that he always wipes his feet before he enters the house, that it has become a matter of conscience with him; and those exactions are to me pathetic. These reflections are uncommonly like the popular conception as to how an old-maid aunt should reflect, had she not ceased to exist. Sometimes I wish she were still existing and that I carried out her character to the full. I am not at all sure but she, as she once was, coming here, would not have brought more happiness than I have. I must say I thought so when I saw poor Harry Goward turn so pale when he first saw me after my arrival. Why, in the name of common sense, Ada, my sister-in-law, when she wrote to me at the Pollards', announcing Peggy's engagement, could not have mentioned who the man was, I cannot see.

Sometimes it seems to me that only the girl and the engagement figure at all in such matters. I suppose Peggy always alluded to me as "dear Aunt Elizabeth," when that poor young fellow knew me at the Abercrombies', where we were staying a year ago, as Miss Lily Talbert. The situation with regard to him and Peggy fairly puzzles me. I simply do not know what to do. Goodness knows I never lifted my finger to attract him. Flirtations between older women and boys always have seemed to me contemptible. I never particularly noticed him, although he is a charming young fellow, and there is not as much difference in our ages as in those of Harriet Munroe and her husband, and if I am not mistaken there is more difference between the ages of Ned Temple and his wife. Poor soul! she looks old enough to be his mother, as I remember him, but that may be partly due to the way she arranges her hair. However, Ned himself may have changed; there must be considerable wear and tear about matrimony, taken in connection with editing a country newspaper. If I had married Ned I might have looked as old as Mrs. Temple does. I wonder what Ned will do when he sees me. I know he will not turn white, as poor Harry Goward did. That really worries me. I am fond of little Peggy, and the situation is really rather awful. She is engaged to a man who is fond of her aunt and cannot conceal it. Still, the affection of most male things is curable. If Peggy has sense enough to retain her love for frills and bows, and puts on her clothes as well, and arranges her hair as prettily, after she has been married a year— no, ten years (it will take at least ten years to make a proper old-maid aunt of me)—she may have the innings. But Peggy has no brains, and it really takes a woman with brains to keep her looks after matrimony.

Of course, the poor little soul has no danger to fear from me; it is lucky for her that her *fiancé* fell in love with me; but it is the principle of the thing which worries me. Harry Goward must be as fickle as a honey-bee. There is no assurance whatever for Peggy that he will not fall headlong in love— and headlong is just the word for it—with any other woman after he has married her. I did not want the poor fellow to stick to me, but when I come to think of it that is the trouble. How shortsighted I am! It is his perverted fickleness rather than his actual fickleness which worries me. He has proposed to Peggy when he was in love with another woman, probably because he was in love with another woman. Now Peggy, although she is not brilliant, in spite of her co-education (perhaps because of it), is a darling, and she deserves a good husband. She loves this man with her whole heart, poor little thing! that is easy enough to be seen, and he does not care for her, at least not when I am around or when I am in his mind. The question is, is this marriage going to make the child happy? My first impulse, when I saw Harry Goward and knew that he was poor Peggy's lover, was immediately to pack up and leave. Then I really wondered if that was the wisest thing to do. I wanted to see for myself if Harry Goward were really in earnest about poor little Peggy and had gotten over his mad infatuation for her aunt and would make her a good husband. Perhaps I ought to leave, and yet I wonder if I ought. Harry Goward may have turned pale simply from his memory of what an uncommon fool he had been, and the consideration of the embarrassing position in which his past folly has placed him, if I chose to make revelations. He might have known that I would not; still, men know so little of women. I think that possibly I am worrying myself needlessly, and that he is really in love with Peggy. She is quite a little beauty, and she does know how to put her clothes on so charmingly. The adjustments of her shirt-waists are simply perfection. I may be very foolish to go away; I may be even insufferably conceited in assuming that Harry's change of color signified anything which could make it necessary. But, after all, he must be fickle and ready to turn from one to another, or deceitful, and I must admit that if Peggy were my daughter, and Harry had never been mad about me six weeks ago, but about some other woman, I should still feel the same way.

Sometimes I wonder if I ought to tell Ada. She is the girl's mother. I might shift the responsibility on to her. I almost think I will. She is alone in her room now, I know. Peggy and Harry have gone for a drive, and the rest have scattered. It is a good chance. I really don't feel as if I ought to bear the whole responsibility alone. I will go this minute and tell Ada.

Well, I have told Ada, and here I am back in my room, laughing over the result. I might as well have told the flour-barrel. Anything like Ada's ease of character and inability to worry or even face a disturbing situation I have never seen. I laugh, although her method of receiving my tale was not, so to speak, flattering to me. Ada was in her loose white kimono, and she was sitting at her shady window darning stockings in very much the same way that a cow chews her cud; and when I told her, under promise of the strictest secrecy, she just laughed that placid little laugh of hers and said, taking another stitch, "Oh, well, boys are always falling in love with older women." And when I asked if she thought seriously that Peggy might not be running a risk, she said: "Oh dear, no; Harry is devoted to the child. You can't be foolish enough, Aunt Elizabeth, to think that he is in love with you *now?*"

I said, "Certainly not." It was only the principle involved; that the young man must be very changeable, and that Peggy might run a risk in the future if Harry were thrown in much with other women.

Ada only laughed again, and kept on with her darning, and said she guessed there was no need to worry. Harry seemed to her very much like Cyrus, and she was sure that Cyrus had never thought of another woman besides herself (Ada).

I wonder if another woman would have said what I might have said, especially after that imputation of the idiocy of my thinking that a young man could possibly fancy *me*. I said nothing, but I wondered what Ada would say if she knew what I knew, if she would continue to chew her cud, that Cyrus had been simply mad over another girl, and only married her because he could not get the other one, and when the other died, five years after he was married to Ada, he sent flowers, and I should not to this day venture to speak that girl's name to the man. She was a great beauty, and she had a wonderful witchery about her. I was only a child, but I remember how she looked. Why, I fell in love with her myself! Cyrus can never forget a woman like that for a cud-chewing creature like Ada, even if she does keep his house in order and make a good mother to his children. The other would not have kept the house in order at all, but it would have been a shrine. Cyrus worshipped that girl, and love may supplant love, but not worship. Ada does not know, and she never will through me, but I declare I was almost wicked enough to tell her when I saw her placidly darning away, without the slightest conception, any more than a feather pillow would have, of what this ridiculous affair with me might mean in future consequences to poor, innocent little Peggy. But I can only hope the boy has gotten over his feeling for me, that he has been really changeable, for that would be infinitely better than the other thing.

Well, I shall not need to go away. Harry Goward has himself solved that problem. He goes himself to-morrow. He has invented a telegram about a sick uncle, all according to the very best melodrama. But what I feared is true—he is still as mad as ever about me. I went down to the post-office for the evening mail, and was coming home by moonlight, unattended, as any undesirable maiden aunt may safely do, when the boy overtook me. I had heard his hurried steps behind me for some time. Up he rushed just as we reached the vacant lot before the Temple house, and caught my arm and poured forth a volume of confessions and avowals, and, in short, told me he did not love Peggy, but me, and he never would love anybody but me. I actually felt faint for a second. Then I talked. I told him what a dishonor-able wretch he was, and said he might as well have plunged a knife into an innocent, confiding girl at once as to have treated Peggy so. I told him to go away and let me alone and write friendly letters to Peggy, and see if he would not recover his senses, if he had any to recover, which I thought doubtful; and then when he said he would not budge a step, that he would remain in Eastridge, if only for the sake of breathing the same air I did, that he would tell Peggy the whole truth at once, and bear all the blame which he deserved for being so dishonorable, I arose to the occasion. I said, "Very well, remain, but you may have to breathe not only the same air that I do, but also the same air that the man whom I am to marry does." I declare that I had no man whatever in mind. I said it in sheer desperation. Then the boy burst forth with another torrent, and the secret was out.

My brother and my sister-in-law and Grandmother Evarts and the chil-dren, for all I know, have all been match-making for me. I did not suspect it of them. I supposed they esteemed my case as utterly hopeless, and then I knew that Cyrus knew about—well, never mind; I don't often mention him to myself. I certainly thought that they all would have as soon endeav-ored to raise the dead as to marry me, but it seems that they have been

thinking that while there is life there is hope, or rather, while there are wid-
owers there is hope. And there is a widower in Eastridge—Dr. Denbigh.
He is the candle about which the mothlike dreams of ancient maidens and
widows have fluttered, to their futile singeing, for the last twenty years. I
really did not dream that they would think I would flutter, even if I was an
old-maid aunt. But Harry cried out that if I were going to marry Dr. Denbigh he would go away. He never would stay and be a witness to such sacrilege. "That *old* man!" he raved. And when I said I was not a young girl myself he got all the madder. Well, I allowed him to think I was going to marry
Dr. Denbigh (I wonder what the doctor would say), and as a consequence
Harry will flit to-morrow, and he is with poor little Peggy out in the grape-
arbor, and she is crying her eyes out. If he dares tell her what a fool he is I
could kill him. I am horribly afraid that he will let it out, for I never saw
such an alarmingly impetuous youth. Young Lochinvar out of the west was
mere cambric tea to him. I am really thankful that he has not a gallant
steed, nor even an automobile, for the old-maid aunt might yet be captured
as the Sabine woman were.

Well, thank fortune, Harry has left, and he cannot have told, for poor little
Peggy has been sitting with me for a solid hour, sniffing, and sounding his
praises. Somehow the child made me think of myself at her age. I was
about a year old when my tragedy came and was never righted. Hers, I
think, will be, since Harry was not such an ass as to confess before he went
away. But all the same, I am concerned for her happiness, for Harry is either fickle or deceitful. Sometimes I wonder what my duty is, but I can't tell
the child. It would do no more good for me to consult my brother Cyrus
than it did to consult Ada. I know of no one whom I can consult. Charles
Edward and his wife, who is just like Ada, pretty, but always with her shirt-
waist hunching in the back, sitting wrong, and standing lopsided, and not
worrying enough to give her character salt and pepper, are there. (I should
think she would drive Charles Edward, who is really an artist, only out of
his proper sphere, mad.) Tom and Maria are down there, too, on the piazza, and Ada at her everlasting darning, and Alice bossing Billy as usual. I
can hear her voice. I think I will put on another gown and go for a walk.
   I think I will put on my pink linen, and my hat lined with pink chiffon
and trimmed with shaded roses. That particular shade of pink is just right
for my hair. I know quite well how I look in that gown and hat, and I know,
also, quite well how I shall look to the members of my family assembled

below. They all unanimously consider that I should dress always in black silk, and a bonnet with a neat little tuft of middle-aged violets, and black ribbons tied under my chin. I know I am wicked to put on that pink gown and hat, but I shall do it. I wonder why it amuses me to be made fun of. Thank fortune, I have a sense of humor. If I did not have that it might have come to the black silk and the bonnet with the tuft of violets, for the Lord knows I have not, after all, so very much compared with what some women have. It troubles me to think of that young fool rushing away and poor, dear little Peggy; but what can I do? This pink gown is fetching, and how they will stare when I go down!

Well, they did stare. How pretty this street is, with the elms arching over it. I made quite a commotion, and they all saw me through their eye-glasses of prejudice, except, possibly, Tom Price, Maria's husband. I am certain I heard him say, as I marched away, "Well, I don't care; she does look stunning, anyhow," but Maria hushed him up. I heard her say, "Pink at her age, and a pink hat, and a parasol lined with pink!" Ada really looked more disturbed than I have ever seen her. If I had been Godiva, going for my sacrificial ride through the town, it could not have been much worse. She made her eyes round and big, and asked, in a voice which was really agitated, "Are you going out in that dress, Aunt Elizabeth?" And Aunt Elizabeth replied that she certainly was, and she went after she had exchanged greetings with the family and kissed Peggy's tear-stained little face. Charles Edward's wife actually straightened her spinal column, she was so amazed at the sight of me in my rose-colored array. Charles Edward, to do him justice, stared at me with a bewildered air, as if he were trying to reconcile his senses with his traditions. He is an artist, but he will always be hampered by thinking he sees what he has been brought up to think he sees. That is the reason why he has settled down uncomplainingly in Cyrus's "Works," as he calls them, doing the very slight æsthetics possible in such a connection. Now Charles Edward would think that sunburned grass over in that field is green, when it is pink, because he has been taught that grass is green. If poor Charles Edward only knew that grass was green not of itself, but because of occasional conditions, and knew that his aunt looked—well, as she does look—he would flee for his life, and that which is better than his life, from the "Works," and be an artist, but he never will know or know that he knows, which comes to the same thing.

Well, what does it matter to me? I have just met a woman who stared at me, and spoke as if she thought I were a lunatic to be afield in this array. What does anything matter? Sometimes, when I am with people who see straight, I do take a certain pleasure in looking well, because I am a woman, and nothing can quite take away that pleasure from me; but all the time I know it does not matter, that nothing has really mattered since I was about Peggy's age and Lyman Wilde quarrelled with me over nothing and vanished into thin air, so far as I was concerned. I suppose he is comfortably settled with a wife and family somewhere. It is rather odd, though, that with all my wandering on this side of the water and the other I have never once crossed his tracks. He may be in the Far East, with a harem. I never have been in the Far East. Well, it does not matter to me where he is. That is ancient history. On the whole, though, I like the harem idea better than the single wife. I have what is left to me—the little things of life, the pretty effects which go to make me pretty (outside Eastridge); the comforts of civilization, travelling and seeing beautiful things, also seeing ugly things to enhance the beautiful. I have pleasant days in beautiful Florence. I have friends. I have everything except—well, except everything. That I must do without. But I will do without it gracefully, with never a whimper, or I don't know myself. But now I *am* worried over Peggy. I wish I could consult with somebody with sense. What a woman I am! I mean, how feminine I am! I wish I could cure myself of the habit of being feminine. It is a horrible nuisance; this wishing to consult with somebody when I am worried is so disgustingly feminine.

Well, I have consulted. I am back in my own room. It is after supper. We had three kinds of cake, hot biscuits, and raspberries, and—a concession to Cyrus—a platter of cold ham and an egg salad. He will have something hearty, as he calls it (bless him! he is a good-fellow), for supper. I am glad, for I should starve on Ada's New England menus. I feel better, now that I have consulted, although, when I really consider the matter, I can't see that I have arrived at any very definite issue. But I have consulted, and, above all things, with Ned Temple! I was walking down the street, and I reached his newspaper building. It is a funny little affair; looks like a toy house. It is all given up to the mighty affairs of the Eastridge *Banner*. In front there is a piazza, and on this piazza sat Ned Temple. Changed? Well, yes, poor fellow! He is thin. I am so glad he is thin instead of fat; thinness is not nearly so disillusioning. His hair is iron-gray, but he is, after all, distinguished-looking, and his manners are entirely sophisticated. He shows at a glance, at a word, that he is a brilliant man, although he is stranded upon such a petty little editorial island. And—and he saw *me* as I am. He did not change color. He is too self-poised; besides, he is too honorable. But he saw *me*. He rose immediately and came to speak to me. He shook hands. He looked at my face under my pink-lined hat. He saw it as it was; but bless him! that stupid wife of his holds him fast with his own honor. Ned Temple is a good man. Sometimes I wonder if it would not have been better if he, instead of Lyman— Well, that is idiotic.

He said he had to go to the post-office, and then it was time for him to go home to supper (to the cake and sauce, I suppose), and with my permission he would walk with me. So he did. I don't know how it happened that I consulted with him. I think he spoke of Peggy's engagement, and that led up to it. But I could speak to him, because I knew that he, seeing me as I really am, would view the matter seriously. I told him about the miserable affair, and he said that I had done exactly right. I can't remember that he offered any actual solution, but it was something to be told that I had done exactly right. And then he spoke of his wife, and in such a faithful fashion, and so lovingly of his two commonplace little girls. Ned Temple is as good as he is brilliant. It is really rather astonishing that such a brilliant man can be so good. He told me that I had not changed at all, but all the time that look of faithfulness for his wife never left his handsome face, bless him! I believe I am nearer loving him for his love for another woman than I ever was to loving him for himself.

And then the inconceivable happened. I did what I never thought I should be capable of doing, and did it easily, too, without, I am sure, a change of color or any perturbation. I think I could do it, because faithfulness had become so a matter of course with the man that I was not ashamed should he have any suspicion of me also. He and Lyman used to be warm friends. I asked if he knew anything about him. He met my question as if I had asked what o'clock it was, just the way I knew he would meet it. He knows no more than I do. But he said something which has comforted me, although comfort at this stage of affairs is a dangerous indulgence. He said, very much as if he had been speaking of the weather, "He worshipped you, Lily, and wherever he is, in this world or the next, he worships you now." Then he added: "You know how I felt about you, Lily. If I had not found out about him, that he had come first, I know how it would have been with me, so I know how it is with him. We had the same views about matters of that kind. After I did find out, why, of course, I felt different—although always, as long as I live, I shall be a dear friend to you, Lily. But a man is unfaithful to himself who is faithful to a woman whom another man loves and whom she loves."

"Yes, that is true," I agreed, and said something about the hours for the mails in Eastridge. Lyman Wilde dropped out of Ned's life as he dropped out of mine, it seems. I shall simply have to lean back upon the minor joys of life for mental and physical support, as I did before. Nothing is different, but I am glad that I have seen Ned Temple again, and realize what a good man he is.

Well, it seems that even minor pleasures have dangers, and that I do not always read characters rightly. The very evening after my little stroll and renewal of friendship with Ned Temple I was sitting in my room, reading a new book for which the author should have capital punishment, when I heard excited voices, or rather an excited voice, below. I did not pay much attention at first. I supposed the excited voice must belong to either Maria or Alice, for no others of my brother's family ever seem in the least excited, not to the extent of raising their voices to a hysterical pitch. But after a few minutes Cyrus came to the foot of the stairs and called. He called Aunt Elizabeth, and Aunt Elizabeth, in her same pink frock, went down. Cyrus met me at the foot of the stairs, and he looked fairly wild. "What on earth, Aunt Elizabeth!" said he, and I stared at him in a daze.

"The deuce is to pay," said he. "Aunt Elizabeth, did you ever know our next-door neighbor before his marriage?"

"Certainly," said I; "when we were both infants. I believe they had gotten him out of petticoats and into trousers, but much as ever, and my skirts were still abbreviated. It was at Harriet Munroe's before she was married."

"Have you been to walk with him?" gasped poor Cyrus.

"I met him on my way to the post-office last night, and he walked along with me, and then as far as his house on the way home, if you call that walking out," said I. "You sound like the paragraphs in a daily paper. Now, what on earth do you mean, if I may ask, Cyrus?"

"Nothing, except Mrs. Temple is in there raising a devil of a row," said Cyrus. He gazed at me in a bewildered fashion. "If it were Peggy I could understand it," he said, helplessly, and I knew how distinctly he saw the old-maid aunt as he gazed at me. "She's jealous of you, Elizabeth," he went on in the same dazed fashion. "She's jealous of you because her husband walked home with you. She's a dreadfully nervous woman, and, I guess, none too well. She's fairly wild. It seems Temple let on how he used to know you before he was married, and said something in praise of your looks, and she made a regular header into conclusions. You have held your own remarkably well, Elizabeth, but I declare—" And again poor Cyrus gazed at me.

"Well, for goodness' sake, let me go in and see what I can do," said I, and with that I went into the parlor.

I was taken aback. Nobody, not even another woman, can tell what a woman really is. I thought I had estimated Ned Temple's wife correctly. I had taken her for a monotonous, orderly, dull sort of creature, quite incapable of extremes; but in reality she has in her rather large, flabby body the characteristics of a kitten, with the possibilities of a tigress. The tigress was uppermost when I entered the room. The woman was as irresponsible as a savage. I was disgusted and sorry and furious at the same time. I cannot imagine myself making such a spectacle over any mortal man. She was weeping frantically into a mussy little ball of handkerchief, and when she saw me she rushed at me and gripped me by the arm like a mad thing.

"If you can't get a husband for yourself," said she, "you might at least let other women's husbands alone!"

She was vulgar, but she was so wild with jealousy that I suppose vulgarity ought to be forgiven her.

I hardly know myself how I managed it, but, somehow, I got the poor thing out of the room and the house and into the cool night air, and then I talked to her, and fairly made her be quiet and listen. I told her that Ned Temple had made love to me when he was just out of petticoats and I was in short dresses. I stretched or shortened the truth a little, but it was a case of necessity. Then I intimated that I never would have married Ned Temple, anyway, and *that* worked beautifully. She turned upon me in such a delightfully inconsequent fashion and demanded to know what I expected, and declared her husband was good enough for any woman. Then I said I did not doubt that, and hinted that other women might have had their romances, even if they did not marry. That immediately interested her. She stared at me, and said, with the most innocent impertinence, that my brother's wife had intimated that I had had an unhappy love-affair when I was a girl. I did not think that Cyrus had told Ada, but I suppose a man *has* to tell his wife everything.

I hedged about the unhappy love-affair, but the first thing I knew the poor, distracted woman was sobbing on my shoulder as we stood in front of her gate, and saying that she was so sorry, but her whole life was bound up in her husband, and I was so beautiful and has so much style, and she knew what a dowdy she was, and she could not blame poor Ned if— But I hushed her.

"Your husband has no more idea of caring for another woman besides you than that moon has of travelling around another world," said I; "and you are a fool if you think so; and if you are dowdy it is your own fault. If you have such a good husband you owe it to him not to be dowdy. I know you keep his house beautifully, but any man would rather have his wife look well than his house, if he is worth anything at all."

Then she gasped out that she wished she knew how to do up her hair like mine. It was all highly ridiculous, but it actually ended in my going into the Temple house and showing Ned's wife how to do up her hair like mine. She looked like another woman when it was puffed softly over her forehead— she has quite pretty brown hair. Then I taught her how to put on her corset and pin her shirt-waist taut in front and her skirt behind. Ned was not to be home until late, and there was plenty of time. It ended in her fairly purring around me, and saying how sorry she was, and ashamed, that she had been so foolish, and all the time casting little covert, conceited glances at herself in the looking-glass. Finally I kissed her and she kissed me, and I went home. I don't really see what more a woman could have done for a rival who had supplanted her. But this revelation makes me more sorry than ever for poor Ned. I don't know, though; she may be more interesting than I thought. Anything is better than the dead level of small books on large ones, and meals on time. It cannot be exactly monotonous never to know whether you will find a sleek, purry cat, or an absurd kitten, or a tigress, when you come home. Luckily, she did not tell Ned of her jealousy, and I have cautioned all in my family to hold their tongues, and I think they will. I infer that they suspect that I must have been guilty of some unbecoming elderly prank to bring about such a state of affairs, unless, possibly, Maria's husband and Billy are exceptions. I find that Billy, when Alice lets him alone, is a boy who sees with his own eyes. He told me yesterday that I was handsomer in my pink dress than any girl in his school.

"Why, Billy Talbert!" I said, "talking that way to your old aunt!"

"I suppose you *are* awful old," said Billy, bless him! "but you are enough-sight prettier than a girl. I hate girls. I hope I can get away from girls when I am a man."

I wanted to tell the dear boy that was exactly the time when he would not get away from girls, but I thought I would not frighten him, but let him find it out for himself.

Well, now the deluge! It is a week since Harry Goward went away, and Peggy has not had a letter, although she has haunted the post-office, poor child! and this morning she brought home a letter for *me* from that crazy boy. She was white as chalk when she handed it to me.

"It's Harry's writing," said she, and she could barely whisper. "I have not had a word from him since he went away, and now he has written to you instead of me. What has he written to you for, Aunt Elizabeth?"

She looked at me so piteously, poor, dear little girl! that if I could have gotten hold of Harry Goward that moment I would have shaken him. I tried to speak, soothingly. I said:

"My dear Peggy, I know no more than you do why he has written to me. Perhaps his uncle is dead and he thought I would break it to you."

That was rank idiocy. Generally I can rise to the occasion with more success.

"What do I care about his old uncle?" cried poor Peggy. "I never even saw his uncle. I don't care if he is dead. Something has happened to Harry. Oh, Aunt Elizabeth, what is it?"

I was never in such a strait in my life. There was that poor child staring at the letter as if she could eat it, and then at me. I dared not open the letter before her. We were out on the porch. I said:

"Now, Peggy Talbert, you keep quiet, and don't make a little fool of yourself until you know you have some reason for it. I am going up to my own room, and you sit in that chair, and when I have read this letter I will come down and tell you about it."

"I know he is dead!" gasped Peggy, but she sat down.

"Dead!" said I. "You just said yourself it was his handwriting. Do have a little sense, Peggy." With that I was off with my letter, and I locked my door before I read it.

Of all the insane ravings! I put it on my hearth and struck a match, and the thing went up in flame and smoke. Then I went down to poor little Peggy and patched up a story. I have always been averse to lying, and I did not lie then, although I must admit that what I said was open to criticism when it comes to exact verity. I told Peggy that Harry thought that he had done something to make her angry (that was undeniably true) and did not dare write her. I refused utterly to tell her just what was in the letter, but I did succeed in quieting her and making her think that Harry had not bro-ken faith with her, but was blaming himself for some unknown and imag-inary wrong he had done her. Peggy rushed immediately up to her room to write reassuring pages to Harry, and her old-maid aunt had the horse put in the runabout and was driven over to Whitman, where nobody knows her—at least the telegraph operator does not. Then I sent a telegram to Mr. Harry Goward to the effect that if he did not keep his promise with regard to writing F. L. to P. her A. would never speak to him again; and that A. was about to send L., but he must keep his promise with regard to P. by next M.

It looked like the most melodramatic Sunday personal ever invented. It might have meant burglary or murder or a snare for innocence, but I sent it. Now I have written. My letter went in the same mail as poor Peggy's, but what will be the outcome of it all I cannot say. Sometimes I catch Peggy looking at me with a curious awakened expression, and then I wonder if she has begun to suspect. I cannot tell how it will end.

Old Woman Magoun

1905

The hamlet of Barry's Ford is situated in a sort of high valley among the mountains. Below it the hills lie in moveless curves like a petrified ocean; above it they rise in green-cresting waves which never break. It is *Barry's* Ford because at one time the Barry family was the most important in the place; and *Ford* because just at the beginning of the hamlet the little turbulent Barry River is fordable. There is, however, now a rude bridge across the river.

Old Woman Magoun was largely instrumental in bringing the bridge to pass. She haunted the miserable little grocery, wherein whiskey and hands of tobacco were the most salient features of the stock in trade, and she talked much. She would elbow herself into the midst of a knot of idlers and talk.

"That bridge ought to be built this very summer," said Old Woman Magoun. She spread her strong arms like wings, and sent the loafers, half laughing, half angry, flying in every direction. "If I were a *man*," said she, "I'd go out this very minute and lay the fust log. If I were a passel of lazy men layin' round, I'd start up for once in my life, I would." The men cowered visibly—all except Nelson Barry; he swore under his breath and strode over to the counter.

Old Woman Magoun looked after him majestically. "You can cuss all you want to, Nelson Barry," said she; "I ain't afraid of you. I don't expect you to lay ary log of the bridge, but I'm goin' to have it built this very summer." She did. The weakness of the masculine element in Barry's Ford was laid low before such strenuous feminine assertion.

Old Woman Magoun and some other women planned a treat—two

sucking pigs, and pies, and sweet cake—for a reward after the bridge should be finished. They even viewed leniently the increased consumption of ardent spirits.

"It seems queer to me," Old Woman Magoun said to Sally Jinks, "that men can't do nothin' without havin' to drink and chew to keep their sperits up. Lord! I've worked all my life and never done nuther."

"Men is different," said Sally Jinks.

"Yes, they be," assented Old Woman Magoun, with open contempt.

The two women sat on a bench in front of Old Woman Magoun's house, and little Lily Barry, her granddaughter, sat holding her doll on a small mossy stone near by. From where they sat they could see the men at work on the new bridge. It was the last day of the work.

Lily clasped her doll—a poor old rag thing—close to her childish bosom, like a little mother, and her face, round which curled her long yellow hair, was fixed upon the men at work. Little Lily had never been allowed to run with the other children of Barry's Ford. Her grandmother had taught her everything she knew—which was not much, but tending at least to a certain measure of spiritual growth—for she, as it were, poured the goodness of her own soul into this little receptive vase of another. Lily was firmly grounded in her knowledge that it was wrong to lie or steal or disobey her grandmother. She had also learned that one should be very industrious. It was seldom that Lily sat idly holding her doll-baby, but this was a holiday because of the bridge. She looked only a child, although she was nearly fourteen; her mother had been married at sixteen. That is, Old Woman Magoun said that her daughter, Lily's mother, had married at sixteen; there had been rumors, but no one had dared openly gainsay the old woman. She said that her daughter had married Nelson Barry, and he had deserted her. She had lived in her mother's house, and Lily had been born there, and she had died when the baby was only a week old. Lily's father, Nelson Barry, was the fairly dangerous degenerate of a good old family. Nelson's father before him had been bad. He was now the last of the family, with the exception of a sister of feeble intellect, with whom he lived in the old Barry house. He was a middle-aged man, still handsome. The shiftless population of Barry's Ford looked up to him as to an evil deity. They wondered how Old Woman Magoun dared brave him as she did. But Old Woman Magoun had within her a mighty sense of reliance upon herself as being on the right track in the midst of a maze of evil, which gave her courage. Nelson Barry had manifested no interest whatever in his daughter.

Lily seldom saw her father. She did not often go to the store which was his favorite haunt. Her grandmother took care that she should not do so.

However, that afternoon she departed from her usual custom and sent Lily to the store.

She came in from the kitchen, whither she had been to baste the roasting pig. "There's no use talkin'," said she, "I've got to have some more salt. I've jest used the very last I had to dredge over that pig. I've got to go to the store."

Sally Jinks looked at Lily. "Why don't you send her?" she asked.

Old Woman Magoun gazed irresolutely at the girl. She was herself very tired. It did not seem to her that she could drag herself up the dusty hill to the store. She glanced with covert resentment at Sally Jinks. She thought that she might offer to go. But Sally Jinks said again, "Why don't you let her go?" and looked with a languid eye at Lily holding her doll on the stone.

Lily was watching the men at work on the bridge, with her childish delight in a spectacle of any kind, when her grandmother addressed her.

"Guess I'll let you go down to the store an' git some salt, Lily," said she.

The girl turned uncomprehending eyes upon her grandmother at the sound of her voice. She had been filled with one of the innocent reveries of childhood. Lily had in her the making of an artist or a poet. Her prolonged childhood went to prove it, and also her retrospective eyes, as clear and blue as blue light itself, which seemed to see past all that she looked upon. She had not come of the old Barry family for nothing. The best of the strain was in her, along with the splendid stanchness in humble lines which she had acquired from her grandmother.

"Put on your hat," said Old Woman Magoun; "the sun is hot, and you might git a headache." She called the girl to her, and put back the shower of fair curls under the rubber band which confined the hat. She gave Lily some money, and watched her knot it into a corner of her little cotton handkerchief. "Be careful you don't lose it," said she, "and don't stop to talk to anybody, for I am in a hurry for that salt. Of course, if anybody speaks to you answer them polite, and then come right along."

Lily started, her pocket-handkerchief weighted with the small silver dangling from one hand, and her rag doll carried over her shoulder like a baby. The absurd travesty of a face peeped forth from Lily's yellow curls. Sally Jinks looked after her with a sniff.

"She ain't goin' to carry that rag doll to the store?" said she.

"She likes to," replied Old Woman Magoun, in a half-shamed yet defiantly extenuating voice.

"Some girls at her age is thinkin' about beaux instead of rag dolls," said Sally Jinks.

The grandmother bristled. "Lily ain't big nor old for her age," said she. "I ain't in any hurry to have her git married. She ain't none too strong."

"She's got a good color," said Sally Jinks. She was crocheting white cotton lace, making her thick fingers fly. She really knew how to do scarcely anything except to crochet that coarse lace; somehow her heavy brain or her fingers had mastered that.

"I know she's got a beautiful color," replied Old Woman Magoun, with an odd mixture of pride and anxiety, "but it comes an' goes."

"I've heard that was a bad sign," remarked Sally Jinks, loosening some thread from her spool.

"Yes, it is," said the grandmother. "She's nothin' but a baby, though she's quicker than most to learn."

Lily Barry went on her way to the store. She was clad in a scanty short frock of blue cotton; her hat was tipped back, forming an oval frame for her innocent face. She was very small, and walked like a child, with the clap-clap of little feet of babyhood. She might have been considered, from her looks, under ten.

Presently she heard footsteps behind her; she turned around a little timidly to see who was coming. When she saw a handsome, well-dressed man, she felt reassured. The man came alongside and glanced down carelessly at first, then his look deepened. He smiled, and Lily saw he was very handsome indeed, and that his smile was not only reassuring but wonderfully sweet and compelling.

"Well, little one," said the man, "where are you bound, you and your dolly?"

"I am going to the store to buy some salt for grandma," replied Lily, in her sweet treble. She looked up in the man's face, and he fairly started at the revelation of its innocent beauty. He regulated his pace by hers, and the two went on together. The man did not speak again at once. Lily kept glancing timidly up at him, and every time that she did so the man smiled and her confidence increased. Presently when the man's hand grasped her little childish one hanging by her side, she felt a complete trust in him. Then she smiled up at him. She felt glad that this nice man had come along, for just here the road was lonely.

After a while the man spoke. "What is your name, little one?" he asked, caressingly.

"Lily Barry."

The man started. "What is your father's name?"

"Nelson Barry," replied Lily.

The man whistled. "Is your mother dead?"

"Yes, sir."

"How old are you, my dear?"

"Fourteen," replied Lily.

The man looked at her with surprise. "As old as that?"

Lily suddenly shrank from the man. She could not have told why. She pulled her little hand from his, and he let it go with no remonstrance. She clasped both her arms around her rag doll, in order that her hand should not be free for him to grasp again.

She walked a little farther away from the man, and he looked amused.

"You still play with your doll?" he said, in a soft voice.

"Yes, sir," replied Lily. She quickened her pace and reached the store.

When Lily entered the store, Hiram Gates, the owner, was behind the counter. The only man besides in the store was Nelson Barry. He sat tipping his chair back against the wall; he was half asleep, and his handsome face was bristling with a beard of several days' growth and darkly flushed. He opened his eyes when Lily entered, the strange man following. He brought his chair down on all fours, and he looked at the man—not noticing Lily at all—with a look compounded of defiance and uneasiness.

"Hullo, Jim!" he said.

"Hullo, old man!" returned the stranger.

Lily went over to the counter and asked for the salt, in her pretty little voice. When she had paid for it and was crossing the store, Nelson Barry was on his feet.

"Well, how are you, Lily? It is Lily, isn't it?" he said.

"Yes, sir," replied Lily, faintly.

Her father bent down and, for the first time in her life, kissed her, and the whiskey odor of his breath came into her face.

Lily involuntarily started, and shrank away from him. Then she rubbed her mouth violently with her little cotton handkerchief, which she held gathered up with the rag doll.

"Damn it all! I believe she is afraid of me," said Nelson Barry, in a thick voice.

"Looks a little like it," said the other man, laughing.

"It's that damned old woman," said Nelson Barry. Then he smiled again at Lily. "I didn't know what a pretty little daughter I was blessed with," said he, and he softly stroked Lily's pink cheek under her hat.

Now Lily did not shrink from him. Hereditary instincts and nature itself were asserting themselves in the child's innocent, receptive breast.

Nelson Barry looked curiously at Lily. "How old are you, anyway, child?" he asked.

"I'll be fourteen in September," replied Lily.

"But you still play with your doll?" said Barry, laughing kindly down at her.

Lily hugged her doll more tightly, in spite of her father's kind voice. "Yes, sir," she replied.

Nelson glanced across at some glass jars filled with sticks of candy. "See here, little Lily, do you like candy?" said he.

"Yes, sir."

"Wait a minute."

Lily waited while her father went over to the counter. Soon he returned with a package of the candy.

"I don't see how you are going to carry so much," he said, smiling. "Suppose you throw away your doll?"

Lily gazed at her father and hugged the doll tightly, and there was all at once in the child's expression something mature. It became the reproach of a woman. Nelson's face sobered.

"Oh, it's all right, Lily," he said; "keep your doll. Here, I guess you can carry this candy under your arm."

Lily could not resist the candy. She obeyed Nelson's instructions for carrying it, and left the store laden. The two men also left, and walked in the opposite direction, talking busily.

When Lily reached home, her grandmother, who was watching for her, spied at once the package of candy.

"What's that?" she asked, sharply.

"My father gave it to me," answered Lily, in a faltering voice. Sally regarded her with something like alertness.

"Your father?"

"Yes, ma'am."

"Where did you see him?"

"In the store."

"He gave you this candy?"

"Yes, ma'am."

"What did he say?"

"He asked me how old I was, and —"

"And what?"

"I don't know," replied Lily; and it really seemed to her that she did not know, she was so frightened and bewildered by it all, and, more than anything else, by her grandmother's face as she questioned her.

Old Woman Magoun's face was that of one upon whom a long-anticipated blow had fallen. Sally Jinks gazed at her with a sort of stupid alarm.

Old Woman Magoun continued to gaze at her grandchild with that look of terrible solicitude, as if she saw the girl in the clutch of a tiger. "You can't remember what else he said?" she asked, fiercely, and the child began to whimper softly.

"No, ma'am," she sobbed. "I—don't know, and—"

"And what? Answer me."

"There was another man there. A real handsome man."

"Did he speak to you?" asked Old Woman Magoun.

"Yes, ma'am; he walked along with me a piece," confessed Lily, with a sob of terror and bewilderment.

"What did *he* say to you?" asked Old Woman Magoun, with a sort of despair.

Lily told, in her little, faltering, frightened voice, all of the conversation which she could recall. It sounded harmless enough, but the look of the realization of a long-expected blow never left her grandmother's face.

The sun was getting low, and the bridge was nearing completion. Soon the workmen would be crowding into the cabin for their promised supper. There became visible in the distance, far up the road, the heavily plodding figure of another woman who had agreed to come and help. Old Woman Magoun turned again to Lily.

"You go right up-stairs to your own chamber now," said she.

"Good land! ain't you goin' to let that poor child stay up and see the fun?" said Sally Jinks.

"You jest mind your own business," said Old Woman Magoun, forcibly, and Sally Jinks shrank. "You go right up there now, Lily," said the grandmother, in a softer tone, "and grandma will bring you up a nice plate of supper."

"When be you goin' to let that girl grow up?" asked Sally Jinks, when Lily had disappeared.

"She'll grow up in the Lord's good time," replied Old Woman Magoun, and there was in her voice something both sad and threatening. Sally Jinks again shrank a little.

Soon the workmen came flocking noisily into the house. Old Woman Magoun and her two helpers served the bountiful supper. Most of the men had drunk as much as, and more than, was good for them, and Old Woman Magoun had stipulated that there was to be no drinking of anything except coffee during supper.

"I'll git you as good a meal as I know how," she said, "but if I see ary one of you drinkin' a drop, I'll run you all out. If you want anything to drink, you can go up to the store afterward. That's the place for you to go to, if you've got to make hogs of yourselves. I ain't goin' to have no hogs in my house."

Old Woman Magoun was implicitly obeyed. She had a curious authority over most people when she chose to exercise it. When the supper was in full swing, she quietly stole up-stairs and carried some food to Lily. She found the girl, with the rag doll in her arms, crouching by the window in her little rocking-chair—a relic of her infancy, which she still used.

"What a noise they are makin', grandma!" she said, in a terrified whisper, as her grandmother placed the plate before her on a chair.

"They've 'most all of 'em been drinkin'. They air a passel of hogs," replied the old woman.

"Is the man that was with—with my father down there?" asked Lily, in a timid fashion. Then she fairly cowered before the look in her grandmother's eyes.

"No, he ain't; and what's more, he never will be down there if I can help it," said Old Woman Magoun, in a fierce whisper. "I know who he is. They can't cheat me. He's one of them Willises—that family the Barrys married into. They're worse than the Barrys, ef they *have* got money. Eat your supper, and put him out of your mind, child."

It was after Lily was asleep, when Old Woman Magoun was alone, clearing away her supper dishes, that Lily's father came. The door was closed, and he knocked, and the old woman knew at once who was there. The sound of that knock meant as much to her as the whir of a bomb to the defender of a fortress. She opened the door, and Nelson Barry stood there.

"Good-evening, Mrs. Magoun," he said.

Old Woman Magoun stood before him, filling up the doorway with her firm bulk.

"Good-evening, Mrs. Magoun," said Nelson Barry again.

"I ain't got no time to waste," replied the old woman, harshly. "I've got my supper dishes to clean up after them men."

She stood there and looked at him as she might have looked at a rebellious animal which she was trying to tame. The man laughed.

"It's no use," said he. "You know me of old. No human being can turn me from my way when I am once started in it. You may as well let me come in."

Old Woman Magoun entered the house, and Barry followed her.

Barry began without any preface. "Where is the child?" asked he.

"Up-stairs. She has gone to bed."

"She goes to bed early."

"Children ought to," returned the old woman, polishing a plate.

Barry laughed. "You are keeping her a child a long while," he remarked, in a soft voice which had a sting in it.

"She *is* a child," returned the old woman, defiantly.

"Her mother was only three years older when Lily was born."

The old woman made a sudden motion toward the man which seemed fairly menacing. Then she turned again to her dish-washing.

"I want her," said Barry.

"You can't have her," replied the old woman, in a still stern voice.

"I don't see how you can help yourself. You have always acknowledged that she was my child."

The old woman continued her task, but her strong back heaved. Barry regarded her with an entirely pitiless expression.

"I am going to have the girl, that is the long and short of it," he said, "and it is for her best good, too. You are a fool, or you would see it."

"Her best good?" muttered the old woman.

"Yes, her best good. What are you going to do with her, anyway? The girl is a beauty, and almost a woman grown, although you try to make out that she is a baby. You can't live forever."

"The Lord will take care of her," replied the old woman, and again she turned and faced him, and her expression was that of a prophetess.

"Very well, let Him," said Barry, easily. "All the same I'm going to have her, and I tell you it is for her best good. Jim Willis saw her this afternoon, and—"

Old Woman Magoun looked at him. "Jim Willis!" she fairly shrieked. "Well, what of it?"

"One of them Willises!" repeated the old woman, and this time her voice was thick. It seemed almost as if she were stricken with paralysis. She did not enunciate clearly.

The man shrank a little. "Now what is the need of your making such a fuss?" he said. "I will take her, and Isabel will look out for her."

"Your half-witted sister?" said Old Woman Magoun.

"Yes, my half-witted sister. She knows more than you think."

"More wickedness."

"Perhaps. Well, a knowledge of evil is a useful thing. How are you going to avoid evil if you don't know what it is like? My sister and I will take care of my daughter."

The old woman continued to look at the man, but his eyes never fell. Suddenly her gaze grew inconceivably keen. It was as if she saw through all externals.

"I know what it is!" she cried. "You have been playing cards and you lost, and this is the way you will pay him."

Then the man's face reddened, and he swore under his breath.

"Oh, my God!" said the old woman; and she really spoke with her eyes aloft as if addressing something outside of them both. Then she turned again to her dish-washing.

The man cast a dogged look at her back. "Well, there is no use talking. I have made up my mind," said he, "and you know me and what that means. I am going to have the girl."

"When?" said the old woman, without turning around.

"Well, I am willing to give you a week. Put her clothes in good order before she comes."

The old woman made no reply. She continued washing dishes. She even handled them so carefully that they did not rattle.

"You understand," said Barry. "Have her ready a week from to-day."

"Yes," said Old Woman Magoun, "I understand."

Nelson Barry, going up the mountain road, reflected that Old Woman Magoun had a strong character, that she understood much better than her sex in general the futility of withstanding the inevitable.

"Well," he said to Jim Willis when he reached home, "the old woman did not make such a fuss as I expected."

"Are you going to have the girl?"

"Yes; a week from to-day. Look here, Jim; you've got to stick to your promise."

"All right," said Willis. "Go you one better."

The two were playing at cards in the old parlor, once magnificent, now squalid, of the Barry house. Isabel, the half-witted sister, entered, bringing some glasses on a tray. She had learned with her feeble intellect some tricks, like a dog. One of them was the mixing of sundry drinks. She set the tray on a little stand near the two men, and watched them with her silly simper.

"Clear out now and go to bed," her brother said to her, and she obeyed.

Early the next morning Old Woman Magoun went up to Lily's little sleeping-chamber, and watched her a second as she lay asleep, with her yellow locks spread over the pillow. Then she spoke. "Lily," said she—"Lily, wake up. I am going to Greenham across the new bridge, and you can go with me."

Lily immediately sat up in bed and smiled at her grandmother. Her eyes were still misty, but the light of awakening was in them.

"Get right up," said the old woman. "You can wear your new dress if you want to."

Lily gurgled with pleasure like a baby. "And my new hat?" asked she.

"I don't care."

Old Woman Magoun and Lily started for Greenham before Barry Ford, which kept late hours, was fairly awake. It was three miles to Greenham. The old woman said that, since the horse was a little lame, they would walk. It was a beautiful morning, with a diamond radiance of dew over everything. Her grandmother had curled Lily's hair more punctiliously than usual. The little face peeped like a rose out of two rows of golden spirals. Lily wore her new muslin dress with a pink sash, and her best hat of a fine white straw trimmed with a wreath of rosebuds; also the neatest black open-work stockings and pretty shoes. She even had white cotton gloves. When they set out, the old, heavily stepping woman, in her black gown and cape and bonnet, looked down at the little pink fluttering figure. Her face was full of the tenderest love and admiration, and yet there was something terrible about it. They crossed the new bridge—a primitive structure built of logs in a slovenly fashion. Old Woman Magoun pointed to a gap.

"Jest see that," said she. "That's the way men work."

"Men ain't very nice, be they?" said Lily, in her sweet little voice.

"No, they ain't, take them all together," replied her grandmother.

"That man that walked to the store with me was nicer than some, I guess," Lily said, in a wishful fashion. Her grandmother reached down and took the child's hand in its small cotton glove. "You hurt me, holding my hand so tight," Lily said presently, in a deprecatory little voice.

The old woman loosened her grasp. "Grandma didn't know how tight she was holding your hand," said she. "She wouldn't hurt you for nothin', except it was to save your life, or somethin' like that." She spoke with an undertone of tremendous meaning which the girl was too childish to grasp. They walked along the country road. Just before they reached Greenham they passed a stone wall overgrown with blackberry-vines, and, an unusual thing in that vicinity, a lusty spread of deadly nightshade full of berries.

"Those berries look good to eat, grandma," Lily said.

"At that instant the old woman's face became something terrible to see. "You can't have any now," she said, and hurried Lily along.

"They look real nice," said Lily.

When they reached Greenham, Old Woman Magoun took her way straight to the most pretentious house there, the residence of the lawyer, whose name was Mason. Old Woman Magoun bade Lily wait in the yard for a few moments, and Lily ventured to seat herself on a bench beneath an oak-tree; then she watched with some wonder her grandmother enter the lawyer's office door at the right of the house. Presently the lawyer's wife came out and spoke to Lily under the tree. She had in her hand a little tray containing a plate of cake, a glass of milk, and an early apple. She spoke very kindly to Lily; she even kissed her, and offered her the tray of refreshments, which Lily accepted gratefully. She sat eating, with Mrs. Mason watching her, when Old Woman Magoun came out of the lawyer's office with a ghastly face.

"What are you eatin'?" she asked Lily, sharply. "Is that a sour apple?"

"I though she might be hungry," said the lawyer's wife, with loving, melancholy eyes upon the girl.

Lily had almost finished the apple. "It's real sour, but I like it; it's real nice, grandma," she said.

"You ain't been drinkin' milk with a sour apple?"

"It was real nice milk, grandma."

"You ought never to have drunk milk and eat a sour apple," said her grandmother. "Your stomach was all out of order this mornin', an' sour apples and milk is always apt to hurt anybody."

"I don't know but they are," Mrs. Mason said, apologetically, as she stood on the green lawn with her lavender muslin sweeping around her. "I am real sorry, Mrs. Magoun. I ought to have thought. Let me get some soda for her."

"Soda never agrees with her," replied the old woman, in a harsh voice. "Come," she said to Lily, "it's time we were goin' home."

After Lily and her grandmother had disappeared down the road, Lawyer Mason came out of his office and joined his wife, who had seated herself on the bench beneath the tree. She was idle, and her face wore the expression of those who review joys forever past. She had lost a little girl, her only child, years ago, and her husband always knew when she was thinking about her. Lawyer Mason looked older than his wife; he had a dry, shrewd, slightly one-sided face.

"What do you think, Maria?" he said. "That old woman came to me with the most pressing entreaty to adopt that little girl."

"She is a beautiful little girl," said Mrs. Mason, in a slightly husky voice.

"Yes, she is a pretty child," assented the lawyer, looking pityingly at his wife; "but it is out of the question, my dear. Adopting a child is a serious measure, and in this case a child who comes from Barry's Ford."

"But the grandmother seems a very good woman," said Mrs. Mason.

"I rather think she is. I never heard a word against her. But the father! No, Maria, we cannot take a child with Barry blood in her veins. The stock has run out; it is vitiated physically and morally. It won't do, my dear."

"Her grandmother had her dressed up as pretty as a little girl could be," said Mrs. Mason, and this time the tears welled into her faithful, wistful eyes.

"Well, we can't help that," said the lawyer, as he went back to his office.

Old Woman Magoun and Lily returned, going slowly along the road to Barry's Ford. When they came to the stone wall where the blackberry-vines and the deadly nightshade grew, Lily said she was tired, and asked if she could not sit down for a few minutes. The strange look on her grandmother's face had deepened. Now and then Lily glanced at her and had a feeling as if she were looking at a stranger.

"Yes, you can set down if you want to," said Old Woman Magoun, deeply and harshly.

Lily started and looked at her, as if to make sure that it was her grandmother who spoke. Then she sat down on a stone which was comparatively free of the vines.

"Ain't you goin' to set down, grandma?" Lily asked, timidly.

"No; I don't want to get into that mess," replied her grandmother. "I ain't tired. I'll stand here."

Lily sat still; her delicate little face was flushed with heat. She extended her tiny feet in her best shoes and gazed at them. "My shoes are all over dust," said she.

"It will brush off," said her grandmother, still in that strange voice.

Lily looked around. An elm-tree in the field behind her cast a spray of branches over her head; a little cool puff of wind came on her face. She gazed at the low mountains on the horizon, in the midst of which she lived, and she sighed, for no reason that she knew. She began idly picking at the blackberry-vines; there were no berries on them; then she put her little fingers on the berries of the deadly nightshade. "These look like nice berries," she said.

Old Woman Magoun, standing stiff and straight in the road, said nothing.

"They look good to eat," said Lily.

Old Woman Magoun still said nothing, but she looked up into the ineffable blue of the sky, over which spread at intervals great white clouds shaped like wings.

Lily picked some of the deadly nightshade berries and ate them. "Why, they are real sweet," said she. "They are nice." She picked some more and ate them.

Presently her grandmother spoke. "Come," she said, "it is time we were going. I guess you have set long enough."

Lily was still eating the berries when she slipped down from the wall and followed her grandmother obediently up the road.

Before they reached home, Lily complained of being very thirsty. She stopped and made a little cup of a leaf and drank long at a mountain brook. "I am dreadful dry, but it hurts me to swallow," she said to her grandmother when she stopped drinking and joined the old woman waiting for her in the road. Her grandmother's face seemed strangely dim to her. She took hold of Lily's hand as they went on. "My stomach burns," said Lily, presently. "I want some more water."

"There is another brook a little farther on," said Old Woman Magoun, in a dull voice.

When they reached that brook, Lily stopped and drank again, but she whimpered a little over her difficulty in swallowing. "My stomach burns, too," she said, walking on, "and my throat is so dry, grandma." Old

Woman Magoun held Lily's hand more tightly. "You hurt me holding my hand so tight, grandma," said Lily, looking up at her grandmother, whose face she seemed to see through a mist, and the old woman loosened her grasp.

When at last they reached home, Lily was very ill. Old Woman Magoun put her on her own bed in the little bedroom out of the kitchen. Lily lay there and moaned, and Sally Jinks came in.

"Why, what ails her?" she asked. "She looks feverish."

Lily unexpectedly answered for herself. "I ate some sour apples and drank some milk," she moaned.

"Sour apples and milk are dreadful apt to hurt anybody," said Sally Jinks. She told several people on her way home that Old Woman Magoun was dreadful careless to let Lily eat such things.

Meanwhile Lily grew worse. She suffered cruelly from the burning in her stomach, the vertigo, and the deadly nausea. "I am so sick, I am so sick, grandma," she kept moaning. She could no longer see her grandmother as she bent over her, but she could hear her talk.

Old Woman Magoun talked as Lily had never heard her talk before, as nobody had ever heard her talk before. She spoke from the depths of her soul; her voice was as tender as the coo of a dove, and it was grand and exalted. "You'll feel better very soon, little Lily," said she.

"I am so sick, grandma."

"You will feel better very soon, and then—"

"I am sick."

"You shall go to a beautiful place."

Lily moaned.

"You shall go to a beautiful place," the old woman went on.

"Where?" asked Lily, groping feebly with her cold little hands. Then she moaned again.

"A beautiful place, where the flowers grow tall."

"What color? Oh, grandma, I am so sick."

"A blue color," replied the old woman. Blue was Lily's favorite color. "A beautiful blue color, and as tall as your knees, and the flowers always stay there, and they never fade."

"Not if you pick them, grandma? Oh!"

"No, not if you pick them; they never fade, and they are so sweet you can smell them a mile off; and there are birds that sing, and all the roads have gold stones in them, and the stone walls are made of gold."

"Like the ring grandpa gave you? I am so sick, grandma."

"Yes, gold like that. And all the houses are built of silver and gold, and the people all have wings, so when they get tired walking they can fly, and—"

"I am so sick, grandma."

"And all the dolls are alive," said Old Woman Magoun. "Dolls like yours can run, and talk, and love you back again."

Lily had her poor old rag doll in bed with her, clasped close to her agonized little heart. She tried very hard with her eyes, whose pupils were so dilated that they looked black, to see her grandmother's face when she said that, but she could not. "It is dark," she moaned, feebly.

"There where you are going it is always light," said the grandmother, "and the commonest things shine like that breastpin Mrs. Lawyer Mason had on to-day."

Lily moaned pitifully, and said something incoherent. Delirium was commencing. Presently she sat straight up in bed and raved; but even then her grandmother's wonderful compelling voice had an influence over her.

"You will come to a gate with all the colors of the rainbow," said her grandmother; "and it will open, and you will go right in and walk up the gold street, and cross the field where the blue flowers come up to your knees, until you find your mother, and she will take you home where you are going to live. She has a little white room all ready for you, white curtains at the windows, and a little white looking-glass, and when you look in it you will see—"

"What will I see? I am so sick, grandma."

"You will see a face like yours, only it's an angel's; and there will be a little white bed, and you can lay down an' rest."

"Won't I be sick, grandma?" asked Lily. Then she moaned and babbled wildly, although she seemed to understand through it all what her grandmother said.

"No, you will never be sick any more. Talkin' about sickness won't mean anything to you."

It continued. Lily talked on wildly, and her grandmother's great voice of soothing never ceased, until the child fell into a deep sleep, or what resembled sleep; but she lay stiffly in that sleep, and a candle flashed before her eyes made no impression on them.

Then it was that Nelson Barry came. Jim Willis waited outside the door. When Nelson entered he found Old Woman Magoun on her knees beside the bed, weeping with dry eyes and a might of agony which fairly shook Nelson Barry, the degenerate of a fine old race.

"Is she sick?" he asked, in a hushed voice.

Old Woman Magoun gave another terrible sob, which sounded like the gasp of one dying.

"Sally Jinks said that Lily was sick from eating milk and sour apples," said Barry, in a tremulous voice. "I remember that her mother was very sick once from eating them."

Lily lay still, and her grandmother on her knees shook with her terrible sobs.

Suddenly Nelson Barry started. "I guess I had better go to Greenham for a doctor if she's as bad as that," he said. He went close to the bed and looked at the sick child. He gave a great start. Then he felt of her hands and reached down under the bedclothes for her little feet. "Her hands and feet are like ice," he cried out. "Good God! why didn't you send for some one—for me—before? Why, she's dying; she's almost gone!"

Barry rushed out and spoke to Jim Willis, who turned pale and came in and stood by the bedside.

"She's almost gone," he said, in a hushed whisper.

"There's no use going for the doctor; she'd be dead before he got here," said Nelson, and he stood regarding the passing child with a strange, sad face—unutterably said, because of his incapability of the truest sadness.

"Poor little thing, she's past suffering, anyhow," said the other man, and his own face also was sad with a puzzled, mystified sadness.

Lily died that night. There was quite a commotion in Barry's Ford until after the funeral, it was all so sudden, and then everything went on as usual. Old Woman Magoun continued to live as she had done before. She supported herself by the produce of her tiny farm; she was very industrious, but people said that she was a trifle touched, since every time she went over the log bridge with her eggs or her garden vegetables to sell in Greenham, she carried with her, as one might have carried an infant, Lily's old rag doll.

The Selfishness of Amelia Lamkin

1908

It was a morning in late February. The day before there had been a storm of unusually damp, clogging snow, which had lodged upon everything in strange, shapeless masses. The trees bore big blobs of snow, caught here and there in forks or upon extremities. They looked as if the northwester had pelted them with snowballs. Below the rise of ground on which the Lamkin house stood there was a low growth of trees, and they resembled snowball bushes in full bloom. Amelia Lamkin at her breakfast-table could see them. There were seven persons at the breakfast-table: Josiah Lamkin and his wife Amelia; Annie Sears, the eldest daughter, who was married and lived at home; Addie Lamkin, the second daughter, a pretty girl of eighteen; Tommy Lamkin, aged thirteen; little Johnny Field, a child of four, an orphan grandchild of Amelia Lamkin; and Jane Strong, Amelia's unmarried sister, who was visiting her. Annie Sears was eating, with dainty little bites, toast and eggs prepared in a particular way. She was delicate, and careful about her diet. The one maid in the household was not trusted to prepare Annie's eggs. Amelia did that. She was obliged to rise early in any case. Harry Sears, Annie's husband, left for the city at seven o'clock, and he was also particular about his eggs, although he was not delicate. Addie loathed eggs in any form except an omelet, and Hannah, the maid, could not achieve one. Therefore, Amelia cooked Addie's nice, fluffy omelet. Tommy was not particular about quality, but about quantity, and Amelia had that very much upon her mind. Johnny's rice was cooked in a special way which Hannah had not mastered, and Amelia prepared that. Josiah liked porterhouse beefsteak broiled to an exact degree of rareness, and Hannah could not be trusted with that. Hannah's coffee was always muddy, and the Lamkins detested muddy coffee; therefore, Amelia made the coffee.

Hannah's morning duties resolved themselves into standing heavily about, resting her weight first upon one large flat foot, then upon the other, while her mistress prepared breakfast, then waiting upon the table in an absent, desultory fashion. There was a theory in the Lamkin household that poor Hannah worked very hard, since she was the only maid in a family of seven. The neighbors also acquiesced in that opinion, and Hannah herself felt pleasantly and comfortably injured. Nobody pitied Amelia Lamkin, least of all her own family. She had always waited upon them and obliterated herself to that extent that she seemed scarcely to have a foothold at all upon the earth, but to balance timidly upon the extreme edge of existence. Now and then Amelia's unmarried sister, Jane Strong, visited the Lamkins, and always expressed her unsolicited opinion. The Lamkins were justly incensed, and even Amelia herself bristled her soft plumage of indignation. She would say privately to her sister that she realized that she meant well, but she did wish that she would let her live her own way without interference; that she, Amelia, got her happiness in ways that Jane could not understand. Amelia would be quite disagreeable, and her references to Jane's single condition would be obvious; then later, being gentle to the very core, she would beg Jane's pardon, which would be granted stiffly, without the slightest retreat from the position of attack. "Of course I don't mind a straw about what you threw out about my not being married," said Jane. "You know as well as I do that it was my own choice."

"Of course," responded Amelia, meekly, but she looked reminiscent. She was trying to remember what serious suitors Jane had really had. Jane saw the expression and understood. She was nothing if not honest.

"Land! I don't mean to say there was a line of men on their knees to marry me," she said, brusquely. "There wasn't a run as there was on that New York bank, and men hanging round from dawn till dark. Most of them got married afterward, and I guess they were pretty well satisfied, and I don't believe one of them lost a meal of victuals or a night's sleep. But you know as well as I do that there were chances I might have followed up if I wanted to."

"Yes, I know," returned Amelia, with more assurance. Really she had no doubt that if her sister had chosen to follow up any man, even her own husband Josiah, he might have capitulated. There had always been something fascinating about Jane, and she had been and was still handsome. She was much handsomer than Amelia, although she was ten years older. Amelia was faded almost out as to color, and intense solicitude for others and perfect meekness had crossed her little face with deep lines, and bowed her slender figure like that of a patient old horse, accustomed to having his lameness ignored, and standing before doors in harness through all kinds of weather. Amelia's neck, which was long and slender, had the same curve of utter submission which one sees in the neck of a weary old beast of burden. She would slightly raise that drooping neck to expostulate with Jane. There would be a faint suggestion of ancient spirit; then it would disappear. Jane, her own chin raised splendidly, eyed her sister with a sort of tender resentment and contempt.

"Of course you know," said Jane, "that I'm enough sight better off the way I am. I'm freer than any married woman in the world. Then I've kept my looks. My figure is just as good as it ever was, and my hair's just as thick and not a thread of gray. I suppose the time's got to come, if I live long enough, that I shall look in my glass, and see my skin yellow and flabby; but now the only change is that I'm settled *past* change. I know that means I'm not young, and some may think not as good-looking, but I *am*." Jane regarded her sister with a sort of defiance. What she said was true. Her face was quite as handsome as in her youth; all the change lay in the fact of its impregnability to the shift and play of emotions. A laugh no longer transformed her features. These reigned triumphant over mirth and joy, even grief. She was handsome, but she was not young. She was immovably Jane Strong.

"I think you are just as good-looking as you ever were," replied Amelia. As she spoke she gave a gentle sigh. Amelia, after all, was human. As a girl she had loved the soft, sweet face, suffused with bloom like an apple blossom, which she had seen in her looking-glass. She had enjoyed arranging the pretty, fair hair around it. Now that enjoyment was quite gone out of her life. The other face had been so dear and pleasant to see. She could not feel the same toward this little seamed countenance, with its shade of grayish hair over the lined temples, and its meek, downward arc of thin lips. However, she told herself, with a little feeling of self-scorn, that she, Josiah Lamkin's wife, and mother and grandmother, could not possibly be so foolish as to regret the loss of her beauty when she could see it renewed so many-fold in the faces of her loved ones. She told herself that she was so thankful that her husband had kept his looks so well. Josiah, although older than she, was still fresh-colored and full-faced, and he had not a gray hair. Amelia knew that it would have been harder for her to see her husband's face grown old and worn in the faithful mirror of her heart than to view her own altered face in her looking-glass.

When Amelia sighed, Jane looked at her with a sort of angry pity. "You might be just as good-looking as you ever were if you had taken decent care of yourself, and not worn yourself out for other folks," said she. "There was no real need of your getting all bent over, no older than you were, and no need of your hair getting so thin and gray. You ought to have taken the time to put a tonic on it, and you ought to have stretched yourself out on the bed a good hour every afternoon, and remembered to hold your shoulders back."

"I haven't had much time to lie down every afternoon."

"You might have had if you had set others to doing what they ought, instead of doing it yourself."

Amelia bristled again, this time with more vigor. "You know," said she, "that Hannah can't cook. It isn't in her."

"I'd get a girl who could cook," returned Jane, setting her lips hard and doubling her chin in an obstinate fashion.

"I can't discharge Hannah after all the years she has been with me. She is honest and faithful."

"Faithful nothing!"

"She is faithful," said Amelia, with decision. "She is cranky, too, and I doubt if she could stay long with anybody except me. I know just how to manage her."

"She knows just how to manage you. They all do."

"Jane Strong, I won't hear you talk so about my family and poor Hannah."

"I should think it was poor Amelia."

"I have everything to be thankful for," said Amelia. "I have the best husband and children that ever a woman had, and Hannah is just as faithful as she can be; and as for the cooking, you know I always liked to do it, Jane."

"Yes, you always liked to do everything that everybody else didn't; no doubt about that. And you always pretended you liked to eat everything that everybody else didn't."

"I have everything I want to eat."

"What did you make your breakfast of this morning?" demanded Jane.

Amelia reflected. She colored a little, then she looked defiantly at her sister. "Beefsteak, and omelet, and biscuit, and coffee," said she.

Jane sniffed. "Yes, a little scraggy bit of steak that Josiah didn't want, and that little burnt corner of Addie's omelet, and that under crust of Tommy's biscuit, and a muddy cup of watered coffee, after all the others had had two cups apiece. You needn't think I didn't see. Amelia Lamkin, you are a fool! You are killing yourself, and you are hurting your whole family and that good-for-nothing Hannah thrown in."

Then Amelia looked at Jane with sudden distress. "What do you mean, Jane?" she quavered.

"Just what I say. You are simply making your whole family a set of pigs, and Hannah too, and you know you have an awful responsibility toward an ignorant person like that, and you are ruining your own health."

"I am very well, indeed, Jane," said Amelia, but she spoke with a slight hesitation.

"You are not well. No mortal woman who has lived her whole life on the fag ends of food and rest and happiness that nobody else had any use for can be well. You hear about dogs feeding on crumbs, and I suppose they may thrive on them, though I never saw a dog yet that didn't seem to me to get along better on bones with considerable meat sticking to them; but you don't hear about human beings living in such a fashion, and it isn't required of them. You've been doing your duty all your life so hard that you haven't given other people a chance to do theirs. You've been a very selfish woman as far as duty is concerned, Amelia Lamkin, and you have made other people selfish. If Addie marries Arthur Henderson, what kind of a wife will she make after the way you have brought her up? He's a poor man, and Addie has no more idea of waiting on herself than if she were a millionairess."

"I don't know that they have come to an understanding yet," said Amelia, and as she spoke she blushed softly. She was as delicate over her daughter's romance as over her own.

"Oh, they will," said Jane, with a sniff, "though I don't see, for my part, what Addie Lamkin, with her looks, is in such a hurry for. I don't mean that Arthur Henderson isn't well enough, but Addie might do better when it comes to money."

"Money isn't everything."

"It is a good deal," responded Jane, sententiously, "and I guess Addie Lamkin will find it is if she marries Arthur Henderson and has to live on next to nothing a year, with everything going up the way it is now, when you have to stretch on your tiptoes and reach your arms up as if you were hanging for dear life to a strap on a universe trolley-car to keep going at all."

"Oh, I don't think they have even thought of marriage yet," said Amelia.

"*Lord!*" said Jane, with infinite scorn. After a little she continued: "I don't care. You *are* miserable. You can't hide it from me. You have lost flesh. You needn't pretend you haven't. You don't weigh nearly as much as you did when I was here last fall."

"I haven't been weighed lately."

"You don't need to get weighed. You can tell by your clothes. That gray silk dress you wore last night fairly hung on you."

"I always went up and down in my weight; you know I did, Jane."

"One of these days you will go down and never come up," retorted Jane, with grim assurance. Then Addie Lamkin, young and vigorous and instinct with beauty and health, marched into the room, and in her wake trailed Annie, sweet and dainty in a pale blue cashmere wrapper.

Addie, with her young cheeks full of roses, with her young yellow hair standing up crispy above her full temples, with her blue eyes blazing, with her red mouth pouting, opened fire. "Now, Aunt Jane," said Addie, "you know we always like to have you visit us, but Annie and I couldn't help overhearing—the door has been open all the time—and we have made up our minds to speak right out and tell you what we think. We love to have you here, don't we, Annie?"

"Yes, indeed, we love to have you, Aunt Jane," assented Annie, in her soft voice, which was very like her mother's.

Amelia made a little distressed noise.

"Don't you say a word, mother," said Addie. "We are going to say just what we think. We have made up our minds." Addie's face had the expression of one who dives. "We simply can't have you making mother miserable, Aunt Jane," said she, "and you might just as well understand. Don't you agree with me, Annie?"

"Yes," said Annie.

"Don't, dear," said Amelia.

"I must," Addie replied, firmly. "We both feel that it is our duty. We both love Aunt Jane, and we are not lacking in respect to her as to an older woman, but we must do our duty. We must speak. Aunt Jane, you simply must not interfere with mother. We will not have it."

Jane's face wore a curious expression. "How do I interfere?" asked she.

"You interfere with mother's having her own way and doing exactly what she likes," said Addie.

"And you never do?"

"No," replied Addie, "we never do. None of us do."

"No, we really don't," said Annie. She spoke apologetically. She was not as direct as Addie.

"You are quite right," said Jane Strong. "I don't think any of you ever do interfere with your mother. You let her have her own way about slaving for you and waiting upon you. Your father has, ever since he was married, and all you children have, ever since you were born; not the slightest doubt of it."

Addie looked fairly afire with righteous wrath. "Really, Aunt Jane," said she, "I don't feel that, as long as it makes mother's whole happiness to live as she does, you are called upon to hinder her."

Amelia in her turn was full of wrath. "I am sure I don't want to be hindered," said she.

"We know you don't, mother dear," said Addie, "and you shall not be."

"You need not worry," Jane said, slowly. "*I* shall not hinder your mother, but I miss my guess if she isn't hindered." Then she went out of the room, her head up, her carriage as majestic as that of a queen.

"Aunt Jane is hopping," said Addie, "but I don't care; as for having poor mother teased and made miserable every time she comes here, I won't, for one!"

"Your aunt has never had a family and she doesn't understand, dear," said Amelia. She was a trifle bewildered by her daughter's partisanship. She was not well, and had had visions of Addie's offering to assist about luncheon. Now she realized that Addie would consider that such an offer would make her unhappy.

"No, mother dear, you shall have your own way," Annie said, caressingly. "Your own family knows what makes you happy, and you shall do just what you like." Annie put her arm around her mother's poor little waist and kissed her softly. "I am feeling wretchedly this morning," said Annie. "I think I will follow Doctor Emerson's advice to wrap myself up and sit out on the piazza an hour. I can finish that new book."

"Mind you wrap up well," Amelia said, anxiously.

"I think I will finish embroidering my silk waist," said Addie. "I want to wear it to the Simpsons' party Saturday night."

Then the daughters went away, and Amelia Lamkin went into the kitchen and prepared some scalloped fish and a cake for luncheon. She attended to some soup stock, and had consultations with the butcher and grocer. She also assisted Hannah about the breakfast dishes.

Amelia worked all the morning. She did not sit down for a moment until lunch-time. Then suddenly the hindrance which Jane Strong had foretold that morning came without a moment's warning. There had not been enough fish left from the dinner of the day before to prepare the ramekins for the family and allow Tommy two, unless Amelia went without. She was patiently eating a slice of bread and butter and drinking tea when she fell over in a faint. The little, thin creature slid gently into her swoon, not even upsetting her teacup. She fainted considerately, as she had always done everything else. Jane, who sat next her sister, caught her before she had fallen from her chair. Josiah sprang up, and stood looking intensely shocked and perfectly helpless. Addie ran for a smelling-bottle, and Annie leaped back and gasped, as if she were about to faint herself. Tommy stared, with a spoon half-way to his mouth. Then he swallowed the contents of the spoon from force of habit. Then he stared again, and turned pale under his freckles. The baby cried and pounded the table with his fists.

Amelia's face, under its thin film of gray hair, was very ghastly. Jane, supporting that poor head, looked impatiently at Josiah standing inert, with his fresh countenance fixed in that stare of helpless, almost angry, astonishment. "For goodness' sake, Josiah Lamkin," said his sister-in-law, "don't stand there gaping like a nincompoop, but go for Doctor Emerson, if you've got sense enough!" Jane came from New England, and in moments of excitement she showed plainly the influence of the land of her birth. She spoke with forcible, almost vulgar, inelegance, but she spoke with the effect of an Ethan Allen or a Stark.

Josiah moved. He made one stride for the door. Then he shot past the window on his way for the doctor.

"Stop fainting away, Annie Sears," said Jane, "and hand me that glass of water for your mother, then spank that bawling young one. You are no more faint than I am. Tommy, tell Hannah to march up-stairs lively and get your mother's bed ready." Hannah at that moment appeared in the doorway, and she promptly dropped a cup of coffee, which crashed and broke into fragments with a gush of brown liquid. At the sound of that crash there was a slight flicker of poor Amelia Lamkin's eyelids, but they immediately closed. "Let that coffee and that cup be, now you have smashed it," said Jane Strong to Hannah, "and, for goodness' sake, stop staring, and get up-stairs lively and get Mrs. Lamkin's bed ready. Why don't you move?"

Hannah moved, and the house shook with the trembling thud of her steps on the stairs. Annie came falteringly around with the glass of water. Tommy, who, once awakened to the situation, showed remarkable sense, caught up the morning paper, and fanned his mother, while the tears rolled over his hard, boyish cheeks, and he gulped convulsively.

"Oh, what ails her?" gasped Annie, holding the glass of water to her mother's white lips.

Jane was pitiless. "She's dead, for all I know," said she. "She's an awful time coming to. For the land's sake, don't spill that water all over her! Dip your fingers in and sprinkle some on her forehead. Haven't you got any sense at all?"

Annie sprinkled her mother's forehead as if she were baptizing her. "Oh, what is it?" she moaned again.

"She's dead if she ain't fainted away," said Jane. "How do I know? But I can tell you what the matter is, Annie Sears, and you too, Addie Lamkin" (for Addie was just returning with the little green smelling-bottle): "your mother is worn out with hard work because you've all been so afraid to cross her in slaving for everybody else and having nothing for herself. She's worked out and starved out."

Addie, holding the green bottle to her mother's little pinched nostrils, aroused at that, although her pretty, healthy young face retained a pale, shocked expression. "Mother isn't starved," she whispered.

"Yes, she is, too, living on odds and ends. She hasn't eaten a good square meal since I've been here. Hens can live on such truck, but your mother can't. She ain't a hen. Here, for goodness' sake, set down that old smelling-bottle, and, Tommy, you come here and help hold her head, and, Annie, you stop sniffing and shaking and help Addie, and we'll lay her down on the floor. She'll never come to, sitting up."

"I knew that all the time," volunteered Tommy, in a shaking voice. "Teacher said to lay Jim Addison down that time when he bumped his nose against his desk reaching down for a marble he dropped."

Between them they lowered the little inanimate form to the floor, and Tommy got a sofa cushion from the sitting-room and put it under his mother's head. Then Jane broke down completely. She became hysterical.

"Oh, Amelia, Amelia!" she wailed, in a dreadful voice of ascending notes, "my sister, the only sister I've got! Amelia, speak to me! Amelia, can't you hear? Speak to me!"

Annie sank down on the floor beside her unconscious mother and wept weakly. Addie, with her lips firmly set, rubbed her mother's hands. Tommy fanned with all his might! The morning paper made a steady breeze above the still, white face. The baby had succeeded in reaching the sugar-bowl and had stopped crying. He was eating the lumps in the bowl, with one wary eye of mischief on the group.

Amelia did not revive. Those around her became more and more alarmed. Hannah stood in the door. She stammered out that the bed was ready; then she, too, wailed the wail of her sort, lifting high a voice of un-couth animal woe.

"She's dead, she's dead!" at last sobbed Jane. "She'll never speak to any of us again. Oh, Amelia, Amelia, to think it should come to this!"

Addie, with one furious glance at her aunt, stopped rubbing her mother's hands. She stood back. She looked very stiff and straight. Her face was still, but tears rolled over her cheeks as if they had been marble. Annie wept with gentle grief. Jane continued to lament, as did Hannah. The baby steadily ate sugar. Tommy was the only one who held steadfast. He never whimpered, and he fanned as if life depended upon the news-paper gale.

Then there was a quick rattle of wheels, and Jane rushed to the door and shrieked out, as the doctor was fumbling for his medicine chest:

"You're too late, doctor, you're too late!"

Poor Josiah, who had driven back with the doctor and was already out of the buggy, turned ghastly white.

"Oh, my God, doctor, she's gone!" he gasped.

The doctor, who was young and optimistic, clapped him on the shoul-der. "Brace up, man!" he said, in a loud voice. Then he entered the house and the dining-room where poor Amelia lay. He pushed rather rudely past Jane and Hannah and Addie and Annie. He knelt down beside the pros-trate woman, looked at her keenly, felt her wrist, and held his head to her breast. Then he addressed Tommy. "How long has your mother been un-conscious?" he asked.

Tommy glanced up at the clock. "Most half an hour," he replied. His mouth and eyes and nose twitched, but he spoke quite firmly. There was the making of a man in Tommy.

"Oh, she's dead!" wailed Jane. "Oh, Amelia! Oh, my sister, my sister!"

Doctor Emerson rose and looked at Jane Strong with cool hostility. "She is not dead unless you make her so by your lack of self-control," said he. "You must all be as quiet as you can."

Jane stopped wailing and regarded him with awed eyes, the eyes of a feminine thing cowed by the superior coolness in adversity of a male. She was afraid of that clear, pink-and-white, young masculine face, with its steady outlook of rather cold blue eyes and its firm mouth. All became quiet and obeyed Doctor Emerson's orders. Josiah, Hannah, and the doctor carried Amelia to her room, and laid her, still unconscious, upon her bed. Then, after a while, she awakened, but she was a broken creature. They hardly recognized her as Amelia. Amelia without her ready hand for them all, her ready step for their comfort, seemed hardly credible. She lay sunken among her pillows in a curious, inert fashion. She was very small and slight, but she gave an impression of great weight, so complete was her abandonment to exhaustion, so entirely her bed sustained her, without any effort upon her part.

Addie cornered the doctor in the front hall on his way out. "What do you think is the matter with mother?" she whispered. The doctor looked at Addie's pretty, pale face. He was unmarried, and had had dreams about Addie Lamkin. He had dismissed those dreams upon the advent of Arthur Henderson. Still, the girl had almost the interest of an old love for him.

"Your mother is simply worn out, Miss Lamkin," said Doctor Emerson, curtly; yet his eyes, regarding that pretty face, were pitying.

"Worn out?" repeated Addie.

"Yes. To put it plainly, she has worked too hard for everybody else, and not hard enough for herself."

Soft rose suffused Addie's face and neck. She looked piteously at the doctor, with round eyes like a baby's, pleading not to be hurt. The doctor's tone softened a little.

"Of course I realize how almost impossible it is to prevent self-sacrificing women like your mother from offering themselves up," he said.

Tears stood in Addie's eyes. "Mother never complained, and she seemed to want—" she returned, brokenly.

"Yes, she seemed to want to do everything and not let anybody else do anything, and everybody indulged her."

"I don't think any of us realized," said Addie.

"Of course you didn't," said Doctor Emerson, and his voice, while slightly sarcastic, was still almost caressing.

"Of course now we shall see that mother does not overdo," said Addie.

"She can't—now."

Addie turned very white. "You don't mean—"

"I don't know. I shall do everything I can, but she is very weak. I never saw a case of more complete exhaustion."

After Doctor Emerson had driven out of the yard, Addie and Annie talked together, Jane Strong made gruel, and Tommy sat beside his mother. Josiah paced up and down the front walk. He had a feeling as if the solid ground was cut from under his feet. He had not known for so many years what it was to live without the sense of Amelia's sustaining care that he felt at once unreasoning anger with her, a monstrous self-pity, and an agony of anxious love. The one clear thing in his mind was that Amelia ever since their marriage had put in his sleeve-buttons and shirt-studs. Always he saw those little, nervous, frail hands struggling with the stiff linen and the studs and buttons. It seemed to him that of all her wrongs, that was the one which he should definitely grasp. He felt that she was worn out, maybe come to her death, through putting in those buttons and studs. Josiah was a great, lumbering masculine creature, full of helpless tenderness. He paced up and down the walk. He looked at his thick fingers, and he saw always those little, slender, nervous ones struggling with his linen and buttons, and he knew what remorse was. Finally he could bear it no longer, and he entered the house and the kitchen where Jane was making the gruel.

"Doctor Emerson says she is all worn out," he said, thickly.

Jane looked at him viciously. "Of course she is worn out."

"Jane, do you think putting in my sleeve-buttons and studs hurt her?"

Jane stared at him. "Everything has hurt her together, I suppose," she replied, grimly.

Josiah went into the dining-room, where Addie and Annie stood talking together in low voices, and sobbing softly between the words. The baby was asleep in his chair, his curly head hanging sidewise. "Your mother seems to be all worn out," Josiah said to his daughters.

"Yes, she is, I am afraid," Annie said, tearfully. "If *I* had only been stronger."

"If mother had only known *she* wasn't strong," Addie said, fiercely, and Annie did not resent it. "Here I've been saying mother must be let alone to do things because it worried her not to," said Addie. "Great fool, great hypocrite!" She gave a sob of fury at herself.

"I have been thinking how she has always put in my sleeve-buttons and shirt-studs," said Josiah.

Neither Annie nor Addie seemed to hear what he said.

"If only *I* had been stronger," repeated Annie.

Addie turned on her. "You have always been enough sight stronger than mother, Annie Sears," said she. "You fairly enjoy thinking you are delicate. You think it is a feather in your cap; you know you do!"

Annie was so astonished she fairly gaped at her sister. She could not speak. Addie made a dart toward Johnny and caught him up in her arms. "Here we are letting mother's baby break his neck," said she, furiously, "standing here like great gumps. Next thing he would have tumbled out of his chair." Johnny began to wail, and Addie kissed him, then shook him. "Johnny, hush up for mercy's sake," said she. "Grandma's very sick. Here, don't cry, and auntie will give you a lump of sugar." With that Addie poked a lump of sugar into the little, soft, red mouth, and Johnny was appeased and began sucking it.

"She's always put in my sleeve-buttons and studs," said Josiah, in his miserable monotone. Then he returned to the front walk, and began pacing up and down.

Addie turned to Annie. "Annie Sears," said she, "do you know mother is up there all alone with Tommy? Why don't you go up there?"

"'Let me take Johnny, and you go Addie," Annie said, faintly.

Addie thrust Johnny upon Annie, and turned and went up-stairs. Tommy looked up as she entered the room and gave an inaudible "hush!" "Mother is asleep," he motioned with his lips. Amelia, indeed, lay as if asleep, with her eyes partly open, and a ghastly line of white eyeball showing. Addie sat beside the bed and looked at her mother. Tommy broke down, and curved his arm in its rough sleeve around his freckled face and wept bitterly. Addie did not weep. Gradually the expression of those who renunciate stole over her face. She was making up her mind to relinquish all thoughts of marriage, to live at home single, and devote her life to her mother. Addie's face, which had been pretty with a rather hard prettiness, grew beautiful. She looked as her mother had done as a girl. The possibilities of entire self-renunciation lit it with spiritual glory. She realized that she was very unhappy; she thought of Arthur Henderson, but she said to herself that he was a man and young, and men could forget. She knew quite well that his character was not one capable of going through life without snatching at one sweet if he could not obtain another. She felt glad that it was so. She had never been so miserable and so blissful in her whole life as she was, sitting beside her mother's bed; for she, for the first time, saw beyond her own self, and realized the unspeakable glory there. She reached out a hand and patted Tommy's heaving shoulder.

"We'll all take care of her, and she'll get well; don't cry, dear," she whispered, very softly.

But Tommy gave his shoulder an impatient shrug and wept on. He was remembering how he had worn so many holes in his mittens and his mother had mended them, and it seemed to him as if mending those mittens was the one thing which had tired her out. He made up his mind, whether she lived or died, that he would never get holes in his mittens again for anybody to mend. He would start to school with mittens on his hands, and when once out of sight of home, into his pockets they would go, and he would use his bare hands if they did get frost-bitten.

Down-stairs Annie Sears sat beside little Johnny and told him a story. She never knew what the story was about. Johnny had eaten all the sugar in the bowl, and he nestled his little curly head against Annie's shoulder while she talked in her unhappy voice. After a while Johnny's eyes closed, and Annie lifted him and carried him up-stairs and laid him on her own bed. He was a heavy child, and she bent painfully beneath his weight, and reflected, the while she did so, how many times she had seen her mother toil up-stairs with him—her little mother, whose shoulders were narrower than her own.

Jane finished the bowl of gruel, while Hannah stood looking on. Jane turned upon the girl with sudden fury.

"For the land's sake, get to work, can't you?" she said. "What are you standing there for? Clear off the table, and wash the dishes, and sweep up the kitchen!"

Hannah did not resent the angry voice. She began to weep without covering her face, bawling aloud like a baby. "Oh, Lord! oh, Lord!" she wailed. "Here's that poor blessed soul all wore out doing my work while I've been standing watching her!"

"Well, you haven't got her to watch now," said Jane. "Get to work!" Hannah paddled into the dining-room, and the clatter of dishes accompanied her loud sobs. Jane carried the bowl of gruel to her sister, but poor Amelia was too spent to take more than a spoonful or two, for all her gentle willingness. "There's no use," said Jane, grimly. "She's got to have something to put some life in her. There's that bottle of port wine down cellar that the doctor ordered for Annie, and she didn't like. I'm going to put some in this gruel."

"Won't it be an awful mess?" whispered Addie.

"Mess or not, she's got to take it. She's got to have something to put some life in her."

The cellar in the Lamkin house was approached by a trap-door in a pantry opening out of the parlor. It was a strange arrangement, but there were many strange arrangements in the Lamkin house, which was very old, had suffered many alterations, and had been built originally by an eccentric man. Nobody saw Jane Strong enter the parlor and the pantry, raise the trap-door, and descend the main stairs. Jane knew just where the port wine was kept. It was standing by itself, giving out a dusky red glow like a carbuncle, in the southwest corner of the very neat cellar. Jane had her hand on the bottle when she heard a thud, and realized that the trap-door had fallen. She did not feel at all dismayed, but when she had climbed the stairs with her wine-bottle she found herself in difficulty. The trap-door was very heavy, and there was nothing whatever to take hold of on the under side. Jane raised herself as near the top of the stairs as she could and pushed in vain with her hands, then she butted the door with her little head banded with sleek black hair. Jane's neck was very slender, and her head was very small. She could not make the slightest impression upon the door. She descended the stairs and found a clean, empty stone jar in the northwest corner of the cellar. Jane took the lid of the jar, and with the wine-bottle still under her arm, she climbed the stairs again. Then she pounded upon the door viciously with the lid of the jar, until it suddenly broke in halves, and she, taken by surprise, fell down the stairs, with the wine-bottle, which broke. Jane Strong sat on the cellar floor and felt faint. Then came the consciousness of extreme pain in her foot and ankle. "I have spilled all that wine over my dress, I am soaked to my skin with wine, and I've sprained my ankle, maybe I've broken it; and there's Amelia up-stairs the way she is," said Jane Strong aloud, in a curiously cool, reflective voice. She had a judicial turn of mind, and she pulled herself together and considered the whole situation. "I've got to make somebody hear somehow," she said, also aloud. Jane had a very thin, reedy voice which did not carry far. She raised it as loud as she possibly could, and she called by name, each in turn, the members of the family. She thought that possibly Tommy had the most acute hearing, and she called, "Tommy! Tommy!" oftener than any other name. Nobody came. After a while she got incensed. "Might as well give it up," said she. She wore cloth shoes with elastic at the sides, and succeeded in pulling the one on the injured foot off, although it caused her agony. She eyed the swollen foot and ankle sternly. She felt of the ankle, and became almost sure that a bone was broken. She sat still, thinking. It seemed to her that she had never really thought in all her life before. Jane Strong had kept all the commandments from her youth up. She had always been considered a most exemplary woman by other people, and she had acquiesced in their opinion. Now suddenly she differed with other people and with her own previous estimation of herself. She had blamed her sister Amelia Lamkin for her sweet, subtle selfishness, which possibly loved the happiness of other people rather than their own spiritual gain; she had blamed all the Lamkin family for allowing a martyr to live among them, with no effort to save her from the flame of her own self-sacrifice. Now suddenly she blamed herself. She pictured to herself her easy, unhampered life in her nice little apartment, and was convicted of enormous selfishness in her own righteous person. "Lord!" she said, "what on earth have I been thinking about? I knew Amelia was overworked. What was to hinder my coming here at least half the year and taking some of the burden off her? I knew Addie was young, and Annie none too strong, and Josiah fussy, like all men. Why didn't I come? And now here she is flat on her back, and maybe she'll never get up; and here I am with a broken ankle, and can't do a thing. You've made a nice mess of it, Jane Strong! Instead of snooping around to find the sins of other folks, you'd better have looked at home. Good land!" Tears rolled down Jane's cheeks. Then she wiped them away with a hand wet with port wine, and she raised her voice and called again. She sat there vainly calling until the light began to wane; then it was Josiah who heard. Josiah, who had been in the house, gazing at his prostrate wife, and going to his daughters for comfort, and then returned to his miserable promenade on the front walk, heard her through the cellar window. He hurried into the house and met Addie.

"Somebody's calling me, and it sounds like it came from the cellar," he stammered. His nerves were so unstrung that he felt a shiver of superstition.

Addie also felt an answering thrill of horror. "What do you think it is, father?" she whispered, fearfully.

"Don't know. Sounds like a cat calling 'Josiah!' as near as anything else."

The two stood looking at each other.

"Where is Aunt Jane?" asked Addie.

"I don't know."

"Annie and I have been looking for her, and she doesn't seem to be in the house."

"If she were here she would go down cellar and see what it was," said Josiah, with open weakness.

Addie straightened herself. "Nonsense, father! We will go together," said she.

When they had opened the trap-door in the parlor pantry, and peered down into the gloom, and heard the faint voice from below, Addie gave a cry and hurried down the stairs.

"Goodness, Aunt Jane!" said she, "is that you?"

"Yes, it's me," groaned Jane. Then she began to weep. "Oh, Lord, it's a judgment on me!" said she.

"Are you hurt? How did you come down here?"

"Fell down. Oh, Lord, it's a judgment on me!"

"What did you come here for? How came the trap-door shut?"

"It fell down. I came for that bottle of port wine for your poor mother. It broke when I fell. I was trying to knock on the trap-door with the lid of that jar, and I fell. I'm all wine from head to foot."

"Are you hurt?"

"Guess my ankle is broken. It pains me something dreadful, but I don't care. It's a judgment on me! I've been terrible selfish about your mother. It's a judgment on me!"

"Seems to me there's judgments on all of us," said Addie, rather sharply, although there was pity in her voice as she stooped over her aunt, but she was wondering what could be done, with her mother so ill and her aunt crippled.

Josiah stood over his sister-in-law, a helpless bulk of a man, drooping in every muscle before this new calamity.

"Can't you get up, Jane?" he inquired, quaveringly.

"For the land's sake, Josiah Lamkin, do you suppose I'd sit here catching my death of cold on this cellar floor if I could get up?" responded Jane.

"Father, you had better run as fast as you can and get Doctor Emerson. He said he would come again to see mother, but he may not until after his office hour," said Addie. "I'll get some pillows and a shawl, and Hannah can make some hot tea. Then I think you and Doctor Emerson can get her up-stairs. Hannah and I will have everything ready in her room."

Josiah, for the second time that day, raced for the doctor. Annie came and sat on the cellar stairs, while poor Jane drank her tea, and wept softly at this disaster.

Jane gulped down the tea in a sort of fury. "I don't deserve this tea," said she, "and I wouldn't touch it, but I've got to make trouble enough as it is without getting pneumonia. I don't know whether it is as dangerous to set soaked through with wine as it is with water, but I'm wet to the skin, any-how, and all of a shake. How is she?"

"She just lies there, and she looks like death," moaned Annie.

"We've all been killing her, and now she's *killed*, I guess," said Jane.

"We didn't realize," said Annie. "If only I had been stronger!"

"For the Lord's sake, don't talk any more about being strong," said Jane. "You'd better hustle round and *get* strong. You've been as strong as your mother right along, and she has never said a word."

"I know it," Annie said. She bent over, and her whole slender body shook with sobs.

"For the land's sake," said Jane, "stop crying! You don't want to make yourself sick and have another to take care of. There's enough as it is. If Harry comes home and finds you've been crying, there'll be an awful to-do. He acts like a pox fool about you, and always did. I believe he's put it into your head about not being strong, anyhow. He's seen your mother getting up and getting his early breakfast for him, and he hasn't thought it was anything."

"I'm going to get Harry's breakfast now."

"You'd better. If a woman has married a man who has to gulp his break-fast and race for an early train, it's her place to get it for him, and not her poor old mother's."

"I am going to," said Annie. Then she wept again.

Meanwhile, Amelia Lamkin was lying in her peaceful bed up-stairs in a very trance of happiness. She was quite conscious. She had not a pain. She realized an enormous weakness and sheer inability to move, but along with it came the blessed sense of release from hard duties. Almost for the first time in her life Amelia Lamkin's conscience did not sting her because she was not up and doing for others. She knew that it was impossible. She felt like one who has received absolution. The weight of her life had slipped from her shoulders. She regarded Tommy's pale, disturbed face, but even that did not trouble her, so sunken was she in the peace of weakness and sweet irresponsibility. She made one effort to speak to him, to comfort him; then she gave it up, and lay smiling the ghost of a smile. It did not seem to her that he could be really distressed when she was not suffering and was relieved of the weight of existence under which she had staggered so long. The faces of the other members of her family came before her mental vi-sion, and she beheld them with immense love and no anxiety. The sense of being herself so entirely in the arms of Providence, of being undriven by any lash of duty, filled her with peace concerning them. She was beatifically happy, while the others were bemoaning her condition, and while Jane was being attended to in another room for her badly sprained ankle, which would disable her for weeks, perhaps for life. They worried lest Amelia should hear some noise which would awaken her suspicion, lest she should ask for her sister, and be alarmed at her absence, but they had no occasion for worry. Amelia, for the time being, was past alarm. She missed nobody. She wanted nothing except to lie there in her clean white bed and feel that she need not move. The days went on, and her condition did not change.

She lay still day after day, opening her mouth obediently for the spoonfuls of sustenance which were given her, half dozing, half waking, and wholly happy. All her life she had done what she could, and all her life she had been anxious lest she should not do what she could. Now that she knew that she could do no more there came upon her a perfect peace. She did not know that Jane was confined to her bed with her injured foot. She did not know that Addie had turned a cold shoulder to Arthur Henderson, and that he was already engaged to Eliza Loomis. She did not know of the harrowing anxiety concerning her. She knew naught but her conviction that nothing was required of her except to lie still, that other people required nothing except that, that God required nothing except that. Addie always wore a cheerful face when with her mother. Indeed, the readiness with which Arthur Henderson had given her up had caused her pride to act as a tonic, and her eyes had been opened. She knew that she had never cared for a man who could relinquish her without more effort, and whose loss had caused her no more pain. At first she thought that her love and anxiety for her mother had made her callous, but after a little she knew. She even laughed at herself because she had once thought it possible for her to marry Arthur Henderson. She could not yet laugh at the prospect of the life of self-immolation which she ordered for herself since the day her mother had been taken ill, but she was schooling herself to contemplate it cheerfully, although the doctor, with his daily visits to her mother, was now making it hard. Addie began to realize that this man, had she allowed herself to think of him, might have been more difficult to relinquish than the other. After a while she saw him as little as possible, and received his directions through Annie. Addie and Annie had their days full. They were glad when Tommy's spring vacation came. Tommy was of much assistance, and he developed a curious aptitude for making Hannah work. "Now, Hannah, if you are any girl at all, if you ever mean to get married yourself and not have your fellow light out the first week, it's time for you to brace up and hustle," said Tommy; and the next morning Hannah achieved surprising biscuits and well-cooked eggs. Addie ate her eggs cooked any way now, and so did Annie, and Josiah Lamkin never said a word if his steak were not quite as rare as usual, and Johnny ate his rice half-cooked, and survived.

Amelia's window-shades were up all day, for the doctor said she should have all the light and sun possible; and as spring advanced she could see, with those patient eyes which apparently saw nothing, the blue sky crossed with tree branches deepening in color before they burst into leaf and flower. Amelia saw not only those branches, but beyond them, as though they were transparent, other branches, but those other branches grew on the trees of God, and were full of wonderful blooms; and beyond the trees she saw the far-away slope of mountains, and through them in turn the curves of beauty of the Delectable Hills. When Amelia closed her eyes, the picture of those trees beyond trees, those mountains beyond mountains, was still with her, and she saw also heavenly landscapes, rich green meadows, and pearly floods, and gardens of lilies, and her vision, which had been content for years with only the dear simple beauties of her little village, was fed to her soul's delight and surfeit. But she was too weak to speak more than a word at a time, and she scarcely seemed to know one of her dear ones. Poor Amelia Lamkin was so tired out in their service that she had gone almost out of their reach for her rest.

At last came a warm day during the first of May, when people said about the village that Mrs. Amelia Lamkin was very low indeed. The air was very soft and full of sweet languor, and those partly opened eyes of Amelia's saw blossoms through blossoms on the tree branches. In the afternoon Doctor Emerson came, and Addie did not shun him. Her mind was too full of her mother for a thought of any human soul beside. She and the young man stood in Amelia's room over the prostrate little figure, and the doctor took up the slender hand and felt for the pulse in the blue-veined wrist. Then he went over by the window, and stood there with Addie, and Amelia's eyes, which had been closed, opened slowly, and she saw the blooming boughs of the trees of heaven through *them* also. Addie was weeping softly, but her mother did not know it, at first, in her rapt contemplation. She did not see Doctor Emerson put an arm around the girl's waist, she did not hear what he said to her but suddenly she *did* hear what the girl said. She heard it more clearly than anything since she had been taken ill. "I can't think of such things with mother lying there the way she is," Addie said, in a whisper. "I wonder at you."

"She can't hear a word; she does not know," said the young man; and Amelia, listening, was surprised to learn how little a physician really knows himself, when she was hearing and understanding every word, and presently seeing. "I would not speak now," Doctor Emerson continued. "I know it must seem untimely to you, but you have been through so much all these weeks, and it is possible that more still is before you soon, and I feel that if you can consent to lean upon me as one who loves you more than anybody else in the world, I may take it all easier. You know I love you, dear."

"You can't love me. I have been an unworthy daughter," Addie sobbed.

"An unworthy daughter? I have never seen such devotion."

"The devotion came too late," Addie replied, bitterly. "If mother had had a little more devotion years ago, she would be up and about now. There is no use talking, Doctor Emerson; you don't know me as I know myself or you wouldn't once think of me; but, anyway, it is out of the question."

"Why?"

"Because," said Addie, firmly, "I have resolved never to marry, never to allow any other love or interest to come between me and my own family. If mother—" Addie could not finish the sentence. She went on, with a word omitted: "I must make all the restitution to her in my power by devoting my whole life to her dear ones, to Tommy and the baby and father. Annie is delicate, although now she tries to think she isn't, and is doing so much, and Aunt Jane will never be able to walk as well as before she sprained her ankle falling down those cellar stairs. You know that."

Amelia heard. It was the first she had known of Jane's accident.

"She is getting on very well," Doctor Emerson said, rather evasively.

"Yes, but she is lame. That is the reason she won't come in here, though I have told her poor mother wouldn't notice. Aunt Jane has said that if it were not for her lameness she would come here and keep house, but she is a woman older than mother, and she *is* lame. There is nobody except myself to keep up the home here, and any other arrangement is out of the question."

"We could live here, dear," said the young man, and his voice sounded young and pleasing and pitiful. Amelia herself loved him as he spoke. But Addie turned upon him with a sort of fierceness.

"Don't talk to me any more," she said. "Haven't you eyes? Don't you see

I can't bear it? We *could* live here, but you—and maybe others—would come between me and my sacred trust. It can't be, Edward. If mother had lived—" (she spoke of her mother as already dead). "Of course with Aunt Jane—I think she will live here now, anyway, and she *can* do a good deal—and with Annie, they could have got along, and I don't say I would not have. Of course it must cost me something to give up the sort of life a girl naturally expects. Don't talk to me any more."

Then Amelia sat up in bed. Her eyes were opened wide; they had seen her last of heavenly visions until the time when they should close forever. In a flash she saw how selfish it was for her, this patient, loving woman, who had thought of others all her life, to be happy in giving up her life. She realized, too, what she had never felt when in the midst of them, the torture and the fires of martyrdom in which her life had been spent. Now that the unselfishness of others had quenched those fires, she knew what had been, and saw how fair the world might yet be for her. She reached back her loving, longing, willing hands to her loved ones of earth and her earthly home. Amelia spoke in quite a clear, strong voice. Addie turned with a great start, and screamed, "Mother!" and Doctor Emerson was by her side in an instant. Amelia looked at them and smiled the smile of a happy, awakening infant.

"I am better," said she; "I am going to get well now. I have lain here long enough."

The Balking of Christopher

1912

The spring was early that year. It was only the last of March, but the trees were filmed with green and paling with promise of bloom; the front yards were showing new grass pricking through the old. It was high time to plow the south field and the garden, but Christopher sat in his rocking-chair beside the kitchen window and gazed out, and did absolutely nothing about it.

Myrtle Dodd, Christopher's wife, washed the breakfast dishes, and later kneaded the bread, all the time glancing furtively at her husband. She had a most old-fashioned deference with regard to Christopher. She was always a little afraid of him. Sometimes Christopher's mother, Mrs. Cyrus Dodd, and his sister Abby, who had never married, reproached her for this attitude of mind. "You are entirely too much cowed down by Christopher," Mrs. Dodd said.

"I would never be under the thumb of any man," Abby said.

"Have you ever seen Christopher in one of his spells?" Myrtle would ask.

Then Mrs. Cyrus Dodd and Abby would look at each other. "It is all your fault, mother," Abby would say. "You really ought not to have allowed your son to have his own head so much."

"You know perfectly well, Abby, what I had to contend against," replied Mrs. Dodd, and Abby became speechless. Cyrus Dodd, now deceased some twenty years, had never during his whole life yielded to anything but birth and death. Before those two primary facts even his terrible will was powerless. He had come into the world without his consent being obtained; he had passed in like manner from it. But during his life he had ruled, a petty monarch, but a most thorough one. He had spoiled Christopher, and his wife, although a woman of high spirit, knew of no appealing.

"I could never go against your father, you know that," said Mrs. Dodd, following up her advantage.

"Then," said Abby, "you ought to have warned poor Myrtle. It was a shame to let her marry a man as spoiled as Christopher."

"I would have married him, anyway," declared Myrtle with sudden defiance; and her mother-in-law regarded her approvingly.

"There are worse men than Christopher, and Myrtle knows it," said she.

"Yes, I do, mother," agreed Myrtle. "Christopher hasn't one bad habit."

"I don't know what you call a bad habit," retorted Abby. "I call having your own way in spite of the world, the flesh, and the devil rather a bad habit. Christopher tramples on everything in his path, and he always has. He tramples on poor Myrtle."

At that Myrtle laughed. "I don't think I look trampled on," said she; and she certainly did not. Pink and white and plump was Myrtle, although she had, to a discerning eye, an expression which denoted extreme nervousness.

This morning of spring, when her husband sat doing nothing, she wore this nervous expression. Her blue eyes looked dark and keen; her forehead was wrinkled; her rosy mouth was set. Myrtle and Christopher were not young people; they were a little past middle age, still far from old in look or ability.

Myrtle had kneaded the bread to rise for the last time before it was put into the oven, and had put on the meat to boil for dinner, before she dared address that silent figure which had about it something tragic. Then she spoke in a small voice. "Christopher," said she.

Christopher made no reply.

"It is a good morning to plow, ain't it?" said Myrtle.

Christopher was silent.

"Jim Mason got over real early; I suppose he thought you'd want to get at the south field. He's been sitting there at the barn door for 'most two hours."

Then Christopher rose. Myrtle's anxious face lightened. But to her wonder her husband went into the front entry and got his best hat. "He ain't going to wear his best hat to plow," thought Myrtle. For an awful moment it occurred to her that something had suddenly gone wrong with her husband's mind. Christoper brushed the hat carefully, adjusted it at the little looking-glass in the kitchen, and went out.

"Be you going to plow the south field?" Myrtle said, faintly.

"No, I ain't."

"Will you be back to dinner?"

"I don't know—you needn't worry if I'm not." Suddenly Christopher did an unusual thing for him. He and Myrtle had lived together for years, and outward manifestations of affection were rare between them. He put his arm around her and kissed her.

After he had gone, Myrtle watched him out of sight down the road; then she sat down and wept. Jim Mason came slouching around from his station at the barn door. He surveyed Myrtle uneasily.

"Mr. Dodd sick?" said he at length.

"Not that I know of," said Myrtle, in a weak quaver. She rose and, keeping her tear-stained face aloof, lifted the lid off the kettle on the stove.

"D'ye know am he going to plow to-day?"

"He said he wasn't."

Jim grunted, shifted his quid, and slouched out of the yard.

Meantime Christopher Dodd went straight down the road to the minister's, the Rev. Stephen Wheaton. When he came to the south field, which he was neglecting, he glanced at it turning emerald upon the gentle slopes. He set his face harder. Christopher Dodd's face was in any case hard-set. Now it was tragic, to be pitied, but warily, lest it turn fiercely upon the one who pitied. Christopher was a handsome man, and his face had an almost classic turn of feature. His forehead was noble; his eyes full of keen light. He was only a farmer, but in spite of his rude clothing he had the face of a man who followed one of the professions. He was in sore trouble of spirit, and he was going to consult the minister and ask him for advice. Christopher had never done this before. He had a sort of incredulity now that he was about to do it. He had always associated that sort of thing with womankind, and not with men like himself. And, moreover, Stephen Wheaton was a younger man than himself. He was unmarried, and had only been settled in the village for about a year. "He can't think I'm coming to set my cap at him, anyway," Christopher reflected, with a sort of grim humor, as he drew near the parsonage. The minister was haunted by marriageable ladies of the village.

"Guess you are glad to see a man coming, instead of a woman who has doubts about some doctrine," was the first thing Christopher said to the minister when he had been admitted to his study. The study was a small room, lined with books, and only one picture hung over the fireplace, the portrait of the minister's mother—Stephen was so like her that a question concerning it was futile.

Stephen colored a little angrily at Christopher's remark—he was a hot-tempered man, although a clergyman; then he asked him to be seated.

Christopher sat down opposite the minister. "I oughtn't to have spoken so," he apologized, "but what I am doing ain't like me."

"That's all right," said Stephen. He was a short, athletic man, with an extraordinary width of shoulders and a strong-featured and ugly face, still indicative of goodness and a strange power of sympathy. Three little mongrel dogs were sprawled about the study. One, small and alert, came and rested his head on Christopher's knee. Animals all liked him. Christopher mechanically patted him. Patting an appealing animal was as unconscious with the man as drawing his breath. But he did not even look at the little dog while he stroked it after the fashion which pleased it best. He kept his large, keen, melancholy eyes fixed upon the minister; at length he spoke. He did not speak with as much eagerness as he did with force, bringing the whole power of his soul into his words, which were the words of a man in rebellion against the greatest odds on earth and in all creation—the odds of fate itself.

"I have come to say a good deal, Mr. Wheaton," he began.

"Then say it, Mr. Dodd," replied Stephen, without a smile.

Christopher spoke. "I am going back to the very beginning of things," said he, "and maybe you will think it blasphemy, but I don't mean it for that. I mean it for the truth, and the truth which is too much for my comprehension."

"I have heard men swear when it did not seem blasphemy to me," said Stephen.

"Thank the Lord, you ain't so deep in your rut you can't see the stars!" said Christopher. "But I guess you see them in a pretty black sky sometimes. In the beginning, why did I have to come into the world without any choice?"

"You must not ask a question of me which can only be answered by the Lord," said Stephen.

"I am asking the Lord," said Christopher, with his sad, forceful voice. "I am asking the Lord, and I ask why?"

"You have no right to expect your question to be answered in your time," said Stephen.

"But here am I," said Christopher, "and I was a question to the Lord from the first, and fifty years and more I have been on the earth."

"Fifty years and more are nothing for the answer to such a question," said Stephen.

Christopher looked at him with mournful dissent; there was no anger about him. "There was time before time," said he, "before the fifty years and more began. I don't mean to blaspheme, Mr. Wheaton, but it is the truth. I came into the world whether I would or not; I was forced, and then I was told I was a free agent. I am no free agent. For fifty years and more I have thought about it, and I have found out that, at least. I am a slave—a slave of life."

"For that matter," said Stephen, looking curiously at him, "so am I. So are we all."

"That makes it worse," agreed Christopher—"a whole world of slaves. I know I ain't talking in exactly what you might call an orthodox strain. I have got to a point when it seems to me I shall go mad if I don't talk to somebody. I know there is that awful why, and you can't answer it; and no man living can. I'm willing to admit that sometime, in another world, that why will get an answer, but meantime it's an awful thing to live in this world without it if a man has had the kind of life I have. My life has been harder for me than a harder life might be for another man who was different. That much I know. There is one thing I've got to be thankful for. I haven't been the means of sending any more slaves into this world. I am glad my wife and I haven't any children to ask 'why?'

"Now, I've begun at the beginning; I'm going on. I have never had what men call luck. My folks were poor; father and mother were good, hard-working people, but they had nothing but trouble, sickness, and death, and losses by fire and flood. We lived near the river, and one spring our house went, and every stick we owned, and much as ever we all got out alive. Then lightning struck father's new house, and the insurance company had failed, and we never got a dollar of insurance. Then my oldest brother died, just when he was getting started in business, and his widow and two little children came on father to support. Then father got rheumatism, and was all twisted, and wasn't good for much afterward; and my sister Sarah, who had been expecting to get married, had to give it up and take in sewing and stay at home and take care of the rest. There was father and George's widow—she was never good for much at work—and mother and Abby. She was my youngest sister. As for me, I had a liking for books and wanted to get an education; might just as well have wanted to get a seat on a throne. I went to work in the grist-mill of the place where we used to live when I was only a boy. Then, before I was twenty, I saw that Sarah wasn't going to hold out. She had grieved a good deal, poor thing, and worked too hard, so we sold out and came here and bought my farm, with the mortgage hitching it, and I went to work for dear life. Then Sarah died, and then father. Along about then there was a girl I wanted to marry, but, Lord, how could I even ask her? My farm started in as a failure, and it has kept it up ever since. When there wasn't a drought there was so much rain everything mildewed; there was a hail-storm that cut everything to pieces, and there was the caterpillar year. I just managed to pay the interest on the mortgage; as for paying the principal, I might as well have tried to pay the national debt.

"Well, to go back to that girl. She is married and don't live here, and you ain't like ever to see her, but she was a beauty and something more. I don't suppose she ever looked twice at me, but losing what you've never had sometimes is worse than losing everything you've got. When she got married I guess I knew a little about what the martyrs went through.

"Just after that George's widow got married again and went away to live. It took a burden off the rest of us, but I had got attached to the children. The little girl, Ellen, seemed 'most like my own. Then poor Myrtle came here to live. She did dressmaking and boarded with our folks, and I begun to see that she was one of the nervous sort of women who are pretty bad off alone in the world, and I told her about the other girl, and she said she didn't mind, and we got married. By that time mother's brother John— he had never got married—died and left her a little money, so she and my sister Abby could screw along. They bought the little house they live in and left the farm, for Abby was always hard to get along with, though she is a good woman. Mother, though she is a smart woman, is one of the sort who don't feel called upon to interfere much with men-folks. I guess she didn't interfere any too much for my good, or father's, either. Father was a set man. I guess if mother had been a little harsh with me I might not have asked that awful 'why?' I guess I might have taken my bitter pills and held my tongue, but I won't blame myself on poor mother.

"Myrtle and I get on well enough. She seems contented—she has never said a word to make me think she wasn't. She isn't one of the kind of women who want much besides decent treatment and a home. Myrtle is a good woman. I am sorry for her that she got married to me, for she deserved somebody who could make her a better husband. All the time, every waking minute, I've been growing more and more rebellious.

"You see, Mr. Wheaton, never in this world have I had what I wanted, and more than wanted—needed, and needed far more than happiness. I have never been able to think of work as anything but a way to get money, and it wasn't right, not for a man like me, with the feelings I was born with. And everything has gone wrong even about the work for the money. I have been hampered and hindered, I don't know whether by Providence or the Evil One. I have saved just six hundred and forty dollars, and I have only paid the interest on the mortgage. I knew I ought to have a little ahead in case Myrtle or I got sick, so I haven't tried to pay the mortgage, but put a few dollars at a time in the savings-bank, which will come in handy now."

The minister regarded him uneasily. "What," he asked, "do you mean to do?"

"I mean," replied Christopher, "to stop trying to do what I am hindered in doing, and do just once in my life what I want to do. Myrtle asked me this morning if I wasn't going to plow the south field. Well, I ain't going to plow the south field. I ain't going to make a garden. I ain't going to try for hay in the ten-acre lot. I have stopped. I have worked for nothing except just enough to keep soul and body together. I have had bad luck. But that isn't the real reason why I have stopped. Look at here, Mr. Wheaton, spring is coming. I have never in my life had a chance at the spring nor the summer. This year I'm going to have the spring and the summer, and the fall, too, if I want it. My apples may fall and rot if they want to. I am going to get as much good of the season as they do."

"What are you going to do?" asked Stephen.

"Well, I will tell you. I ain't a man to make mystery if I am doing right, and I think I am. You know, I've got a little shack up on Silver Mountain in the little sugar-orchard I own there; never got enough sugar to say so, but I put up the shack one year when I was fool enough to think I might get something. Well, I'm going up there, and I'm going to live there awhile, and I'm going to sense the things I have had to hustle by for the sake of a few dollars and cents."

"But what will your wife do?"

"She can have the money I've saved, all except enough to buy me a few provisions. I sha'n't need much. I want a little corn meal, and I will have a few chickens, and there is a barrel of winter apples left over that she can't use, and a few potatoes. There is a spring right near the shack, and there are trout-pools, and by and by there will be berries, and there's plenty of fire-wood, and there's an old bed and a stove and a few things in the shack. Now, I'm going to the store and buy what I want, and I'm going to fix it so Myrtle can draw the money when she wants it, and then I am going to the shack, and"—Christopher's voice took on a solemn tone—"I will tell you in just a few words the gist of what I am going for. I have never in my life had enough of the bread of life to keep my soul nourished. I have tried to do my duties, but I believe sometimes duties act on the soul like weeds on a flower. They crowd it out. I am going up on Silver Mountain to get once, on this earth, my fill of the bread of life."

Stephen Wheaton gasped. "But your wife, she will be alone, she will worry."

"I want you to go and tell her," said Christopher, "and I've got my bank-book here; I'm going to write some checks that she can get cashed when she needs money. I want you to tell her. Myrtle won't make a fuss. She ain't the kind. Maybe she will be a little lonely, but if she is, she can go and visit somewhere." Christopher rose. "Can you let me have a pen and ink?" said he, "and I will write those checks. You can tell Myrtle how to use them. She won't know how."

Stephen Wheaton, an hour later, sat in his study, the checks in his hand, striving to rally his courage. Christopher had gone; he had seen him from his window, laden with parcels, starting upon the ascent of Silver Mountain. Christopher had made out many checks for small amounts, and Stephen held the sheaf in his hand, and gradually his courage to arise and go and tell Christopher's wife gained strength. At last he went.

Myrtle was looking out of the window, and she came quickly to the door. She looked at him, her round, pretty face gone pale, her plump hands twitching at her apron.

"What is it?" said she.

"Nothing to be alarmed about," replied Stephen.

Then the two entered the house. Stephen found his task unexpectedly easy. Myrtle Dodd was an unusual woman in a usual place.

"It is all right for my husband to do as he pleases," she said with an odd dignity, as if she were defending him.

"Mr. Dodd is a strange man. He ought to have been educated and led a different life," Stephen said, lamely, for he reflected that the words might be hard for the woman to hear, since she seemed obviously quite fitted to her life, and her life to her.

But Myrtle did not take it hardly, seemingly rather with pride. "Yes," said she, "Christopher ought to have gone to college. He had the head for it. Instead of that he has just stayed round here and dogged round the farm, and everything has gone wrong lately. He hasn't had any luck even with that." Then poor Myrtle Dodd said an unexpectedly wise thing. "But maybe," said Myrtle, "his bad luck may turn out the best thing for him in the end."

Stephen was silent. Then he began explaining about the checks.

"I sha'n't use any more of his savings than I can help," said Myrtle, and for the first time her voice quavered. "He must have some clothes up there," said she. "There ain't bed-coverings, and it is cold nights, late as it is in the spring. I wonder how I can get the bedclothes and other things to him. I can't drive, myself, and I don't like to hire anybody; aside from its being an expense, it would make talk. Mother Dodd and Abby won't make talk outside the family, but I suppose it will have to be known."

"Mr. Dodd didn't want any mystery made over it," Stephen Wheaton said.

"There ain't going to be any mystery. Christopher has got a right to live awhile on Silver Mountain if he wants to," returned Myrtle with her odd, defiant air.

"But I will take the things up there to him, if you will let me have a horse and wagon," said Stephen.

"I will, and be glad. When will you go?"

"To-morrow."

"I'll have them ready," said Myrtle.

After the minister had gone she went into her own bedroom and cried a little and made the moan of a loving woman sadly bewildered by the ways of man, but loyal as a soldier. Then she dried her tears and began to pack a load for the wagon.

The next morning early, before the dew was off the young grass, Stephen Wheaton started with the wagon-load, driving the great gray farm-horse up the side of Silver Mountain. The road was fairly good, making many winds in order to avoid steep ascents, and Stephen drove slowly. The gray farm-horse was sagacious. He knew that an unaccustomed hand held the lines; he knew that of a right he should be treading the plowshares instead of climbing a mountain on a beautiful spring morning.

But as for the man driving, his face was radiant, his eyes of young manhood lit with the light of the morning. He had not owned it, but he himself had sometimes chafed under the dull necessity of his life, but here was excitement, here was exhilaration. He drew the sweet air into his lungs, and the deeper meaning of the spring morning into his soul. Christopher Dodd interested him to the point of enthusiasm. Not even the uneasy consideration of the lonely, mystified woman in Dodd's deserted home could deprive him of admiration for the man's flight into the spiritual open. He felt that these rights of the man were of the highest, and that other rights, even human and pitiful ones, should give them the right of way.

It was not a long drive. When he reached the shack—merely a one-roomed hut, with a stove-pipe chimney, two windows, and a door—Christopher stood at the entrance and seemed to illuminate it. Stephen for a minute doubted his identity. Christopher had lost middle age in a day's time. He had the look of a triumphant youth. Blue smoke was curling from the chimney. Stephen smelled bacon frying, and coffee.

Christopher greeted him with the joyousness of a child. "Lord!" said he, "did Myrtle send you up with all those things? Well, she is a good woman. Guess I would have been cold last night if I hadn't been so happy. How is Myrtle?"

"She seemed to take it very sensibly when I told her."

Christopher nodded happily and lovingly. "She would. She can understand not understanding, and that is more than most women can. It was mighty good of you to bring the things. You are in time for breakfast. Lord! Mr. Wheaton, smell the trees, and there are blooms hidden somewhere that smell sweet. Think of having the common food of man sweetened this way! First time I fully sensed I was something more than just a man. Lord, I am paid already. It won't be so very long before I get my fill, at this rate, and then I can go back. To think I needn't plow to-day! To think all I have to do is to have the spring! See the light under those trees!"

Christopher spoke like a man in ecstasy. He tied the gray horse to a tree and brought a pail of water for him from the spring near by.

Then he said to Stephen: "Come right in. The bacon's done, and the coffee and the corn-cake and the eggs won't take a minute."

The two men entered the shack. There was nothing there except the little cooking-stove, a few kitchen utensils hung on pegs on the walls, an old table with a few dishes, two chairs, and a lounge over which was spread an ancient buffalo-skin.

Stephen sat down, and Christopher fried the eggs. Then he bade the minister draw up, and the two men breakfasted.

"Ain't it great, Mr. Wheaton?" said Christopher.

"You are a famous cook, Mr. Dodd," laughed Stephen. He was thoroughly enjoying himself, and the breakfast was excellent.

"It ain't that," declared Christopher in his exalted voice. "It ain't that, young man. It's because the food is blessed."

Stephen stayed all day on Silver Mountain. He and Christopher went fishing, and had fried trout for dinner. He took some of the trout home to Myrtle.

Myrtle received them with a sort of state which defied the imputation of sadness. "Did he seem comfortable?" she asked.

"Comfortable, Mrs. Dodd? I believe it will mean a new lease of life to your husband. He is an uncommon man."

"Yes, Christopher is uncommon; he always was," assented Myrtle.

"You have everything you want? You were not timid last night alone?" asked the minister.

"Yes, I was timid. I heard queer noises," said Myrtle, "but I sha'n't be alone any more. Christopher's niece wrote me she was coming to make a visit. She has been teaching school, and she lost her school. I rather guess Ellen is as uncommon for a girl as Christopher is for a man. Anyway, she's lost her school, and her brother's married, and she don't want to go there. Besides, they live in Boston, and Ellen, she says she can't bear the city in spring and summer. She wrote she'd saved a little, and she'd pay her board, but I sha'n't touch a dollar of her little savings, and neither would Christopher want me to. He's always thought a sight of Ellen, though he's never seen much of her. As for me, I was so glad when her letter came I didn't know what to do. Christopher will be glad. I suppose you'll be going up there to see him off and on." Myrtle spoke a bit wistfully, and Stephen did not tell her he had been urged to come often.

"Yes, off and on," he replied.

"If you will just let me know when you are going, I will see that you have something to take to him—some bread and pies."

"He has some chickens there," said Stephen.

"Has he got a coop for them?"

"Yes, he had one rigged up. He will have plenty of eggs, and he carried up bacon and corn meal and tea and coffee."

"I am glad of that," said Myrtle. She spoke with a quiet dignity, but her face never lost its expression of bewilderment and resignation.

The next week Stephen Wheaton carried Myrtle's bread and pies to Christopher on his mountainside. He drove Christopher's gray horse harnessed in his old buggy, and realized that he himself was getting much pleasure out of the other man's idiosyncrasy. The morning was beautiful, and Stephen carried in his mind a peculiar new beauty, besides. Ellen, Christopher's niece, had arrived the night before, and, early as it was, she had been astir when he reached the Dodd house. She had opened the door for him, and she was a goodly sight: a tall girl, shaped like a boy, with a fearless face of great beauty crowned with compact gold braids and lit by unswerving blue eyes. Ellen had a square, determined chin and a brow of high resolve.

"Good morning," said she, and as she spoke she evidently rated Stephen and approved, for she smiled genially. "I am Mr. Dodd's niece," said she. "You are the minister?"

"Yes."

"And you have come for the things aunt is to send him?"

"Yes."

"Aunt said you were to drive uncle's horse and take the buggy," said Ellen. "It is very kind of you. While you are harnessing, aunt and I will pack the basket."

Stephen, harnessing the gray horse, had a sense of shock; whether pleasant or otherwise, he could not determine. He had never seen a girl in the least like Ellen. Girls had never impressed him. She did.

When he drove around to the kitchen door she and Myrtle were both there, and he drank a cup of coffee before starting, and Myrtle introduced him. "Only think, Mr. Wheaton," said she, "Ellen says she knows a great deal about farming, and we are going to hire Jim Mason and go right ahead." Myrtle looked adoringly at Ellen.

Stephen spoke eagerly. "Don't hire anybody," he said. "I used to work on a farm to pay my way through college. I need the exercise. Let me help."

"You may do that," said Ellen, "on shares. Neither aunt nor I can think of letting you work without any recompense."

"Well, we will settle that," Stephen replied. When he drove away, his usually calm mind was in a tumult.

"Your niece has come," he told Christopher, when the two men were breakfasting together on Silver Mountain.

"I am glad of that," said Christopher. "All that troubled me about being here was that Myrtle might wake up in the night and hear noises."

Christopher had grown even more radiant. He was effulgent with pure happiness.

"You aren't going to tap your sugar-maples?" said Stephen, looking up at the great symmetrical efflorescence of rose and green which towered about them.

Christopher laughed. "No, bless 'em," said he, "the trees shall keep their sugar this season. This week is the first time I've had a chance to get acquainted with them and sort of enter into their feelings. Good Lord! I've seen how I can love those trees, Mr. Wheaton! See the pink on their young leaves! They know more than you and I. They know how to grow young every spring."

Stephen did not tell Christopher how Ellen and Myrtle were to work the farm with his aid. The two women had bade him not. Christopher seemed to have no care whatever about it. He was simply happy. When Stephen left, he looked at him and said, with the smile of a child, "Do you think I am crazy?"

"Crazy? No," replied Stephen.

"Well, I ain't. I'm just getting fed. I was starving to death. Glad you don't think I'm crazy, because I couldn't help matters by saying I wasn't. Myrtle don't think I am, I know. As for Ellen, I haven't seen her since she was a little girl. I don't believe she can be much like Myrtle; but I guess if she is what she promised to turn out she wouldn't think anybody ought to go just her way to have it the right way."

"I rather think she is like that, although I saw her for the first time this morning," said Stephen.

"I begin to feel that I may not need to stay here much longer," Christopher called after him. "I begin to feel that I am getting what I came for so fast that I can go back pretty soon."

But it was the last day of July before he came. He chose the cool of the evening after a burning day, and descended the mountain in the full light of the moon. He had gone up the mountain like an old man; he came down like a young one.

When he came at last in sight of his own home, he paused and stared. Across the grass-land a heavily laden wagon was moving toward his barn. Upon this wagon heaped with hay, full of silver lights from the moon, sat a tall figure all in white, which seemed to shine above all things. Christopher did not see the man on the other side of the wagon leading the horses; he saw only this wonderful white figure. He hurried forward and Myrtle came down the road to meet him. She had been watching for him, as she had watched every night.

"Who is it on the load of hay?" asked Christopher.

"Ellen," replied Myrtle.

"Oh!" said Christopher. "She looked like an angel of the Lord, come to take up the burden I had dropped while I went to learn of Him."

"Be you feeling pretty well, Christopher?" asked Myrtle. She thought that what her husband had said was odd, but he looked well, and he might have said it simply because he was a man.

Christopher put his arm around Myrtle. "I am better than I ever was in my whole life, Myrtle, and I've got more courage to work now than I had when I was young. I had to go away and get rested, but I've got rested for all my life. We shall get along all right as long as we live."

"Ellen and the minister are going to get married come Christmas," said Myrtle.

"She is lucky. He is a man that can see with the eyes of other people," said Christopher.

It was after the hay had been unloaded and Christopher had been shown the garden full of lusty vegetables, and told of the great crop with no drawback, that he and the minister had a few minutes alone together at the gate.

"I want to tell you, Mr. Wheaton, that I am settled in my mind now. I shall never complain again, no matter what happens. I have found that all the good things and all the bad things that come to a man who tries to do right are just to prove to him that he is on the right path. They are just the flowers and sunbeams, and the rocks and snakes, too, that mark the way. And—I have found out more than that. I have found out the answer to my 'why?'"

"What is it?" asked Stephen, gazing at him curiously from the wonder-height of his own special happiness.

"I have found out that the only way to heaven for the children of men is through the earth," said Christopher.

The Outside of the House

1914

Barr Center almost always excited the amusement of strangers. "Why Barr Center?" they would inquire, and follow up the query, if they were facetious, with another: "The center of what?"

In reality, Barr Center, the little village where lived the Edgewaters, the Ellertons, the Dinsmores, and a few more very good old New England families, was hardly anything but a center, and almost, regarded geographically, the mere pinprick of a center of four villages. As a matter of fact, the apex of a triangle would have been a more accurate description. The village came first on the old turnpike from the city; Barr-by-the-Sea was on the right, three miles away; Leicester, which had formerly been West Barr, was three miles to the left; South Barr was three miles to the south.

There was a popular saying that Barr Center was three miles from everywhere. All four villages had, of course, been originally one, the Precinct of Barr. Leicester had been the first to revolt and establish a separate township and claim a different name. Leicester was the name of the one wealthy old family of the village, which had bestowed its soldiers' monument, its town hall, and its library, and had improved the cemetery and contributed half of the high school.

Barr-by-the-Sea came next, and that had serious and legitimate reasons for individuality. From being a mere summer colony of tents and rude cottages it had grown to be almost a city, frequented by wealthy city folk, who had beautiful residences along the shore. Barr-by-the-Sea was so large and important that it finally made an isosceles triangle of the original Precinct of Barr. All summer long it hummed with gay life, ending in the autumn with a carnival as a grand crescendo. Barr-by-the-Sea was, however, not the center. It boasted no old family, resident all the year round, as did Barr Center.

South Barr was the least important of all. It was simply the petering out of the Barrs. It was a little farming hamlet, which humbly sold butter, fresh eggs, and garden truck to Barr-by-the-Sea for the delectation of the rich folk who dwelt in the hotels and boarding-houses and stately residences on the ocean front.

Barr-by-the-Sea was an exclusive summer resort. Its few permanent inhabitants were proud of it, and none were prouder than old Captain Joe Dickson and his wife, Martha. The Dicksons lived in a tiny house beyond the fashionable limits. They were on the opposite side of the road from the sea. The house stood in a drift of sandy soil, pierced by coarse beach grass like green swords. Captain Joe, however, had reclaimed a little garden from the easily conquered waste, and his beans, his cucumbers, and his tomatoes were flourishing.

In front of the house Martha had two great tubs of hydrangeas, which she colored a ghastly blue with bluing water from her weekly wash. Captain Joe did not approve of the unnatural blue.

"Why didn't ye leave the posies the way the Lord made 'em?" he inquired.

"They have them this way at a lot of the grand places," replied Martha. "The big-bugs color them."

"Ruther guess the big-bugs ain't any bigger than the Lord A'mighty," returned Captain Joe. "I guess if He had thought them posies would look better blue He would have made 'em blue in the fust place."

Captain Joe, having spoken his mind, puffed his pipe amiably over the tops of the blue flowers. He sat on his bit of a porch, tipping back comfortably in his old chair.

Martha did not prolong the discussion. She was not much of a talker. Captain Joe always claimed that a voyage with him around the world in a sailing-vessel had cured her of talking too much in her youth.

"Poor Marthy used to be a regular buzz-saw at the talk," he would say, "but rockin' round the world with such a gale that she couldn't hear her own tongue wag, and bein' scared 'most to death, cured her."

Whether the great, primeval noises of the world had, in fact, subdued the woman to silence, rendering her incapable of much sounding of her own little note all through her life, or not, she was a very still woman. She went silently about her household tasks. When they were done there was much mending while her husband smoked.

Over across the road the littered, wave-marked beach sloped broadly to the sea. There were several boats anchored. One was Captain Joe's, the *Martha Dickson*. He had been out in it fishing that very morning, had had a good catch, and sold well to the customers who flocked on the beach when the fishing-boats came in. The rich people sent their servants with baskets for the fresh fish.

Joe had sold his catch, with the exception of one fine cod, which Martha was making into a savory chowder. Captain Joe sniffed with pleasure the odor of frying onions which were to make the foundation of the good dish. He gazed at the sea, which now and then lapped into view with a foaming crest over the beach. There was no passing, as a rule. The fine road for driving and motoring stopped several yards before Joe's house was reached. He was mildly surprised, therefore, when a runabout with a red cross on the front, with a young man at the wheel and a pretty young girl by his side, came skidding over the sand and stopped.

"Any fresh fish?" inquired the young man, who was Dr. Tom Ellerton. Joe shook his head.

"Know where I can get any?"

"Guess mebbe you can get a cod at the third house from me. He was late gettin' in, and didn't sell the hull. But you'll capsize if you try to go there in that."

Tom eyed the road billowing with sand. "Sit here while I find out," he told Margy, his sister. She nodded.

After Tom had gone, plowing through the sand, Captain Joe rose stiffly. He was not a very old man, but a broken leg had not been set properly, and kept him from his life-work of cruising the high seas.

He limped up to the car. "Pooty hot day," he remarked.

"Very," replied Margy.

"Wish I'd had the fish. Sold all my catch except the cod Marthy's cookin'." Margy sniffed appreciatively. "A chowder?" she inquired.

Joe nodded. "About the only way to cook a cod. Goin' to have yourn cooked that way?"

"It isn't for us," explained Margy. "My brother is trying to find some really fresh fish for an old lady who is ill. My brother is a doctor. He has just been to see her. She wanted fresh fish, and he said he would try to find some. Their servants are all busy because they are closing the house. They are going to sail for Europe to-morrow."

"What house?" inquired Joe, eagerly.

"The very large house on the ocean side of the road, about half a mile back."

"The one with all them yaller flowers in the front yard, and a garden of 'em on the roof, with vines hangin' over?"

Margy nodded. "That sounds like it," said she. "There are two square towers, one on each side, then the flowers and vines are on the balcony between; and there is a roof-garden, too; and there are quantities of beautiful flowers on the grounds. It is a lovely place."

"Know the name of the folks that live there?"

"Willard," replied Margy. She eyed Joe with surprise.

"Lord!" said he. "They goin' away so soon?"

He paid no more attention to Margy, but limped into the house, and the girl heard loud exclamations. Then she saw Tom coming with a fine glistening fish in each hand.

"I have one for us, too," he said as he got into the car. "They are fine fish."

Tom put on power, as he wished not only to deliver the fish to the Willards fresh, but to reach home with his own in good condition, and it was a scorching day. Margy clung to her side of the car as they spun along. After the fish had been left at the grand Willard house, and a beautiful young lady in a pale-blue gown had thanked the young doctor charmingly, and they were on a smooth road, Margy asked Tom why he thought the lame man, of whom he had inquired about the fish, had been so interested in the Willard family.

"Oh, probably he is one of the old residents here. I discovered some time ago that they feel a queer interest in the comings and goings of the summer folk," said Tom. "Their lives are pretty narrow eight months of the year. They have to be interested in something outside themselves. I think lots of them have a feeling that they own a good deal that they only have liberty to look at."

"I can see how a fisherman can feel that he owns the sea," said Margy. "Maybe it is because so many of them are fishermen."

She looked reflective with her deep-set blue eyes. Tom cast a quick glance at her. "Maybe," he said.

Tom was not imaginative. When Margy said things like that he always wondered if she were well. He began to plan a prescription for her as they sped along.

He did not know how intensely Margy had felt that she owned the sea, just from looking at it, when she had sat in the car waiting for him when he was making professional calls, and that her reasoning was quite logical and not unnecessarily imaginative. If she considered that she owned the sea, which is the vast untaxed asset of the world, how much more would the fisherman who got his daily bread from it?

Meantime, the fisherman with whom she had talked was in excited colloquy with his wife in the kitchen and living-room of the little house. The room, though comfortable and clean, was poorly equipped, with the exception of various articles that were at direct odds with all else. There was a cooking-stove, on which the chowder was steaming. There was a kitchen table, set for a meal with the commonest utensils, save that in the center, ready for the chowder, was a bowl of old Japanese pottery which would have adorned a palace. Martha did not think much of this bowl, which Joe had brought home from one of his voyages. She considered the decorations ugly, and used it to save a lovely one from the ten-cent store, decorated with pink rosebuds. Martha could understand pink rosebuds, but she could not fathom dragons and ugly, grinning faces of Oriental fancy.

There was a lounge with a hideous cover, two old chairs worn into hollows of comfort, two kitchen chairs, an old clock, and a superb teakwood table. Martha did not care for that, either. The contortions of the carved wood gave her a vague uneasiness. She kept it covered with an old fringed spread, and used to set her bread to rise on it. On the mantel, besides the clock and three kerosene-lamps, was a beautiful old Satsuma vase, and a pressed glass one, which Martha loved. The glass one was cracked, and she told Joe she did not see why the other vase could not have suffered instead. Joe agreed with her. He did not care much for the treasures which he had brought from foreign ports, except the shells—lovely, pinked-lipped ones that were crowded on the shelf between the other things, and completely filled more shelves which Joe had made expressly to hold them. The shelves were in three tiers, and the shells were mounted on them, catching the light from broken surfaces of rose and pearl and silver. Martha privately considered that the shells involved considerable work. She washed them carefully, and kept them free from dust, but she also admired them.

In front of the outer door was a fine old prayer-rug of dull, exquisite tones. Martha kept it there for Joe to wipe his feet on, because it was so faded, but she had a bright red one in the center of the room. Joe never stepped on that until his shoes were entirely clean. He had made quite sure there was not a speck of dust to injure this brilliant rug before he entered to give Martha the intelligence.

"They are goin' away from Our House to-morrow," said he.

Martha, standing over the chowder, turned, spoon in hand. She waved the spoon as if it were a fan. "Before the carnival?" said she.

Martha was a small, wide-eyed woman with sleek hair. She was not pretty, but had a certain effect of being exactly in place which gave the impression of prettiness to some people.

"They are goin' to sail for Europe," said Joe.

"I suppose for His health," said Martha. Nobody could excel the air of perfect proprietorship with which she uttered the masculine pronoun. The man indicated might have been her own father, or her brother, or her son.

"I guess so," said Joe. "He has looked pooty bad lately when I've seen him."

"I suppose They are goin'?"

"I s'pose so, because they are closin' the house. That young doctor from the Center stopped out here just now, and wanted to know where he could get fresh fish, and I told him I guessed Mac had some left; and whilst he was gone his sister—she was with him—told me they were closin' the house, and Old Lady Willard wanted fresh fish, and they were out huntin' for it, because all the help was busy."

"That means Old Lady Willard's goin', and Him, and his Wife, and the three girls, Grace and Marie and Maud, and the two little boys."

"Yes."

"And they will take the ladies'-maids, and His man. Maybe that pretty young lady that visits there so much will go, too."

"Maybe; and the lady that teaches the little boys will go."

"O Lord, yes! They couldn't get on without her. My! there will be 'most enough to fill the ship."

"About enough to sink my old one I sailed around when you was aboard," said Joe, and laughed.

Martha never laughed. The seriousness of New England was in her very soul. She was happy and good-natured, but she saw nothing whatever to laugh at in all creation. She never had.

"Land, yes!" said she. "You know there wa'n't any room in that little cabin."

"Not more'n enough to hold you and your Bible and sewin'-machine," said Captain Joe. He cast a glance at the old sewing-machine as he spoke, and laughed again. It was perfectly useless because of that long-ago voyage, and the fact always amused him. Martha considered it no laughing matter. The sewing-machine was dear to her, even in its wrecked state. She kept the Bible on it, and a little cup and saucer.

"The chowder's done," said she. "Draw up, Joe."

Joe drew up a chair to the table. "Smells prime," said he.

"Guess it's all right."

"Ef your chowders ever wa'n't all right I'd think the sun was goin' to rise in the west next mornin'," said Joe.

Martha ladled the chowder into the beautiful bowl, then into heavy, chipped plates. The two ate with relish.

"To-morrow's Saturday," said Joe. "That means we can go to Our House come Sunday."

Martha nodded. Her good mouth widened in the semblance of a smile. Her steady eyes gleamed with happy intelligence at her husband.

"It will seem nice," said she. "Land! I'd been thinkin' we might have to wait till 'way into October, the way we did last year, and now it's only the first of August."

"I'm feelin' jest as set up as you be about it," said Joe.

That night all the family from the great house where Tom Ellerton had called went by train to Boston. They were to stay in the city overnight to be ready for the steamer. Not one of the numerous company even noticed Captain Joe Dickson and his wife Martha, who were at the station watching them closely, hearing everything that was said, noting all details—the baggage, the host of servants.

All the servants were to be out of the house next day, the Dicksons heard Her tell another lady who inquired. "Only a caretaker, the same old colored man we always employ," stated Mrs. Richard Willard, tall, elegant, a bit weary of manner. "The servants will finish closing the house to-morrow, then some of them have vacations, and the rest will be in our Boston house. We take only our maids and Mr. Willard's man up to-night. We shall not go to the city house at all ourselves. It will be much more sensible to stay at the hotel."

"Of course," said the lady. Then she said something about an unexpected start, and so early in the season, and Mrs. Willard replied that to her nothing was ever unexpected. That had ceased with her youth, and Mr. Willard was not quite well, and there were seasons all over creation. She said that with a pleasant smile—weary, however.

Martha eyed her keenly when she and Joe, after the train with all the Willards on board had pulled out, were walking home.

"She said that She didn't look none too strong, and she guessed it was a good thing She was going." Martha said that as if Mrs. Richard Willard, who had never heard of her, was her dearly beloved friend or relative.

Joe nodded solemnly. "She did look sorter peaked," he agreed. "As for Him, he didn't look no worse than usual to me, but I guess it's jest as well for them they're off, let alone us."

The remark seemed enigmatic, but Martha understood. They walked home from the station. They passed the Willard house, standing aloof from the highway like a grand Colonial lady.

"The awnin's are down," said Martha, "and they've begun to board up the winders."

Joe nodded.

"It is unlooked for, as far as we are concerned," said Martha, with a happy widening of her lips.

"Day arter to-morrer—only think of it!" said Captain Joe.

"Goin' out fishin' to-morrer?"

"Reckon not; got in considerable to-day, and I want to git my hair cut to-morrer."

"I'm goin' to trim my bunnit over, and fix my best dress a little, too; and I guess your best suit needs brushin'."

"There's a spot on the coat."

"I'll git it off. Land! I do hope Sunday is pleasant."

"Goin' to be. It's a dry moon," declared Joe.

However, Sunday, although fair, was one of those fervid days of summer which threatened storm.

"It's goin' to shower," declared Martha. She was clad in her best black silk, hot, and tightly fitted, trimmed with cascades of glittering jet. A jet aigrette on her bonnet caught the light. She had fastened a vivid rose on one side of the bonnet to do honor to the occasion. Crowning glory—she wore her white gloves, her one pair, which was the treasure of her wardrobe.

"Better take the umbrell', I guess," said Joe.

"Guess you'd better."

Joe held his head stiffly because of his linen collar. He wore a blue suit much too large for him, but it was spotless. He took the umbrella from behind the door. It was distinctly not worthy of the occasion, although it was entirely serviceable. Still, it was large, and greenish-black, and bulged determinedly from its mooring of rubber at the top.

Martha, as they walked along, looked uncomfortably at the umbrella. "Can't ye roll the umbrell' up tight, the way I see 'em?" she inquired.

Joe stopped, unfastened the rubber strap, and essayed to roll it. It was in vain. "The umbrell' is too thick," he said. "No use, Marthy. It's a good umbrell'. If it showers it will keep it off, but I can't make it look slim."

"Well, don't show it any more than you can help," admonished Martha.

Joe henceforth carried the umbrella between himself and Martha. It continually collided with their legs, but Martha's black-silk skirt flopped over its green voluminousness and it was comparatively unseen.

"I declare; it does seem like showerin'," said Joe.

"You said it was a dry moon."

"Ef thar's anything in nature to be depended on least of anything else it's a dry moon," said Joe, with an air of completely absolving himself from all responsibility in the matter of the moon.

"Of course in such hot weather nobody can tell when a thunder-tempest is goin' to come up," said Martha. She was extremely uncomfortable in her tight black raiment. Drops of perspiration stood on her forehead.

"If we were goin' anywhere else I'd take off my gloves," said she.

"Well, Marthy, long as it's the first time this year, reckon you'd better stand it, if you can," returned Joe. "My collar is about chokin' me, but its the first time this year we're goin' there, you know, Marthy."

"That's just the way I feel," agreed Martha.

The sun beat upon their heads. "Ef the umbrell' was a little better-lookin' I'd h'ist her," said Joe.

"Now, Joe, you know you can't."

"I know it, Marthy. I can't."

They were now in the midst of a gay, heterogeneous Sunday throng. The church-bells were ringing. A set of chimes outpealed the rest. Elegantly arrayed people—the ladies holding brilliant parasols at all angles above their heads crowned with plumes and flowers; the gentlemen in miraculously creased trousers, many of them moving with struts, swinging sticks—met and went their way. The road was filled with a never-ending procession of motor-cars, carriages, horses, and riders. Barr-by-the-Sea was displaying her charms like a beauty at a ball.

Many were bound for church; more for pleasure. There were country people dressed in cheap emulation of the wealthy, carrying baskets with luncheon, who had come to Barr-by-the-Sea to spend Sunday and have an outing. They were silent, foolishly observant, and awed by the splendors around them.

Joe Dickson and his wife Martha moved as the best of them. There was no subserviency in them. They had imbibed the wide freedom and lordliness of the sea, and at any time moved among equals; but to-day their errand made them move as lords. By what childlike sophistry it had come to pass none could tell, but Joe Dickson, poor ex-captain of a sailing-vessel, and his wife Martha were, in their own conviction, on their way to re-establishment in the best mansion on that coast, inhabited by the wealthy of the country.

When they reached the Willard house Joe and Martha ducked under the iron chain across the carriage-drive, and proceeded along the glittering smoothness bordered by brilliant flowers, having no realization of the true state of affairs.

"I declare, it does seem good to get back," said Joe.

"It certainly does," said Martha, "and so much earlier than we'd looked forward to."

"I calculated they might stay till late in October, the way they did last year," said Joe, joyously. "Just see that red-geranium bed, Marthy."

"Them ain't geraniums; them is begonias," said Martha, haughtily.

"It always seems to me as if all the flowers was geraniums," said Joe. He laughed.

Martha did not smile. "They ain't," said she.

They passed around to the back of the grand house. The wide veranda was cleared except for two weather-beaten old chairs. The windows, except one on the second floor, were boarded over. The house looked as if asleep, with closed eyes, before that magnificent ocean, a vast brilliance as of gemlike facets reflecting all the glory of the whole earth and the heavens above the earth. The tide was coming in. Now and then a wave broke with a rainbow toss, quite over the sea wall of the beach. The coast in places— and this was one of them—was treacherous.

Captain Joe and his Martha sat down in the rude chairs. Martha sighed a sigh of utter rapture.

"Land! it is certainly nice to be here again," said she.

Joe, however, scowled at the sea wall. "They had ought to have seen to that wall afore they went off," he said.

"Land! It's safe, ain't it?"

"I dunno. Nobody never knows nothin' when the sea's consarned. Ef they had asked me I'd said: 'Hev a lot of men on the job, and make sure there ain't no shaky places in that 'ere wall; and whilst you're about it, build it up about six foot higher. It wouldn't cut off your view none.' The hull of it is, the sea never quits the job. Everything on earth quits the job, one way or t'other, but that sea is right on, and she's goin' to be right on it; and bein' right on the job, and never quittin', means somethin' doin' and somethin' bein' done, and nobody knows just what."

"I guess it's all right," said Martha. "It ain't likely that They would have gone off and left this house unless it was; and money ain't no object."

"Sometimes folks with money gits the wrong end of the bargain," said Joe. "Money don't mean nothin' to the sea. It's swallowed more'n the hull earth holds, and it's ready to swallow till the day of jedgment. That wall had ought to be looked arter."

There was a sound of the one unboarded window being opened, and it immediately framed an aged colored face, with a fringe of gray beard like wool. The owner of the face could not be seen, and, because of the veranda roof, he could not see, but, his ears being quick to note sounds above the rush of the waters, he heard Joe and Martha talking on the veranda. Presently he came up the veranda steps. He was the caretaker, and his door of entrance and exist was in the basement, under the veranda. He was a tall old colored man with an important mien.

When his head appeared above the veranda floor Joe and Martha rose. "Good day, Sam," they said almost in concert.

Sam bowed with dignity. "I 'lowed it was you," he said, then sat down on a fixed stone bench near the chairs.

"So they've gone," said Joe, as he and Martha resumed their seats.

"Yassir. Mr. Richard is kind of pindlin', and the doctor 'lowed he'd better get away. They went day before yesterday, and all the help last night."

Joe nodded. Martha nodded. They all sat still, watching the waves dash at the sea wall and break over it.

"They had ought to have looked at that wall," said Joe, presently.

The colored man laughed with the optimism of his race. "That wall has held more'n twenty year—eber since the house was built," said he. "Wall all right."

"Dunno," said Joe.

Martha was not as optimistic as the colored man, but she was entirely happy. "Seems sorter nice to be settin' here ag'in, Sam," said she.

"Yes'm," said Sam.

"We've got a baked fish for dinner, and some fresh beans," said Martha. "We thought you'd come and have dinner with us, the way you always do the first day."

"I 'lowed you'd ask me, thank ye, marm," said Sam, with his wonderful dignity.

"Seems nice to be settin' here ag'in," repeated Martha, like a bird with one note.

"Yes'm." Sam's own face wore a pleased expression. He, too, felt the charm of possession. All three, the man and wife and the colored retainer, realized divine property rights. The outside of that grand house was as much theirs as it was any soul's on the face of the earth. They owned that and the ocean. Only Joe's face was now and then disturbed when a wave, crested in foam, came over the sea wall. He knew the sea well enough to love and fear it, while he owned it.

The three sat there all the morning. Then they all went away to the little Dickson house. The thunder was rumbling in the northwest. They walked rapidly. Joe spread the umbrella, but no rain came. There was a sharp flash of lightning and a prodigious report. All three turned about and looked in the direction of the Willard house.

"Struck somewheres, but it didn't strike thar," said Joe.

When they reached home Martha immediately changed her dress and set about preparing dinner. The two men sat on Joe's upturned boat, on the sloping beach opposite, and smoked and watched the storm. It did not rain for a long time, although the thunder and lightning were terrific. The colored man cringed at the detonations and flashes, but Joe was obdurate. He had sailed stormy seas too much to be anything but a cool critic of summer showers. However, after each unusual flash and report the two stared in the direction of the Willard house.

"Seems as if I had ought to have stayed there," remarked Sam, trembling, after one great crash.

"What could you have done? That didn't strike no house. Struck out at sea. I'm keepin' an ear out for the fire-alarm," said Joe.

"Have you got it ready?" inquired Sam, mysteriously.

Joe nodded. He flushed slightly. Sam was under orders to keep secret the fact that the poor old sailorman had the preceding year purchased a fire-extinguisher, with a view to personally protecting the House. "You can run faster than I can, and you know how to use it," said Joe.

Then another storm came up swiftly. Martha came to the door. "It's another!" cried she.

Joe rose. "Get it for me, Marthy," said he.

Martha brought the fire-extinguisher.

"Guess you and me had better be on the bridge ef another's comin'," said Joe, grimly, to Sam.

The two disappeared down the road in a gray drive of rain. Martha screamed to Joe to take the umbrella, his best suit would get wet, but he did not hear her. Sam went on a run and Joe hobbled after. They stood on the Willard veranda and kept watch. Both men were drenched. The waves broke over the sea wall, and the salt wind drove the rain in the faces of the men.

At last it was over, and they went back to the Dickson house. The odor of fish and beans greeted them. Martha had continued her dinner preparations. She was not in the least afraid of storms. She, too, only thought of danger to the grand house, but she had great faith in her husband and the fire-extinguisher, whose unknown virtues loomed gigantic to her feminine mind.

She made Joe change his best suit, which she hung carefully to dry on the clothes-line, and she gave Sam a ragged old suit, and hung up his drenched attire also. "You couldn't do much about taking care of things if you got the rheumatiz," said she.

They ate their dinner in comfort, for the thunder-storm had conquered the heat. Afterward, while Martha cleared away, the men sat on the porch and went to sleep. Martha herself slept on the old lounge. She dreamed that she was on the veranda of the Willard house and she awoke to no disillusion. Next day, and all the following days, for nearly a whole year, she and Joe could be there if they chose. They were in possession; for so long that dispossession seemed unreality.

That was the happiest summer Joe and Martha had ever known in Barr-by-the-Sea. There were long afternoons, when Joe had been out and sold his catch; there were wonderful moonlit nights, when they lived on the outside of the beautiful house and inherited the earth.

The fall was late that year. Long into October, and even during warm days in November, they could assemble on the veranda and enjoy their wealth. There came a storm in October, however, which increased Joe's fears concerning the stanchness of the sea wall. He conferred with Sam. Sam was hard to move from his position that the past proved the future, but finally his grudging assistance was obtained. The two worked hard. They did what they could, but even then Joe would look at the wall and shake his head.

"She ought to be six foot higher," he told Martha.

If Sam could have written, he would have pleaded with him to write the Willards abroad, urging that they order the raising of the wall, but Sam could not write. Joe went to a real-estate agent and talked, but the man laughed at him.

"Don't butt in, Joe," he advised. "Nobody is going to thank you. I think the wall is all right."

"It ain't," declared Joe.

Joe was right. In December there came the storm and the high tide. Joe was up at two o'clock in the morning, awakened by the wild cry of the sea, that wildest of all creation, which now and then runs amuck and leaps barriers and makes men dream of prehistoric conditions.

He hastened along the road, with that terrible menace in his ears, dragging a great length of rope. Martha stayed behind on her knees, praying. Nobody ever knew quite what happened; that is, all the details. They did know that in some miraculous fashion the sea wall of the Willard house had been strengthened by frantic labor of poor men who owned not a stick as valuable as the poorest beam in the house, and that they were urged on by Captain Joe Dickson, with his lame leg and his heart of a lover and a hero. They knew that strange things had been piled against that wall; all the weighty articles from the basement of the Willard house—wood, boats, sandbags, stones, everything which had power to offer an ounce of resistance. They knew that the wall stood and the house was saved, and old Sam was blubbering over old Captain Joe Dickson lying spent almost to death on the veranda where he had been carried.

"Tell Marthy Our House is safe," stammered old Captain Joe. Then he added something which was vaguely made out to be a note of triumph. "The sea didn't git me."

When they took him home to Martha she was very calm. All her life, since she had married Joe, she had had in her heart the resolution which should be in the hearts of the wives of all poor sailormen and fishermen, who defy the splendid, eternal danger of the sea to gain their sustenance.

It was Dr. Tom Ellerton, spinning over from Barr Center, at the risk of his neck and his car, who saved Captain Joe, although the old man was saved only to spend the rest of his life in bed or wheel-chair, and never could sail the seas again. It was Dr. Tom Ellerton who told the Willards, and it was they who sent the wheel-chair and gave Joe a pension for saving their house. Mrs. Richard Willard (Richard had died during their stay abroad) came out on purpose to see Joe. She was sad, and weary, and elegant in her deep black.

She told Joe and Martha what was to be done, and they thanked her and gave her daughter some of their choicest shells. They were quite dignified and grateful about her bounty. On the train going home Mrs. Willard told her daughter that they were evidently superior people. "They belong to the few who can take with an air of giving and not offend," said Mrs. Willard.

Neither of them dreamed of the true state of the case: that subtly and happily the old man and his wife possessed what they called their own home in a fuller sense than they ever could. More than the announcement of the comfortable annuity had meant Mrs. Willard's statement that they would not open the House at all next summer; they would visit with relatives in the Berkshires, then go abroad.

Joe and Martha looked at each other, and their eyes said: "We can go to Our House as soon as you can wheel me over there. We can stay there as much as we like, all one year."

Mrs. Willard saw the look, and did not understand. How could she? It was inconceivable that these two people should own the outside of her home to such an extent that their tenure became well-nigh immortal.